What Should Be Taxed:
Income or Expenditure?

D1591191

Studies of Government Finance: Second Series

TITLES PUBLISHED

What Should Be Taxed: Income or Expenditure?

JOSEPH A. PECHMAN
Editor

*A report of a conference sponsored by
the Fund for Public Policy Research
and the Brookings Institution*

Studies of Government Finance

THE BROOKINGS INSTITUTION

WASHINGTON, D.C.

Library of Congress Cataloging in Publication Data:

Main entry under title:

What should be taxed, income or expenditure?
  (Studies of government finance: Second series)
  Includes bibliographical references and index.
    1. Income tax—United States—Congresses.
2. Spendings tax—United States—Congresses.
I. Pechman, Joseph A., 1918–   II. Fund for Public
Policy Research.   III. Brookings Institution,
Washington, D.C. IV. Series.
HJ4652.W59   336.2′4′0973   79-22733
ISBN 0-8157-6966-0
ISBN 0-8157-6965-2 pbk.

9 8 7 6 5 4 3 2 1

THE BROOKINGS INSTITUTION is an independent organization devoted to nonpartisan research, education, and publication in economics, government, foreign policy, and the social sciences generally. Its principal purposes are to aid in the development of sound public policies and to promote public understanding of issues of national importance.

The Institution was founded on December 8, 1927, to merge the activities of the Institute for Government Research, founded in 1916, the Institute of Economics, founded in 1922, and the Robert Brookings Graduate School of Economics and Government, founded in 1924.

The Board of Trustees is responsible for the general administration of the Institution, while the immediate direction of the policies, program, and staff is vested in the President, assisted by an advisory committee of the officers and staff. The by-laws of the Institution state: "It is the function of the Trustees to make possible the conduct of scientific research, and publication, under the most favorable conditions, and to safeguard the independence of the research staff in the pursuit of their studies and in the publication of the results of such studies. It is not a part of their function to determine, control, or influence the conduct of particular investigations or the conclusions reached."

The President bears final responsibility for the decision to publish a manuscript as a Brookings book. In reaching his judgment on the competence, accuracy, and objectivity of each study, the President is advised by the director of the appropriate research program and weighs the views of a panel of expert outside readers who report to him in confidence on the quality of the work. Publication of a work signifies that it is deemed a competent treatment worthy of public consideration but does not imply endorsement of conclusions or recommendations.

The Institution maintains its position of neutrality on issues of public policy in order to safeguard the intellectual freedom of the staff. Hence interpretations or conclusions in Brookings publications should be understood to be solely those of the authors and should not be attributed to the Institution, to its trustees, officers, or other staff members, or to the organizations that support its research.

Foreword

IN RECENT YEARS many economists and lawyers have taken renewed interest in proposals for taxing expenditure as an alternative to taxing income. The idea, which dates back to John Stuart Mill, is to deduct saving from income in computing the personal tax base. The tax rates may be proportional or graduated, although it is generally understood that expenditure tax rates would be graduated.

The expenditure tax was proposed by the U.S. Treasury Department during World War II, but it was not given serious consideration because of its novelty and complexity. It has been used only briefly in India and Sri Lanka and is not now used anywhere in the world.

The expenditure tax, advocated either to supplement or to replace the graduated income tax, is strongly supported by those who believe that saving should be encouraged. It is just as strongly opposed by many who believe that the exemption for saving would reduce the progressivity of the tax system. Some maintain that the expenditure tax would be extremely difficult to administer; others conclude that the exemption of saving would ease the burdens of compliance and administration.

This book presents five papers that set forth what must be considered in making judgments about the economic merits, relative fairness, administrative complexity, and compliance problems of the income tax and the expenditure tax. The book opens with an analysis

of the role of the interest rate in determining saving by E. Philip
Howrey and Saul H. Hymans, both of the University of Michigan.
Richard Goode of the International Monetary Fund then offers a
defense of the income tax, after which David F. Bradford of Princeton
University defends the expenditure tax. William D. Andrews of the
Harvard Law School presents the case for using an expenditure tax
as a supplement to the income tax, and Michael J. Graetz of the California Institute of Technology and the University of Southern California examines the problem of implementing an expenditure tax and
of making the transition from an income tax to an expenditure tax.

These papers were presented at a conference of experts jointly
sponsored by the Brookings Institution and the Fund for Public Policy Research. The conference, held at Brookings on October 19 and
20, 1978, was attended by the economists, tax lawyers, federal exec-
utives, and congregressional tax officials listed on pages 325–26. The
Howrey and Hymans paper was originally presented before a meeting
of the Brookings Panel on Economic Activity in September 1978 and
first published in *Brookings Papers on Economic Activity, 3:1978*.
Joseph J. Minarik of the Brookings Economic Studies staff wrote the
summary of the conference discussion that concludes the book. Caro-
line Lalire edited the manuscript for publication; Evelyn P. Fisher
and Penelope Harpold verified its factual content; Diana Regenthal
prepared the index.

The project was supported with funds provided by the Fund for
Public Policy Research, Washington, D.C. This is the eleventh volume in the second series of Brookings Studies of Government Finance. Both series are devoted to examining issues in taxation and
public policy.

The views expressed in this book are those of the authors and the
conference participants and should not be ascribed to the Fund for
Public Policy Research or to the trustees, officers, or other staff members of the Brookings Institution.

BRUCE K. MACLAURY
President

January 1980
Washington, D.C.

Contents

Tables

E. PHILIP HOWREY *and* SAUL H. HYMANS

The Measurement
and Determination
of Loanable-Funds Saving

Saving is taken to be the source of the resources needed to produce capital. It represents new materials and labor which could have been used for current consumption but which, instead, are held back (saved) in order to make possible the production of larger outputs in the future. Thus savings are the supply side of the supply and demand for new capital.—William J. Baumol[1]

WHILE there may be many reasons to be concerned about what determines the flow of saving in the U.S. economy, it is the role of saving as the supply side in the process of capital accumulation that seems to lie at the heart of the renewed interest in saving behavior in recent literature. That same view of saving is the focus of our attention and guides the choices we make in the empirical analysis presented here. Our major objective is to investigate the proposition that saving—in the

This paper was presented to the Brookings Panel on Economic Activity three weeks before the conference on income and expenditure taxation was held. See *Brookings Papers on Economic Activity, 3:1978,* pp. 655–706. The discussion by the Brookings panel is summarized below by Robert Z. Lawrence.

The authors thank David M. Garman for his exceptionally competent research assistance. Their colleague, Theodore C. Bergstrom, and members of the Brookings panel made many helpful suggestions on earlier versions of this article.

1. William J. Baumol, *Economic Theory and Operations Analysis,* 4th ed. (Prentice-Hall, 1977), pp. 650–51.

sense of the flow of resources available for capital formation, or "loanable funds"—is determined in part by the rate of interest.

A critically important policy problem is at issue here. Suppose, as Feldstein has claimed, that the United States saves too little and therefore forgoes the benefits of unrealized additions to productive capacity.[2] Suppose further that, as a number of writers have recently suggested, part of the reason that the United States does not save a sufficiently large fraction of its income is that the tax structure drives a wedge between the marginal rate of return to private capital formation and the after-tax of return to private saving, and thus the latter is low relative to the former.[3] In that case, a change in the tax laws could be expected to change the ratio of saving to income. Specifically, if saving is positively related to the after-tax rate of return to saving, a reduction in the marginal tax rate on earnings from saving would raise saving at any given level of income; in other words, the reduction would raise the saving rate. For such a prescription to be useful to policymakers, two findings must emerge from the empirical analysis. First, it must be demonstrated that a positive, reliably measured partial derivative exists connecting loanable-funds saving and the appropriate interest rate. And if this can be shown, the second requirement is that the positive relationship must be "important" as well as significant. That is, policymakers cannot have much interest if the estimated response of the saving rate to a unit change in the rate of return to saving is 0.0001, regardless of how small the standard error on that 0.0001 might be.[4]

2. See Martin Feldstein, "Does the United States Save Too Little?" *American Economic Review,* vol. 67 (February 1977, *Papers and Proceedings, 1976*), pp. 116–21. Feldstein argues that realizing those additional benefits would increase economic welfare so that existing saving is inefficiently small.

3. See the excellent survey article on this and related topics: George M. von Furstenberg and Burton G. Malkiel, "The Government and Capital Formation: A Survey of Recent Issues," *Journal of Economic Literature,* vol. 15 (September 1977), pp. 835–78. Also see Michael J. Boskin, "On Some Recent Econometric Research in Public Finance," *American Economic Review,* vol. 66 (May 1976, *Papers and Proceedings, 1975*), pp. 102–09; Michael J. Boskin, "Taxation, Saving, and the Rate of Interest," *Journal of Political Economy,* vol. 86 (April 1978), pt. 2, pp. S3–S27; and Feldstein, "Does the United States Save Too Little?"

4. Presumably the fiscal issue here is not a net tax cut, but a tax reform that lowers the tax rate on interest income and then raises other tax rates (say, taxes on wage and salary income) to maintain fixed total tax revenue. We would then want to measure the responsiveness of saving to a change in the after-tax rate of return

It is by no means true that all writers on this topic claim the existence of a positive relation between saving and the interest rate. In the Fisherian gospel that forms the theoretical basis for the analysis of saving behavior, it is well recognized that the response of an individual who is a net saver at interest rate R_0 to a change in the rate to $R_0 +$ ΔR is, in general, indeterminate because the substitution and income effects are of opposite signs. Indeed the recent attack on neoclassical capital theory from Cambridge (England) includes the view that the effect of the interest rate on saving is likely to be negligible, and focuses on business decisions and the division of national income between workers and entrepreneurs as the major determinants of saving.[5]

To shed light on the role of the interest rate in determining loanable-funds saving, it is important that we know what interest rate to consider and that we are able to observe an empirical counterpart of loanable-funds saving. There is fair agreement, at least in principle, that the relevant rate of return to saving should be an expected, after-tax, real rate of return. There is less agreement on precisely how to measure the expected after-tax real rate.[6] As we indicate in the next section, the results can be quite sensitive to the choice of data on interest and inflation rates.

---

to saving, given the level of total tax revenue. This means that the fiscal authorities would have to raise the tax rate on wage and salary income by enough to offset the tax revenue lost on interest income from the entire stock of consumer saving, not just from the flow of saving from current income. Our final empirical results below measure such an effect by treating the after-tax rate of return and personal tax payments as separate independent variables in a multiple regression explaining saving. This procedure is not the same as the one implied in the usual conceptual experiment of isolating the income and substitution effects of a change in the after-tax interest rate.

5. A concise and insightful discussion of the capital theory controversy may be found in Baumol, *Economic Theory and Operations Analysis,* pp. 653–70. Baumol concludes that *"a priori* surmise" cannot tell us what determines the flow of saving; "It is a matter for empirical investigation, and the issue is still far from being settled" (p. 657).

6. In the presence of uncertainty, is it only the expectation of a probability distribution that matters? If the interest rate, tax rate, and inflation rate are perceived to be random variables, is it appropriate simply to combine them into a single random variable (the after-tax real rate of return), or is the saving decision a more complex function of all three variables? Is a single interest rate all that matters, or is there an array of interest rates on alternative assets that affects the saving decision? In this paper we cannot treat all these issues, but we look at some of them.

And what is loanable-funds saving? Observations of two saving flows are published regularly: saving in the national income and product accounts (hereafter NIPA) and saving in the flow-of-funds accounts (hereafter FF). We claim that neither of these is the appropriate measure of saving for the proposition under consideration. No firm interested in borrowing (through the bond or equity markets or from the banking system) to finance capital formation can borrow either NIPA personal or FF personal saving. The former includes expenditure on owner-occupied dwellings and a number of imputations; the latter, expenditure on owner-occupied dwellings and all other consumer durables, and several imputations. What individuals contribute directly to the loanable funds available for business capital formation—and the quantity that might be affected by tax changes that alter the rate of return to saving—is their cash saving. This saving is the difference between total cash receipts and total cash expenditures on anything except those financial assets providing funds for capital expenditures either directly (such as corporate bonds) or indirectly (such as time deposits). Individuals spend money to purchase claims to retirement income, say, by participation in a private pension plan, and some or all of that may well be regarded by these individuals as a part of their personal saving. But is it part of personal loanable-funds saving? To the extent that the pension funds accumulate cash in excess of their operating expenditure (including the payment of pension benefits), those funds may become available for capital formation; if they do, they should be viewed as a component of the net cash flow in the business or nonpersonal sector of the economy.[7] How pension funds hold their net cash flow is a separate issue from whether the interest rate is a determinant of personal cash saving.[8]

7. We do not deny that the purchase of pension rights may affect personal cash saving or that business cash flow may affect personal cash saving. Rather, we assert that the expenditure on such claims is not itself a component of personal loanable-funds saving. The behavioral relationship between business saving and personal saving has been treated in Paul A. David and John L. Scadding, "Private Savings: Ultrarationality, Aggregation and 'Denison's Law,' " *Journal of Political Economy,* vol. 82 (March–April 1974), pt. 1, pp. 225–49, and we address this in our empirical work below.

8. It is possible that changes in the interest rate may lead individuals to vary the amount saved in cash and through private pension funds. We treat such behavior at least indirectly by allowing for the possibility of substitution between these forms of saving.

Table 1. Derivation of Alternative Concepts of Personal Saving, 1975

Billions of dollars

Item[a]	Amount	Source[b]
NIPA personal saving	80.2	*SCB*, table 2.1
Minus: Gross investment in owner-occupied buildings	43.6	*SCB*, table 8.3 (80 + 81)
Margin on owner-built houses	0.7	*SCB*, table 8.3 (87)
Plus: Capital consumption allowances with adjustment on owner-occupied buildings	28.0	*SCB*, table 8.3 (64 + 70 + 76)
Equals: NIPA personal saving, excluding imputations	**63.8**	*SCB*, table 8.3 (60)
Minus: Change in reserves of private pension and insurance plans	27.8	*FF* (13 + 14 + 15)
Equals: Personal cash saving	**36.0**	
Plus: Gross investment in owner-occupied buildings	43.6	*SCB*, table 8.3 (80 + 81)
Minus: Capital consumption allowances with adjustment on owner-occupied buildings	28.0	*SCB*, table 8.3 (64 + 70 + 76)
Plus: Net investment in consumer durables	22.7	*FF* (41)
Equals: FF personal saving[c]	**74.3**	

a. NIPA refers to items from the national income and product accounts; FF, to items from the flow-of-funds accounts of the Federal Reserve System.

b. *SCB* is *Survey of Current Business*, vol. 57 (July 1977), and *FF* is *Flow of Funds Accounts, 4th Quarter 1977* (Board of Governors of the Federal Reserve System, February 1978), p. 53. The numbers in parentheses refer to line numbers in the source table. Figures are rounded.

c. This item does not equal the category "personal saving, F/F basis" in the flow-of-funds accounts, which was $104.9 billion in 1975.

In what follows we use the terms "personal cash saving" and "personal loanable-funds saving" interchangeably. Our empirical analysis makes use of NIPA, FF, and cash saving, but our main focus is on cash saving.

Table 1 provides a detailed description of personal cash saving as it relates to NIPA personal saving and our concept of FF personal saving, using 1975 data.[9] Briefly, the major difference between NIPA personal saving and our definition of personal cash saving is that the

9. The FF saving as defined here is conceptually the same as that in the published data of the Federal Reserve Board, but we have not reconciled it exactly with the published series.

Table 2. Derivation of Alternative Concepts of Gross Private Saving, 1975
Billions of dollars

Item	Amount	Source[a]
Change in reserves of private pension and insurance plans	27.8	*FF* (13 + 14 + 15)
Plus: Undistributed corporate profits with inventory valuation and capital consumption adjustments	16.7	*SCB*, table 5.1
Wage accruals less disbursements	0.0	*SCB*, table 5.1
Corporate capital consumption allowances with adjustment	101.7	*SCB*, table 5.1
Noncorporate capital consumption allowances with adjustment	60.8	*SCB*, table 5.1
Minus: Capital consumption allowances with adjustment on owner-occupied buildings	28.0	*SCB*, table 8.3 (64 + 70 + 76)
Equals: Nonpersonal (business) private cash saving	**179.0**	
Plus: Personal cash saving	36.0	Authors' calculations from table 1
Equals: Gross private cash saving	**215.0**	
Plus: Gross investment in owner-occupied buildings	43.6	*SCB*, table 8.3 (80 + 81)
Margin on owner-built houses	0.7	*SCB*, table 8.3 (87)
Equals: NIPA gross private saving[b]	**259.4**	*SCB*, table 5.1

a. See table 1, note b.
b. NIPA refers to items from the national income and product accounts.

net investment in owner-occupied buildings and the net contribution to private pension and insurance plans are included in NIPA personal saving but excluded from personal cash saving.[10] Our FF personal saving adds net purchases of consumer durables and net investment in owner-occupied buildings to personal cash saving. In this way we treat purchases of consumer durables and housing consistently. Table 2 makes the transition to gross private cash saving and NIPA gross private saving; the former is obtained by adding personal cash saving and the nonpersonal (business) gross cash saving. Table 3 outlines personal cash receipts and NIPA disposable personal income; table 4, private cash receipts and NIPA private receipts. All calculations are

10. Our treatment of private pension and insurance plans is thus consistent with the NIPA treatment of social insurance funds.

Table 3. Relation of NIPA Personal Income to Personal Cash Receipts before and after Tax and Cash Flows Plus Noncash Receipts after Tax, 1975[a]

Billions of dollars

Item	Amount	Source[b]
Personal income without imputations[c]	1,217.0	*SCB*, table 8.3 (42)
Minus: Investment income of private pension and insurance funds	20.6	*SCB*, table 8.2 (43) minus table 8.3 (35 + 38 + 56)
Employer contributions for private pension and insurance funds	56.8	*SCB*, table 6.13
Plus: Personal contributions for social insurance	50.4	*SCB*, table 2.1
Benefits paid from private pension and insurance funds	45.2	*SCB*, table 6.13
Equals: Personal cash receipts[d]	**1,235.2**	
Minus: Personal tax and nontax payments	169.0	*SCB*, table 2.1
Equals: Personal cash receipts after tax	**1,066.2**	
Plus: Imputations[e]	36.2	*SCB*, table 8.3 (68 − 66 + 79 + 82 + 84 + 85 + 86 + 87)
Employer contributions for social insurance and private pension and insurance funds	116.6	*SCB*, tables 1.13 and 6.13
Equals: Personal cash and noncash receipts after tax	**1,219.0**	
Plus: Investment income of private pension and insurance funds	20.6	*SCB*, table 8.2 (43) minus table 8.3 (35 + 38 + 56)
Minus: Employer contributions for social insurance	59.8	*SCB*, table 1.13
Benefits paid from private pension and insurance funds	45.2	*SCB*, table 6.13
Personal contributions for social insurance	50.4	*SCB*, table 2.1
Equals: NIPA disposable personal income	**1,084.4**	*SCB*, table 2.1

a. NIPA refers to items from the national income and product accounts.
b. *SCB* is *Survey of Current Business*, vol. 57 (July 1977). The numbers in parentheses refer to line numbers in the source table. Figures are rounded.
c. Personal income without imputations, as published, does not correspond to personal cash receipts because of the attribution of investment income of private pension and insurance funds to individuals (not regarded as an imputation by national income accountants), the inclusion of employer contributions to private pension and insurance funds, and the exclusion of personal contributions for social insurance (but not personal contributions for private pension and insurance) and benefits paid from private pension and insurance funds. We have simply reversed these items so that private pension and insurance contributions are treated exactly the same as social insurance contributions, and private "transfer payments" to individuals are treated exactly the same as government transfer payments.
d. Includes personal contributions for social and private pension and insurance funds.
e. Includes net imputed profit-type income on owner-occupied buildings, income in kind, and services furnished without payment by financial intermediaries except life insurance carriers.

Table 4. Relation of NIPA Private Receipts to Private Cash and Noncash Receipts after Tax, 1975[a]

Billions of dollars

Item	Amount	Source[b]
Nonpersonal private cash saving	179.0	Authors' calculations from table 2
Plus: Personal cash receipts after tax	1,066.2	Authors' calculations from table 3
Equals: Private cash receipts after tax	**1,245.2**	
Plus: Imputations	36.2	*SCB*, table 8.3 (68 − 66 + 79 + 82 + 84 + 85 + 86 + 87)
Employer contributions for social insurance and private pension and insurance funds	116.6	*SCB*, tables 1.13 and 6.13
Capital consumption allowances with adjustment on owner-occupied buildings	28.0	*SCB*, table 8.3 (64 + 70 + 76)
Equals: Private cash and noncash receipts after tax	**1,426.0**	
Plus: Investment income of private pension and insurance funds	20.6	*SCB*, table 8.2 (43) minus table 8.3 (35 + 38 + 56)
Minus: Employer contributions for social insurance	59.8	*SCB*, table 1.13
Benefits paid from private pension and insurance funds	45.2	*SCB*, table 6.13
Personal contributions for social insurance	50.4	*SCB*, table 2.1
Interest paid by consumers to business	22.9	*SCB*, table 2.1
Personal transfer payments to foreigners	0.9	*SCB*, table 2.1
Change in reserves of private pension and insurance plans	27.8	*FF* (13 + 14 + 15)
Equals: NIPA gross receipts of individuals and business	**1,239.8**	*SCB*, table 8.1

a. NIPA refers to items from the national income and product accounts.
b. *SCB* is *Survey of Current Business*, vol. 57 (July 1977), and *FF* is *Flow of Funds Accounts, 4th Quarter 1977*, p. 53. The numbers in parentheses refer to line numbers in the source table. Figures are rounded.

illustrated for calendar year 1975, based on published data as indicated. Variables such as personal cash saving or personal cash receipts are available only on an annual basis, and we calculated annual observations on all the relevant variables in tables 1 through 4 for the period 1951–74 for purposes of the empirical analysis. The last year we included was 1974 because that was the most recent year (as of the start of this research) for which the data would no longer be subject to regular annual revision. Because the Korean War period may have been "special," we used 1955–74 as a separate subperiod in some cases.[11]

Review of Previous Studies

As a basis for our empirical work, we begin with a review of recent contributions to the empirical study of the role of interest rates in aggregate consumption and saving behavior. We compare and integrate three general approaches that appear in the literature. The first concentrates on aggregate consumption expenditure and introduces the interest rate in the consumption function. This approach is used by Boskin and others.[12] The second approach is based on the Houthakker-Taylor saving function in which aggregate or per capita saving is the dependent variable.[13] This work has led to the use of disaggregated income flows as separate independent variables in the saving function.[14] The third approach is concerned, at least implicitly, with a disaggregation of saving into personal and nonpersonal components. The work of Denison and David and Scadding is illustrative of this approach.[15]

These three approaches reach widely different conclusions about the interest elasticity of saving. It is therefore necessary to analyze each and, if possible, consolidate the approaches or at least understand how they differ.

11. This argument seems less compelling than it once did in view of the extraordinary economic events that have occurred since the latter part of the 1960s.

12. Boskin, "Taxation, Saving, and the Rate of Interest." The studies by Martin Feldstein, "Social Security, Induced Retirement, and Aggregate Capital Accumulation," *Journal of Political Economy,* vol. 82 (September–October 1974), pp. 905–26, and Robert J. Barro, *The Impact of Social Security on Private Saving: Evidence from the U.S. Time Series* (American Enterprise Institute, 1978), also employ this general approach. Neither of these last studies is specifically concerned with the effects of the interest rate, however.

13. H. S. Houthakker and Lester D. Taylor, *Consumer Demand in the United States: Analysis and Projections,* 2d ed. (Harvard University Press, 1970), pp. 287–303.

14. See, for example, Lester D. Taylor, "Saving out of Different Types of Income," *BPEA, 2:1971,* pp. 383–407.

15. Edward F. Denison, "A Note on Private Saving," *Review of Economics and Statistics,* vol. 40 (August 1958), pp. 261–67, and David and Scadding, "Private Savings."

Aggregate Consumption Functions

In his recent paper, Boskin reports a positive and significant interest elasticity of saving.[16] This conclusion is based on an aggregate annual consumption function of the form

(1) $\ln C = a_0 + a_1 \ln YD + a_2 \ln YD_{-1} + a_3 \ln W_{-1}$
$+ a_4 \ln U + a_5(R - \pi) + a_6\pi,$

where

C = real per capita private consumption
YD = real per capita disposable private income
W = end-of-year real per capita wealth
U = unemployment rate
$R - \pi$ = the expected real after-tax return on capital
π = expected rate of inflation.

Fitting the equation to annual data for the period 1934–69 (excluding 1941–46), Boskin reports the estimated equation (after correction for first-order serial correlation of the residuals) as

(2) $\ln C = -0.456 + 0.569 \ln YD + 0.180 \ln YD_{-1}$
        (-0.34) (4.75) (2.25)

$+ 0.265 \ln W_{-1} - 0.002 \ln U - 1.066(R - \pi) - 0.029 \pi,$
(3.71) (-0.27) (-3.24) (-0.47)

with estimated t-statistics shown in parentheses (here and throughout the paper).[17] Boskin reports that virtually the same results were obtained using different interest rates, sample periods, and estimation techniques.[18]

The important feature of this equation for our purposes is the statistically significant, negative coefficient of the real rate of return. This implies a positive saving elasticity and hence an increase in the

16. Boskin, "Taxation, Saving, and the Rate of Interest."
17. The results shown here correct typographical errors in the coefficients for the inflation rate and the unemployment rate appearing in ibid., p. S13. Here and in the remainder of this discussion, the interest and inflation rates are expressed as proportional rather than as percentage rates.
18. Ibid., p. S16.

saving rate in response to an increase in the real interest rate. By defining saving implicitly as $S = Y - C$, it follows that

$$(3) \qquad \ln \left(1 - \frac{S}{Y}\right) = \ln \left(\frac{C}{Y}\right);$$

hence for fixed Y,

$$(4) \qquad \frac{\partial \left(\frac{S}{Y}\right)}{\partial R} = - \left(1 - \frac{S}{Y}\right)\left(\frac{\partial \ln C}{\partial R}\right).$$

An upper bound on the sensitivity of the saving rate to changes in the interest rate is thus $-\partial \ln C/\partial R$ when this quantity is positive. Because equation 2 yields the estimate $-\partial \ln C/\partial R \cong 1.066$, Boskin's work implies that a 1 percentage point increase in the real rate of return (say, from 4 to 5 percent) would be expected to lead to (at most) a 1 percentage point increase in the saving rate (say, from 6 to 7 percent). Thus this estimate of the interest-rate effect is both statistically significant and sufficiently large to be meaningful for policy purposes.

An equation like the one employed by Boskin requires that saving, and hence the saving rate, be defined implicitly by the specific consumption and income data that are used. Boskin's consumption data exclude expenditures on all consumer durables and include the flow of services from durables, including owner-occupied buildings. The saving implicitly defined thereby comes closest to an FF saving concept, rather than a loanable-funds saving concept. It is not obvious to us why such saving should respond positively to the interest rate. In particular, FF saving includes net investment in consumer durables and housing. It is generally thought that purchases of consumer durables and housing would, if anything, vary inversely with the interest rate. Viewing FF saving essentially as an aggregate of cash saving and net investment in housing and other durables, one would expect the coefficient of the interest rate to be an average of the negative value deriving from the net investment component and a possibly positive value taken from the cash-saving component of FF saving. Boskin's finding of a large positive coefficient relating the rate of interest and FF saving is therefore a novel and intriguing result that calls for replication and further scrutiny.

Boskin provided us with the data used in his analysis. Most of these data derive directly from the calculations of Christensen and Jorgen-son.[19] However, Boskin contributed a calculation that is of critical importance for the problem at hand. The real after-tax rate of return $(R - \pi)$, which appears in equation 2, results from Boskin's process-ing of the rate of return and the price data appearing in the work of Christensen and Jorgenson. Boskin applied a process of smoothing and forward projection to produce an $(R - \pi)$ that he regarded as an appropriate measure of the expected after-tax real rate of return. We were struck by two facts in our visual inspection of the $(R - \pi)$ series. The first was that the observation for 1934 seemed to be uniquely different from nearby observations; we therefore dropped it from the sample to determine whether it was exerting a peculiarly strong lever-age on the regression. This experiment produced a coefficient of -0.877 on $(R - \pi)$, rather than the -1.066 reported by Boskin, with an estimated t-statistic of -1.62, which clearly calls into ques-tion the statistical significance of $(R - \pi)$.[20]

The second point we noticed was that the $(R - \pi)$ series resembled the inverted unemployment rate lagged two years. To test whether the interest rate played a purely cyclical role in the equation, we entered the unemployment rate lagged two years rather than the (insignifi-cant) current unemployment rate; the result for the period 1936–40, 1949–69 is

$$(5) \quad \ln C = -3.547 + 0.675 \ln YD - 0.044 \ln YD_{-1}$$
$$(-4.05) \quad (4.73) \qquad\quad (-0.26)$$

$$+ 0.680 \ln W_{-1} - 0.042 \ln U_{-2} - 0.120(R - \pi) + 0.059\,\pi.$$
$$(27.19) \qquad\quad (-4.62) \qquad\quad (-0.17) \qquad\qquad (0.39)$$

Durbin-Watson = 1.70; standard error of estimate = 0.013; ρ = 0.250.

The lagged unemployment rate has a significant negative coefficient, while the real interest rate is no longer statistically significant. A similar result holds for the postwar period; when $\ln U_{-2}$ rather than $\ln U$ is used in the equation, the t-statistic for the coefficient on the interest rate is -0.90, which makes its significance questionable.

As a final check on the sensitivity of the Boskin result, we used several alternative interest rates in place of Boskin's interest rate. These rates were of the form $(R - \pi)$, where π is Boskin's expected

19. See Laurits R. Christensen and Dale W. Jorgenson, "U.S. Income, Saving, and Wealth, 1929–1969," *Review of Income and Wealth*, series 19 (December 1973), pp. 329–62.

20. The remainder of the equation was quite robust when we dropped 1934.

rate of inflation, and R is the Aaa, Baa, or municipal rate. Averaged and exponentially smoothed $(R - \pi)$ rates were also used. We were never able to reproduce Boskin's result using any other interest rates with or without averaging or exponential smoothing. Indeed, when we restricted the consumption regressions to postwar data (1947–69), the coefficients for the interest rate were invariably positive, and in most cases exceeded their standard errors by a factor of two or more.

Perhaps no regression equation would withstand all the sensitivity tests that we performed. In this case, however, we found that the positive and significant saving elasticity reported by Boskin is extremely sensitive to the sample period he used, the timing of variables in the equation, and, finally, to the way in which the interest-rate series was processed. In view of this sensitivity, it is difficult to have much confidence in the reported result for the interest rate. Moreover, as indicated earlier, the saving concept to which this result is appropriate is not the personal or private loanable-funds concept in which we are interested.

Aggregate Saving Functions

In contrast to Boskin, Taylor uses saving rather than consumption as the dependent variable in his work.[21] His basic model draws upon the theory of saving developed by Houthakker and Taylor.[22] In brief, the main premise of this theory is that desired wealth is a function of income and the interest rate,

$$(6) \qquad W^* = b_1^* Y + b_2^* R.$$

Saving is then assumed to be proportional to the difference between desired and actual wealth so that

$$(7) \qquad S = \lambda(W^* - W_{-1}).$$

Differencing 7 and substituting 6 for desired wealth yields the saving equation,

$$(8) \qquad S = b_1 S_{-1} + b_2 \Delta R + b_3 \Delta Y,$$

which forms the basis for empirical work.

21. Taylor, "Saving out of Different Types of Income."
22. Houthakker and Taylor, *Consumer Demand in the United States.* See also Lester D. Taylor, "Price Expectations and Households' Demand for Financial Assets," *Explorations in Economic Research,* vol. 1 (Fall 1974), pp. 258–339, where income and the interest rate are treated in a parallel manner.

The major recent innovation by Taylor is the disaggregation of income by type, based on the NIPA identity,

(9) $$YD = L + P + TR - SI - TX,$$

where

$YD =$ NIPA disposable personal income
$L =$ labor income
$P =$ property income
$TR =$ government transfer payments to individuals
$SI =$ personal contributions for social insurance
$TX =$ personal tax and nontax payments.

This decomposition leads to the extended model,

(10) $$S = b_1 S_{-1} + b_2 \Delta R + b_3 \Delta L + b_4 \Delta P + b_5 \Delta TR + b_6 \Delta SI + b_7 TX.$$

In his empirical work, Taylor found that the coefficients on labor and property income did not differ greatly, and most of his work combined these two sources of income (designated as LP).

The original result reported by Taylor for aggregate personal saving, in constant 1958 dollars, is

(11) $$S = 0.953 \, S_{-1} + 0.418 \, \Delta LP + 0.890 \, \Delta TR - 2.194 \, \Delta SI$$
$$\quad (45.27) \qquad (5.11) \qquad\quad (2.87) \qquad\quad (-4.92)$$

$$- 0.884 \, \Delta TX + 4.011 \, \Delta Baa.$$
$$(-4.92) \qquad\quad (2.50)$$

Two important conclusions emerge from Taylor's analysis. First, the coefficients on different types of income are substantially different. Second, the significance of the interest rate is higher using disaggregated income than when disposable income is used alone in the equation.[23] The variable Baa used by Taylor is the nominal yield on Baa corporate bonds. As we mentioned above, it is generally agreed that the interest rate appropriate in a saving function is the expected real rate. If so, the Taylor equation may be specified incorrectly because it uses a nominal interest rate but no expected rate of inflation.

Juster and Wachtel have extended the Houthakker-Taylor saving model to include consideration of inflationary expectations and un-

23. This last conclusion follows from an examination of the alternative regressions shown in table 1 of Taylor, "Saving out of Different Types of Income," p. 391.

certainty about the rate of inflation.[24] For this purpose, inflationary expectations are measured by the mean expected price change obtained from survey data collected by the Survey Research Center at the University of Michigan. Uncertainty about inflation has been measured by the standard deviation of the observed distribution of expected price changes.[25] Juster and Wachtel have found that uncertainty about inflation has a significant impact on consumer saving, with growing uncertainty leading to an increase in saving. But little is said about the effects of the interest rate in their work and, as in the case of Taylor's research, the focus is on NIPA or FF saving rather than personal cash saving.

Disaggregated Saving Functions

In a recent reexamination of Denison's law, David and Scadding confirm Denison's original finding that the private saving rate, adjusted for the business cycle, has remained remarkably stable over time.[26] The model that forms the basis for their empirical investigation is

(12) $$S = c_1 GNP + c_2 \Delta GNP^*,$$

where

S = NIPA gross private saving
GNP = gross national product
ΔGNP^* = difference between the last "high-employment" year GNP and current GNP.

For the period 1921–64 (excluding 1941–47), they report the following result:

(13) $$S = 0.1552\ GNP - 0.1376\ \Delta GNP^*.$$
$$(161.52) \qquad (-7.407)$$

24. See, for example, F. Thomas Juster, "A Note on Prospective 1977 Tax-Cuts and Consumer Spending" (University of Michigan, Institute for Social Research, January 1977); and Paul Wachtel, "Inflation, Uncertainty, and Saving Behavior since the Mid-1950s," *Explorations in Economic Research,* vol. 4 (Fall 1977), pp. 558–78.

25. The details of the methods used to construct these series as well as the series themselves are given in F. Thomas Juster and Robert Comment, "A Note on the Measurement of Price Expectations" (University of Michigan, Survey Research Center, n.d.).

26. David and Scadding, "Private Savings," and Denison, "Note on Private Saving."

The ratio of the standard error of the regression to the mean value of S is 0.049. This relatively small standard error, together with the stability of the estimated equation over various subperiods, is taken as support for Denison's law—namely, that year-to-year changes in the saving rate are small and that there is no long-run trend in the saving rate.

One explanation offered for the stability of the saving rate thus defined is that households are "ultrarational": personal saving decisions are conditional on the amount of nonpersonal (that is, corporate) saving. Suppose the basic saving equation is rewritten as

$$(14) \qquad S_p = c_1 GNP + c_2 \Delta GNP^* + c_3 S_n,$$

where S_p and S_n are personal and nonpersonal saving, respectively. Then the ultrarationality hypothesis is tantamount to the restriction that $c_3 = -1$. Statistical analysis of this last relationship would provide the basis for a more direct test of the rationality conjecture.

The relative constancy of the private saving rate is sometimes taken as evidence that private saving is insensitive to interest and tax rate changes. As Boskin has argued, such a conclusion is not warranted for a number of reasons.[27] In any event, a direct test of the hypothesis of interest rate insensitivity is clearly desirable. To do this, in the context of the David and Scadding model, it would be necessary to modify the personal saving function above to include the effect of the real interest rate,

$$(15) \qquad S_p = c_1 GNP + c_2 \Delta GNP^* + c_3 S_n + c_4 (R - \pi).$$

A direct test of the hypothesis $c_4 = 0$ is possible using this model.

None of the empirical work that we reviewed provides a direct test of the interest sensitivity of saving decisions within the context of a model that allows for the ultrarationality of David and Scadding. Boskin includes corporate saving as part of income but not as a separate variable. This procedure restricts the corporate saving coefficient to being the same as the income coefficient (presumably positive) and hence does not, in general, allow for rationality of the David and Scadding variety. Taylor uses NIPA personal saving as his dependent variable, which does not have a direct loanable-funds interpretation. Moreover, corporate saving is not included as one of the determinants of personal saving. David and Scadding do not directly

27. Boskin, "Taxation, Saving, and the Rate of Interest."

investigate the potential effect of the interest rate on saving but rather argue indirectly that the effect must be small. Hence previous work is not adequate, in our opinion, to draw any definitive conclusions about the interest elasticity of personal saving decisions. Because the theoretical arguments for the effect of the interest rate are generally given in terms of personal decisions about loanable-funds saving, an investigation of this concept of saving is needed.

A First Look at Loanable-Funds Saving

In this section we take another look at the saving decision in what might be called the new public finance framework that Boskin uses.[28] We have already alluded to two important difficulties with Boskin's work—namely, saving is defined only implicitly and the data used appear to be most relevant to the analysis of FF rather than loanable-funds saving. In our efforts to overcome these difficulties, we first translate the logarithmic consumption function into a saving function and then apply the latter to several alternative saving concepts.

We begin with the logarithmic consumption function of equation 1 and subtract $\ln Y$ from both sides. Using the implicit definition of saving, $S = Y - C$, it follows that

$$(16) \quad \ln \left(1 - \frac{S}{Y}\right) = a_0 + (a_1 - 1) \ln Y + a_2 \ln Y_{-1} + a_3 \ln W_{-1}$$
$$+ a_4 \ln U + a_5(R - \pi) + a_6\pi.$$

For small S/Y, the left-hand side of this equation is closely approximated by $-S/Y$ itself, which implies

$$(17) \quad \frac{S}{Y} \cong - a_0 + (1 - a_1) \ln Y - a_2 \ln Y_{-1} - a_3 \ln W_{-1}$$
$$- a_4 \ln U - a_5(R - \pi) - a_6\pi.$$

Thus the logarithmic consumption function implies an equation for the *saving rate* with the same independent variables.

---

28. A similar econometric approach is found not only in Boskin's work but in that of Feldstein, Barro, and others who have advanced quite dramatically the application of econometrics to crucially important questions in the field of public finance. Interestingly, as far as consumption behavior is concerned and despite the acceptance of a high level of aggregation, these researchers have taken a direction quite different from the familiar one in the long history of work associated with the major macro-econometric models of the U.S. economy.

Table 5. Saving Rate Equations, 1951–74[a]

Equation and concept of saving rate	Independent variable								Summary statistic		
	Constant	ln Y	ln Y_{-1}	ln W	ln U	Baatax	π	SD	Durbin-Watson	$\bar{R}^2$	Standard error of estimate
5-1 NIPA personal	1.131 (3.26)	0.073 (0.90)	0.075 (0.82)	−0.130 (−3.07)	−0.008 (−1.24)	0.002 (0.49)	...	...	2.29	0.403	0.0067
5-2 NIPA personal	1.162 (3.28)	0.102 (1.11)	0.029 (0.26)	−0.132 (−3.07)	−0.006 (−0.94)	0.002 (0.57)	0.001 (0.71)	...	2.24	0.386	0.0068
5-3 NIPA personal	0.962 (2.16)	0.090 (0.96)	0.030 (0.26)	−0.110 (−2.07)	−0.007 (−1.05)	0.0015 (0.36)	−0.001 (−0.24)	0.0025 (0.75)	2.13	0.370	0.0069
5-4 Personal cash	0.106 (0.24)	−0.142 (−1.41)	0.200 (1.78)	−0.015 (−0.29)	−0.016 (−2.13)	0.003 (0.58)	...	...	2.29	0.672	0.0081
5-5 Personal cash	0.114 (0.25)	−0.130 (−1.12)	0.180 (1.26)	−0.016 (−0.29)	−0.015 (−1.85)	0.003 (0.60)	0.0005 (0.24)	...	2.26	0.654	0.0084
5-6 Personal cash	0.219 (0.38)	−0.123 (−1.02)	0.178 (1.22)	−0.028 (−0.40)	−0.015 (−1.73)	0.004 (0.64)	0.002 (0.38)	−0.001 (−0.30)	2.32	0.634	0.0086
5-7 FF personal	1.573 (4.09)	0.237 (2.69)	−0.037 (−0.37)	−0.183 (−3.93)	−0.026 (−3.97)	0.004 (0.84)	...	...	2.01	0.773	0.0071
5-8 FF personal	1.574 (3.97)	0.238 (2.35)	−0.038 (−0.31)	−0.183 (−3.82)	−0.026 (−3.60)	0.004 (0.81)	0.0000 (0.02)	...	2.01	0.760	0.0073
5-9 FF personal	1.002 (2.23)	0.200 (2.14)	−0.029 (−0.25)	−0.119 (−2.23)	−0.028 (−4.26)	0.0015 (0.35)	−0.005 (−1.75)	0.007 (2.13)	1.87	0.801	0.0067

Sources: The NIPA personal saving rate is NIPA personal saving divided by NIPA disposable personal income; the personal cash and FF personal saving rates use personal cash and noncash receipts after tax as the denominator. These series are defined in tables 1 through 4 and are from national income and product accounts data of the U.S. Department of Commerce and flow-of-funds accounts data of the Board of Governors of the Federal Reserve System. The income variables, Y and Y_{-1}, are the personal income concept that appears in the denominator of the corresponding saving rate, expressed in real per capita terms. W is the real per capita net worth of households and is from Robert J. Barro, *The Impact of Social Security on Private Saving: Evidence from the U.S. Time Series* (American Enterprise Institute, 1978). The unemployment rate, U, is from the U.S. Bureau of Labor Statistics. π, the mean expected price change, and SD, the standard deviation of the observed distribution of expected price changes, are from F. Thomas Juster and Robert Comment, "A Note on the Measurement of Price Expectations (University of Michigan, Survey Research Center, n.d.). *Baatax* equals $(1 - t)$ *Baa*, where *Baa* is the corporate bond rate and is from Moody's Investors Service, Inc., while t, the marginal federal tax rate applicable to income from capital, was provided by Joseph A. Pechman.
a. The numbers in parentheses are t-statistics.

We applied 17 to three basic saving rates derivable from the definitions contained in tables 1 through 4:

NIPA personal saving rate = *NIPA personal saving* divided by NIPA disposable personal income

personal cash saving rate = *personal cash saving* divided by personal cash and noncash receipts after tax

FF personal saving rate = *FF personal saving* divided by personal cash and noncash receipts after tax.[29]

The income variable, Y, used on the right-hand side is the personal income concept that appears in the denominator of the corresponding saving rate, adjusted to be measured in real per capita terms; W is real per capita net worth of households at the beginning of the year;[30] and U is the unemployment rate. The results of estimating 17 for various saving rates are given in table 5.

We experimented with interest rate data that included the municipal bond rate (which should already be an after-tax rate), the corporate Aaa rate, and the corporate Baa rate measured in percent. The best results (in the sense of the strongest effects of the interest rate on saving) were obtained using an after-tax Baa rate defined as

$$Baatax = (1 - t)Baa,$$

where the tax rate, t, is the marginal federal tax rate applicable to income from capital.[31] We employed the mean expected price change

29. The basic summary statistics for these three saving rates for 1951–74 are as follows.

Saving rate	Mean	Standard deviation
NIPA personal saving rate	0.0636	0.0086
Personal cash saving rate	0.0022	0.0142
FF personal saving rate	0.0559	0.0149

The regression results in table 5 are rather insensitive to whether the FF personal saving rate is defined with personal cash and noncash receipts after tax or with NIPA disposable personal income in the denominator.

30. The data correspond to that used in the Fed-MIT-Penn model and were taken from Barro, *Impact of Social Security on Private Saving.*

31. The original data for this tax rate appear in Colin Wright, "Saving and the Rate of Interest," in Arnold C. Harberger and Martin J. Bailey, eds., *The Taxation of Income from Capital* (Brookings Institution, 1969), p. 300. Joseph A. Pechman provided us with an updated series.

variable, π, derived from Survey Research Center data cited in the preceding section, as a separate variable to allow for both the effect of a real rate of return on saving and a separate inflation effect. To measure uncertainty about inflation we used the standard deviation, *SD,* of the expected inflation variable defined above. The equations were estimated using annual data for the period 1951–74 as well as for the subperiod 1955–74. The same basic story is told in both cases, and the results are shown only for 1951–74.

Table 5 shows that the form of the equation under consideration explains little of the variation in the NIPA saving rate. Only the wealth variable makes any significant contribution. Personal cash saving is not explained well either. Only the FF personal saving rate —and that is the one closest to the saving rate implicit in Boskin's work—seems to be explained by this form of equation. Allowing for the parameter transformations implicit in the use of S/Y rather than $\ln C$ as the dependent variable, the coefficients on current income and wealth in the regressions for the FF personal saving rate are generally similar to those reported by Boskin. The effect of the unemployment rate on FF saving is negative and significant, rather than insignificantly positive, as reported by Boskin. The coefficient on the interest rate is always positive, whether or not inflation variables are included, but it never becomes statistically significant. Inflation is a significant determinant of the FF personal saving rate if both π and *SD* are included (making the coefficient on the interest rate zero). In that event, it appears that higher expected inflation reduces FF saving, while greater uncertainty about inflation increases it.

If a negative relation exists between the interest rate and expenditures on durable goods, one would expect that to be evident in the FF saving rate equations because FF saving includes net expenditures on all consumer durables, including housing. One would also expect, however, that the cash saving rate, which contains no expenditures on durable goods, would be the most likely to show a positive relation with the interest rate. It might be possible to find a hint of such an outcome in equations 5-3, 5-6, and 5-9. Judging by the coefficient values alone, a 1 percentage point increase in the after-tax interest rate increases the FF and NIPA saving rates by 0.15 percentage point (say, from 6 percent to 6.15 percent), while the corresponding increase for the cash saving rate is 0.4 percentage point. These are small compared with Boskin's point-for-point outcome; none of them is anywhere near statistical significance. In fact, no coefficient on the interest-rate variable in table 5 has a t-statistic greater than 0.84. From the table it seems that no personal saving rate—whether cash or some other form—responds to variations in the real after-tax rate of return.

In the following section we investigate the determination of cash saving in more detail by bringing together the most promising aspects of the research reviewed above.

A Closer Look at Loanable-Funds Saving

One framework that has been used successfully for the analysis of saving is the Houthakker-Taylor model as expanded by the work of Juster, Wachtel, and others to include consideration of the effects of inflation—an issue long discussed in the work of Katona.[32] We apply a similar framework, with further modification, to the analysis of cash or loanable-funds saving. The theory underlying the Houthakker-Taylor analysis implies an estimating equation of the form (including the stochastic error term, u)

$$(18) \qquad S = a_1 S_{-1} + a_2 \Delta Y + a_3 \Delta R + u$$

if the level of income, Y, and the interest rate, R, determine the desired or equilibrium level of personal wealth. To this basic model we add the disaggregation of income (from the work of Taylor), expectations about inflation and uncertainty regarding inflation (from Katona, Juster, and others), the interrelations of personal and nonpersonal saving (the ultrarationality hypothesis from David and Scadding), and our own views on the most appropriate definitions of the saving and income flows.

To cover all these issues we must rely on annual data for the calculation of cash or loanable-funds saving and the corresponding cash income flows. Earlier successes with the Houthakker-Taylor saving model, by Taylor himself and by Juster in the incorporation of inflation variables into the analysis, have been achieved within the framework of quarterly data. If a calendar quarter is the appropriate time frame from the viewpoint of the underlying economic behavior, the

---

32. Some of the relevant work of Juster and Wachtel has already been cited. See also George Katona, *The Powerful Consumer: Psychological Studies of the American Economy* (McGraw-Hill, 1960).

use of calendar-year data as though they were quarterly data involves a time-aggregation error of specification that is potentially serious. If we begin with 18 for the basic equation with quarterly data and average the four successive quarters referring to a given year, say 1970, we obtain

$$(19) \qquad \bar{S}_{70} = a_1 S_{69:4-70:3} + a_2 \frac{1}{4} (Y_{70:4} - Y_{69:4})$$

$$+ a_3 \frac{1}{4} (R_{70:4} - R_{69:4}) + \bar{u}_{70}.$$

The dependent variable, $\bar{S}$, is saving for calendar year 1970 as usually measured (assuming the quarterly flow data are seasonally adjusted at annual rates). But the lagged dependent variable is now a calendar year of saving defined over the four quarters from 1969:4 to 1970:3, and the quarterly change variables (ΔY and ΔR in the original equation) are transformed into changes measured from 1969:4 to 1970:4.[33] Plainly, this is not the same set of independent variables that would result from the use of calendar-year data on all variables, and we know of no way to derive an equation using calendar-year saving as the dependent variable that does not also require observations on within-year data (assuming that the quarterly specification is appropriate). In order to use the saving and income concepts defined in tables 1 through 4, we are limited to calendar-year data. The same is not true of data on the interest rate (and inflation). Changes in the interest rate are readily available, as shown in the aggregated equation 19 above. We experimented with annual equations of the following two types:

$$(20\text{-}A) \qquad \bar{S}_{70} = a_1^* \bar{S}_{69} + a_2^*(Y_{70} - Y_{69})$$
$$+ a_3^*(R_{70} - R_{69}) + a_4^*(\pi_{70} - \pi_{69})$$
$$+ \cdots$$

$$(20\text{-}B) \qquad \bar{S}_{70} = a_1^{**} \bar{S}_{69} + a_2^{**}(Y_{70} - Y_{69})$$
$$+ a_3^{**}(R_{70:4} - R_{69:4}) + a_4^{**}(\pi_{70:4} - \pi_{69:4})$$
$$+ \cdots .$$

Almost uniformly, the type B forms that employ "proper aggregation" for interest rate and inflation variables outperform the type A forms

---

33. If the quarterly error term, u, is homoscedastic and serially independent, so is the average calendar-year error term, $\bar{u}$. If u is first-order serially correlated, the serial properties of $\bar{u}$ are considerably more complicated.

when judged on the basis of overall fit and the significance of the interest rate and inflation variables as a set. In addition—and of greatest importance—the conclusions that would be drawn about the significance of the interest rate are not sensitive to whether type A or type B equations are estimated. The measurement of the effects of the interest rate is sensitive to the inflation and ultrarationality issues but not to whether changes in the interest rate are measured on the basis of a calendar year or from fourth quarter to fourth quarter.[34] The results given below correspond to the type B form of the equation.

The income decomposition used by Taylor follows the NIPA breakdown shown in 9. We begin instead with the definitions

(21) $YCASH = LPCASH + TRCASH + SI - TX$

(22) $YCNC = YCASH + IMP + FRINGE,$

where

$YCASH$ = personal cash receipts after tax (table 3)
$LPCASH$ = labor and property cash income (defined implicitly in 21 above)
$TRCASH$ = cash transfers to individuals (the sum of government transfers and benefits paid from private pension and insurance funds (the latter shown in table 3)
SI, TX = as in 9
$YCNC$ = personal cash and noncash receipts after tax (table 3)
IMP = imputations (table 3)
$FRINGE$ = employer contributions for social insurance and private pension and insurance funds (table 3).

We then combine 21 and 22 to obtain

(23) $YCNC = LPCASH + TRCASH$
$$+ (SI + FRINGE) + IMP - TX$$

as our basic income decomposition. A number of fundamental differences between our components and the NIPA components are of

---

34. The time aggregation may even have some advantages. Suppose the quarterly framework is correct, but that the interest rate enters as ΔR_{-1}, rather than ΔR. The use of ΔR could produce serious errors in the parameter estimates of the incorrectly specified quarterly equation. In contrast, the use of $(R_{70:4} - R_{69:4})$ rather than the appropriate $(R_{70:3} - R_{69:3})$ in the type B annual equation may involve a minor specification error compared to the corresponding error in the quarterly equation.

interest. *LPCASH* excludes imputations, personal contributions for social insurance, and the change in reserves of private pension and insurance funds; *LP* includes all three.[35] *TRCASH* includes social insurance benefit payments (as does *TR*) and private pension and insurance benefit payments that are logically similar. The variable (*SI* + *FRINGE*) includes payments to private and social pension and insurance funds made on behalf of individuals, as well as the social insurance payments made by the individuals.

To address the issue of ultrarationality, we modify the Houthakker-Taylor saving model in the following way. We first define aggregate personal income, Y^T, as

$$(24) \qquad Y^T = YCNC + \theta_1 BCS + \theta_2 GCS,$$

where

BCS = business cash saving
GCS = government cash saving.

This formulation allows for the possibility that individuals impute to themselves the fraction θ_1 of business cash saving and the fraction θ_2 of government cash saving as income. Similarly, aggregate personal saving is defined as

$$(25) \qquad S^T = S + \mu_1 BCS + \mu_2 GCS,$$

where S is personal cash saving. Again, the coefficients μ_1 and μ_2 are presumably nonnegative, but their values are not prescribed a priori. If households perceive that some fraction of the saving of business and government ultimately accrues to them as individuals, that would imply $0 < \mu_1 \leq 1$ and $0 < \mu_2 \leq 1$.

We then assume that the saving decision is described by

$$(26) \qquad S^T = d_1 Y^T + d_2(W^* - W_{-1}),$$

where

W = personal cash wealth
W^* = desired personal cash wealth.

Thus we postulate two major determinants of saving: the level of income, broadly defined, and the discrepancy between desired and

---

35. *LPCASH* (and *LP*) includes personal contributions for private pension and insurance plans that we were unable to separate.

actual personal cash wealth. Finally, following Houthakker and Taylor, desired wealth is specified as

(27) $$W^* = b_1^* Y^T + b_2^* R.$$

When 24 through 27 are combined and differenced to eliminate the stock of personal cash wealth, the saving equation that forms the basis of our empirical work is obtained:

(28) $$\begin{aligned} S = {} & (d_1 + d_2 b_1^*)\Delta YCNC + d_2 b_2^* \Delta R + (1 - d_2)S_{-1} \\ & + [\theta_1(d_1 + d_2 b_1^*) - \mu_1]\Delta BCS \\ & + [\theta_2(d_1 + d_2 b_1^*) - \mu_2]\Delta GCS. \end{aligned}$$

The equation for personal cash saving that we propose to estimate can now be written as

(29) $$\begin{aligned} S = {} & a_0 + a_1 S_{-1} + a_2 \Delta(LPCASH) + a_3 \Delta(TRCASH) \\ & + a_4 \Delta(SI + FRINGE) + a_5 \Delta(IMP) + a_6 \Delta(TX) \\ & + a_7 \Delta(BCS) + a_8 \Delta(GCS) + a_9 \Delta(Baatax - \pi) \\ & + a_{10} \Delta(\pi) + a_{11} \Delta(SD) + u. \end{aligned}$$

The dependent variable, S, is calendar-year personal cash measured in 1967 dollars per capita; the income components are changes in calendar-year values measured in 1967 dollars per capita; and the interest rate and inflation are measured as changes from fourth quarter to fourth quarter as in 20-B. The variable BCS is business cash saving as defined in table 2 above, and GCS is cash saving of the federal government, defined as the government surplus (NIPA basis) minus the surplus in the social insurance account. Both BCS and GCS are measured in 1967 dollars per capita.

The variable BCS is directly relevant to the ultrarationality argument of David and Scadding. This hypothesis maintains that business saving is viewed by the rational consumer as a component of income and saving, with θ_1 and μ_1 both equal to unity. Thus we should find that $a_2 = a_7 - 1$, provided that the coefficient of labor and property cash income is also appropriate for the business cash saving component of income.[36] David and Scadding do not consider government cash saving to be a substitute for personal cash saving; rather, they propose that government saving and private investment are substi-

36. This follows directly from 28 in which a_2 is identified as $d_1 + d_2 b_1^*$ and $a_7 = d_1 + d_2 b_1^* - 1$ if $\theta_1 = \mu_1 = 1$.

Table 6. Personal Saving Equations Based on Authors' Income Decomposition, 1951–74

Independent

Equation, sample period, and concept of saving	Constant	S_{-1}	Δ (LPCASH)	Δ (TRCASH)	Δ (SI + FRINGE)	Δ (IMP)	Δ (TX)
6-1 Personal cash 1951–74	−4.657 (−0.61)	0.550 (4.05)	0.278 (2.75)	0.682 (1.73)	−0.842 (−1.73)	−0.693 (−0.60)	−0.121 (−0.49)
6-2 Personal cash 1951–74	−3.068 (−0.31)	0.649 (3.63)	0.369 (2.80)	0.082 (0.17)	0.327 (0.43)	−0.550 (−0.35)	−0.562 (−2.12)
6-3 Personal cash 1951–74	−7.403 (−0.61)	0.355 (1.79)	0.095 (0.78)	1.390 (2.54)	−1.573 (−2.26)	0.634 (0.41)	0.233 (0.79)
6-4 Personal cash 1955–74	−8.274 (−0.92)	0.609 (5.23)	0.387 (4.35)	0.893 (2.34)	−0.848 (−2.16)	1.444 (1.32)	−0.475 (−2.28)
6-5 NIPA personal 1951–74	27.547 (1.60)	0.771 (5.46)	0.344 (3.38)	0.573 (1.59)	−0.671 (−1.42)	−0.819 (−0.72)	−0.363 (−1.33)
6-6 FF personal 1951–74	2.391 (0.27)	0.894 (12.88)	0.521 (6.15)	0.810 (3.03)	−0.643 (−1.50)	−2.037 (−1.97)	−0.387 (−1.72)

Sources: Derived from data in the national income and product accounts (NIPA) of the U.S. Department of Commerce. In addition, S uses data from the flow-of-funds accounts (FF) of the Board of Governors of the Federal Reserve System. For definitions and sources of *Baatax*, π, and SD, see table 5.

a. *TRCASH* is cash transfers to individuals; *SI* is personal contributions for social insurance; and *TX* is personal tax and nontax payments. *LPCASH* is labor and property income and equals personal cash receipts after tax (defined in table 3) minus *TRCASH* and *SI*. *FRINGE* is employer contributions for social insurance and private pension and insurance funds; *IMP* is the NIPA imputations included in table 3;

tutes. We take an agnostic position on this issue and include government cash saving in the saving function.

The variable (*SI* + *FRINGE*) is relevant to the controversy between Feldstein and Barro about whether social security depresses personal saving.[37] This variable combines the corresponding social and private contributions because it seems unlikely that individuals are more aware of their social security rights than they are of their private pension rights.

The result of estimating the personal cash saving equation as specified in 29 is shown in table 6. The estimate shown in 6-1 was obtained using annual data for the period 1951–74. Several variations of the basic equation were also examined. Equation 6-2 gives the results when the variables for inflation and uncertainty are omitted. When the cash saving variables for business and government are deleted, the results shown in 6-3 are obtained. Finally, 6-4 indicates what happens when the sample is limited to the 1955–74 period.

The overall impression that emerges from these parameter estimates can be characterized as follows. The coefficients of the income

37. This may be viewed as another part of the ultrarationality argument. See Feldstein, "Social Security, Induced Retirement, and Aggregate Capital Accumulation," and Barro, *Impact of Social Security on Private Saving*. Feldstein claims that social security depresses personal saving; Barro says the claim is unwarranted.

and Subperiod[a]

variable					Summary statistic		
Δ (BCS)	Δ (GCS)	Δ (Baatax-π)	Δ (π)	Δ (SD)	Durbin-Watson	R^2	Standard error of estimate[b]
−0.484 (−2.10)	−0.336 (−4.04)	7.079 (0.69)	−0.724 (−0.07)	29.966 (3.12)	2.00	0.908	12.45
−1.014 (−4.25)	−0.394 (−3.61)	−3.344 (−0.76)	...	...	2.36	0.833	16.75
...	...	14.853 (0.92)	−2.469 (−0.16)	51.547 (4.08)	1.76	0.766	19.82
−0.701 (−3.66)	−0.191 (−2.18)	8.469 (0.96)	0.348 (0.04)	26.247 (3.24)	2.01	0.955	9.15
−0.169 (−0.78)	−0.288 (−3.56)	−1.455 (−0.14)	−7.228 (−0.72)	23.549 (2.42)	1.99	0.919	12.15
−0.095 (−0.50)	−0.085 (−1.15)	−11.286 (−1.22)	−22.177 (−2.45)	20.681 (2.29)	2.25	0.974	11.00

BCS is business cash saving as defined in table 2; and *GCS* is the NIPA government surplus less the surplus on the social insurance account. *S* is either personal cash, FF personal, or NIPA personal saving, as defined in table 1. All the above variables are expressed in real (1967 dollars), per capita terms. Δ(*LPCASH*), Δ(*TRCASH*), Δ(*SI* + *FRINGE*), Δ(*IMP*), Δ(*TX*), Δ(*BCS*), and Δ(*GCS*) are first differences of calendar-year data. Δ(*Baatax-π*), Δ(*π*), and Δ(*SD*) are measured as changes from fourth quarter to fourth quarter. The numbers in parentheses are *t*-statistics.
  b. In 1967 dollars per capita.

components are broadly consistent with previous results but not all are estimated with sufficient precision to warrant sharp distinctions. Business and government cash savings are significant determinants of personal cash saving. Neither the real interest rate nor the rate of inflation is an important determinant of personal cash saving, but the uncertainty with which inflationary expectations are held is in itself a significant determinant of saving.

When we compared 6-1 and 6-4 for instances of coefficient instability between 1951–74 and 1955–74, we found the following. The variables S_{-1}, (*SI* + *FRINGE*), and *SD* are highly significant and their coefficients are robust with respect to the sample period. *LPCASH* is highly significant, and although its coefficient increases from about 0.3 to about 0.4 when the early years are dropped from the sample, the change is clearly not statistically significant. The coefficient of the imputations variable, *IMP*, is particularly unstable, but the variable is insignificant. The tax variable, *TX*, is insignificant in the full sample period (6-1) but is quite significant in the 1955–74 period (6-4), when its absolute value differs little from the coefficient of labor and property cash income, *LPCASH*. It is also clear that the size of the coefficient on tax payments is heavily dependent on whether or not the inflation variables are included, indicating an obvious correlation between real taxes and inflation.

The variable measuring cash receipts from social and private pensions and insurance, *TRCASH,* has a marginally significant coefficient of about 0.7 in the full sample, but a clearly significant coefficient of about 0.9 for 1955–74. This may not be much of a mystery because the coefficients are insignificantly different from unity in each of the periods; if 1.0 is the true value, in the short run every dollar reduction in pension and insurance benefits results in a dollar reduction in cash saving.

Table 6 contains some important results for the ultrarationality hypothesis. For the full sample (6-1) the point estimate implies that a one dollar increase in business cash saving reduces personal cash saving by about 48 cents. The corresponding result for the 1955–74 period indicates a substitution of about 70 cents. In either case it is not possible to reject the hypothesis that business cash saving is regarded as both "personal" income and "personal" saving in the sense of David and Scadding. A formal statement of this rationality hypothesis is $a_2 - a_7 = 1$ in equation 29, on the assumption that business cash saving is viewed as an addition to labor and property income. The data do not reject this hypothesis for either sample period. Government cash saving also has a significant negative impact on personal cash saving, although it is somewhat less pronounced than the business saving effect. The point estimate in equation 6-1 implies a reduction of 34 cents in personal cash saving per dollar increase in government saving in the full sample period. The shorter sample period yields a corresponding effect of 19 cents. These results indicate that there is less than complete substitution of government saving for personal saving.

The evidence on social plus private pensions and insurance seems to favor the view that there is substitution between $(SI + FRINGE)$ and personal cash saving. However, the estimate of this effect is quite sensitive to whether the inflation variables appear in the equation.

Finally, we turn to the major question of whether there exists an interest rate effect. By this time we think it is unlikely. In the presence of our income decomposition and the variables measuring cash saving by business and government, inflation, and uncertainty, the interest rate is clearly insignificant. Indeed, the real after-tax interest rate is insignificant even if we drop the expected inflation and uncertainty variables (π, SD) or the variables for business and government saving (BCS, GCS). It is possible that equations indicating a strong effect of the interest rate on saving give inadequate attention to nonpersonal saving and inflation. An obvious negative correlation exists between *BCS* and the interest rate because higher interest charges reduce profits; and there is a positive correlation between the interest rate and the inflation rate. This implies the potential for spurious correlation with a vengeance.

For the sake of completeness, we review the last two equations in table 6. Equation 6-5 presents the results obtained using NIPA personal saving as the dependent variable, and 6-6 shows the results for FF personal saving. We have argued that neither of these saving concepts is relevant for an analysis of the supply of loanable funds. In any event, these equations show that our result for the interest elasticity of saving is not unique to our use of personal cash saving. Neither NIPA saving nor FF saving shows a significant effect of the interest rate. Indeed, as we anticipated earlier when we discussed the effect of including durable goods and purchases of homes in these saving concepts, the coefficients on the interest rate in these equations are both negative, with FF saving having a particularly high value.

Principal Findings

In this paper we address the interest sensitivity of the resources that individuals make available for financing business capital formation. We argue that neither of the traditional measures of saving, NIPA personal saving or FF personal saving, is the appropriate empirical counterpart for personal loanable-funds saving. We believe that the appropriate loanable-funds concept is personal cash saving, which, unlike NIPA and FF saving, excludes expenditures on both owner-occupied buildings and consumer durables.

If this view is correct, the empirical evidence of previous studies is not directly relevant to the major question regarding interest sensitivity. Virtually all the studies of which we are aware are concerned with the more traditional saving concepts. Our review of previous research produces a number of reasons to question the conclusion that there is a significant positive relationship between personal saving, however defined, and the rate of interest. The sensitivity of these empirical results to small variations in the sample period, to the definitions of variables, and to the dynamic specification of the saving equation weaken substantially our confidence in such results. Moreover, none of the previous studies we reviewed has dealt adequately with the ultrarationality hypothesis discussed by David and Scadding.

Based on this review and our empirical work we conclude that David and Scadding were correct in claiming that the current data uphold Denison's law. Stated more conservatively, the data we examined are consistent with the following formulation of the equilibrium function for personal loanable-funds saving:

$$(30) \quad S \cong d_1(YCNC + \theta_1 BCS + \theta_2 GCS) - \mu_1 BCS - \mu_2 GCS.$$

Our empirical results are consistent with $\theta_1 = \mu_1 = 1$, but not with $\theta_2 = \mu_2 = 1$; rather, they suggest that θ_2 and μ_2 are less than unity but not zero. Thus the results are not in conflict with the proposition that business saving is a nearly perfect substitute for personal saving. Government saving is also apparently viewed as a substitute for personal saving, though not to the same extent as business saving is. In general, the parameter estimates are sensitive both to the sample period used and to the way inflation and uncertainty are treated, but the following approximation appears to tell the essence of the story. With $\mu_1 \cong 1$ and $\theta_1 \cong 1$, equation 30 can be rewritten as

$$(31) \qquad \frac{S + BCS}{YCNC + BCS} \cong d_1 + (d_1\theta_2 - \mu_2) \frac{GCS}{YCNC + GCS}.$$

This implies that the gross private loanable-funds saving rate is approximately constant in the long run. Approximate constancy follows both because $(d_1\theta_2 - \mu_2)$ is estimated to be small and because GCS is negligible in comparison with $(S + BCS)$. Over the 1951–74 period, for example, GCS averaged only 8 percent of the average value of gross private loanable-funds saving. Equations 30 and 31 neglect short-run variability arising from variability in the relative shares of the components of total income and in changes in uncertainty about inflation.[38] As for the major question, there simply is no strong evidence that loanable-funds saving can be manipulated by policy aimed at changing the after-tax rate of return to saving.

Our nonresult—that we have been unable to isolate a significant interest rate effect—is not surprising. There are good reasons to find the nonresult believable. The microeconomic theory of saving permits

---

38. Variation in income components relative to total income and in the inflation variables are obviously more detailed, and perhaps behavioral, alternatives to adjusting for the business cycle by means of the unemployment rate or the GNP gap.

any effect from interest rates (positive, negative, or none) for a net saver, and the net cash savers surely outweigh the net cash dissavers. Two factors in our analysis cancel the positive effect of the interest rate that others have found. The first is the effect of inflation on saving. Taking advantage of the recently developed option of measuring both expectations and uncertainty about inflation, we find evidence in support of the proposition long espoused by Katona, Juster, and others. The incentive to "save for a rainy day" has a strong effect when uncertainty (*SD*) increases. And it is easy to see how the interest rate could enter the picture as a proxy for the direct influence of uncertainty effects in saving equations. The second factor is ultrarationality: the apparent substitutability of direct personal saving and saving done "on an individual's behalf" by the business sector. One could argue, we suppose, that the significance of business cash saving derives from sources unrelated to ultrarationality; for example, times are bad or are getting bad when *BCS* declines, so individuals save more. Because *BCS* has a greater negative impact on saving in the absence of *SD* than when *SD* is present in the saving function (table 6), the possibility exists that the *BCS* variable represents the reaction to uncertainty. But *SD* should and apparently does pick that up and still leaves *BCS* with a statistically significant effect. And even if the *BCS* effect does not measure ultrarationality, but rather a different aspect of uncertainty than that contained in *SD,* it is clearly doing so better than the interest rate with which it is correlated. It is difficult to turn the argument around and claim that there is an important effect of the rate of return that is better measured by *BCS* than by the rate of return itself.

There are many good reasons for tax reform, but there is no good evidence to support the view that a positive interest elasticity of loanable-funds saving is one of them.

Comments by Robert Z. Lawrence

The discussion of the Howrey-Hymans paper at the recent meeting of the Brookings panel was concerned with four main questions, which will form an organizing framework for this summary:

1. What are the theoretic predictions about the effects on saving of changes in the rate of return?

2. Which variables belong in empirical estimates of saving behavior?

3. What can be learned from these aggregate regressions about saving behavior?

4. What are the policy implications of these findings?

Economic theory is agnostic on the relation between saving and the interest rate. When the rate of return on saving rises, there is both a substitution effect and an income effect, and the sum of these effects may be either positive or negative. However, it was pointed out in the discussion that even when a compensating tax is levied to make up the taxes on capital income forgone, the effect upon personal saving will be ambiguous. If a person consumes more in the future, he or she may actually give up less in the present to do so. Feldstein has argued, however, that aggregate (as opposed to personal) saving will rise in response to such a compensated change. But he assumes that the government does two things: maintains its own consumption patterns and applies the tax relief only to new saving (otherwise it will find itself out of pocket during the transitional phase until the existing capital stock depreciates to zero).[39] If the government does not act in this way, one cannot be sure what the saving response will be.

The variables that the authors used in their regressions generated considerable discussion. A number of panel members raised questions about the authors' focus on what they call "personal cash saving." It was felt that this variable amounts to only a small part of aggregate saving and that it would be misleading to infer the overall effects of changes in interest rates on saving from the response to this variable. The authors pointed out that the variance in personal cash saving was almost as large as the variance in the flow-of-funds measure, but others responded that for the question at hand it was the size of the long-run equilibrium response rather than the variable's historic variation that was relevant.

Much of the discussion focused on the possible measurement errors associated with the authors' (and Boskin's) proxies for the expected real net yield relevant to saving behavior. It was noted that an entire schedule of rates belongs in the equation. Very few savers actually hold Baa bonds in their portfolios, and the use of other rates might give very different answers. One suggestion was to use time de-

39. Martin Feldstein, "The Rate of Return, Taxation and Personal Savings," *Economic Journal,* vol. 88 (September 1978), pp. 482–87.

posit rates, as these are widely held, but it was pointed out that the measured return on time assets excludes the substantial liquidity premium that these assets command.

It was pointed out, too, that consumer credit rates belong in the equation and that when one looks at the cost of consumer credit one gets a very different picture about people's rates of time preference. In addition, the difficulties of coming up with appropriate measures of the relevant expected return measure were mentioned. Questions were also raised about the appropriateness of the particular tax variable the authors had used. It was argued that this variable might not be applicable to the return on personal cash saving. One panel member felt that the authors ought to have distinguished between the permanent and the transitory components of their income variable.

Howrey and Hymans agreed that a broader range of asset yields was appropriate but explained that the small number of observations dictated the use of only one. The Baa rate has dominated all other rates in the equations. One participant suggested that the great sensitivity of this rate to changes in uncertainty might explain both its strong performance and the subsequent decline in its significance once an explicit uncertainty measure was entered.

It should also be mentioned that panel members were unsure about how Boskin had generated his interest rate variable; some felt that this was more cause for concern than the fact that his equation did not stand up unchanged to the reestimations the authors had subjected it to.

More serious questions were raised about how useful this entire exercise had been. Many participants believed that the meager data base precluded taking account of the numerous factors relevant to lifetime saving decisions. And the authors agreed that a richer data base, with panel data, was really needed to derive a structural model to explore how reactions differ by wealth, income, and demographic characteristics. As the authors noted, these weaknesses apply to *all* studies using only aggregate data, not just their own.

The panel also discussed what the policy implications of findings of a particular interest elasticity of saving would be. There is a general impression, it was said, that when economists talk about that question they ignore the issue of income distribution and rely upon vague theoretical suggestions that there might be some benefits from reducing taxation on capital. But to make such a measure politically acceptable, one would need a sounder empirical knowledge of what the distribution effects of such a measure might be. Moreover, several participants thought it necessary to distinguish between two very different social goals. The first is the goal of the optimal quantity of social saving, and the second the goal of the most efficient way of raising taxes. It was pointed out that, given the high degree of uncertainty about the aggregate response of saving to interest rates, as well as the availability of far more effective tools to influence aggregate saving and capital formation and its distribution between the private and public sectors, changing the rate of return on saving is not really a suitable tool for changing the aggregate quantity of social savings. On the other hand, the compensated interest elasticity of saving is relevant to the issue of how a given quantity of tax revenue can be raised so as to minimize the misallocation of resources incurred by so doing.

The question of how heavily capital should be taxed depends essentially upon the (compensated) supply elasticity of saving. It is this quantity elasticity (on future consumption) that is the relevant indicator of intertemporal distortion. A zero elasticity with respect to the real rate of return would imply a unitary elasticity of substitution between present and future consumption; that is, when the interest rate rises by 1 percent, the amount of future consumption will rise by 1 percent even if savings are not increased. However, as a number of panel members noted, if the government is to raise an equivalent amount of revenue elsewhere, it will presumably impose inefficiencies on the economy. In the case of an income tax these costs will influence the choice between labor and leisure and must be taken into account in this second-best exercise.

Comments by Michael J. Boskin

My comments on the paper by Howrey and Hymans are divided into three parts: comments on their critique of my study; comments on their estimates of saving equations and on Denison's law; and discussion about the relation of the interest elasticity of saving to the desirability of income or consumption taxation.

My first reaction to seeing such eminent authors as Howrey and Hymans devote so much attention to my early work on the consumption-saving choice was that I was flattered. Unfortunately, as I continued studying their paper, I noted that they did not cover in any detail the most important parts of my work. Therefore my first comment is that they have totally ignored—to the extent of not even discussing—the most important results from my *Journal of Political Economy* paper or *any* of the results from my Treasury compendium paper with Lawrence Lau.[40] In each of these—the latter half of my *JPE* paper and the entire compendium paper—I estimated interest elasticities much larger than those contained in the equation Howrey and Hymans sought to reestimate. One of the major points in my *JPE* paper was that it was not reasonable to estimate consumption functions by single-equation methods; indeed, it was necessary to use an instrumental variables technique. In the second half of that paper I did so, using as instruments principal components of a variety of exogenous variables from the major macroeconometric models. This resulted in a doubling of the estimated interest elasticity from about 0.2 to 0.4, with one estimate as high as 0.6. In my paper with Lau, we embedded the consumption-saving choice in a full model that allowed for a labor-leisure choice; this too resulted in precise estimates of an interest elasticity of saving of about 0.4. Once again, the instruments used were principal components of exogenous variables of macroeconomic models. This procedure not only accounts for cyclical fluctuations but in principle distinguishes our saving (or consumption) function from investment behavior. Hence I am in the somewhat embarrassing position of commenting on a critique of my study that focuses on the issue of the interest elasticity of saving and uses my equations with the lowest estimated interest elasticity—equations that I personally, for the economic and statistical reasons discussed in the papers mentioned above, do not claim to be my best results. In brief, the authors have been very selective in the part of my work they have chosen to review, and under no circumstances would I consider their results and reestimations a satisfactory discussion of my previous work.

I do not even believe that the authors' interpretation of their reestimation of my equations casts serious doubt on the basic estimates. Any battery of reestimates of any time-series equation is likely to

40. Boskin, "Taxation, Saving, and the Rate of Interest"; Michael J. Boskin and Lawrence J. Lau, "Taxation and Aggregate Factor Supply: Preliminary Estimates," in Department of the Treasury, Office of Tax Analysis, *1978 Compendium of Tax Research* (GPO, 1978), pp. 1–15.

change the results. For example, in runs where the t-statistics are reduced to only marginal significance, Howrey and Hymans make much more of this than is reasonable. Reducing the t-statistic so that the estimated elasticity of approximately 0.2 is only marginally significant is not the same as demonstrating that it is remarkably small and economically insignificant. Indeed, most of the estimates confirm my previous results; for example, taking a Koyck lag results in estimates that are similar to my original equations. Dropping observations, lagging observations, changing the sample period, and so forth sometimes reduce the estimated coefficient to statistical insignificance (usually because the number of observations has decreased or because the variability of the right-hand variable is so reduced that a precise estimate of the coefficient could not be obtained). There are a number of suggestions given as to why the authors have chosen to lag unemployment and so on, but again I must point out that the instrumental variables technique used in the second half of my *JPE* paper essentially accounts for the cyclical pattern of the economy, its growth, and the interaction of saving and investment. Hence I must conclude that even if the work they review were all I had presented, the Howrey-Hymans paper would not alter my conclusions very much. Indeed, their results reflect exactly what I would have expected would happen from a variety of transformations, dropping observations, changing sample periods, and the like. But again, more important, the selective nature of their critique ignores the most important sets of estimates that, coincidentally, are those with the largest estimated elasticities. This renders their analysis somewhat less relevant than it might appear.

Next I turn to Denison's law. It was pointed out to me by my colleague Victor Fuchs that the female–male wage ratio in both 1960 and 1970, holding other things constant, was approximately 0.6 and that if one looked at the Bible, in particular Leviticus, one would note that female slaves sold for 30 shekels of silver while male slaves sold for 50. I would attach no more structural interpretation to Denison's law—the alleged constancy of the gross private saving rate and the inability of any economic policies to affect it—than to the much longer apparent constancy of the female–male wage ratio. One of the two main points of my *JPE* paper was the foolishness of trying to draw strong structural inferences about saving behavior from the apparent constancy of the gross private saving rate.

I do not see how anyone could disagree with this point. I am glad to see that Howrey and Hymans seem to agree with it, although it deserves more than their casual mention.

And what problems exist in the structural interpretation of Denison's law? First, neither the numerator nor the denominator, gross private saving or gross national product, measure the economically relevant concepts. Human capital is omitted from the analysis, even though John Kendrick, Jacob Mincer, and others have indicated that much saving, especially early in life, is in the form of human capital. Also missing is the net saving of U.S. citizens overseas, which has greatly increased in recent years. Saving theory relates to net income and net saving, and again these vary markedly. Indeed, an interest in gross saving would only occur in the United States if we were strong believers in embodied technical change and cared about the rate of turnover of the capital stock. My own estimate suggests that the coefficient of variation of net saving is a large multiple of the coefficient of variation of gross saving for the postwar period. Further, this coefficient of variation would increase substantially if saving were adjusted to reflect replacement rather than historical cost depreciation. I take this to be a strong indictment of the simplest structural interpretation of Denison's law.

It is also worth observing that a constancy has never been noted in the private saving rate of any other country for a sustained period of time. Michael Edelstein has noted a substantial interest elasticity of saving in the United Kingdom, and Paul David has found that true of the United States in the nineteenth century. Even if the view were taken that public consumption and private consumption were perfect substitutes for each other, so that the share of total consumption, public and private, out of income was a constant share of wealth (as David and Scadding have argued), the fraction of wealth consumed would still be a function of the *net* rate of interest, whereas income would be a flow from wealth at the gross rate of interest. As a consequence, policies that affected the ratio of the net rate to the gross rate of interest would affect the consumption-saving choice.

Moreover, important changes affecting saving have occurred in the U.S. economy in the last few decades. The changing age structure of the population has been marked. The ratio of retirees to workers will go up 75 percent shortly after the turn of the century because of the combination of the post–World War II "baby boom" and the recent "baby bust." Since World War II the life expectancy at age 60 has increased about a year and a half for men and three years for women, and the average retirement age has gone down substantially. For example, in 1948 one-half of men over the age of 65 were in the labor force. That number is now about one in five. This implies perhaps a 30 percent increase in the average retirement period. A large increase in the female labor force participation rate has occurred. The huge growth in the public sector includes a large rise in both average and marginal tax rates and an enormous growth in social insurance programs, such as those for social security and unemployment, that may substitute for private saving. The increase in inflation in the last ten years affects saving decisions. There has been a sizable decrease in the average workweek—about 22 percent since 1929. This alone renders GNP suspect as an income measure. The saving rate out of "full income" has fallen substantially. And tremendous changes have occurred in typical family patterns. Each of these factors, if it had happened alone, would have resulted in substantial changes in saving. The fact that they have balanced out one another is what leads to the apparent constancy in the gross private saving rate, and I see no reason to give a structural interpretation to that fact.

Efforts ought to be devoted to disentangling these effects rather than to giving strong structural interpretations to the reduced-form outcome. My own current research is specifically designed to disentangle such age and household effects from interest rate, income, and other effects on saving.

I now turn to the second half of the Howrey-Hymans paper, in which the authors discuss their estimates of saving equations. They look at only a small fraction of saving. Though this does account for a substantial fraction of the total variance, they essentially regress one component of saving on other components of saving, or the sum of other components of saving. This is the same as regressing the consumption of automobiles on the consumption of cigarettes, the consumption of food, and so forth. That is, it results in the usual kinds of specification bias and correlation between right-hand variables and the error terms in such estimated equations. Hence the estimated coefficients are biased, and I can give no statistical interpretation to their results. Ideally what ought to be done—and I think Howrey and Hymans would agree with me—is to disaggregate saving into its numerous components, include the rates of return of all types of saving in the economy and their covariances as well as a variety of other determinants of aggregate saving, and estimate a system of such equations. Unfortunately, this puts extreme data demands on the researcher, demands that are well beyond current capabilities. That is why I focused on aggregate consumption functions in the first place.

The Howrey-Hymans interest rate variable suffers from a major conceptual error. *They subtracted a one-year expected inflation rate from a long-term bond rate.* Obviously, an expected inflation rate over the time horizon of the bond is necessary. In my *JPE* paper I contributed such estimates of long-term expected inflation rates. I also constructed estimates of the long-term expected return to capital from the Jorgenson-Christensen data on actual returns to capital. I used alternative measures of the long-run expected real net rate of return based on Moody's bond rates, high-grade municipal bond rates, and the expected long-run return to capital. Though the results differed slightly, each estimate of the long-run expected net-of-tax rate of return to saving produced a modest positive estimated interest elasticity of private saving. In view of the inconsistency in the generation of the Howrey-Hymans interest rate series and the likelihood that measurement error biases the estimated coefficients (in addition to the biases noted above), I do not believe much weight should be given to the equations they report with their own generated rates of return.

A number of other issues relate to the interest elasticity of saving. To begin, it is simply not the case that a positive interest elasticity of saving implies that a consumption tax is preferable to an income tax and that a negative interest elasticity or a zero interest elasticity implies that an income tax is preferable. It could be that a consumption tax, or even an interest income subsidy, is desirable with a negative interest elasticity of saving; and a saving tax or a high interest tax—perhaps one even heavier than that at present—could be desirable with a positive interest elasticity of saving. As pointed out in papers by Joseph Stiglitz and me, by Martin Feldstein, and by A. B. Atkinson and Stiglitz,[41] for example, this choice depends upon the relative substitutability and complementarity with leisure of consumption

41. Joseph E. Stiglitz and Michael J. Boskin, "Some Lessons from the New Public Finance," *American Economic Review*, vol. 67 (February 1977, *Papers and Proceedings, 1976*), pp. 295–301; Martin Feldstein, "The Welfare Cost of Capital Income Taxation," *Journal of Political Economy*, vol. 86 (April 1978), pt. 2, pp. S29–S51; A. B. Atkinson and J. E. Stiglitz, "The Design of Tax Structure: Direct versus Indirect Taxation," *Journal of Public Economics*, vol. 6 (July–August 1976), pp. 55–75.

early in working life and consumption during retirement. The full set of such compensated cross-price elasticities must be known in order to reach a conclusion about the desirable, or efficient, degree of taxation of capital income. Lighter taxation, or subsidization, of capital income increases with the interest elasticity of saving only if all other things remain unchanged.

Next, general equilibrium growth effects imply that the interest elasticity of saving in the overall economy is likely to be larger than that embedded in single-equation consumption estimates such as mine, or estimates of the elasticity of substitution in utility functions between consumption now and consumption in the future. The growth of the population and the likely growth of income because of technical change implies that, to obtain the total derivative of saving with respect to the interest rate, researchers would have to take account of the fact that a large fraction of total saving is being done by the young; and that it has to be compared with the dissaving being done by the elderly. Evidence of an enormous amount of dissaving done by young workers would be a strong indictment of a large estimated interest elasticity. Actually it appears that there is a substantial amount of saving done by young workers, although it is mostly in the form of investment in human capital.

I should also note that there are two issues in saving efficiency. The first is the "golden rule" rate, in which the marginal product of capital will equal the rate of growth of the effective labor force, or the profit share in the economy will equal the net saving rate. If saving were below this golden rule rate, as Arthur Okun and others have mentioned, a variety of policy instruments could be used to deal with the problem: for example, by changes in government fiscal policy like running a surplus and modifying social security financing. There is still the issue of the misallocation of consumption during individuals' lifetimes if their lifetime consumption-saving choices are distorted by the heavy taxation of interest income. The second-best problem, as pointed out repeatedly by Feldstein, Atkinson, Stiglitz, Diamond, myself, and others, also needs to account for misallocations in the labor market. These misallocations are purely a function of the compensated elasticities, not the uncompensated ones. Even if the total interest elasticity were zero, the compensated elasticity might be positive; if the total interest elasticity were negative, the compensated forward-price elasticity of the demand for future consumption could still be negative. In either of these cases a situation would result in which a consumption tax or a lighter taxation of interest than labor income might be desirable.

If through dynastic families or any other means, households took a much longer run view and, for example, maximized the sum of discounted utility à la Ramsey, all the problems under consideration would be transitory, and the economy would converge to a new steady state with the same real net rate of return.

Finally, Howrey and Hymans do point out that my work on consumption functions—like all other work on consumption functions, with few exceptions—does not explicitly build a dynamic model of saving behavior. I concur with this observation, and I am working on this problem now. I only report that my original results did not do so because I was hoping to compare them with the traditional consumption function estimates. And there are few parameters of more interest in the economy than the interest elasticity of saving. This parameter affects our notions about the long-run efficacy of fiscal and monetary policy, the effect of inflation on the real economy, the incidence of various taxes, the desirability of consumption versus income taxes, and the social rate of discount or the social opportunity cost of public funds. Further research is desperately needed, and I look forward to adding Howrey and Hymans to the list of people who are working hard to increase our knowledge about the subject.

Comments by John A. Brittain

Economists have lived a long time on a priori assumptions about the interest elasticity of saving and investment. Moreover, these largely untested assumptions have continued to play a key role in macro-economics. The shortage of serious empirical analysis of the interest elasticity of saving used to be a mystery, but that is no longer the case. After the Howrey and Hymans paper and much astute discussion, one's chief impression is that the empirical problem is quite intractable.

The authors deserve much credit for tackling this central problem and making an important contribution despite endless difficulties. In my opinion, they have looked conscientiously and skillfully for persuasive evidence against the null hypothesis of zero interest elasticity of saving, and they have found very little. As though the authors' task were not arduous enough, some of the discussion at the BPEA meeting in September 1978 appeared to fault them for what they did not do, or for having too modest an objective.[42] Of course, they did not "prove" that the null hypothesis is correct, nor did they assert that the interest elasticity of saving is the sole relevant consideration in comparing income and expenditure taxes. Nevertheless, their case against earlier findings of positive elasticity remains an important contribution. Their objectives should be put in perspective.

The Relation of the Paper to the Conference Topic

What is the relevance of the interest elasticity of saving to the choice between income and expenditure taxation? The exclusion of saving from the tax base, whether or not compensated by increases in other taxes, would raise the after-tax yield on saving. Among the potential consequences of this are increased capital formation *and* favorable welfare effects. Howrey and Hymans have stressed the former and take for granted that any positive interest elasticity of saving will have a stimulating effect on capital accumulation, productivity, and growth. They are especially addressing those who are already convinced that saving and capital formation are too low and believe that a positive interest elasticity of saving would therefore constitute one argument for the expenditure tax.

Feldstein and Shoven have put forth significant qualifications to the analysis of Howrey and Hymans. Shoven noted that it is the elasticity of substitution between present and future consumption that is most directly relevant to policy on the taxation of income from capital; for example, a zero uncompensated elasticity of saving with respect to the real rate of return would imply a unitary elasticity of substitution. Moreover, he assumes that an uncompensated reduction of the taxation on saving would promote efficiency, but warns that in practice another tax would usually replace it and detract from this gain in efficiency. However, in response to the discussants' assumption that they were estimating uncompensated elasticities, the authors claim that they have actually estimated compensated elasticities in table 6—their last set of estimates. They base that claim on their inclusion of the after-tax rate of return and personal tax payments as explanatory variables. In these models, however, they have only 12 to 15 degrees of freedom in estimating their coefficients; for this reason and others, the lack of significance of their interest rate coefficient in this par-

---

42. See the discussion by Martin Feldstein, John Shoven, and others in *BPEA, 3:1978*, pp. 686–705.

ticular table is not very persuasive. Feldstein notes the uncertain effects on personal saving of any substitution of a consumption or payroll tax for the tax on capital income. But he argues that a *compensated* tax change that raises the real net return on personal saving must necessarily increase the total of government and private saving.

At times Feldstein appears to downgrade the importance of the interest elasticity of saving. He argues that even under a zero uncompensated interest elasticity of saving, a welfare gain might still be achieved by cutting the tax on interest income. This would change the pattern of consumption over the life cycle even if saving did not increase. If the supply elasticity of work effort were also zero, a gain in welfare could also be attained by a compensating substitution of a tax on wages for a tax on interest. Boskin concluded earlier that the welfare effect of such an offsetting tax change is only moderately sensitive to the compensated interest elasticity of the saving rate.[43]

The comments by Shoven, Feldstein, and others on the general objectives of Howrey and Hymans and the implications of their findings appear to be more like qualifications and refinements than fundamental criticism. It seems generally agreed that empirical estimates of the effect on saving of uncompensated changes in the real net rate of return would be useful. There is also no reason to believe that the authors' emphasis on saving as a source of capital accumulation is at all misplaced. The extent to which the authors and others before them have achieved their objectives is considered next.

The Focus on Personal Cash Saving

The authors offer a useful reconciliation of three different variants of personal saving (see table 4). They argue pragmatically and per-

43. Boskin, "Taxation, Saving, and the Rate of Interest," p. S19. Boskin's conclusion depends on a function of "the tax-induced increase in the price of future consumption and the compensated change in future consumption." For example, when he assumes that the interest elasticity is 0.4 while making many other assumptions, he finds an annual welfare loss of $56 billion attributable to the tax-induced distortion of consumption over the life cycle. Although skepticism about such estimates may be rather common, it may be worth noting that the insertion of a zero compensated interest elasticity of saving in the same formula yields a welfare loss of $40 billion. Thus, according to this calculation, a compensated interest elasticity of 0.4 increases the welfare loss by 40 percent over that implied for zero elasticity. (Boskin's use of 0.4 in this formula is questionable, since his empirically derived estimate of 0.4 is presumably an uncompensated elasticity.)

suasively that only cash saving can be borrowed by firms to finance capital formation and that this is the form of saving that might be influenced by tax policy affecting the rate of return. In other words, those who believe that the personal saving rate is too low to contribute adequately to capital formation would probably like to try to influence cash saving rather than such saving components as investment in owner-occupied homes. Their exclusion of changes in reserves of private pension plans, however, is debatable. Even though these funds may become available for capital formation, the authors exclude them on the ground that they are a part of the net cash flow of the business sector. But their cost is probably met by firms only nominally. Their exclusion seems inappropriate if pension accumulations are regarded as part of the claims by individuals to their total compensation—claims that have been accepted by individuals in place of cash wages. Insofar as they are traded off against wages and salaries, they represent personal saving as surely as money in the bank does. Their inclusion would increase the Howrey-Hymans personal saving estimate for 1975 by 77 percent.

Shoven made the important observation that the authors' variant of personal cash saving is relatively small—only 20 percent of business cash saving in 1975, for example. In effect, any given elasticity pertaining only to personal saving would be a misleading indication of the potential impact of tax policy on total saving. The authors replied that personal saving is more important than it looks because of its relatively large variance. In evaluating the tax policy lever, however, the expected value of any predicted saving increase is important, and that would be small if personal cash saving were small.

The revelation by Howrey and Hymans of the relatively minor role of personal cash saving has other implications. Given the various methodological problems of their study, their conclusion that there is now no evidence of a substantial interest elasticity of personal cash saving must be tentative. But the small size of that component of saving backs up their finding because it suggests that even a significant positive elasticity would be of little moment if applicable only to personal cash saving.[44] In that case, measures affecting business saving, such as corporation income taxes, tax credits, and dividend taxation, would be more effective policy levers in promoting capital formation.

44. This point would lose some force if pension fund accumulations were included in personal saving.

The Consumption Function Models

The important methodological problems faced by all investigators, including the present authors, have already been spelled out chillingly by Feldstein and Shoven. Perhaps the most important is the difficulty of defining and measuring the expected real net rate of return that could be observed by individuals and possibly affect their saving behavior. Also important are the shortness of the series available and the limitations of the single equation models. It will suffice here to add a few generalizations.

Howrey and Hymans start with the work Boskin did in showing significant positive and large saving elasticities, estimated within plausible consumption functions.[45] The authors are, of course, far more successful in their attempts to refute those findings than they are at persuading others that the evidence indeed shows that the elasticity *is* small. Because of the many methodological problems, it is easier to undermine an allegedly significant coefficient than to gain support for the hypothesis of no elasticity. Moreover, in my opinion, even the authors' generally successful critique of Boskin's findings has lost some force with each of their revisions.

As the paper now stands, the evidence against Boskin's concept of positive elasticity is only moderately persuasive. The technique of adding variables and dropping observations is a perfectly appropriate procedure, but it should be emphasized that it somewhat favors the authors' position by sacrificing degrees of freedom and making it harder to salvage significant coefficients. Even so, I find quite impressive the halving of the *t*-ratio on the elasticity coefficient when autocorrelated residuals are allowed for and 1934 is dropped. However, the Boskin coefficient did not finally succumb until a new executioner—the unemployment rate lagged two years—was included.[46] The reason for its inclusion was to cancel out any cyclical role played by the rate of return variable. But this highly effective executioner was discovered simply by inspection, and no rationale was given for the two-year lag. Although I believe the authors have been scrupulously

45. Boskin, "Taxation, Saving and the Rate of Interest."
46. There is a contradiction between two versions of the paper. The last indicated that Boskin had already corrected for the autocorrelation of residuals and that simply dropping 1934 cut the *t*-ratio from 3.24 to 1.62. The previous version had indicated that the coefficient was only undermined to this extent by correcting for autocorrelation *and* dropping 1934.

fair, this particular example tends to nourish Boskin's complaint that many things were tried simply to destroy his coefficient.

Despite these reservations, it is fair to say that in the total of their work Howrey and Hymans have cast great doubt on Boskin's elasticity estimate. Yet their case has gradually lost force with each revision. They dropped all the persuasive analysis they did with Boskin's model before receiving his data. In the last version of the paper, the lagged dependent variable (consumption) was also dropped. It is not easy to fault brevity, but this mountain of earlier regressions with no significant interest elasticities constituted a more impressive exhibit; it should at least be given passing reference in support of the Howrey-Hymans conclusion.

Some questions remain about Boskin's result. First, the authors report that his implied saving variable was close to the flow-of-funds variant and thus included net investment in consumer durables and housing. These are assumed likely to vary *inversely* with the rate of interest. Their exclusion, as in the Howrey-Hymans saving variant, should therefore increase the positive saving elasticity found by Boskin. Apparently this was never tested. No version of equation 2, with the Howrey-Hymans implied saving and Boskin's rate of return, is ever reported. Excluding these variants of saving that were perhaps negatively correlated with the interest rate might have raised the estimated interest elasticity and strengthened Boskin's case before it was subjected to Howrey and Hymans' sensitivity tests.

The second question relates to the first. If Boskin's saving variant leads to a preliminary underestimate of the elasticity, as suggested above, his result for the Howrey-Hymans variant will depart even further from theirs. What can account for this great difference between the Boskin result and the many other results reported in this paper? For example, in table 5 equations 5-1, 5-4, and 5-7 report results for the amended Boskin framework explaining savings with a nominal interest rate. The lack of significance of this rate and the expected real rates of return elsewhere suggest that the key to Boskin's result may be the particular rate of return series he used. This series is described by the authors as smoothed and processed. It would be helpful to know more about this measure of the expected real rate of return. Indeed, the mystery that continues to shroud the generation of this series augments the Howrey-Hymans tests as grounds for great skepticism concerning Boskin's reported positive elasticity.

Further Tests and Analysis of Earlier Work

The adaptive expectations saving model of Houthakker and Taylor is congenial, except for its disconcerting injection of nominal interest rates in place of the expected real rate of return. Howrey and Hymans suggest that the significant interest elasticity of saving reported by Taylor may thus be due to misspecification. Again the authors have dropped some of their important earlier work, which showed that the interest elasticity disappears when a plausible measure of uncertainty about price changes is included.

The discussion of David and Scadding on Denison's law and "ultra-rationality" seems uncontroversial. Certainly Howrey and Hymans should not be accused of taking the relative constancy of the total private saving rate as evidence of interest inelasticity. Boskin's rejection of any structural interpretation of Denison's law is a red herring in this context—inapplicable to the paper under review.

Further Elaborations of Saving Models

The authors amend the Boskin consumption function model to explain saving explicitly. They find no significant interest elasticity. However, the meaning of this result is minimized by the fact that they switch at the same time from the expected real rate of return to the actual Baa interest rate. No explanation is given for their change to this new variable, which they interpreted earlier as a misspecification on the part of Houthakker and Taylor.

The authors go on to a "deeper look" in which they integrate some features of the models previously discussed, including Houthakker-Taylor and the ultrarationality hypothesis involving a trade-off between business and personal saving. By this time there are so many variables in the model that Howrey and Hymans are left with only 12 to 15 degrees of freedom in their regressions. The consistent lack of significance of the rate of return variable is thus not very impressive. Moreover, Shoven has made a telling point about the joint determination of personal and business saving and the implausibility of having the latter explain the former.

It would be easy to discount these last findings of the authors for the reasons mentioned. However, one saving grace of table 6, despite the paucity of degrees of freedom, is the high *t*-ratios and plausible signs on a number of the explanatory variables. These do indeed make the rate of return variable look like a poor relation.

Concluding Remarks

Howrey and Hymans have greatly undermined the only currently strong evidence of a substantial interest elasticity of saving. On the other hand, the argument that this elasticity differs little from zero is inevitably less persuasive, given the few degrees of freedom in the regressions and other methodological problems. Even so, the appropriate behavior and significance of other plausible variables in these models do contrast rather sharply with the weak explanatory power of the rate of return. The authors have done very well with what they had to work with.

One suggestion made at the BPEA meeting was that an analysis across countries might be a more fruitful basis for a study of the interest elasticity of saving than the U.S. time series. Some immediate problems come to mind there also, but the approach deserves consideration.

Finally, Howrey and Hymans have discredited the interest elasticity of saving as a reason for adopting an expenditure tax. Obviously, however, many considerations are involved in the choice of a tax base other than capital formation and growth. One that seems rarely discussed in recent years is the effect on income distribution of exempting capital income from taxation. One argument is that a shift from the taxation of capital income to the taxation of labor income will change the relative price of the factors and increase the relative share of labor. A cursory look at one such demonstration suggests that, though this may be true on a pretax basis, the after-tax result is likely to be different. This question deserves attention along with the many other pros and cons brought out at this conference.

RICHARD GOODE

The Superiority
of the Income Tax

ALTHOUGH the possibility of a direct tax on consumption expenditures has attracted support from distinguished economists since John
Stuart Mill, it has not figured prominently in public or political debate. Recently efforts have been made to broaden interest in the subject in the United States, the United Kingdom, and Sweden. The
report of the U.S. Department of the Treasury, *Blueprints for Basic
Tax Reform* (Government Printing Office, 1977), and in the United
Kingdom the Meade committee report[1] supported the principle of
expenditure taxation and treated in some detail the design of an expenditure tax and its effects. In Sweden a Government Commission
on Taxation requested a study of the expenditure tax, and its final
report, presented in 1977, noted advantages of that tax, though it
remained uncertain whether personal expenditure is a more suitable
tax base than income.[2] These reports and other recent discussions

1. Institute for Fiscal Studies, *The Structure and Reform of Direct Taxation,* Report of a Committee chaired by Professor J. E. Meade (London: Allen and Unwin,
1978) (hereafter Meade committee report).
2. The study, by Sven-Olof Lodin, was published in Swedish in 1976 under the
title *Progressiv utgiftsskatt—ett alternativ?* (Stockholm: Statens Offentliga Utredningar [Public Reports of the Government] 1976:62) and in an English translation
in 1978: *Progressive Expenditure Tax—an Alternative?* A Report of the 1972 Government Commission on Taxation (Stockholm: LiberFörlag, 1978). The commission's final report, *Översyn av skattesystemet* (Review of the Tax System), was
presented in December 1977 (Statens Offentliga Utredningar 1977:91).

may help attract the attention of molders of public opinion and politicians.

Only two countries—India and Sri Lanka (formerly Ceylon)—have actually experimented with an expenditure tax. In each country the tax was adopted as a minor supplement to the income tax, in response to a persuasive report by Nicholas Kaldor.[3] Both countries abandoned the expenditure tax after brief trials. Sri Lanka tried it again in 1976, but in 1977 decided to give it up a second time. In proposing its repeal for the second time, the minister of finance of Sri Lanka characterized the expenditure tax as "unworkable and impractical in an economy like that of Sri Lanka."[4]

This paper argues that the income tax is superior to the expenditure tax. After brief comments on the nature of the two taxes, there follows a comparison of them with respect to equity, efficient allocation of economic resources, and compatibility with the full utilization of resources. The discussion is conducted initially on the assumption that both taxes are well designed and administered and without regard to the special problems arising from the existing remediable defects of the income tax or from the transition to an expenditure tax. Consideration is then given to some of these problems and to the complications caused by inflation. This leads to some remarks on the practicality of the expenditure tax and on the combination of that tax with other taxes. These sections, however, are greatly abbreviated, since the technical features of the expenditure tax and the possibility of using the expenditure tax as a supplement to other taxes are treated in more detail in other papers. The concluding section contains some comments on the semantics of the debate.

General Comparison of the Taxes

The income tax is initially assumed to be a comprehensive tax, with income defined essentially as proposed by Schanz-Haig-Simons (S-H-S) and many other supporters of the tax.[5] According to this

3. *Indian Tax Reform: Report of a Survey* (New Delhi: Ministry of Finance, Government of India, 1956); *Suggestions for a Comprehensive Reform of Direct Taxation,* Sessional Paper IV—1960 (Colombo, Ceylon: Government Publications Bureau, 1960).

4. Ronnie de Mel, *Budget Speech, 1978* (Colombo, Sri Lanka: Office of Minister of Finance and Planning, November 15, 1977), p. 52.

5. See Richard Goode, "The Economic Definition of Income," in Joseph A. Pechman, ed., *Comprehensive Income Taxation* (Brookings Institution, 1977), pp. 1–30.

definition, income is the accretion to power to consume. It consists of a person's actual consumption plus or minus any increase or decrease in the value of his power to consume in the future as measured by his net worth.

The base of an expenditure tax has been less discussed. Here it is initially assumed to equal S-H-S income less net saving (or plus net dissaving). Broadly, net saving is equal to the increase in a person's net worth (net dissaving, to the decrease in net worth). Certain difficult conceptual problems, having mainly to do with the distinction between intermediate and final goods and with fringe benefits of employment, relate to the definition of both income and consumption. But some of the troublesome problems in the measurement of S-H-S income would be irrelevant or unimportant in the measurement of taxable consumption. The most prominent of these are depreciation (capital consumption) allowances and increases or decreases in the value of investments held at the end of the tax period (accrued but unrealized capital gains or losses). Appreciation in the value of a dwelling, a work of art, or another durable good used by the owner should be taken into account in assessing his taxable consumption because the appreciation implies that the annual service value of the durable good has increased. Except for increases in nominal values caused by inflation, however, these gains appear to constitute only a small part of consumption. Their omission from the base of an expenditure tax would be far less significant than is the omission of accrued capital gains on all kinds of assets from the base of the income tax.

Recent discussions have maintained that an expenditure tax is equivalent to an income tax on a base excluding the yield of capital. This proposition and its implications are examined in a later section.

Equity

An equitable tax system must take proper account of ability to pay. This may be defined as "the capacity for paying without undue hardship on the part of the person paying or an unacceptable degree of interference with objectives that are considered socially important by other members of the community."[6] The idea that ability should be measured by a comprehensive index is attractive. Lately it has been argued that a person's "endowment" is the best indicator of

6. Richard Goode, *The Individual Income Tax*, rev. ed. (Brookings Institution, 1976), p. 17.

ability to pay. Endowment, in a broad sense, includes not only the value of the marketable goods one can consume but also the value of the time one can devote to leisure activities and household production.[7] The restriction of taxation to marketable activities omits important aspects of welfare and therefore results in an incomplete measure of ability to pay. However, the concept of endowment is nonoperational, since all will agree that no practicable way of evaluating it exists.

Indicators of ability to pay. The meaningful question is whether actual income or consumption is a better indicator of ability to pay. In my view, the total increase in a person's power to consume marketable output has greater intuitive appeal as an indicator of ability to pay than the exercise of the power to consume has. The former, which is of course income, is broader (though not truly comprehensive); the latter comprises only a part of the former. A person's decision to save a portion of his income is an individual choice and does not lessen his capacity to satisfy his private wants or to contribute to the public budget.

At this basic level, the arguments for selecting consumption rather than income as the tax base can be resolved into variants of Hobbes's assertion (which, I suspect, most writers on the subject discovered from Kaldor) that it is just for a person to be taxed on what he takes out of the common pool rather than on what he contributes to it.[8] A literal version is Andrews's statement that the principal purpose of taxation is to force a curtailment of private consumption in order to make way for government expenditure.[9] But private investment, no less than consumption, is a withdrawal from the pool, a form of utilization of production. Investment is motivated not by benevolence but by the self-regard that Adam Smith relied on to induce the butcher, the brewer, and the baker to supply him his dinner.[10] Inves-

7. Richard A. Musgrave, "ET, OT and SBT," *Journal of Public Economics,* vol. 6 (July–August 1976), pp. 3–16; Peter Mieszkowski, "The Cash Flow Version of an Expenditure Tax," OTA Paper 26 (U.S. Department of the Treasury, Office of Tax Analyses, 1977), pp. 2–3.

8. Thomas Hobbes, *Leviathan,* Everyman's Library ed. (London: J. M. Dent & Sons, 1934), chap. 30, p. 184; Nicholas Kaldor, *An Expenditure Tax* (London: Allen and Unwin, 1955; Westport, Conn.: Greenwood Press, 1977), p. 5.

9. William D. Andrews, "A Consumption-Type or Cash Flow Personal Income Tax," *Harvard Law Review,* vol. 87 (April 1974), p. 1121.

10. *An Inquiry into the Nature and Causes of the Wealth of Nations,* Edwin Cannan, ed. (Modern Library, 1937), bk. 1, chap. 2, p. 14.

tors may not capture the total benefits resulting from their activities, but neither do other participants in economic life. An objective of taxation is to restrain the private use of economic resources, including both consumption and private investment. Whether consumption or investment should give way to make room for government expenditure is a separate question that should be considered on its merits.

Lifetime income and consumption. If income and consumption are defined as suggested above, they will be equal over a person's lifetime, provided that gifts and bequests are considered income of the recipients and consumption of the donors. Under the S-H-S definition of income, gifts and bequests received would be classified as income, but it is not clear that they would be classified as consumption by the donors. Simons thought these transfers should be regarded as consumption of the donors and hence included in their income as well as in the income of the recipients.[11] If so, the differences between the income tax and the expenditure tax, with both bases comprehensively defined, would reduce to differences in the timing of tax payment. Neither *Blueprints for Basic Tax Reform* nor the Meade committee report proposes to include gifts and bequests in the taxable consumption of donors; Lodin in his study for the Swedish tax commission suggests that gifts inter vivos, but not bequests, should be treated as taxable consumption of donors.[12] Even if gifts and bequests are not included in income receipts or in consumption expenditures, it is true that the difference between lifetime income and consumption usually is relatively small. Most people do not receive or make large gifts or bequests. Hence for them the difference between the bases of an income and an expenditure tax would be mainly a matter of timing. But differences in timing are highly important, particularly in a period of inflation and high interest rates. Furthermore, in some conspicuous cases large accumulations of wealth are built up out of income and passed on to heirs; the opportunities for doing so would be greatly increased under the expenditure tax unless action were taken to prevent it.

The expenditure tax is likely to have more appeal to those who

11. Henry C. Simons, *Personal Income Taxation: The Definition of Income as a Problem of Fiscal Policy* (University of Chicago Press, 1938), pp. 125, 139–40.

12. *Progressive Expenditure Tax,* pp. 94–100. Lodin recommends that an inheritance tax apply to assets left by deceased persons.

think that taxpaying ability should be measured from a lifetime perspective than to those who look at shorter time periods. The differences in approach are associated with, among other things, beliefs about the efficiency of the capital market and the degree of rationality people exercise. If the capital market were perfect in the sense that everyone could borrow and lend at the same interest rate without transaction costs, and if people were rational planners, then the case for a lifetime perspective would be plausible, though not necessarily compelling. In the absence of these conditions I find the case weak.[13] The substitution of an expenditure tax for an income tax in the real world would mean higher taxes for the young and the old—and heavier burdens on them than on the middle-aged. This hardly accords with prevailing value judgments in our society.

Double taxation of saving. From the time of Mill, supporters of the expenditure tax have argued that it is fairer than an income tax because the latter results in the double taxation of saving. Basically the argument is simple. The income tax applies both to the receipt of income and to the return obtained by lending or investing any savings made out of after-tax income. Under the expenditure tax, tax is payable only when consumption occurs; hence no tax is due on the part of income that is saved. Although this difference may be economically significant, I consider it irrelevant to the question of fairness. The income tax does not involve double taxation in the literal sense. Both the original income and interest on savings are taxed because they represent distinct increases in the power to consume. The act of saving as such does not attract tax. No tax is due if the savings are hoarded, or if the investment is unsuccessful and the return is zero.[14] A gain obtained by lending or investing is an accretion to economic power just as wages earned by working overtime are. (No allowance

13. Richard Goode, "Long-Term Averaging of Income for Tax Purposes," in Henry J. Aaron and Michael J. Boskin, eds., *The Economics of Taxation* (Brookings Institution, forthcoming).

14. It is noteworthy—and discouraging—that many writers appear to have forgotten the important insight into the nature of individual saving that John Maynard Keynes stated so clearly in 1936. Among the relevant passages in *The General Theory of Employment, Interest, and Money* (Harcourt, Brace, 1936), two short ones may be quoted: "It should be obvious that the rate of interest cannot be a return to saving or waiting as such. For if a man hoards his savings in cash, he earns no interest, though he saves just as much as before" (pp. 166–67), and "An act of individual saving . . . is not a substitution of future consumption-demand for present consumption-demand,—it is a net diminution of such demand" (p. 210).

is made here for the possibility that nominal returns due solely to inflation will be subjected to income tax.) The term "double taxation of saving" is pejorative and should be deleted from the vocabulary of tax debate. (I shall have more to say on the subject of the treatment of saving in the section on the allocation of economic resources.)

Timing of consumption. A related but distinguishable argument is that the expenditure tax is fairer than the income tax because the first treats persons equally regardless of when they choose to consume, whereas the second favors those who consume early. To support this conclusion, it is asserted that the present value of consumption—and hence of a proportional expenditure tax—is independent of the taxpayer's choice about when he consumes, but that the present value of income—and of a proportional income tax—is increased if consumption is postponed.

To illustrate, assume that A and B have equal earned incomes in periods 1 and 2 and that A consumes all of his income as received, while B saves part of his period 1 income and consumes it together with his period 2 earnings in period 2. The assertion is that the present value of the consumption of A and B will be equal but the present value of B's income will be greater than the present value of A's income. In this form, the argument is elliptical and possibly misleading. The present value of the consumption of A and B will be equal only if B invests his savings at a rate of return equal to the discount rate used in computing present values. If this occurs, B's income will exceed A's income in period 2 by the amount of return received on B's savings. Since the cumulative amount of B's income and its present value are greater than the cumulative amount and present value of A's income, it is appropriate that B should pay more tax if income is an acceptable measure of ability to pay. B pays more tax than A, not because he postpones consumption, but because he obtains interest income, thereby enhancing his power to consume in period 2. The same result would have occurred if B had held his savings in currency and supplemented his period 2 income by working more.

To generalize, a comprehensive income tax curtails all opportunities for obtaining consumption power, whether by work or by investment. The argument under consideration implies that taxation should fall on the rewards of work but not on the return from saving-and-investing. It would be possible to avoid reducing the return from saving-and-investing, while maintaining tax revenue, only by taxing other parts of income more heavily than under a comprehensive income tax.

Tax progressivity. Another aspect of equity and ability to pay is that of tax progressivity (often called vertical equity). If progressivity is thought to be justified by some version of the sacrifice theory, it appears that the satisfactions attributable to income as a whole, including immediate consumption and additions to wealth, should be taken into account. Insofar as the justification for progressivity is considered to be that of reducing potential inequalities in economic power or status, the appropriate measure is less clear. To some, gross inequalities of consumption seem more conspicuous and more offensive than differences in income. I would stress that both consumption and wealth accumulation are exercises of economic power and that wealth accumulation confers additional power and also prestige and influence at high income levels. In the United States, the power of the rich to make investment decisions affecting the location of industry and employment, their political power, and their influence on nongovernmental educational and cultural institutions seem to me to present far more sensitive issues than their conspicuous consumption does. Power is reflected in wealth as well as in income and consumption. A case exists for an independent tax on wealth as a supplement to an income tax and a stronger case for combining it with an expenditure tax. A wealth tax ought to be more congenial to supporters of the income tax than to advocates of an expenditure tax, because it is the second group who argue that current savings, which are additions to wealth, should not be taxed.

Although there are no fully satisfactory statistics on the size distribution of comprehensively defined income and consumption, the available evidence indicates that the ratio of consumption to current income declines as income rises. A proportional expenditure tax would therefore be regressive with respect to income. To offset this effect and achieve the same degree of overall progressivity with respect to income, an expenditure tax would have to incorporate more steeply graduated rates than the income tax.[15]

Efficient Allocation of Resources

Both the income tax and the expenditure tax favor leisure, household production and consumption, and barter over activities that are

15. Goode, *Individual Income Tax,* pp. 62–65, 317–20.

channeled through the market. Therefore, under either tax more resources will be directed to nonmarket uses than would be the case if taxes could be raised in a neutral way. Especially with high tax rates, economic efficiency in both production and consumption will suffer. If their rates were the same, the income tax and the expenditure tax would equally encourage the consumption of goods and services produced by nonmarket activities. The expenditure tax might be less biased in favor of leisure (or undemanding jobs), because some work is motivated by a desire to accumulate wealth rather than to consume. However, since aggregate saving is positive and total consumption is smaller than income, expenditure tax rates would have to be higher than income tax rates to obtain equal revenue or equal effectiveness in preventing excess demand (provided the base of each tax were comprehensively defined). This would make for a greater distortion of choices between the consumption of marketed and nonmarketed goods and services under the expenditure tax and would make nontaxable fringe benefits that substitute for other consumption more attractive. The expenditure tax would be more likely to discourage entry into the labor force by housewives and other second earners, or overtime work by the primary earner, when the motivation was to obtain additional income for immediate consumption. In general, however, the higher rate of the expenditure tax would not mean a proportionately greater reduction in after-tax earnings, since a part of earnings is saved and would not be immediately subject to that tax.[16]

Saving. As noted above, the two taxes differ in their treatment of savers. Under the expenditure tax a person who saves part of his income postpones tax payment until the savings are consumed. He can, if he chooses, lend or invest his savings—including the amount that would have been paid in taxes if the income had been immediately consumed—and obtain a return by doing so. With a proportional expenditure tax, the net-of-tax rate of return from saving-and-lending

---

16. A person whose marginal saving is s percent of before-tax earnings ($0 < s < 100$) would pay the same amount of tax on an increment of earnings under an income tax at rate t_i percent as under an expenditure tax at rate $100\ t_i/(100 - s)$ percent (on a tax-inclusive base). For taxes of equal yield and similar progressivity, this relation between s and the tax rates would exist for representative individuals. I am indebted to Gerard M. Brannon and Martin J. Bailey for bringing this point to my attention and thus helping me improve the treatment in an earlier version of this paper.

or saving-and-investing (measured in relation to the amount of immediate consumption forgone) will be the same as the before-tax rate of return on loans or investments. Under the income tax, on the other hand, the after-tax rate of return will be lower than the before-tax rate. It should be emphasized that the difference is due solely to the later payment of the expenditure tax. A numerical illustration may help bring out the point. With an expenditure tax of 50 percent (on a tax-inclusive base; equivalent to 100 percent on a tax-exclusive base) a person who receives $100 of income either can enjoy $50 of consumption immediately and pay $50 of tax or can save $100. If he saves and lends the $100 at an 8 percent interest rate, he can increase his consumption by $4 a year, which is 8 percent of the amount of immediate consumption forgone by saving. With a 50 percent income tax, the amount that can be immediately consumed or saved is $50. If this is saved and lent, the before-tax return is $4, and the after-tax return is $2, which is only 4 percent of the immediate net consumption forgone.

On the assumption that, if it were not for taxation, individual responses to market rates of return would bring about the optimum amounts of saving, lending, and investing, the difference between gross and net rates of return under the income tax creates an inefficiency that does not occur under the expenditure tax. And even though the capital market has serious imperfections, their existence does not necessarily destroy the argument that the expenditure tax is more efficient in this respect. Because of the imperfections and other inefficiencies, it cannot be confidently affirmed that the removal of one tax distortion—that relating to the choice between immediate consumption and saving-and-lending to finance future consumption—would produce a net gain in economic efficiency. In my view, however, a gain would be likely if an adequate level of resource utilization were maintained.

The size of any gain in efficiency would depend on the elasticity of individual saving with respect to the rate of return received by savers, the influence of an increase in individual saving propensities on the cost of capital for investors, and their responsiveness to a reduction in capital costs. The interest elasticity of saving is treated in the Howrey-Hymans paper. The other factors deserve attention, but a systematic consideration of them would be outside the scope of my paper. Here I shall only say that the less elastic the various responses are, the smaller would be any gain in efficiency from substituting an expenditure tax for an income tax.

Risky investments. Kaldor argued that an economic advantage of the expenditure tax is that, unlike the income tax, it does not discriminate against risky investment, essentially because the expenditure tax does not reduce the part of the reward for risk-taking that is saved.[17] This argument, however, is not wholly convincing. Kaldor did not take into account the mitigating effects of loss offsets under the income tax. As is well known, under a proportional income tax the possibility of fully offsetting losses against taxable income will equally reduce the investor's risk and the reward for assuming risk. The government will, in effect, share the risks as well as the returns. Whether the total amount of risk assumed, including both the private risk of the investor and the risk borne by the treasury, will increase, decrease, or remain the same depends on reactions that cannot be confidently predicted.[18] With graduated income tax rates, the gains on successful investments are taxed at rates higher than those against which losses are offset, and this is likely to shift the balance against risk assumption. Inasmuch as both the expenditure tax and the income tax would have graduated rates, and the rates of the expenditure tax would be higher, this point does not strengthen the case for that tax. There remains the question whether loss offsets would be as complete under an income tax as under an expenditure tax. Opportunities for offsetting under the income tax are greatly enhanced by carry-backs and carry-forwards of losses, such as exist in the United States and many other countries; nevertheless, the expenditure tax seems to have the edge in this respect unless lifetime averaging is available under the income tax. Under the expenditure tax the investor, through his saving decisions, can establish a tax-free reserve against losses; if this reserve later proves inadequate, he can still reduce his tax liability by cutting his consumption.

Human capital. W. A. Klein has pointed to what he considers an unfairness and inefficiency in the income tax arising out of the treat-

17. *Expenditure Tax,* pp. 118–22.
18. Evsey D. Domar and Richard A. Musgrave, "Proportional Income Taxation and Risk-Taking," *Quarterly Journal of Economics,* vol. 58 (May 1944), pp. 388–422, reprinted in Richard A. Musgrave and Carl S. Shoup, eds., *Readings in the Economics of Taxation* (Irwin for the American Economic Association, 1959), pp. 493–524; E. Cary Brown, "Mr. Kaldor on Taxation and Risk Bearing," *Review of Economic Studies,* vol. 25 (October 1957), pp. 49–52.

ment of human capital formation.[19] In creating human capital by de-
voting time to education and the acquisition of experience, a person
forgoes taxable income. In a sense, he may be said to benefit from
instantaneous depreciation of this part of his investment in an asset
that will yield returns in the future.[20] Inasmuch as it would not be
feasible to require people to report as current income their forgone
earnings in such circumstances and to amortize the investment over
its productive life, Klein considers this characteristic of the income
tax to be an inherent defect. Under the expenditure tax, on the other
hand, investment in human capital and investment in other capital
are treated alike in that tax is payable only when the returns are consumed.

This ingenious argument implies that none of the out-of-pocket
costs of education would be classified as consumption and subjected
to expenditure tax. Even if this is granted, the argument neglects
other decisively important considerations. First, the present income
tax discriminates against investment in education by failing to allow
deductions for many of the out-of-pocket costs associated with it.
Second, earnings in occupations that require long and expensive education and training are likely in practice to be subject to higher graduated income tax rates than other earnings, because they are concentrated in a shorter time period. Third, investment in education is an
area in which rational calculation is notoriously difficult. And fourth,
the imperfections of the capital market limit opportunities for borrowing to finance the creation of human capital. Considerations of
this kind have led governments throughout the world to conclude that
education should be subsidized by the state. The allegedly favorable
treatment accorded to education by the income tax is not, in my
judgment, a reason for preferring the expenditure tax.

Labor income. An important development in the discussion of the
expenditure tax in recent years is the attention being given to the
proposition that it is equivalent to a tax on income with the return on
savings excluded from the base. The Meade committee report gives
great prominence to this proposition and extends it to other taxes

19. William A. Klein, "Timing in Personal Taxation," *Journal of Legal Studies*,
vol. 6 (June 1977), pp. 461–81.
20. Gary S. Becker, *Human Capital: A Theoretical and Empirical Analysis, with
Special Reference to Education* (Columbia University Press for National Bureau of
Economic Research, 1964), pp. 14–15, 149.

that on the basis of certain assumptions are considered equivalent to an expenditure tax: a value-added tax and an income tax with capital investment written off immediately. Though some earlier comments indicated that in certain respects introducing an expenditure tax would be equivalent to exempting from income tax the return on savings,[21] this point was not emphasized. Whether the failure to stress it was due to analytical considerations or to a prudent regard for public opinion is unclear. A recommendation that property income (unearned income) be taxed less heavily than labor income (earned income) is contrary to a long tradition. A widely held opinion is that earned income should be more lightly taxed because its receipt depends on human effort and the sacrifice of leisure and because its duration is limited to a person's working life. Although I do not find these arguments persuasive reasons for applying a lower tax rate to labor income, they have some appeal. Their persistence suggests that a widely shared perception that an expenditure tax goes in the opposite direction would hinder its acceptance.

The basis for the claim that an expenditure tax is equivalent to a tax on income from sources other than property (that is, a tax on labor income) is that the two taxes would have the same effect on the net return from saving-and-lending or saving-and-investing. From the illustration given on page 58, it can be seen that if the interest received on a loan were free of tax, the lender could consume as much under the truncated income tax as under the expenditure tax.

It does not follow, however, that an expenditure tax would be exactly equivalent to a tax on labor income. A priori there is no reason to expect the bases of the two taxes to be of equal size. For them to be equal, the amount of income from property in any time period would have to equal the amount of net saving. In a rich country, in fact, the annual return on the stock of capital and financial claims is usually much greater than the annual addition to the stock. Even if the similarity of the effects of the two taxes on rates of return on loans and investments should cause the marginal additions to returns and to the stock to be equal, a large part of total property income would be derived from the old stock for a long time after the introduction of the new tax. Equality at the margin would imply that the amount consumed by the recipients of additional income from

21. For example, A. C. Pigou, *A Study in Public Finance*, 3d ed. (London: Macmillan, 1949), p. 129.

capital and claims was exactly matched by the addition to the stock originating in the savings of others. But the behavior of these groups is not linked in any direct way. My conclusion is that, though it is true that an expenditure tax would favor property income over labor income, the expenditure tax would have a larger base than a tax on labor income and a lower rate of expenditure tax would be needed to obtain the same revenue.

Conclusions on efficiency. The lower average and marginal rates of a comprehensive income tax would give it some advantages over a comprehensive expenditure tax. In particular, the income tax would do less damage to the efficiency of resource allocation by diverting activity from the market to household production of consumption goods and services, by favoring nontaxable fringe benefits in the form of consumption goods and services, and by discouraging work in certain cases. However, a simple comparison of nominal rates overstates the difference between the incentive effects of the two taxes; the higher rate of expenditure tax would be offset in many cases by the exclusion of savings. The expenditure tax appears to be superior to the income tax in the treatment of saving-and-lending to finance future consumption and in the completeness of loss offsets for unsuccessful investments. It is not clear which tax is preferable on balance in regard to efficiency of resource allocation.

Resource Utilization

Many advocates of an expenditure system seem to have assumed that the encouragement of saving is a preeminent objective of public policy. Irving Fisher made this value judgment fairly explicit.[22] Pigou believed that aggregate saving tended to fall below the optimum level.[23] Contemporary supporters of the expenditure tax may not so readily accept these preconceptions, but they do take it for granted that the problem of unemployment or the underutilization of economic resources has been solved—or at least is not a proper concern of tax policy. Hence they confidently expect an increase in the propensity to save to result in a faster rate of income growth.

I am less sanguine on this point. Underemployment has been a prevalent problem in the 1970s. I do not think it should be taken for

22. Irving Fisher and Herbert W. Fisher, *Constructive Income Taxation: A Proposal for Reform* (Harper, 1942), pp. 61–91.
23. *Study in Public Finance,* pp. 96–99, 121.

granted that a revision of the tax system that increased the propensity to save would, in fact, result in an increased total amount of saving and investment and a consequent acceleration of the rate of economic growth. On the contrary, it might either decrease activity or lead to efforts to combat unemployment that would offset the possible gain from an increased propensity to save.

If it is thought that full utilization of resources can safely be assumed, it seems likely that a small increase in the amount of tax revenue relative to government expenditure (that is, a reduction of the budget deficit) would be a more powerful means of bringing about a desired increase in total saving than a big change in the composition of revenue caused by the replacement of the income tax with an expenditure tax.

Special Problems

Advocates of an expenditure tax tend to contrast an idealized version of that tax with the existing imperfect income tax. Experience has familiarized us with the problems associated with the taxation of income but not with those that would arise in taxing consumption. It may be reasonable to prefer the expenditure tax if careful consideration leads to the judgment that it would be easier to apply a comprehensive expenditure tax than to remedy the defects of the income tax. Acceptance or rejection of such a judgment should take into account conceptual problems, practical difficulties, and politics. While recognizing that a more thorough study and extended discussion are needed, I shall touch on some of the issues.

Gifts and Bequests

The treatment of gifts and bequests poses similar problems under the income tax and the expenditure tax. If these items are included in income and consumption, the need for a suitable averaging system is accentuated. In my opinion, gratuitous transfers can be better treated under a separate tax on gifts and estates, or on accessions, than under either the income tax or the expenditure tax. Legislators have shown no inclination to classify receipts of gifts and bequests as income, and there is no reason to expect them to consider these items as consumption of the donors.

Inflation

The Meade committee report makes much of the argument that it would not be feasible to make a satisfactory adjustment for inflation under the income tax. Although some of the main items in the income statements and balance sheets of business enterprises and the basis of assets for capital gains tax could be adjusted—the argument runs —appropriate allowances for changes in the real value of cash balances and certain other monetary assets and liabilities could not be made. Under the expenditure tax it might be advisable to index the rate brackets and personal exemptions, but items entering into the tax base would need much less adjustment than under the income tax. This is a valid argument so far as it goes. But it should be noted that, according to the recommendations of *Blueprints for Basic Tax Reform,* the items that would be most difficult to index for inflation under the income tax—currency holdings and checking accounts— would not be registered or qualified assets for the expenditure tax, and they might not be so classified under the Meade committee proposals. If they were not registered, saving in the form of additions to cash balances would be taxed as consumption, regardless of whether the additions were necessary to maintain the real value of the holdings.

I find it remarkable, moreover, that advocates of the expenditure tax, who are ready to base tax policy on the assumptions of efficient capital markets, rational planning by individuals, and full employment, presume that inflation will continue. If other problems can be solved or assumed away, why not inflation too? More seriously, I doubt that it would be prudent to adjust the tax system to make us more comfortable with chronic inflation. Much can be said for the contention that, in conditions of moderate inflation, an unadjusted income tax helps compensate for inequities and also slows inflation.

Capital Gains

The prevailing, though not unanimous, opinion is that the application of the income tax to capital gains and losses on an accrual rather than a realization basis would not be practicable. Taxing gains only when realized diminishes the equity of the income tax and imposes a tax penalty on changing investments. This penalty may lock in investors in appreciated assets. It would not occur under the expenditure tax (except for owner-occupied dwellings and other durables if their imputed service value were included in taxable consumption, as it should be). Although the economic damage done by locking-in is often greatly exaggerated, it does contribute to inefficiency in the capital market. Short of taxation of capital gains and losses on an accrual basis or adoption of a radical scheme like Vickrey's cumulative averaging proposal,[24] the lock-in problem under the income tax could be abated by a provision for constructive realization by gift or at death and further reduced by a requirement that gains be written up according to the length of time the asset was held, to reflect roughly the value of tax postponement.[25]

International Aspects

International aspects of the choice between an income tax and an expenditure tax extend from technical complexities to sensitive political issues. These have been largely neglected by American advocates of the expenditure tax. They have been considered systematically by the Meade committee and by Lodin, but on several points doubts and difficulties have not been fully resolved.[26]

The income tax has the advantage of being widely accepted; international tax relations, as formalized in legislation and treaties and as influenced by tradition, are based on its general application. Countries tax income on the basis of both its place of origin and the place of residence of the recipient. But double taxation is usually avoided, or mitigated, because the residence country recognizes the prior claim of the origin country and offers relief by exemption, tax credit, or deduction. The expenditure tax, it appears, would have to be applied solely on a residence basis. A country that adopted an expenditure tax would have to decide whether to give relief for income tax applied by other countries to the foreign-source income of its residents. To do so might appear inconsistent, but failure to do so would discourage foreign investment and interfere with the flow of capital to its most profitable uses. The country with the expenditure tax would also have to decide whether it was content not to tax income of

24. William Vickrey, *Agenda for Progressive Taxation* (Ronald Press, 1947; reprinted, Kelley, 1972), pp. 172–95.

25. Roger Brinner, "Inflation, Deferral and the Neutral Taxation of Capital Gains," *National Tax Journal*, vol. 26 (December 1973), pp. 570–71.

26. Meade committee report, pp. 411–74; Lodin, *Progressive Expenditure Tax*, pp. 108–14.

domestic origin received by nonresidents. Probably it would wish to continue taxing this income. The corporation income tax would be needed for this purpose (and might be supported for other reasons as well). Hence the problems of income measurement, including inflation adjustment, would persist—though in a less acute form—even if the expenditure tax should become the main form of personal taxation.

Emigration and immigration would also create more problems under the expenditure tax than under the income tax. A person who moved to an income tax country after having accumulated large savings under an expenditure tax regime would avoid tax unless some kind of compensatory levy were applied. It is not clear, however, how a compensatory levy could be equitably assessed. If the levy were excessive, it could infringe on an important civil right. A somewhat similar question arises under an income tax applying to capital gains on a realization basis in the case of emigrants who hold appreciated assets. It is, however, less serious, because unrealized capital gains are much smaller than total accumulated savings. Furthermore, if a tax is considered necessary, its assessment can be more objectively made under the income tax because the computation can properly relate only to the taxpayer's current and previous situation, not to the conjectural matter of his future consumption.[27] Immigration of wealthy persons into an expenditure tax country would be discouraged unless special relief were granted for the consumption of savings accumulated under an income tax regime in the former place of residence. But such a provision would be either crude or complex and almost certainly unpopular. Additional complications would arise in determining when a permanent change of residence occurred and in dealing with persons who stayed for some time in a country without taking up permanent residence. Some high-income persons who move about frequently already attract a good deal of attention from the popular press, which could be relied on to keep in view the implica-

27. Canada deems that a person who ceases to be a resident has disposed of his property at its fair market value and applies a capital gains tax or allows a loss deduction. The first Can$5,000 of gains is exempt. The emigrant may elect not to pay the departure tax if he agrees to be taxed as a resident when the disposition of his property occurs (at his death if not earlier) and posts security for the payment of the tax. If taxed at departure, he may pay in six annual installments. See Canadian Income Tax Act, S.C. 1970–71–72, c. 63, as amended, sec. 48.

tions of their movements for the expenditure tax and ancillary measures.

Transition to an Expenditure Tax

Important transition problems would affect persons of mature years who had accumulated savings under the income tax regime in the expectation that these could be drawn down to finance consumption during retirement. They would be faced with a radical change in the rules of the game and would have to pay a graduated expenditure tax on the use of their savings. This seems unfair. In principle, relief should be given, through either a reduced expenditure tax rate or full tax exemption, for consumption financed by using up assets held at the transition date. A major issue to be resolved would be whether the relief should be uniform or should depend on the effective rate of income tax paid in the past or the kind of asset held. Another issue would be whether it would be acceptable to insulate the group that qualified for relief from future changes in the tax burden. Administrative and compliance difficulties would arise because most versions of transition relief would require inventories of assets and liabilities at the transition date and segregation of these from items acquired later. Without going into details, I may say that I am not reassured by the treatment of these transition problems in the Treasury's *Blueprints,* the Meade committee report, and the Swedish study.[28]

Unless it were considered acceptable to allow full exemption from expenditure tax of consumption financed out of assets held at the time of transition—which seems to me quite unlikely—widespread tax evasion could occur. At the time of transition a person might conceal his assets and later liquidate them without reporting the proceeds, thereby financing consumption that would not enter into the tax base, computed either by the comparison of balance sheets or on the basis of cash flows. Tax evasion would be facilitated under a system that provided for a class of unregistered assets, as suggested in *Blueprints* and the Meade committee report. When the intention to adopt the expenditure tax became known, there would be a great incentive to transform assets into an unregistered form and later to use these to

28. *Blueprints for Basic Tax Reform,* pp. 204–12; Meade committee report, pp. 187–92, 199–200; Lodin, *Progressive Expenditure Tax,* pp. 123–27.

finance consumption that would escape taxation. Chaotic market conditions could well result.

Erosion of the Tax Base

Finally, the items that are commonly classified as examples of the erosion of the income tax base, or "tax expenditures," should be considered. Is it likely that they would be more rigorously and equitably treated under an expenditure tax? Although some of them—notably tax deferral through qualified pension plans, retirement plans for the self-employed, and individual retirement accounts—move the income tax in the direction of an expenditure tax, I do not think they reflect a deliberate decision by Congress to favor saving, nor do I detect any trend in that direction. In the United States, tax is not deferred on employees' contributions to pension plans established by employers, as it is in some other countries; the failure to include employers' contributions and interest in the current income of employees can be explained by the lack of current availability and by the absence of vesting, in many plans, of these amounts. The other provisions are examples of the tendency to attack inequities by extending preferential treatment rather than by eliminating it—a tendency shared by proponents of the expenditure tax. In my opinion, it is no more realistic to expect that the adoption of an expenditure tax would overcome opposition to the elimination of tax loopholes than to expect that the familiar proposal to combine the broadening of the income tax base with the reduction of nominal rates will soon become law. To be sure, some of the defects of the income tax may owe more to inertia or lack of understanding than to conviction or the power of vested interests. Possibly these defects could be remedied under an expenditure tax, but inertia and lack of appreciation of the fine points of tax theory are formidable barriers to agreement on the expenditure tax.

Without suggesting that U.S. choices would be the same, I think it may be instructive to note the items that were omitted from taxable expenditures in the two countries that have used the expenditure tax. In India the following items were not taxable: expenditures out of an entertainment allowance granted by an employer; interest payments except on "any loan or other borrowing utilized for incurring expenditure liable to tax"; premiums for insurance on the life of the taxpayer or his dependents and for most other forms of insurance; purchases of books; purchases of works of art or products of cottage industries of India whose price exceeds Rs1,000; expenditures for the purchase or maintenance of livestock; expenditures for a public purpose of a religious or charitable nature; gifts, donations, or settlements; most taxes; expenditures in connection with the candidacy of the taxpayer or his dependents for elective public office; expenditures lawfully incurred in any civil or criminal proceedings to which the taxpayer is a party; expenditures for the marriage of the taxpayer or his dependents; expenditures for medical treatment; expenditures for education outside India (several of these exemptions were subject to limits fixed in money amounts).[29]

In Sri Lanka many, but not all, of the same items were exempt from tax. Special mention may be made of exclusions or deductions for expenditures for the acquisition, construction, repair, or improvement of any immovable property other than the repair of a house owned and occupied by the taxpayer; expenditures for the acquisition of bullion, precious stones, or jewelry; all gifts; ground rent; payments of any sum under a court order; funeral expenses, subject to a limit; expenditures incurred wholly and necessarily in connection with "the discharge of any duties assigned . . . by the State."[30] India did not include in taxable expenditure the imputed rent of owner-occupied dwellings, though it allowed deductions or exclusions for the cost of acquiring such dwellings and from 1957 to 1959 for the cost of repairing, maintaining, and improving them.[31] Sri Lanka included imputed rent in taxable expenditure under its first tax but not under its second one.

The examples of India and Sri Lanka seem to me to corroborate my belief that the factors that have led to the erosion of the income tax base in the United States would operate similarly to narrow the base of an expenditure tax. I do not believe it can be safely assumed that taxable consumption would be defined broadly enough to allow

29. Walter W. Brudno and others, *Taxation in India,* World Tax Series, Harvard Law School (Little, Brown, 1960), pp. 425–30.

30. Sri Lanka, Inland Revenue (Amendment) Law, No. 16 of 1976.

31. Central Board of Revenue, Government of India, *Expenditure-tax Manual,* First Edition (New Delhi, 1960), p. 5; but see also the statement on p. 44, which is open to the interpretation that the exclusion of the cost of acquisition of owner-occupied dwellings was ended in 1959.

the expenditure tax rates to be lower than the present income tax rates[32] or to eliminate inequities and inefficiencies.

Practicality of the Expenditure Tax

It is not my assignment to go into the details of tax design, administration, and compliance. However, since the expenditure tax has often been rejected as impractical, and since recent discussion appears to suggest that new insights into its feasibility have been gained, I feel that I should write a few words on this subject. Andrews's article in the *Harvard Law Review* in 1974 has attracted much attention to the possibility of taxing consumption solely on the basis of cash flows, though Andrews, like Fisher before him, chose to call the tax so levied an income tax rather than an expenditure tax.[33] Mieszkowski has developed this approach for the Treasury Department.[34]

The possibility of measuring consumption by cash flows is not a new idea; it is essentially the method suggested by previous writers. Some earlier writers, however, emphasized the usefulness of having balance sheets as a check on the completeness and consistency of cash flow information.[35] I still consider balance sheets indispensable for this purpose. For the expenditure tax, however, it would not be necessary to adjust the value of investment assets owned at the end of the accounting period as it would be for a wealth tax or an income tax in which capital gains and losses were taxed on an accrual basis. Balance sheets would be more necessary for the expenditure tax than

---

32. A report of the U.S. Advisory Commission on Intergovernmental Relations included statistics showing that in 1968 "the *conceptual base* for an expenditure tax would have been somewhat larger than the *actual* base for the Federal income tax," but added that in practice the conceptual base of an expenditure tax would probably be eroded by exclusions and that "a meaningful estimate" cannot be made of what the base of an expenditure tax would be. *The Expenditure Tax: Concept, Administration and Possible Applications* (GPO, 1974), pp. 24–25 for the statistics, p. 31 for the quotation.

33. "A Consumption-Type or Cash Flow Personal Income Tax."

34. "The Cash Flow Version of an Expenditure Tax."

35. In his report on India, Kaldor stressed the desirability of a "single, comprehensive return," covering wealth, property transactions, income, and personal expenditure, which would produce "a self-checking system" for income tax, capital gains tax, annual wealth tax, personal expenditure tax, and gift tax (*Indian Tax Reform*, pp. 13–16). See also Richard Goode, *The Individual Income Tax* (Brookings Institution, 1964), pp. 30–31.

they are for the present income tax because of the number and variety of transactions affecting consumption and saving. And also, the omission of transactions would often have a greater effect on expenditure tax liability than it has on income tax liability. For example, failure to report the sale of a capital asset allows the omission from the income tax base of the gain realized on the sale but omits the gross proceeds from the expenditure tax base. The importance of balance sheets for the assessment of the expenditure tax and the difficulty of obtaining and verifying them for a large number of people make the proposal to replace the income tax with an expenditure tax impractical in my judgment.

Combination of the Expenditure Tax with Other Taxes

An income tax imposes a check on both consumption and wealth accumulation. Replacement of the income tax by an expenditure tax would allow accumulations of wealth that, in my opinion, would be objectionable unless a significant wealth tax were also levied. The expenditure tax would impose a check on accumulation only if gifts and bequests were included in the taxable consumption of donors— a step that has not generally been proposed. In the absence of an annual wealth tax or heavy taxes on gifts and bequests or accessions, the substitution of an expenditure tax for the income tax would be likely to result in an unacceptable degree of inequality of wealth. But, as mentioned above, the taxation of wealth is inconsistent with some of the principal arguments advanced for the expenditure tax. This is true of both nonrecurrent taxes on property transfers and an annual wealth tax, since the first can in some sense be equated with the second.[36]

Kaldor visualized the expenditure tax as a comparatively minor supplement to the income tax, and the two countries that accepted his advice, India and Sri Lanka, took that approach. In the United Kingdom the maintenance of lavish standards of living by rich people using up their wealth impressed Kaldor as a social evil that should be combated by taxation. In India agricultural income and the privy purses of the former rulers of the princely states were exempt from income tax, but their recipients could be reached by the expenditure tax. These problems are unimportant or nonexistent in the United

36. Meade committee report, pp. 322–26.

States and in most other industrial countries. In these circumstances, would it be worthwhile to incur heavy burdens of administration and compliance to introduce an expenditure tax of limited coverage? I think not.

Conclusion

On examination the arguments in favor of the expenditure tax are incorrect, doubtful, or valid but unconvincing. The brilliance and literary ability of its advocates cannot be denied. Indeed, they have been far cleverer than the supporters of the income tax. The members of the expenditure tax faction speak of the double taxation of saving and the justness of taxing people on what they withdraw from the common pool. They use harvest metaphors that have a reassuring sound of rustic virtue. They compare a perfect expenditure tax with an income tax whose defects are well known, thanks to the efforts of its supporters. And they sometimes call the tax that they favor an income tax. The members of the income tax faction have not responded by talking about the exemption of unearned income under the expenditure tax or by being ironical about the "abstinence" of the rich. They are preoccupied with financially sophisticated transactions and sound like city slickers. They are acutely conscious of the shortcomings of the existing income tax and are busy measuring and publicizing these. Perhaps they do not bother to attack the expenditure tax because they know they have both good arguments and the weight of inertia on their side.

I am convinced that the income tax is clearly superior to the expenditure tax. Without trying to be complete, I can summarize my reasons as follows.

Income is better than consumption as a measure of ability to pay, and the reduction of income inequality is a more meaningful political objective of taxation than the lessening of consumption inequality. As regards efficiency of resource allocation, both a comprehensive income tax and a comprehensive expenditure tax have advantages; here a clear-cut choice between the two taxes does not emerge. If full utilization of resources could be assured, any increase in saving that might be desired could more easily and certainly be obtained by reducing the budget deficit than by replacing the income tax with an expenditure tax. Although it would be much less difficult to adjust for inflation under the expenditure tax than under the income tax, some versions of the expenditure tax that have recently been proposed would not go much beyond what would be feasible under the income tax, because they would not exclude from the tax base additions to cash balances needed to maintain their real value. Furthermore, the advisability of inflation adjustment is questionable. A shift to the expenditure tax would involve transition problems and could be disturbing to international tax relations, capital flows, and the movement of people. It is unrealistic to expect that in practice the expenditure tax would be free of loopholes and other special provisions similar to those that have caused dissatisfaction with the income tax. The substitution of an expenditure tax for the income tax would open the way to unacceptable accumulations of personal wealth unless special taxes on wealth were introduced. Although such taxes would have merits of their own, their use would be inconsistent with some of the principal arguments for the expenditure tax and would entail considerable problems of administration and compliance. Recent attention to the cash flow version of the expenditure tax has not turned up any ideas that, in my opinion, could eliminate the long-held doubts about the practicality of a personal expenditure tax with wide coverage and large yield.

Comments on this paper follow the Bradford paper.

DAVID F. BRADFORD

The Case for a Personal Consumption Tax

THE PUBLICATION of the U.S. Treasury's *Blueprints for Basic Tax Reform* in 1977 and of the Meade committee report in the United Kingdom in 1978[1] reflects the renewed interest in the idea of an expenditure or consumption tax as a practical and desirable alternative to an income tax.[2] These reports have much in common. Both regard the remarkably varied treatment of different forms of saving, the unnecessary complexity of tax rules, and the great sensitivity of relative

I wish to thank W. D. Andrews, A. B. Atkinson, J. A. Kay, M. A. King, M. S. Feldstein, and J. E. Stiglitz for the benefit of discussions on the subject of this paper.

1. U.S. Department of the Treasury, *Blueprints for Basic Tax Reform* (Government Printing Office, 1977) (hereafter *Blueprints*); Institute for Fiscal Studies, *The Structure and Reform of Direct Taxation*, Report of a Committee chaired by Professor J. E. Meade (London: Allen and Unwin, 1978) (hereafter Meade committee report).

2. In this context the terms "expenditure" and "consumption" are usually interchangeable. I shall hereafter stick to "consumption." There have been other recent contributions to the literature, including a 1976 report prepared by Sven-Olof Lodin for a government commission in Sweden, available in an English translation, *Progressive Expenditure Tax—an Alternative? A Report of the 1972 Government Commission on Taxation* (Stockholm: LiberFörlag, 1978); a paper by William D. Andrews, "A Consumption-Type or Cash Flow Personal Income Tax," *Harvard Law Review*, vol. 87 (April 1974), pp. 1113–88; and two papers by Peter Mieszkowski: "The Choice of Tax Base: Consumption versus Income Taxation," in Michael J. Boskin, ed., *Federal Tax Reform: Myths and Realities* (San Francisco: Institute for Contemporary Studies, 1978), chap. 2, and "On the Advisability and Feasibility of an Expenditure Tax System," in Henry J. Aaron and Michael J. Boskin, eds., *The Economics of Taxation* (Brookings Institution, forthcoming).

tax burdens to the rate of inflation as defects of the existing income tax systems of the two countries. Both reports conclude that no simple set of principles—and certainly no consistent concept of income—governs present "income" tax policy.

When one considers the political process by which tax law is made, this is not surprising. But having an effective policy to deal with the hundreds of rule interpretations and proposed rule changes each year requires a clear objective. The dominant approach to tax reform, in the United States at least, has been to aim for comprehensive income taxation.[3] But both the Treasury and Meade committee studies conclude that a comprehensive consumption base has advantages over an income base in terms of both the equity of the ideal form of the tax and the relative ease with which the ideal could be approximated by simple, practical rules. Furthermore, both studies noted that since existing personal income taxes have many features that favor savings, a move to a consistent consumption base might well represent a less radical change than a move to a comprehensive income base.

In this paper I argue the case for a consumption base. "Arguing a case" is something that an economist should perhaps avoid. Tax policy must reflect values, and economics as science cannot resolve the ultimate clashes of interest that are bound to occur. Nonetheless, I believe a strong case can be built for a consumption tax on the basis of values widely shared by the participants in the debate.

In the first section of the paper I define the central concepts of income and consumption. In the second section I examine the relative difficulty of implementing a comprehensive income tax and a comprehensive consumption tax. This issue is given such high priority because it is still apparently widely believed that a consumption base is

3. See, among others, Joseph A. Pechman, *Federal Tax Policy,* 3d ed. (Brookings Institution, 1977), and Pechman, ed., *Comprehensive Income Taxation* (Brookings Institution, 1977); George F. Break and Joseph A. Pechman, *Federal Tax Reform: The Impossible Dream?* (Brookings Institution, 1975); *Report of the Royal Commission on Taxation,* vol. 3 (Ottawa: Queen's Printer, 1966), chap. 8; *Studies of the Royal Commission on Taxation,* no. 25 (Ottawa: Queen's Printer, 1967), and ibid., nos. 26, 28, 29 (1968); Arthur B. Willis, ed., *Studies in Substantive Tax Reform* (Chicago: American Bar Foundation, 1969). Bossons provides a discussion of why, even when Haig-Simons income is the ideal, the impossibility of taxing some components may lead to the omission of others. John Bossons, "The Value of a Comprehensive Tax Base as a Tax Reform Goal," *Journal of Law and Economics,* vol. 13 (October 1970), pp. 327–63.

more difficult to put into practice than an income base.[4] Surprisingly, this is not so. Indeed, many of the most troublesome aspects of income taxation are avoided when consumption is the base. Whereas the discussion in the second section is in terms of hypothetical tax systems, in the third section I look at the existing U.S. income tax and show that some of its more notable defects are in the areas where the theory would lead one to expect them. Together, these two sections make it clear that, because a satisfactory income base is so much more difficult to implement than a satisfactory consumption base, the former should be chosen only if there is some compelling reason to do so. In the final sections I consider two major criteria for judging tax systems: the degree to which they distort resource allocation, and the fairness of the distribution of burdens they produce. I argue that, while firm conclusions are hard to establish, both efficiency and equity considerations probably favor the consumption base.[5]

Background: The Concepts of Income and Consumption

As only two years have passed since the Brookings conference on comprehensive income taxation,[6] it is not necessary here to devote

4. Pechman in 1971 observed: "The expenditure tax is not more widespread than it is primarily because of difficulties of compliance and administration. . . . It is generally agreed that the administrative and compliance problems of an expenditure tax are formidable and that it would be very difficult for most countries to enforce such a tax with the present state of administrative know-how." Significantly, perhaps, no similar view is found in the next edition of Pechman's book. Joseph A. Pechman, *Federal Tax Policy,* rev. ed. (Brookings Institution, 1971), pp. 164–65, and ibid., 3d ed., pp. 66–68, 197–99.

5. Two subjects readers might expect to find addressed have nevertheless been omitted here: the difference in macroeconomic performance of an economy with a consumption tax from that of one with an income tax, and problems of transition from the present system to a consumption base. The latter, in particular, is an unfortunate omission. For even though, as I believe, the advantages of a consumption tax written "on a clean slate" are becoming more widely appreciated, such a tax may still fail as a policy goal if there is no acceptable way to effect the transition. However, an adequate analysis of the subject is dependent upon the particular rules by which a consumption tax is to be realized and is thus beyond the scope of this paper. The Treasury Department's *Blueprints* does provide a detailed plan and includes, in chapter 6, a discussion of the problems of transition. See also Michael Graetz's contribution to the present volume.

6. Pechman, ed., *Comprehensive Income Taxation.*

much attention to the concept of income in its various versions. However, it is important to have firmly in mind the relation between the income concept usually accepted in U.S. tax policy debate, called Haig-Simons income, and the concept of consumption, and to relate both to the accounting systems necessary to translate them into administrable tax bases.[7]

Haig-Simons income is usually defined in terms of the uses to which the tax unit puts its resources during the year, according to the familiar accounting identity

$$(1) \qquad\qquad Y = C + \Delta W,$$

where Y, C, and ΔW stand for income, consumption, and change in net worth ("savings") over the accounting period, respectively. To employ income as a tax base requires putting operational flesh on the concepts of consumption and savings. For example, it must be determined whether outlays for medical treatment constitute consumption. Similarly it must be decided what sort of wealth will be included in net worth; for instance, human capital is usually not included. It should be emphasized that the terms "consumption" and "wealth" are not operationally defined a priori; they are defined in the process of determining tax policy.

To calculate either a consumption or an income tax base, it is normally most convenient to work from the taxpayer's receipts rather than from his outlays. This can be seen most simply by starting with the assumption that the wealth entering the definition of the tax base is an asset like a savings account, with readily identifiable current yield, r. Let W_i stand for the wealth at the beginning of period i, and E_i for the "nonwealth receipts" (wages, transfers, and so forth), understood as occurring at the end of period i, at the same time as returns on wealth, rW_i, and consumption, C_i. For these concepts to form a satisfactory accounting system, it is necessary that

$$(2) \qquad\qquad W_{i+1} = E_i + (1 + r)W_i - C_i$$

7. In an excellent brief survey of the history of the income concept, Richard Goode points out that the Haig-Simons definition was anticipated by Georg von Schanz in 1896 and suggests that the term S-H-S (Schanz-Haig-Simons) be used. Without meaning any disrespect for Shanz, I shall stick to the by now conventional label. Richard Goode, "The Economic Definition of Income," in Pechman, ed., *Comprehensive Income Taxation*, pp. 1–36.

or

(3) $$C_i + \Delta W_i = E_i + rW_i.$$

The left-hand side of 3 is Haig-Simons income; the right-hand side, the sum of nonwealth receipts and returns on wealth accumulated up to date i, is the usual calculation base. The same approach is normally taken to calculate a consumption tax base; savings are subtracted from the sum of nonwealth receipts and returns on wealth:

(4) $$C_i = E_i + rW_i - \Delta W_i.$$

But an important simplification may be effected for a consumption base calculation by substituting for it an equivalent in present-value terms. (I shall return to this point later.)

For the accounting system to balance, a certain consistency among consumption, wealth, and nonwealth receipts is required. If it were determined, for example, that outlays for medical care should not be counted as consumption for tax purposes, accounting consistency would require subtracting these expenses from nonwealth receipts in the period (that is, these expenses should be regarded as negative nonwealth receipts). Consistency also tells us how to treat returns on wealth where the asset is of a type different from the standard savings account. For instance, if the discounted present value of an inheritance at the beginning of period i were to be counted as part of wealth at the beginning of period i-1, the inheritance should not be counted in period i as a nonwealth receipt.[8]

The difference between an income base and a consumption base lies entirely in the treatment of savings. It is sometimes erroneously suggested that gifts and bequests received would be treated differently in income and consumption accounting. This is not so. Assuming their anticipated value is not counted in wealth, these receipts are simply included in E_i in the appropriate period. Referring to accounting relationships 3 and 4, one sees that such an increment in nonwealth receipts leads to the same change in both Haig-Simons income and consumption.

The treatment of gifts and bequests given is less clear, since it may

8. The difference is emphatically *not* just a matter of convention, however, when income is the tax base. The earlier the present value of anticipated receipts is recognized as part of wealth, the larger the tax base in present-value terms. That is simply because the implied returns on wealth are included in the base only when wealth is accounted for.

be argued that amounts given away are not "consumed." If this approach were taken, the corresponding amount would need to be deducted from nonwealth receipts in the period in question, an adjustment much like the one to exclude medical expenses from consumption. Whether or not one thus removes gifts and bequests given from consumption has nothing to do with the choice between income and consumption bases, so that in what follows I assume either that gifts and bequests given are *not* regarded as consumption or that gifts and bequests given are nil.[9]

One conceptual problem with Haig-Simons income should be noted: the appropriate treatment of changes in wealth associated with changes in the discount rate. The problem arises when wealth for tax purposes includes the present value of future receipts (unlike the savings account example), as with a perpetuity bond. To make matters simple, consider a taxpayer who holds a perpetuity yielding $10 a year and who consumes exactly $10 a year. If the interest rate drops from 10 percent to 5 percent, his wealth will instantly jump from $100 to $200, generating Haig-Simons income, even though his potential rate of steady consumption does not change at all.[10] This possibility is perhaps not unimportant in a period, like the present, of highly variable interest rates.

The Relative Difficulty of Implementing Income and Consumption Bases

When turning from definition to practical implementation, one might expect consumption to pose greater problems than income

9. In the terminology of *Blueprints* I assume a "standard of living" concept of income and consumption.

10. For a good discussion of this and other aspects of income definition, see the Meade committee report, chap. 3. The Meade committee considered this defect so serious that it took as its ideal income concept (regarded as impractical for actual tax purposes) a definition that treats the taxpayer as having enjoyed no income at all from the wealth gain in this case. (See also Goode's discussion of definitions stressing capital maintenance in "Economic Definition of Income," pp. 3–5.) This may go too far in the other direction, since the taxpayer *can* enjoy a higher consumption if he is not planning to consume at a steady rate in perpetuity. The problem is one of a changing relative price of future consumption. A similar difficulty arises in a transition from an income- to a consumption-based tax, when, in general, an increase in the price of current relative to future consumption takes place. The appropriate treatment of accumulated wealth then depends upon the time pattern of planned consumption.

(since one normally reckons consumption by subtracting savings from income). Yet I shall argue here[11] that precisely the opposite is the case: a consumption tax can be readily constructed on the basis of current-year cash transactions only, virtually all of them also used in an income tax, while dispensing with the elements of income calculation that are based on transactions in the (sometimes distant) past and are designed to approximate unobservable quantities. These account for many of the most irksome features of income taxation in practice.[12]

In considering the problems of implementation one should keep in mind desirable characteristics of a tax accounting system:[13]

—The transactions used to build up the tax base should be objectively observable. Imputed transactions should be avoided.

—The period over which records of transactions need be kept should be short.

—The rules for constructing the base from recorded transactions should be understandable to ordinary people. Complex transformations of historical data, such as inflation adjustments to put dollar figures on a comparable basis, should be avoided.

All these criteria could be reasonably satisfied by a Haig-Simons income base implemented along the lines suggested by equation 3 if the world resembled the simple model of savings deposit wealth and cash consumption outlays. In practice, unfortunately, instead of using actual annual transactions one must deal with a complex array of imputations to arrive at an estimate of the left-hand side of 3. Such imputations may be subdivided into in-kind or "direct" nonwealth receipts in the form of (a) consumption services (for example, use of the company car) or (b) increments of wealth (for example, additions to the value of pension rights other than those arising from implicitly accruing earnings on pension wealth), and direct returns from wealth, again in the form of (c) consumption services (for example, use of an owner-occupied house) or (d) asset value changes (for example, depreciation of a piece of equipment). The search for practical methods

11. The discussion in this section draws heavily from Andrews, "A Consumption-Type or Cash Flow Personal Income Tax"; J. A. Kay and M. A. King, *The British Tax System* (Oxford: Oxford University Press, 1978); Meade committee report; and *Blueprints*.

12. After discussing these problems, Kaldor concluded it would be impossible to design a fair income tax. Nicholas Kaldor, *An Expenditure Tax* (London: Allen and Unwin, 1955; Westport, Conn: Greenwood Press, 1977), chap. 1.

13. For a detailed discussion, see *Blueprints*, pp. 42–49.

of making those imputations simple enough to permit self-assessment by taxpayers and effective enforcement by the revenue agency has long bedeviled the formulators of income tax rules. Most of the complexity and much of the deviation of the actual personal income tax base from the Haig-Simons ideal stem from the difficulty of measuring consumption services directly rendered by assets and, more important, measuring accruing wealth changes not reflected in current transactions.

A number of difficult imputations, such as the notorious three-martini lunch, fall into category a. Since all are as hard to deal with under a consumption base as under an income base, I devote no further attention to them here. Problems with other imputations will be evident in the discussion that follows. Imputations c and d, in particular, are necessary to measure what is usually called "income from capital."

Accruing Wealth Changes

For those forms of wealth that do not yield any direct consumption service, it is clear that the savings account model is the exception rather than the rule. Particularly under inflationary conditions the cash flow from an investment is a good measure of its yield only by coincidence. But even with stable prices, cash flow—dividends, coupon payments, and so forth—is best regarded as simply a change in form of a portion of the portfolio, to cash, and not as an adequate measure of yield. To use the right-hand side of equation 3 to measure Haig-Simons income, one must track the market value of the components of the balance sheet.

The rules of thumb by which this counsel of perfection is approximated have—not surprisingly in view of the stakes involved—proved enormously troublesome. The most prominent issues are depreciation (the allowance for the reduction in value of assets due to wear and tear, obsolescence, and the like), capital gains (actually unrealized increases in value of all kinds, but usually those associated with earnings retained in corporations, changed expectations about the future, or changed discount rates), and accruing values of claims to future payments like pensions and life insurance.

Depreciation. Although attempts have been made to determine patterns of depreciation through the econometric analysis of used asset markets and although the U.S. Treasury attempts to collect systematic information about actual use patterns of assets under the asset depreciation range (ADR) scheme of depreciation allowances, remarkably little is known about the degree of approximation of such allowances to true depreciation ("economic depreciation").[14]

Capital gains. Another group of changes in asset values not reflected in current market transactions is called "accruing capital gains." To the economist these value changes are no different from those labeled "depreciation," but U.S. tax accounting makes an important distinction between the two.[15] Though it might be possible to measure these accruals currently where active markets exist, as in the case of publicly traded common stock in corporations, such procedures have not interested practical men (in part because they do not seem to consider genuine the wide swings in wealth that these valuations imply). For real estate one could imagine a system of self-assessment—backed up by some sort of implied willingness to sell at the assessed value—but such an approach has never been suggested for an income tax and has never drawn support in the local property tax administration setting. The difficulty of obtaining annual valuations and the potential cash flow problems for taxpayers with large accrued income but no cash income have generally led to the acceptance (for example, in *Blueprints* and in the Meade committee report) of a realization basis for capital gains accounting. Although schemes can be designed to approximate the effect of accrual taxation when the tax is collected on realization (as is proposed in the Meade report),[16] these involve considerable complexity.

Retirement rights and life insurance. When retirement rights are clearly vested in individuals, and particularly when they are "funded,"

14. Econometric techniques have been addressed to this problem, using "second-hand" asset market data, by Frank C. Wykoff and Charles R. Hulten, "Economic Depreciation and the Taxation of Structures in U.S. Manufacturing Industries: An Empirical Analysis," OTA Paper 28 (U.S. Department of the Treasury, Office of Tax Analysis, 1977).

15. Although economists use the term to refer to value changes whether or not accompanied by cash flow, in U.S. tax law "capital gain" refers to the gain from sale or exchange of a capital asset. It is thus explicitly a realization concept, and the notion of "accruing" capital gains is, strictly speaking, nonsense. I stick to the economists' usage here, even though there are some advantages in the other. In particular, when the realization notion is used it becomes clear that the accounting idea of capital gains is essentially a *correction* to past mismeasurement of income, as reflected in an incorrect *basis* (the amount subtracted from sale proceeds in computing gain) of the asset under the tax rules.

16. Meade committee report, pp. 129–35.

they are essentially shares in mutual funds. They present an additional problem for accrual taxation: the need to take into account possible restrictions on access to the market value of the claims, for example, prohibition of or penalty on withdrawal, and limitations on the use of these assets as loan collateral. With such restrictions the appropriate valuation of the rights depends upon the intention of the holder and is thus even more difficult to approximate for tax purposes than the accruing value of other securities.

Much more difficult is the evaluation of pension right accruals under "defined benefit plans," whereby employers agree to provide retirement payments based on a formula related to earnings. Accurately measuring individual wealth in this form is totally out of the question, as is the valuation of accruing social security retirement rights (a significant part of wealth in the United States). Life insurance presents similar, if less extreme, measurement problems.

Corporations. Pensions and life insurance schemes are but two examples of the problem of allocating investment earnings accruing within institutions to the individuals whose wealth is represented. This same problem arises for all corporate income. Ideally, individual income accounts should encompass the performance of corporations in which the individual has an interest. That such an imputation of corporate income to shareholders is not attempted is presumably the chief justification for the separate tax on corporate income, despite its incompatibility with the principle that income should be taxed according to the circumstances of the individual. The Brookings conference on integration of the individual and corporation income taxes showed how complex it would be to impute corporate income to its ultimate beneficiaries in a satisfactory way.[17] None of the proposals considered recently deals with the problem of imputing to shareholders earnings retained in the corporation, and all accept the imperfections in income measurement rules already noted. *Blueprints* does offer a system of full integration of corporate and shareholder accounts, and the Carter Commission in Canada also proposed the allocation of retained earnings to shareholders, but those plans have not drawn much support.[18]

17. Charles E. McLure, Jr., *Must Corporate Income Be Taxed Twice?* (Brookings Institution, 1979), chap. 7.

18. Perhaps this is because they are not designed for the kinds of explicit tax incentives for investment found in the actual U.S. system. The bulk of the discussion at the Brookings conference on integration, for example, concerned the pres-

Advantage of a consumption base. It is in dealing with problems of the sort described above that a consumption base has its most obvious administrative advantage. Under a consumption tax accruing wealth is wholly irrelevant. There is therefore no need to measure it, no need to estimate depreciation, accruing capital gains, or accruing rights in pension systems or life insurance policies. There is no need to measure the effect on shareholder wealth of retained earnings or of any other events at the corporate level. If no cash transaction takes place, there is no need to be concerned about those forms of wealth in calculating the base of a consumption tax. It is that simple.

Wealth Yielding Direct Consumption Services

Owner-occupied housing is the most obvious, and quantitatively the most important, asset that provides most of its yield in the form of direct consumption services. For income tax purposes the owner-occupier should be regarded as being in the business of renting himself housing; then the income from this asset would be measured in the usual way. Otherwise some other method of imputing the return must be adopted if a portion of the income is not to go free of tax and an incentive set up for people to buy "too much" housing and to adopt "too often" the tax-favored form of tenure—ownership. Although housing is the prime example, many others exist: automobiles, boats, household durables, works of art, jewelry, and the like, besides the services of banks that are paid for by interest forgone on checking accounts.

For a while the United Kingdom employed a system of imputing income to owner-occupied dwellings, but it was discontinued. Although a variety of imputation schemes (for example, requiring evaluation of assets and applying a standard assumed rate of return) can be imagined, the practical problems of taxing these direct consumption yields are usually regarded as formidable enough to rule out the attempt.[19]

For these forms of wealth, the consumption base would face exactly the same problems as the income base were it not for the availability of an alternative accounting method—one that yields an

---

ervation of the character of "preference" income in the hands of shareholders. See ibid. For the proposals, see *Blueprints*, pp. 68–75, and *Report of the Royal Commission on Taxation*, vol. 4, pp. 19–30.

19. William F. Hellmuth, "Homeowner Preferences," in Pechman, ed., *Comprehensive Income Taxation*, pp. 163–203; *Blueprints*, pp. 7, 85–89.

equivalent tax base.[20] Under the standard approach an investment—say, in a house—is subtracted from cash receipts from whatever source, whereas all return on the investment is included in the tax base. This approach would require the unattractive imputation of a value to consumption services directly flowing from the asset. Under the alternative approach the investment is *not* subtracted from the base, and none of the subsequent return flow is included. Because this means that the actual tax liability occurs at the time of the investment (which is, in effect, treated as part of consumption), *Blueprints* calls it the "tax prepayment" approach.[21] Given maximizing behavior by the investor, the two methods will produce a tax base of the same discounted value.[22]

By obliging taxpayers to use the prepayment approach in accounting for assets yielding direct services, a consumption tax can achieve at a stroke the neutrality between these investments and business investments that eludes the income tax, while still maintaining a simple, cash-transaction-data-only information requirement. Note, incidentally, the importance of timing. The tax prepayment approach is precisely the one normally accorded consumer durables under an income tax, but it gives the wrong answer in that case. One might describe the result as allowing the corresponding consumption to go tax free; yet the fact that the implicit return goes tax free explains why the same calculation gives the right answer under a consumption tax.

Making the System Inflation Proof

As is now widely understood, thanks to the Brookings conference on inflation and the income tax, two problems need to be distinguished.[23] One is the tendency for taxpayers to be pushed up through the progressive rate schedule by nominal income increases that exceed real income increases. The other is the failure of income measurement rules that function satisfactorily under stable prices to continue to give a reasonable approximation to real income when prices are

20. Naturally there is no sure way to separate the investment and consumption aspects of an outlay for a consumer durable. That it eliminates the necessity of even drawing this distinction is one of the attractions of the alternative accounting method.

21. *Blueprints* spells out in detail how the distinction between the two treatments could be implemented in an easily policed manner (pp. 123–27).

22. This statement requires modification to take into account uncertainty, as will be discussed in the text.

23. See Henry J. Aaron, ed., *Inflation and the Income Tax* (Brookings Institution, 1976).

changing. The first problem is relatively easy to solve, by indexing the parameters of the tax calculation—for example, exemptions, marginal rate bracket boundaries, credits. The same method applies to either an income or a consumption base. The second problem is more difficult. As the discussion at the Brookings conference showed, there is no professional consensus on how to carry out a full-fledged indexing of the measurement of an income base. Yet it is clear that the rates of taxation of various forms of investment depend strongly on the rate of inflation, even when the redistributions caused by changes in prevailing rates of inflation are ignored.

Problems of income measurement in a period of inflation arise because of the need to use market transactions made at different times. In calculating gain from sale, for example, it is necessary to subtract the purchase price from the current sales proceeds. This means subtracting apples from pears if the purchasing power of the unit of account varies, as it may do substantially over a protracted period of inflation like the present one.

Inflation also produces an "inflation premium" in interest rates; a fully satisfactory real income accounting calls for correcting these prices as well, a complex matter involving assumptions about the future rates of change in the price level.[24]

As has been pointed out by Feldstein, in a flat-rate income tax system certain relatively simple corrections could be made—indexing capital gains, depreciation, and inventories—to obtain a satisfactory income base.[25] In a system allowing such adjustments, nonindexed financial yields would include an element of inflation premium *and* an element of compensation for the *tax* on that premium.[26] In a system, like the American one, that regulates the return on savings in certain forms—especially the Regulation Q restriction on savings account in-

24. See, for example, the comprehensive discussion in John B. Shoven and Jeremy I. Bulow, "Inflation Accounting and Nonfinancial Corporate Profits: Physical Assets," *Brookings Papers on Economic Activity, 3:1975*, pp. 557–98; and Shoven and Bulow, "Inflation Accounting and Nonfinancial Corporate Profits: Financial Assets and Liabilities," *BPEA, 1:1976*, pp. 15–57.

25. Martin Feldstein, "Inflation, Income Taxes, and the Rate of Interest: A Theoretical Analysis," *American Economic Review*, vol. 66 (December 1976), pp. 809–20.

26. For example, with a flat 50 percent tax rate both borrowers and lenders will be in the same position with an interest rate of 5 percent and no inflation or an interest rate of 15 percent and an inflation rate of 5 percent. The 7.5 percent after-tax nominal return in the latter case amounts to 2.5 percent in real terms, the same as is realized with no inflation.

terest—this response of financial yields to inflation may be prevented. In any case the ability of financial markets to compensate for the incorrect income measurement no longer precisely holds for progressive taxation, as high-bracket taxpayers would pay too much on their inflation premium and low-bracket taxpayers too little.[27]

In contrast, inflation does not pose any problem for the consumption tax, because the calculation of the base involves only current year transactions. The tax base and tax liabilities are always measured in consistent units. To illustrate, consider a person who purchases a share of stock for $100 that grows in real value to $110 by the next period, when it is sold and the proceeds are consumed. If his tax rate is 50 percent, under the standard treatment he sacrifices $50 of consumption in the first period in return for $55 extra consumption in the second period. If he chooses the tax prepayment approach, he sacrifices $100 of consumption in the first period in return for $110 extra consumption in the second period. The same 10 percent return is obtained under both treatments. If the price level doubles between the two periods, and the price of the stock with it, the second period outcomes will be $110 and $220, respectively, under the two treatments, exactly the same in real terms as when there is no inflation.

Averaging

The problem of averaging arises when a progressive rate structure is applied to a base that is calculated periodically. Normally it is taken for granted that a person with a fluctuating income should not bear a heavier burden of income tax than someone with the same average income experienced at a steady rate. It is not immediately obvious how this objective should be made precise, that is, what the ideal averaging scheme would be. One possibility would be to arrange matters so that income is taxed at a uniform rate over the taxpayer's lifetime, with higher rates for those with "better" income streams. Implementing this would be a complicated matter under an income tax, and, as far as I know, no averaging scheme in use attempts to achieve it.[28]

27. This has been discussed in detail by Martin Feldstein, Jerry Green, and Eytan Sheshinski, "Inflation and Taxes in a Growing Economy with Debt and Equity Finance," *Journal of Political Economy*, vol. 86 (April 1978), pt. 2, pp. S53–S70.

28. For discussion and a proposal for lifetime averaging under an income tax, see William Vickrey, *Agenda for Progressive Taxation* (Ronald Press, 1947; Kelley, 1972), chap. 6.

Interestingly, such an outcome would be exactly what one would expect under a consumption tax in which the two methods of calculating the base—standard and tax prepayment—are simultaneously available, at least for a reasonably broad class of investments. As shown above, the two methods lead to the same present value of the tax base for any given stream of true consumption.[29] It follows that if the tax rate applied to the portion of the base reported in a given year were higher than in other years, the taxpayer could reduce his burden in present-value terms by rearranging his pattern of saving and dissaving in the two allowable forms. For example, a taxpayer whose marginal rate this year is 20 percent and who expects next year to be subject to a marginal rate of 50 percent will naturally use the tax prepayment method for his investments. But he will do more than that: by borrowing according to the standard method this year, raising this year's tax base, and investing on a tax prepaid basis, and then reversing the process next year, he can further reduce his tax burden.

The gain from this profitable arbitrage would be limited by the progressive rate schedule. Thus, as the arbitraging process continues, the present-period marginal tax rate rises, while next year's falls, and the process stops when the two rates are just the same, somewhere between 20 and 50 percent.

In the simple world of a uniform and certain rate of return, with unlimited borrowing and lending capabilities, this self-averaging system produces just the right result: the present value of the tax burden is a function of the present value of lifetime consumption, regardless of the time pattern of earnings or the other features of the lifetime plan. When borrowing and lending are limited, matters become less clear-cut; nevertheless, the general principle would seem still to hold.[30]

Uncertainty introduces a distinction between anticipations and results that has interesting implications. Since the outcome of the investment is not known in advance, the taxpayer cannot assure himself of perfect averaging ex post. Instead in every period he will seek to opti-

29. This statement is precisely true in the simple case of a uniform and certain return on savings. As has been noted above (note 22), uncertainty introduces complications, some of which are discussed in the text.

30. A possible objection that the proposed system puts an undesirable premium on knowledge and forward planning does, however, acquire extra force as the world becomes more complicated. Because of the great complexity of the rules and great differences in the tax treatment of different forms of saving, the present system is perhaps even more vulnerable to this complaint.

mize ex ante. Roughly speaking, the tax burden will be related progressively to the expected value of the taxpayer's consumption stream, as viewed from his perspective. It may be debated whether this ex ante progressivity is as desirable as ex post progressivity—I find it rather appealing—but there is unfortunately not the space to pursue that question here.[31]

Defects of the U.S. Income Tax

It goes without saying that anyone's list of the defects of the U.S. tax system would include many items not germane to the choice between income and consumption bases. However, some of the more egregious faults are relevant for two reasons: (1) they arise from just those measurement problems noted in the previous section that are very difficult to solve in an income tax but easy to solve in a consumption tax; and (2) they reflect the apparent preference of Congress for a system that taxes savings more lightly than a comprehensive income tax would.

Accruing Wealth Changes

The United States subjects ordinary business investments to an extremely complex and varied set of tax treatments. The major features of the law deserving mention are as follows.

—The investment tax credit pays for up to 10 percent[32] of the cost of new equipment (without any reduction in the schedule of depreciation allowances).

—Although no one knows how to measure "true" economic depreciation, the depreciation deduction allowed under U.S. tax laws is widely believed to be too generous. This is especially the case in certain industries, notably real estate. Often the readily visible tax shelter "industry" provides evidence that, indeed, the depreciation allowances are excessive.

—Certain forms of investment are written off immediately, notably

31. I have carried the analysis further in comment on the Meade committee report in David F. Bradford, "The Meade Report from a U.S. Perspective," presentation at the Social Science Research Council/Public Sector Study Group Tax Reform Symposium, University College, London, May 26, 1978.

32. Eleven and a half percent if one counts the extra credit for employee stock ownership plans.

outlays for research and development or mineral exploration (not embodied in personal property), and selling expenses.

—Equity investment in corporations is subject to a separate tax that is unrelated to the circumstances of the investor; dividends are "double taxed."

—Gains and losses from holding assets are not taxed as they accrue; gains and losses "realized" from the sale or exchange of assets— capital gains—are subjected to the income tax according to special rules. The most notable of the rules is the allowance of a deduction for 60 percent of the gain on assets held long enough. On the other hand, severe limits are placed on the netting of realized losses against other elements of income. It has been estimated that the need to distinguish capital gains from ordinary income accounts for half the text of the individual income tax statute.

—Many forms of retirement saving receive preferred tax treatment. Employer contributions to qualified retirement plans are not included in the income of the employees, although the full amount of the ultimate withdrawal on retirement is subjected to tax at that time. This is the classic method of implementing a consumption tax; the effect is to exclude all the accruing yield on retirement wealth from income taxation. Some other forms of retirement saving receive similar treatment, notably saving carried out through an individual retirement account (for those with inadequate employer-provided plans) or a Keogh plan (for the self-employed). The amounts of such tax-preferred saving allowed are, however, limited.

—The buildup of life insurance wealth is also free of income tax. Earnings on the reserves of life insurance companies are free of corporation income tax, and no allocation of accruing wealth to policyholders is registered in the individual income tax calculations.

—Interest from state and local government bonds is not included in the income calculation for tax purposes.

Reasons for the provisions. The extraordinary variety of special provisions has no single explanation. But it is clear that a combination of a policy preference for investment and sheer income measurement problems has played a central role. Of all the features listed, the investment tax credit is most clearly designed as an incentive. No doubt the desire to encourage investment has helped determine the rules for depreciation allowances and write-offs for research and other activities, but the difficulty of measuring the asset value changes these allowances are designed to represent makes them vulnerable to erosion through the political process. Businessmen claim they need more realistic allowances; there is little evidence that they are wrong.

Whatever the origins of a separate tax on corporations—it predates by four years the twentieth century incarnation of the federal tax on individual incomes—it can be rationalized as an answer to the difficult problem of allocating to individual equity owners the income accumulated within the institution of the corporation. The separate tax has serious disadvantages, though, viewed as a component of a system relating tax liabilities to individual circumstances. The anomalous treatment of dividends—which are after all merely a change in portfolio composition, to cash—especially when compared with the treatment of capital gains, puts a premium on retentions or tax-free routes for funds out of the corporation. Indeed the scale of dividend payments in the United States is a continuing puzzle to analysts, in view of the significant tax disadvantages of that payout method. In addition, there are the limitations on the use of tax credits, on loss carry-forward, and so forth. All these rules taken together have undoubtedly had a marked effect on the financial structure and corporate organization of the United States.

The corporation income tax, in turn, provides one justification for the favorable treatment of long-term capital gains. Though by no means all the capital gains realized and recorded on tax returns are earned on corporate stock, the share is substantial, and a reduced rate on such gains compensates for the corporate income tax paid on the underlying retentions. The special treatment of capital gains occurs in the first place because of the difficulty of measuring accruals in the absence of cash transactions. Traditionally, the capital gains preference has been justified as well by its incentive effect on investment, particularly risky investment.

Presumably, the nontaxation of accruals of retirement benefits and of wealth in the form of life insurance has its origin in the income measurement problems noted above. That policy, too, has no doubt had a profound effect on the financial structure of the United States, encouraging the concentration of savings in financial institutions.

Finally, the fact that state and local bond interest is tax free can be explained historically as a phenomenon of U.S. constitutional law. Most legal commentators now regard that reason for the exemption as unsound; the support for the exemption comes from state and local government officials and wealthy individuals—for obvious reasons having nothing to do with either income measurement or any explicit policy to lighten the tax burden on savings.

Shelters. Tax-exempt bonds provide a good example of the kind of problem that occurs because of the lack of a consistent definition of income. In equilibrium, the interest on tax-exempt bonds falls below that on taxable bonds, with the percentage difference representing the marginal tax rate at which it pays to switch savings from one form to the other. Assuming for simplicity that it is possible to borrow at the taxable interest rate, it would pay a person whose marginal tax rate is above the boundary level, but who has no savings or who prefers to hold savings in other forms, to borrow at the higher taxable interest and lend at the lower tax-free interest. In effect, a profit is made on the tax system, with part of the benefit going to the state or local government borrower. The operative mechanism is a "sheltering" of other income—usually income from personal services—by the interest deduction. Such profitable arbitrage could continue until the individual's taxable income fell enough to drive his marginal rate down to the level where the two returns do not differ.

It is debatable whether there is anything objectionable about this arbitrage. After all, what is accomplished is to reduce the top marginal rate on earned income to the rate paid (implicitly) by owners of existing wealth on tax-exempt bond interest. Congress, however, did not take that view and enacted a prohibition against deducting interest on borrowing for the purpose of purchasing or holding tax-exempt bonds. Although to economists it has an odd ring, the attempt is actually made to implement the policy through rules for "tracing" the source of funds to purchase or hold tax exempts. Such rules are typical of the response of tax-law makers to the pressures created by the inconsistent definition of income. Even when the income measurement problem could be solved directly (as in this case, by taxing state and local bond interest), lawmakers tend to enact special rules to counter the perceived "abuse." Thus, for example, the systematically excessive allowances for depreciation in certain sectors—notably real estate—account for much of the complex antishelter legislation.

To see how incorrect measurement rules may affect tax burdens, it may be helpful to look at the functioning of a shelter that uses the depreciation allowances. Suppose that the rules are equivalent to allowing the immediate expensing of one-half the investment in question, and suppose that the going interest rate is 10 percent. This means that by putting up $100 a taxpayer in the 70 percent bracket can buy roughly $154 worth of the investment project, with the government putting in the extra $54 in tax relief (70 percent of the deduction of ½ of $154). If the investment yields 10 percent, the high-bracket taxpayer can pay a deductible $10 a year on $100 of borrowed money and pocket $1.62 a year ($5.40 × [1.0 − 0.7]), with no actual personal investment at all. It is a case of pure arbitrage profit through the tax system; preventing it requires burdensome rules—for example, appropriately limiting interest deductions—which are bound to leave loopholes.

Imputed Consumption Yield

Under U.S. tax law no effort is made to capture the yield in the form of direct services from investment in owner-occupied houses or other consumer durables such as paintings and jewelry, while the price of services of this sort purchased on the market must support income tax.[33] The exemption of the yield on owner-occupied housing, in particular, has long been the target of reformers.

Inflation

The sensitivity of the distribution of real tax burdens to the rate of inflation is also a problem in the current U.S. system. The tendency of inflation to reduce the real value of depreciation allowances based on historical costs has been a powerful argument for accelerated methods. Similarly, objections to the taxation of nominal, inflation-caused increases in the value of assets, when real returns are small or negative, has much to do with the political support for lightly taxing capital gains. That neither of these ways of dealing with inflation is at all satisfactory has not prevented their adoption.

Until recently, there has been little interest in more systematic indexing. This lack is usually attributed to the desire of Congress to claim credit for tax "cuts," made necessary by the fact that inflation pushes households up the progressive rate schedule. However, as

33. Insofar as a wealth accretion results from holding these assets, it also goes untaxed except as realized in the form of capital gains. Even this is allowed to go substantially free of tax in the case of housing, through a "rollover" rule coupled with tax exemption up to specified limits after the owner reaches age fifty-five.

noted above, the mismeasurement of the basis for capital gains and of depreciation allowances tends to raise the effective rate of tax on the return to savings.[34] Present rules also lead to capricious variations in the distribution of the tax burden. In analyzing data from tax returns assembled by the Treasury, Feldstein and Slemrod found an example of this capriciousness by comparing real and nominal capital gains reported.[35] Although the aggregate gain realized from the sale of corporate stock amounted to $4.6 billion in the year analyzed (1973), the real gain was approximately *minus* $0.9 billion (in 1973 dollars). Furthermore, the difference between real and reported gain varied systematically by income class, with a close agreement between the two at the top of the income distribution and a wide divergence at the bottom.[36]

Averaging

Few people regard averaging as a major problem of the U.S. income tax. But it has had an important bearing on policy as an influential argument for the special treatment of capital gains and has probably helped prevent the inclusion in the tax base of gifts and bequests received. Those elements of the Haig-Simons income calculation require averaging provisions because of their typically large size relative to the rest of the income flow.[37]

Explicit provisions for averaging do exist in the individual income tax laws, and an extensive literature deals with the best way to accomplish it. The present rules are simple enough for the taxpayer who does

34. For an estimate of the size of this effect, see Martin Feldstein and Lawrence Summers, "Inflation, Tax Rules, and the Long-Term Interest Rate," *BPEA, 1:1978*, pp. 61–99.

35. Martin Feldstein and Joel Slemrod, "Inflation and the Excess Taxation of Capital Gains on Corporate Stock," *National Tax Journal,* vol. 31 (June 1978), pp. 107–18.

36. Ironically, the political reaction to the effect of inflation on capital gains has most recently taken the form of a reduction in rates on the gains experienced by high-income taxpayers. The tax bill initially approved by the House of Representatives in 1978 did include explicit indexing of gains, starting in 1980, but this provision was struck before the enactment of the Revenue Act of 1978.

37. David has shown that for most people capital gains are actually realized on a fairly regular basis. It is no doubt true, however, that very large realized gains relative to other income are not uncommon, as in the sale of a house. Martin David, *Alternative Approaches to Capital Gains Taxation* (Brookings Institution, 1968), p. 107.

not change his family status, but they are limited and useful only to
even out increases in the individual base, not decreases.[38]

Summary

I have identified three broad problem areas in the present U.S. income tax system: first, the extremely varied taxation of the yields
from ordinary investment, depending on the industrial sector, the
form of business organization, the type of financing, and the purpose
of savings; second, the inconsistent taxation of the yield from owner-
occupied housing and other consumer durables; and third, the sensitivity of the measurement of the real tax base to the rate of inflation.
Correcting these defects fully to meet the Haig-Simons income ideal
is universally conceded to be impractical. Various studies, *Blueprints*
among them, have suggested ways to approximate this ideal. But
there is little evidence that Congress wants to do so. What is clear is
that the present half-way status, with its chains of ad hoc remedies to
problems arising from the basically inadequate income measurement
rules, is unsatisfactory.

Efficiency and the Choice between an Income Base and a Consumption Base

Economic efficiency is commonly regarded as one of the principal
reasons for preferring a consumption to an income base for taxation.
The disincentive to save resulting from the taxation of the returns to
saving under an income tax is eliminated under a consumption tax.[39]
However, all practical tax systems involve some disincentive effects,
so the efficiency issue in the choice between income and consumption
taxation is the relative seriousness of the distortions under the two. As
the discussion just concluded makes clear, the actual income tax in

38. If the rules are intended to deal with *variable* income flows, they are not
well directed, for Treasury studies show that their main effect is to reduce the taxes
of those with easily anticipated life-cycle increases in income. See, for example,
Eugene Steuerle, Richard McHugh, and Emil Sunley, "Income Averaging: Evidence on Benefits and Utilization," in *Compilation of OTA Papers,* vol. 1 (GPO,
1978).

39. This assertion strictly holds only where tax rates do not vary over the taxpayer's lifetime. This is not a negligible qualification when graduated rate schedules
are used, and it is a point in favor of the self-averaging aspect of the consumption
tax system discussed in the text.

the United States must be thought of as a highly complicated array of different taxes on various transactions, but the analysis here must be confined to simple models permitting only combinations of pure income and consumption taxes.

The efficient use of resources requires that the rates at which different desirable goods and services are traded off for one another through changes in production just equal the corresponding trade-offs in the preferences of households. Otherwise a reallocation of resources is available that would produce a better outcome for all households. In the absence of taxes, competitive forces bring about efficient resource use because firms and households face the same prices. But when taxes must be levied to raise revenue, firms and households are presented with different prices, and equilibrium is no longer efficient. The problem of tax policy is how to make as close an approach as possible to efficient resource use and still raise the necessary revenue through price-distorting taxes. This is typical of what has become known in the economics literature as a "problem of the second best."[40]

Second-Best Taxation in a Life-Cycle Saving Model

The essence of the problem is captured by a model in which a person lives for two periods, working and consuming in the first period and consuming from the proceeds of his first-period savings as a retiree in the second period.[41] The budget constraint of this typical taxpayer is then

$$(5) \qquad C^1 + \frac{C^2}{1 + (1 - t_r)r} = (1 - t_w)wL,$$

40. For an elementary discussion and introduction to the literature, see David F. Bradford and Harvey S. Rosen, "The Optimal Taxation of Commodities and Income," *American Economic Review*, vol. 66 (May 1976, *Papers and Proceedings, 1975*), pp. 94–101. For a discussion specifically directed to the issue of the tax treatment of savings, see David F. Bradford, "The Economics of Tax Policy toward Savings," in George M. von Furstenberg, ed., *The Government and Capital Formation* (Ballinger, forthcoming). This paper also goes into the question of how the choice of tax rules affects the accumulation of wealth.

41. See Paul A. Samuelson, "An Exact Consumption-Loan Model of Interest with or without the Social Contrivance of Money," *Journal of Political Economy*, vol. 66 (December 1958), pp. 467–82; Peter A. Diamond, "National Debt in a Neoclassical Growth Model," *American Economic Review*, vol. 55 (December 1965), pp. 1126–50; Martin Feldstein, "The Welfare Cost of Capital Income Taxation," *Journal of Political Economy*, vol. 86 (April 1978), pt. 2, pp. S29–S51.

where

C^1 = consumption in period 1
C^2 = consumption in period 2
L = labor supplied in period 1
r = interest rate
w = wage rate
t_r = tax rate on interest
t_w = tax rate on wages.

This budget constraint reflects a flat-rate income tax if $t_r = t_w$, and a pure consumption tax when $t_r = 0$. (The equivalence between a flat-rate tax on consumption and one on nonwealth receipts is immediately verified by setting $t_r = 0$ and dividing through 5 by $1 - t_w$. The result is the budget constraint for a person facing a flat consumption tax at rate $t_c = t_w/1 - t_w$. Government revenues are also the same in present-value terms under either scheme.)

   The analysis of the second-best problem in this case is made more transparent if the tax on interest is shown as an equivalent tax on second-period consumption, so that the household's budget constraint becomes[42]

$$(6) \qquad C^1 + \frac{(1 + t_2)C^2}{1 + r} - (1 - t_w)wL = 0,$$

where t_2, the tax on second-period consumption, is related to t_r by

$$(7) \qquad t_2 = \frac{1 + r}{1 + (1 - t_r)r} - 1.$$

The problem is to choose t_w and t_2 in such a way as to do the household as little harm as possible while ensuring some specified total of tax revenue. In mathematical terms this is a straightforward problem, and it can be shown that a solution will involve the following relationship between t_w and t_2,

$$(8) \qquad \frac{t_2}{1 + t_2} = \frac{t_w}{1 - t_w}\left[\frac{\sigma_{LL} - \sigma_{2L}}{\sigma_{L2} - \sigma_{22}}\right],$$

where the σ_{ij} are parameters describing the household's preferences among the "commodities" of the problem, first- and second-period consumption, and labor. Economists will recognize them as the com-

---

42. I follow here the treatment in A. B. Atkinson and J. E. Stiglitz, *Lectures on Public Economics* (McGraw-Hill, 1979).

pensated elasticities of the demand for future consumption and the supply of labor.

It should not be surprising that this analysis will imply either pure income or pure consumption taxation only by coincidence. The second-best optimum depends upon the elasticities of demand (including the demand for leisure). This simple model, for example, would imply a consumption base if the compensated supply elasticity of labor (necessarily nonnegative) were just balanced by a positive responsiveness of the (compensated) labor supply to the price of retirement consumption. Such a balancing relationship is not wholly implausible. It holds, for example, if individual preferences imply that an increment of wealth will be used to purchase the three commodities in this problem in proportion to their original quantities, as in the Cobb-Douglas utility function so familiar to economists.[43]

Such a simple model can do no more than offer the roughest sort of assistance to policy, but it does illustrate the severe limitations of unguided intuition in such a complex matter. The Cobb-Douglas utility function offers a particularly striking example, since it is the usual form assumed in life-cycle models of savings, in part because it allows analytical simplification, but also because it has seemed plausible to researchers.[44] In this two-period model it leads, as noted, to the optimality of a consumption base. This holds despite the fact that the (uncompensated) interest elasticity of first-period consumption is zero. In other words, private saving is totally insensitive to changes in the yield on savings, a condition normally thought to favor income taxation.[45]

43. Cobb-Douglas preferences for this case can be written

$$U(C^1, C^2, L) = a_1 \ln C^1 + a_2 \ln C^2 + a_3 \ln (H - L),$$

where ln is the symbol for natural logarithms and H is the total time available for working in the first period. We can think of the household as having $(1 - t_w)wH$ to spend on consumption in the two periods and on leisure. The household with these preferences will spend $a_1(1 - t_w)wH/(a_1 + a_2 + a_3)$ on first-period consumption; $a_2(1 - t_w)wH/(a_1 + a_2 + a_3)$ on claims on second-period consumption, at price $(1 + t_2)/(1 + r)$; and $a_3(1 - t_w)wH/(a_1 + a_2 + a_3)$ on leisure, at price $(1 - t_w)w$.

44. See, for example, Alan S. Blinder, *Toward an Economic Theory of Income Distribution* (MIT Press, 1974).

45. Feldstein explains why an insignificant responsiveness of saving to the rate of return does not imply a low efficiency cost of capital income taxation. He points out that the necessarily nonnegative compensated elasticity of demand for second-period consumption with respect to the rate of return (the basic parameter related to efficiency) is consistent with a zero or even negative elasticity of the demand for *saving*, which is the product of a quantity (second-period consumption) and a price (the present value of a second-period dollar). Feldstein, "Welfare Cost."

Choosing between Income and Consumption

Earlier in this paper I argued that the taxation of capital in the United States is highly variable because of uneasy compromises that have been made between cash flow accounting and Haig-Simons income measurement. The record suggests that, whereas a precise measurement of Haig-Simons income may be difficult, imposing a tax on the return to capital at a rate bearing any systematic relation (other than full equality) to the tax rate on labor earnings is hopeless. It therefore might be argued that the proper question is not what the optimal ratio between tax rates on labor income and capital income is, but what the choice between a pure income tax and a pure consumption tax should be.

In his 1978 paper Feldstein analyzes that question by constructing an estimate of the welfare gain from shifting from a tax of 40 percent on both capital and labor earnings to a tax of equal yield on labor earnings alone. Feldstein employs a set of assumptions that roughly simulate the U.S. economy, including the assumption that the (uncompensated) interest elasticity of savings is zero.[46] He concludes that the differential loss from the income base amounts to 18 percent of the revenue collected from the tax on capital income.[47] In the Feldstein formulation, if savings are more responsive to the rate of return, the efficiency cost will be higher.

Interestingly, as far as the efficiency cost is concerned, Feldstein's formulation does not give any points to the consumption base for what is sometimes considered its chief attraction: encouraging capital formation, where capital is viewed not as the aggregate of individual wealth but as the factor combined with labor to produce output. It is characteristic of second-best optimal tax calculations that when, as in this case, all transactions are potentially subject to tax, only properties of preferences (demand elasticities) enter the solution formulas.[48]

46. Ibid.

47. Green and Sheshinski point out that in comparing both distorted equilibria to a nondistorted equilibrium, Feldstein's approximation to the gain is unnecessarily crude. Their more refined calculations (with slightly different assumptions) place the differential loss at about two-thirds of Feldstein's estimates. Jerry R. Green and Eytan Sheshinski, "Approximating the Efficiency Gain of Tax Reforms," Discussion Paper 516 (Harvard Institute of Economic Research, 1978).

48. See, for example, Peter A. Diamond and James A. Mirrlees, "Optimal Taxation and Public Production II: Tax Rules," *American Economic Review,* vol. 61 (June 1971), pp. 261–78.

Variations in assumptions about the production system will therefore not affect expression 8 for optimal taxes. But since the welfare gain calculations just reviewed treat the before-tax rate of return and wage rate as constant, the results can be interpreted as the efficiency gain when the capital per worker-hour does not change (as in the case of a small open economy, where exchange with a larger system leads to the constancy of factor prices). Usually the price changes that would follow from relaxing this assumption would act to reduce the efficiency effects. (For example, if before-tax prices changed to keep after-tax prices constant, there would be no efficiency gain.)

Various authors have also examined the effect of wage and interest taxes on the properties of steady-state growth paths. Much of this work has been summarized and greatly extended by Atkinson and Sandmo.[49] Their analysis explicitly addresses the problem of compromising between equity and efficiency objectives and is therefore more suitably taken up in the next section, which deals with equity arguments.

Summary

It is hardly to be expected that the conclusions drawn from such simplified models will be persuasive when applied to a complicated real policy issue. The analysis of efficiency just discussed considers a choice between two nonexistent ideals. In particular, the present tax system in the United States deviates so markedly from an income ideal that the more important efficiency effects may well be those related to the misallocation of productive resources across uses and within the household, rather than those related to the life-cycle patterns of consumption and labor.[50] On the other hand, since this volume is concerned with the goal toward which tax policy should aim, the comparison of the pure forms is relevant. Granting the necessary qualifications, I conclude that the efficiency analysis reinforces the administrative considerations in support of a consumption base against an income base.

49. A. B. Atkinson and A. Sandmo, "The Taxation of Savings and Economic Efficiency," Discussion Paper (Bergen, Norway: Norwegian School of Economics and Business Administration, 1977).

50. See, for example, the voluminous literature on the corporate income tax, running from Harberger in 1962 to Shoven in 1976. Arnold C. Harberger, "The Incidence of the Corporation Income Tax," *Journal of Political Economy,* vol. 70 (June 1962), pp. 215–40; John B. Shoven, "The Incidence and Efficiency Effects of Taxes on Income from Capital," ibid., vol. 84 (December 1976), pp. 1261–83.

Equity

If neither practicability nor efficiency leads to a preference for an income base, the case for the superiority of an income tax must be founded on justice or equity. Probably most laymen believe that income represents a fairer basis for taxation than consumption. This has also been the position taken by a number of influential expert commentators, including Goode, Musgrave and Musgrave, and Surrey.[51] In general the preference for income is based on the idea that the accretion of economic power during an accounting period, which may be allocated to either consumption or savings, represents a better measure of ability to pay than consumption, a mere component of total accretion (though the part may be larger than the whole, since savings may be negative).[52] The comparable opposing view is that consumption, a measure of what people take *out* of the economic system, is a more appropriate basis for taxation than income, a measure of what they contribute to the economic system in productive performance.

These arguments are commonly considered persuasive in themselves. They are not, for example, easy to relate to the utilitarian theory that generally underlies welfare arguments in economics. Thus there is no ready answer to the question of why income, which is a measure of *change* in economic power (however that might be defined), should be preferred to some measure of the *level* of economic power.[53] Nor is it obvious how the consumption tax advocate should

51. Richard Goode, *The Individual Income Tax,* rev. ed. (Brookings Institution, 1976), pp. 21–25, and Goode's paper in this volume; Richard A. Musgrave and Peggy B. Musgrave, *Public Finance in Theory and Practice* (McGraw-Hill, 1973), pp. 205–06. More recently Musgrave has offered qualified support for a consumption base that includes gifts and bequests, called an "ability to pay" consumption base in *Blueprints,* p. 36. Richard A. Musgrave, "ET, OT and SBT," *Journal of Public Economics,* vol. 6 (July–August 1976), pp. 3–16.

52. In all of what follows I ignore the possible uses for accretion, such as medical expenses, other than consumption or savings.

53. By taxing all changes, it is presumably possible over a long period to achieve a tax burden roughly related to the level. It is argued below that precisely this effect can be achieved with greater consistency by a consumption base. See also David F. Bradford and Eric Toder, "Consumption vs. Income Base Taxes: The Argument on Grounds of Equity and Simplicity," in National Tax Association–Tax Institute of America, *Proceedings of the Sixty-ninth Annual Conference on Taxation, 1976* (Columbus, Ohio: NTA-TIA, 1977), pp. 25–31.

deal with the view that it is the power to consume, not its exercise, that is the proper basis for taxation. (The miserly millionaire who consumes nothing is usually trotted out at this point.) Furthermore, neither of these lines of argument takes into account the *link* between income and consumption over the life cycle.

Utilitarian Analysis of the Choice of Tax Base

Utilitarian theory has been used to explore the choice of a tax base. I have already noted the paper by Atkinson and Sandmo that surveys and extends one branch of the application of interpersonal utility assumptions to the selection of separate rates of tax on payments to labor and capital.[54] Their analysis focuses on the effect of wage and interest taxes on the equilibrium capital–labor ratio in steady-state growth. They embed the problem of individual maximization subject to a budget constraint of the form of equation 6 in a model of growth in which the generations overlap, like the model introduced by Samuelson and extended by Diamond and others.[55] In such models the capital accumulated by one generation becomes the factor cooperating with the next generation's labor in production. The properties of steady-state growth paths are of prime interest; the usual goal analyzed is that of choosing the path to maximize the utility of a representative individual (or of a representative "effective individual" in the case of productivity growth through technical change).

It is important to recognize that in adopting such a goal these studies move from an efficiency analysis—with efficiency defined strictly according to Pareto optimality—to an explicit interpersonal utility comparison. This issue may be easily understood by looking at the case in which no tax revenue need be raised at all. In that case the second-best analysis discussed above implies zero tax rates, these necessary properties of Pareto optimality being referred to by Atkinson and Sandmo as "static efficiency conditions."[56] By the familiar golden

54. In addition to Atkinson and Sandmo, "Taxation of Savings," see Alan J. Auerbach, "The Optimal Taxation of Heterogeneous Capital" (Harvard University, 1978).

55. Samuelson, "Exact Consumption-Loan Model"; Diamond, "National Debt"; and Diamond, "Taxation and Public Production in a Growth Setting," in James A. Mirrlees and N. H. Stern, eds., *Models of Economic Growth* (London: Macmillan, 1973), pp. 215–35. See Atkinson and Sandmo, "Taxation of Savings," for a compact survey of the literature.

56. Atkinson and Sandmo, "Taxation of Savings."

rule reasoning the resulting path will not be Pareto optimal, however, unless the rate of return on capital exceeds the rate of population growth.[57] When that condition is not satisfied, an excess of capital exists, so that some of the existing stock can be consumed currently at no cost to the consumption of future generations. Except in such a pathological case, however, the path satisfying "static efficiency" will be Pareto optimal. This is true even though the utility of the representative individual will not be maximized. The conditions of production and exchange necessarily characterizing an optimum in the latter sense are called by Atkinson and Sandmo those of "dynamic efficiency,"[58] a somewhat unfortunate term, given the usual meaning of "efficiency" in economics.

When the capital–labor ratio in such a model diverges from the golden rule level, it will usually be possible to raise steady-state utility by a combination of wage and interest taxes that preserve budget balance.[59] In the case of a capital–labor ratio below the golden rule level (rate of return above the rate of population growth), a combination of a tax on interest and a subsidy on wages may raise steady-state utility by causing the capital–labor ratio to rise. Such a result occurs when preferences over combinations of first-period consumption, first-period leisure, and second-period consumption can be described by the Cobb-Douglas form of utility function.[60] With these preferences, labor supply is independent of the wage rate, and the fraction of the after-subsidy wage devoted to capital accumulation is constant, that is, totally insensitive to the after-tax return.

This conclusion, that even with no net government revenue requirement welfare could be improved by taxing interest returns to subsidize wages, is in striking contrast to the efficiency analysis with the same preference structure, as discussed above. In the absence of a need for net government revenue, efficiency called for no taxes at all, whereas a positive government revenue constraint implied a tax on wage income only. In the Atkinson and Sandmo model the pure efficiency analysis characterizes optimal taxes only in the special case where the associated capital–labor ratio is at the golden rule level.

57. Edmund S. Phelps, *Golden Rules of Economic Growth* (Norton, 1966).

58. Atkinson and Sandmo, "Taxation of Savings."

59. This paraphrases the portion of the Atkinson-Sandmo paper in which the capital–labor ratio is allowed to vary. The sections taking the capital–labor ratio as fixed seem to me to accept an inexplicable and unnecessary constraint.

60. See note 43.

Welfare Analysis with Government Saving

Thus far I have been assuming that the only instruments available to the government intent on maximizing welfare are wage and interest taxes. The picture is dramatically changed when the government can issue debt. If so, that instrument alone suffices to attain the golden rule capital–labor ratio (one can imagine the government standing ready to borrow or lend at a rate of interest equal to the growth rate of effective labor), and taxes are zero in the absence of a net revenue requirement. Any net revenue requirement implied should be raised through wage and interest taxes according to the second-best efficiency arguments already summarized.[61] In other words, roughly speaking, when capital accumulation (or decumulation) is the aim, government deficits or surpluses constitute the preferred instrument; pure efficiency arguments determine the structure of distorting taxes, which will be needed only to finance real government expenditures.

Introducing government debt into the Atkinson-Sandmo system is analytically equivalent to allowing an element of lump sum taxation in the second-best problem discussed earlier.[62] In their paper on the design of tax systems, Atkinson and Stiglitz point out that it is in general unrealistic to rule out lump sum taxes, since most tax systems have similar elements (for example, the zero bracket amount in the U.S. income tax).[63] Admitting such taxes into the usual second-best

61. The effect of a person buying a unit of debt in the first life period and selling it for $(1 + r)$ in the second (where r is the rate of return), is equivalent to a lump sum tax of one unit in the first period and a lump sum subsidy of $(1 + r)$ in the second. In a growth setting, part of the second-period lump subsidy to the old can be financed by the lump sum tax on the young, enough to return $(1 + n)$, where n is the rate of population growth. The rest must be raised through transaction taxes (or given away through transaction subsidies). If D_t, G_t, and T_t are per capita government debt, government expenditure (other than interest payments), and tax revenues, respectively, $(1 + n)D_{t+1} = (1 + r_t)D_t + G_t - T_t$. Letting unsubscripted variables denote steady-state values, if $r \neq n$, $D = (G - T)/(n - r)$. If $r = n$, the golden rule condition, there is no steady state unless $G = T$. In this case, the steady-state debt per capita is indeterminate, since the interest payments are exactly covered by the net new debt issue. Thus it is assured that whatever debt level is needed to bring the rate of return on capital into line with population growth can be sustained, but the budget must be balanced for government outlays other than interest payments.

62. See note 61.

63. A. B. Atkinson and J. E. Stiglitz, "The Design of Tax Structure: Direct Versus Indirect Taxation," *Journal of Public Economics*, vol. 6 (July–August 1976), pp. 55–75.

optimality problem leads to the expected conclusion: because of the efficiency advantages, lump sum taxes will be used to the fullest extent possible. This is because the usual analysis in effect assumes that all people are alike. As Atkinson and Stiglitz emphasize, it is the distributional function, inherently deriving from differences in people, that creates the need for taxes on transactions.[64]

While recognizing that a wide range of potentially observable signals—such as income—of differences among people might be used for assessing different tax burdens (thus ruling out conclusions of any great generality), Atkinson and Stiglitz carry out an illustrative analysis in which they assume that people differ only in labor effectiveness, reflected in differences in the wage rate received. Otherwise people are assumed to be identical (for example, they have identical utility functions), and the prices of all goods other than leisure are the same for all.[65] In this model world the government is equipped with a full set of flat-rate transaction taxes and a potentially nonlinear tax schedule applicable to earnings from labor.[66] When taxes are set to maximize a social welfare function, the rather remarkable conclusion emerges that if individual utility functions are weakly separable between labor and all consumption goods taken together, no taxes other than the tax on labor earnings need be employed. This condition says roughly that the rate at which one is willing to trade off future consumption for present consumption is independent of the amount of labor time one puts in. Though such a condition is not empirically established, it does have a certain plausibility (again, Cobb-Douglas preferences provide an illustration), and this suggests the possibility for a fully satisfactory redistributive tax that exempts returns to savings.

Nonutilitarian Equity Arguments

The main contribution of the optimal tax literature has been to make precise certain ideas based on utilitarian premises. The paper by

64. Such factors as the costs of administration might also lead to the use of transaction taxes, as in the case in which a tax burden is placed on residents of other countries by a tariff, lump sum levies on these people being impossible.

65. Note that, as in the preceding growth analysis, consumption in future periods can be included among the goods distinguished by the model.

66. For example, this might consist of a uniform per capita credit plus a flat percentage of labor earnings.

Corlett and Hague, a precursor of the modern optimal commodity tax theory, is a classic example.[67] But outside professional economics circles the debates about tax equity are carried on in terms difficult to analyze in a utilitarian framework. Frequently they hinge on precisely those differences in people—especially differences in taste, health, and so forth—that cast most doubt on the systematic interpersonal comparisons needed for the utilitarian approach. Concepts of "ability to pay" and "horizontal equity" carry great weight. To conclude this section on the equity issues, then, I turn to certain of these less formal but perhaps more persuasive arguments.[68]

The general problem is how to distribute the burden of taxation among people who differ in many respects—health, sex, family status, employment conditions, and so on. It is perfectly legitimate to take any of these differences into account. However, the principle of horizontal equity says that people who are regarded as similar should bear the same tax burden, while the principle of vertical equity says that those who are relatively better situated should bear a relatively greater share of the tax burden. The central questions are *when* people should be regarded as similar for this purpose (and when one person should be considered better situated than another), and *how* the tax burden should be measured.

Although there is no obvious answer to these questions, I would suggest that two related postulates are compelling: (1) events over a short period of time are not an adequate basis for determining the relative "deservingness to pay tax" of two persons; and (2) tax payments over a short period of time are not an adequate basis for comparing the relative tax burdens of two persons. These principles are the more compelling the shorter the "short period of time." None would suggest comparisons based on the events or tax payments of a

67. W. J. Corlett and D. C. Hague, "Complementarity and the Excess Burden of Taxation," *Review of Economic Studies*, vol. 21, no. 1 (1953–54), pp. 21–30.

68. This is not to say that those arguments could not be made more formally. A number of writers have tried to integrate these ideas into conventional welfare economics, including Atkinson and Stiglitz, *Lectures on Public Economics;* Musgrave, "ET, OT and SBT"; and Harvey S. Rosen, "An Approach to the Study of Income, Utility, and Horizontal Equity," *Quarterly Journal of Economics*, vol. 92 (May 1978), pp. 307–22. See also Martin Feldstein, "On the Theory of Tax Reform," *Journal of Public Economics*, vol. 6 (July–August 1976), pp. 77–104, who points out that when tastes are the same virtually any tax will qualify as horizontally equitable.

day or week. A decade seems more reasonable. Yet there is no obvious stopping point short of basing comparisons on a lifetime of circumstances and on a lifetime of tax payments.

To move from these general ideas to a concrete analysis and to isolate the issue of a choice between an income and a consumption base, assume that the lifetime pattern of the labor supply of individuals is fixed, implying for each one a fixed time path of what was called above "nonwealth receipts." People may differ in initial wealth, in the time path of nonwealth receipts, and in the use made of these endowments. How should they be compared? Since people have the same consumption possibilities, it seems compelling that those having the same aggregate of initial wealth and present value of nonwealth receipts should bear the same tax burden, measured in present-value terms. Put another way, because of the lifetime budget constraint, the principle of horizontal equity calls for equal reductions in the discounted value of consumption by people for whom this total would be equal in the absence of tax. The discounted value of nonwealth receipts added to initial wealth might be labeled "lifetime wealth," the operative constraint on lifetime consumption. The principle of horizontal equity amounts to the idea that people should be taxed according to lifetime wealth. Vertical equity, in turn, calls for positively relating tax burdens to lifetime wealth (and, one might add, the principle of progressivity requires that the tax burden, as a fraction of lifetime wealth, be larger the larger is lifetime wealth).

These principles of horizontal and vertical equity are realized by a consumption tax implemented along the lines described above, including the potential for self-averaging by individuals through the alternative methods of accounting for saving. By such a device each person will confront a constant rate of tax on his annual tax base, with the level of the rate a positive function of his lifetime wealth. Further, by the use of a progressive schedule of taxes on the annual base, the burden, measured by the present value of taxes discounted at the rate of interest (the same before and after tax), will be progressively related to lifetime wealth.

By contrast, an annual income tax generates tax burdens that are haphazardly related to individual circumstances, as measured by lifetime wealth. A flat-rate income tax, unlike a flat-rate consumption tax, systematically biases the distribution of tax burdens. Given two persons with the same lifetime wealth, the income tax imposes the lighter burden on the one who consumes early in life, the heavier burden on the one who postpones consumption. Given two persons with the same lifetime wealth, the income tax imposes the lighter burden on the one whose nonwealth receipts occur late in life. If the income tax is levied according to a progressive schedule, the relation between lifetime wealth and lifetime tax burden will be even less systematic. Not only do the timing of receipts and consumption enter the result in the way described but also other characteristics of their time profile now influence relative tax burdens.

All this discussion is based on a highly simplified example. Other aspects of individual circumstances might be considered relevant. For example, to make a distinction between nonwealth receipts due to labor and those due to inheritance or gift might be desirable. Attention to family status is presumably in order. Imperfect capital markets and uncertainty complicate the picture. Yet none of these complications seems to me to point to a preference for income over consumption taxation.

Conclusion

This paper has examined the choice between income and consumption taxes from many angles. In every case a preference, strong or weak, for the consumption base has emerged. In principle, it is much more practical to implement a consumption tax than an income tax. A large number of the most troublesome problems vanish under a consumption tax, and no new problems are evident. This would be a poor basis for choosing a tax—after all, there are even easier taxes to implement—if there were a strong case on other grounds for preferring the income base. Yet it is clear that the two bases are broadly similar and basically attractive. And when efficiency and equity are the criteria by which they are measured, if anything the consumption base proves superior.

In this complex and uncertain world, it is unlikely to find prescriptions for tax policy that will please everyone. Weighty arguments, pro and con, are to be expected. For this reason I am surprised at just how persuasive the case for the consumption base is, on criteria that

I believe are broadly accepted, and I find puzzling the persistent attraction of the income base.

Bibliography

Aaron, Henry J., ed. *Inflation and the Income Tax.* Washington: Brookings Institution, 1976.

Andrews, William D. "A Consumption-Type or Cash Flow Personal Income Tax," *Harvard Law Review,* vol. 87 (April 1974).

Atkinson, A. B., and A. Sandmo. "The Taxation of Savings and Economic Efficiency." Discussion Paper. Bergen, Norway: Norwegian School of Economics and Business Administration, 1977.

Atkinson, A. B., and J. E. Stiglitz. "The Design of Tax Structure: Direct Versus Indirect Taxation." *Journal of Public Economics,* vol. 6 (July–August 1976).

———. *Lectures on Public Economics.* New York: McGraw-Hill, 1979.

Auerbach, Alan J. "The Optimal Taxation of Heterogeneous Capital." Cambridge: Harvard University, 1978.

Blinder, Alan S. *Toward an Economic Theory of Income Distribution.* Cambridge: MIT Press, 1974.

Boskin, Michael J. "Taxation, Saving, and the Rate of Interest," *Journal of Political Economy,* vol. 86 (April 1978), pt. 2.

Bossons, John. "The Value of a Comprehensive Tax Base as a Tax Reform Goal," *Journal of Law and Economics,* vol. 13 (October 1970).

Bradford, David F. "The Economics of Tax Policy toward Savings," in George M. von Furstenberg, ed., *The Government and Capital Formation.* Cambridge, Mass.: Ballinger, forthcoming.

———. "The Meade Report from a U.S. Perspective." Presentation at the Social Science Research Council/Public Sector Study Group Tax Reform Symposium, University College, London, May 26, 1978.

———, and Harvey S. Rosen. "The Optimal Taxation of Commodities and Income," *American Economic Review,* vol. 66 (May 1976, *Papers and Proceedings, 1975*).

———, and Eric Toder. "Consumption vs. Income Base Taxes: The Argument on Grounds of Equity and Simplicity," in National Tax Association–Tax Institute of America, *Proceedings of the Sixty-ninth Annual Conference on Taxation, 1976.* Columbus, Ohio: NTA-TIA, 1977.

Break, George F., and Joseph A. Pechman. *Federal Tax Reform: The Impossible Dream?* Washington: Brookings Institution, 1975.

Corlett, W. J., and D. C. Hague. "Complementarity and the Excess Burden of Taxation," *Review of Economic Studies,* vol. 21, no. 1 (1953–54).

David, Martin. *Alternative Approaches to Capital Gains Taxation.* Washington: Brookings Institution, 1968.

Diamond, Peter A. "National Debt in a Neoclassical Growth Model," *American Economic Review,* vol. 55 (December 1965).

―――. "Taxation and Public Production in a Growth Setting," in James A. Mirrlees and N. H. Stern, eds., *Models of Economic Growth.* London: Macmillan, 1973.

―――, and James A. Mirrlees. "Optimal Taxation and Public Production II: Tax Rules," *American Economic Review,* vol. 61 (June 1971).

Feldstein, Martin. "Inflation, Income Taxes, and the Rate of Interest: A Theoretical Analysis," *American Economic Review,* vol. 66 (December 1976).

―――. "On the Theory of Tax Reform," *Journal of Public Economics,* vol. 6 (July–August 1976).

―――. "The Welfare Cost of Capital Income Taxation," *Journal of Political Economy,* vol. 86 (April 1978), pt. 2.

―――, Jerry Green, and Eytan Sheshinski. "Inflation and Taxes in a Growing Economy with Debt and Equity Finance," *Journal of Political Economy,* vol. 86 (April 1978), pt. 2.

―――, and Joel Slemrod. "Inflation and the Excess Taxation of Capital Gains on Corporate Stock," *National Tax Journal,* vol. 31 (June 1978).

―――, and Lawrence Summers. "Inflation, Tax Rules, and the Long-Term Interest Rate," *Brookings Papers on Economic Activity, 1:1978.*

Goode, Richard. "The Economic Definition of Income," in Joseph A. Pechman, ed., *Comprehensive Income Taxation.* Washington: Brookings Institution, 1977.

―――. *The Individual Income Tax.* Rev. ed. Washington: Brookings Institution, 1976.

Green, Jerry R., and Eytan Sheshinski. "Approximating the Efficiency Gain of Tax Reforms." Discussion Paper 516. Cambridge: Harvard Institute of Economic Research, 1978.

Harberger, Arnold C. "The Incidence of the Corporation Income Tax," *Journal of Political Economy,* vol. 70 (June 1962).

Institute for Fiscal Studies. *The Structure and Reform of Direct Taxation.* Report of a Committee chaired by Professor J. E. Meade. London: Allen and Unwin, 1978.

Kaldor, Nicholas. *An Expenditure Tax*. London: Allen and Unwin, 1955; Westport, Conn: Greenwood Press, 1977.

Kay, J. A., and M. A. King. *The British Tax System*. Oxford: Oxford University Press, 1978.

Lodin, Sven-Olof. *Progressive Expenditure Tax—an Alternative?* A Report of the 1972 Government Commission on Taxation. Stockholm: LiberFörlag, 1978 (originally published as *Progressiv utgiftsskatt—ett alternativ?* Stockholm: Statens Offentliga Utredningar 1976:62).

McLure, Charles E., Jr. *Must Corporate Income Be Taxed Twice?* Washington: Brookings Institution, 1979.

Meade, J. E. See Institute for Fiscal Studies.

Mieszkowski, Peter. "The Choice of Tax Base: Consumption versus Income Taxation," in Michael J. Boskin, ed., *Federal Tax Reform: Myths and Realities*. San Francisco: Institute for Contemporary Studies, 1978.

———. "On the Advisability and Feasibility of an Expenditure Tax System," in Henry J. Aaron and Michael J. Boskin, eds., *The Economics of Taxation*. Washington: Brookings Institution, forthcoming.

Musgrave, Richard A. "ET, OT and SBT," *Journal of Public Economics,* vol. 6 (July–August 1976).

———, and Peggy B. Musgrave. *Public Finance in Theory and Practice*. New York: McGraw-Hill, 1973.

Pechman, Joseph A. *Federal Tax Policy*. Third ed. Washington: Brookings Institution, 1977.

———, ed. *Comprehensive Income Taxation*. Washington: Brookings Institution, 1977.

Phelps, Edmund S. *Golden Rules of Economic Growth: Studies of Efficient and Optimal Investment*. New York: Norton, 1966.

Report of the Royal Commission on Taxation. 6 vols. Ottawa: Queen's Printer, 1966 (vols. 1, 2, 3, 5, 6), and 1967 (vol. 4).

Rosen, Harvey S. "An Approach to the Study of Income, Utility, and Horizontal Equity," *Quarterly Journal of Economics,* vol. 92 (May 1978).

Samuelson, Paul A. "An Exact Consumption-Loan Model of Interest with or without the Social Contrivance of Money," *Journal of Political Economy,* vol. 66 (December 1958).

Shoven, John B. "The Incidence and Efficiency Effects of Taxes on Income from Capital," *Journal of Political Economy,* vol. 84 (December 1976).

———, and Jeremy I. Bulow. "Inflation Accounting and Nonfinancial Corporate Profits: Financial Assets and Liabilities," *Brookings Papers on Economic Activity, 1:1976*.

————, and Jeremy I. Bulow. "Inflation Accounting and Nonfinancial Corporate Profits: Physical Assets," *Brookings Papers on Economic Activity, 3:1975.*

Steuerle, Eugene, Richard McHugh, and Emil Sunley. "Income Averaging: Evidence on Benefits and Utilization," in *Compilation of OTA Papers,* vol. 1. Washington: Government Printing Office, 1978.

Studies of the Royal Commission on Taxation. 30 vols. Ottawa: Queen's Printer, 1966–68.

U.S. Department of the Treasury. *Blueprints for Basic Tax Reform.* Washington: Government Printing Office, 1977.

Vickrey, William. *Agenda for Progressive Taxation.* New York: Ronald Press, 1947; Clifton, N.J.: Kelley, 1972.

Willis, Arthur B., ed. *Studies in Substantive Tax Reform.* Chicago: American Bar Foundation, 1969.

Wykoff, Frank C., and Charles R. Hulten. "Economic Depreciation and the Taxation of Structures in U.S. Manufacturing Industries: An Empirical Analysis," OTA Paper 28. Washington: U.S. Department of the Treasury, Office of Tax Analysis, 1977.

The comments that follow refer to both the Goode and Bradford papers.

Comments by E. Cary Brown

A shift in the basic concept of taxation from income to consumption requires a careful appraisal of all its ramifications. For those who can remember the discussions and controversies leading to the Treasury expenditure tax proposal in 1942 and its flat rejection by the Senate Committee on Finance, its recent recrudescence is of considerable interest. To what should we attribute its greater popularity? What happened on the road to Damascus? Does this call for a major change in policy?

There have always been consumption tax advocates who would favor such a change for almost any reason—in the name of efficiency, growth, or a better distribution of the tax burden. While they may have grown in number, their beliefs do not account for the new interest in the consumption tax. What does account for it is a combination of the tax effects of inflation and a new view about the administration of the consumption tax—a view first advanced by William Andrews regarding a cash flow income tax. This represented a blunting of the earlier position that an expenditure tax had all the difficulties of the income tax plus a few more of its own.

Under a comprehensive income tax many difficult problems arise over the accrual of income; in principle, these can be avoided under a comprehensive consumption tax. But the fussy business of measuring the increase in net worth and subtracting it from income to arrive at consumption expenditure would entail using fairly complete balance sheets. Moreover, in determining the value of the current services of consumer durable goods, imputed consumption would require the inclusion of rental values—net yields *plus* depreciation of the asset—whereas the income concept requires only that the net yields of the asset be added to the tax base. But this can be troublesome under either the income or consumption tax.

Cash flow expenditure tax proposals, such as the Treasury's, that were built on Andrews's cash flow income tax, made the administration easier in many areas—particularly durable goods—by equating the initial outlay with the future expected receipts or flow of services. Tax prepayment, by the inclusion of the durable good expenditure in the current tax base, could be thought of as the equivalent of excluding the outlay from the current tax base and taxing future services to the owner. Under some proposals, this procedure was extended to other investments as an option, and both the outlay and receipts were excluded from the consumption tax.

In a sense this view alters the concept of equity. The equity test becomes one of ex ante equivalence without ex post verification and adjustment of what is rarely a totally accurate set of assumptions. It assumes an omniscient capital market that, for every optimally adjusted durable goods purchaser, has foreseen and adjusted for (1) changes in the price level, (2) changes in the interest rates, (3) changes in the depreciation rates, and (4) changes in the individual tax rates. After the upheavals and uncertainties of this decade, such a set of assumptions may be a long way from reality. Had this method been in effect over the past decades, substantial differences could have arisen in the implied treatment of the current consumption of durable services—for example, among neighbors who purchased homes at different times under different sets of expectations, or between renters and homeowners. The fact that some people bought homes many years ago on the assumption of reasonable stability in the price level means that their implicit present rent could be several times less than that of present buyers or renters. Houses have very long lives; many consumer durables can be expected to last a decade. Some 12 percent of consumption is represented by imputed housing services; some 65 percent of that total is represented by net yields plus depreciation. (Of course, the additional implicit rent is in maintenance and property taxes.) While great inequities may arise in this treatment of durable consumer goods, its application to investments may create even more serious problems, as Michael Graetz points out in his paper.

The present income tax may perform even worse than the tax prepayment method under the consumption tax, but it could perhaps be greatly simplified if certain adjustments like those suggested for the consumption tax were made. For example, in the spirit of the durable goods adjustment under the consumption tax, one could imagine the inclusion in income of a market yield on investments, determined at the time the investment was made and applied throughout the period the asset was held. It would represent an increase in adjusted basis, whereas dividends and other cash returns would reduce the adjusted basis. Gains and losses could be computed after some simple basis adjustment for inflation. Under this principle one could also eliminate the taxation of business units as such and thus not have to worry about the "double taxation" of corporate income. Whether or not a movement in that direction could match the simplification of the consumption tax might be worth further investigation. It would, of course, require some explicit imputations, in violation of Bradford's rule, but they would seem to be relatively straightforward. The new aspect of the debate, then, on the administrative side seems to be the extent to which the equivalence of present and future values needs to be and can be accepted, and what its consequences are when circumstances change.

It is fair to say, however, that the issue of income versus consumption taxation will not be resolved on administrative grounds. The proponents of income taxation have regarded the administrative argument as support for their intrinsically superior position. Reducing the force of this argument merely gives emphasis to the other, more important, aspects of tax policy. It becomes crucially important to understand what is being offered and what is being given up. Here the comparison becomes much more fuzzy because of the different views of what the realistic options are.

Neither Goode nor Bradford seems prepared to make substantial claims for the efficiency of his particular tax, although other economists may take stronger positions. In my opinion, the decisive issues will involve the effects on tax progression and on the distribution of wealth and income, and those issues are hard to see clearly. There are many open questions. For example, will Congress and the public readily tax consumption out of sheltered or exempt income when they will not directly tax such income? Will the United States move from an income tax with special provisions to a consumption tax with these same shelters?

Goode is clearly concerned about this second possibility; Bradford is more sanguine, mainly, I suppose, because he thinks that deviations from the comprehensive income tax stem largely from the difficulty of measuring it. On this issue, I share Goode's concern. Realized capital gains, for example, are not difficult to measure and to average a little, yet they are partially exempt. When introduced in 1962, guideline depreciation was to be accompanied by a reserve ratio test, which was never applied. One could go down the list and note how many special provisions of the income tax could have a mechanically different treatment with substantially different equity consequences.

A second matter for concern is the progression of the tax structure. Many questions arise. What kind of tax substitution will be made? Is the impersonal corporate tax to be eliminated? Will rates on a consumption base be adjusted to provide at least as much progression as the present income tax? How much more heavily would income from personal effort be taxed under a consumption tax as the tax load was being reduced on property income? Goode is worried about the last question and favors additional taxes under a separate wealth tax. Others might prefer to treat gifts and bequests as the consumption of the donor, making the added wealth tax an integral part of the consumption tax proposal. Although the bulk of taxpayers might not be much affected by the change to the consumption tax, those with large intergenerational transfers of assets could have substantially lower taxes.

I would think it essential to add lifetime savings to the tax base in some way if the consumption tax proposal is to get much public support. To the extent that the consumption tax substitutes for income taxes, a base that conformed more closely to lifetime income would seem more acceptable. Such a package would also clarify the policy issues underlying the consumption tax proposal: is it designed as an improvement in tax policy without much redistribution of taxes, or are the benefits as seen by its supporters realized mainly through large changes in the distribution of the tax burden? The principal questions and ambiguities focus on tax changes in the upper-income groups. There is a need for many simulated comparisons of taxpayers with various characteristics regarding income, assets, family status, and the like (comparisons such as Bradford made at the Treasury) before any reasonably informed judgment can be made. It may also be necessary to find ways in which the consumption tax can be partially applied or experimentally tested. Andrews's partial proposal is interesting but runs the danger of enacting a consumption tax that includes present shelters. Perhaps the consumption tax would make a useful minimum tax.

Would it be accurate to say that the appeal of the consumption tax proposal arises from despair about the future, politically or intellectually, of the comprehensive income tax? Is it an acceptance and rationalization of the existing income tax progression rather than an attempt to improve it? Is it a switch rather than a fight? It is hard not to notice the coincidence of the recent interest in consumption taxation in this country, of both value-added and expenditure taxation, with such genuine moves toward a more comprehensive income tax base as the minimum tax and the proposed treatment of capital gains.

Comments by *Arnold C. Harberger*

My comments will be concerned with the real world. I would like to compare the imperfect income tax system that now exists in the United States with the imperfect expenditure tax likely to be adopted as a substitute.

To make the discussion realistic, I have set three ground rules for the comparison. First, the new tax system should have approximately the same degree of progressivity as the present system. As Pechman and Okner have shown, the present system is only moderately progressive.[69] I believe that in considering alternatives to it one should not require or expect them to be different in this respect. (The idea

69. Joseph A. Pechman and Benjamin A. Okner, *Who Bears the Tax Burden?* (Brookings Institution, 1974).

of limiting or significantly redistributing economic power does not seem to be seriously reflected in the present tax system, nor do I think it is a major focus of this conference.) Second, the move to an expenditure tax will be gradual; substantial sums will continue to be raised from corporation income and property taxes. Third, the United States economy is part of an interdependent world economy, with close capital market connections between the major centers.

These ground rules lead me first to the question of efficiency. I agree with Richard Goode that both the satisfactions attributable to immediate consumption and those attributable to additions to wealth should be taken into account in taxing income. But the satisfactions that attach to an addition to wealth today include the present value of any future benefits deriving from it. Therefore, they include the benefits associated with the income which that saving will produce in the future.

If the later income is taxed again, these satisfactions are taxed twice. Thus from the standpoint of resource allocation, one could equally well assess the second tax on savings at the moment when the saving took place and not tax anything deriving therefrom. This double taxation is the basis for the conclusion that, at equal rates (not necessarily at equal revenues), an income tax is substantially more inefficient than a consumption tax (so long as leisure and savings are substitutes). Moreover, the same tax on savings in the presence of other taxes, like the corporate income and property taxes, has a significantly stronger distorting effect than it would have in the absence of those taxes.

Unfortunately, the existence of the world capital market makes it very difficult for the United States to increase domestic capital formation by increasing saving. The reason is that, if the United States saved more, a large part of the extra savings would be funneled abroad; only a fraction would remain in the United States.

If, on the other hand, investment were stimulated directly, say by a reduction in the corporate income tax or by providing a rational investment incentive, saving might be increased at home and capital would be attracted from abroad. So, if additional investment is the goal, the way to achieve it in an interdependent world economy is by stimulating investment rather than saving.

Why then should saving be stimulated? The best answer is that people should begin to be given more of what they want. They are free to take vacations in Europe and Hawaii and have no special tax disincentives to discourage them from doing so. In fact, the airlines are being prodded to lower their fares, so that the cost of vacations is decreasing. If vacations are treated so generously, why should accumulation be discouraged in so many different ways?

The chief purpose of a tax reduction on saving would be to help build up a larger private capital stock to pass on to future generations. It does not matter that the capital may be invested in Eurodollar bonds—it will still benefit Americans.

Goode correctly observes that the federal government could increase national saving by reducing its deficits (or increasing its surpluses). The proponents of expenditure taxation, or of other ways of reducing the tax on private saving, implicitly reject this alternative because they prefer to pass on to future generations capital in forms chosen by the savers rather than by the government.

If I were to design a new tax system, an expenditure tax would be one of its main components. I like the simplicity of the cash flow approach, but I am concerned about some practical problems in the prepayment option suggested by Bradford. Despite its neatness, that option may open the door to manipulation and evasion. Any taxpayer would be able to reduce his tax by electing prepayment on investments with expected high rates of return, while using the cash flow method for investments with low rates of return.

Furthermore, there is a great incentive under an expenditure tax to falsify the prices at which capital transactions take place. A similar incentive exists under the present capital gains tax. It is much smaller than under the expenditure tax, however, because the capital gains rate is lower than any likely expenditure tax rate and the amount involved is only the difference between the purchase and the sale prices of assets, not the full sale prices. Thus, to reduce their expenditure tax liabilities, taxpayers would find it profitable to artificially lower the sale prices of their assets.

I believe that the arguments in favor of an expenditure tax are persuasive, but the tax is really equivalent to lowering the tax on personal income from capital. The United States has already gone a good distance down this road with Keogh and IRA plans, special treatment of capital gains and of the funds invested in the pension plans of companies and trade unions, and so on. My guess is that the natural way to proceed is to go further down that same road rather than to build a new one. My agenda for reform would include a lower corporate income tax, better investment incentives, the reduction or elimination of the tax on dividends, the indexing of capital gains, and perhaps even the taxation of real capital gains at a preferential rate.

My main reason for preferring such changes is that they would probably be more acceptable politically than an expenditure tax. We in the United States have evolved a system that reflects the pressures on our society. By working with the present tax system instead of striving to create an entirely different one, we will probably end up closer to the ideal.

Comments by Alvin C. Warren, Jr.

My comments on the Goode and Bradford papers are limited to five areas: the equity cases for the income and consumption taxes, tax shelters, corporate taxation, and human capital.

The Equity Case for the Income Tax

Richard Goode argues that the income tax is fairer than a personal consumption tax both because the total increase in a person's power to consume marketable output has greater intuitive appeal as an indicator of ability to pay than the exercise of the power to consume has and because wealth as well as consumption gives rise to taxable capacity. To the extent that these are separate arguments, I fully concur with the second. Of course, accretion is only an imperfect substitute for wealth as a tax base, but if wealth is considered an appropriate subject for taxation, then an accretion tax alone is to be preferred to a consumption tax alone. On the other hand, an expenditure tax coupled with a particular wealth tax might be preferable to an income tax alone. That is not, however, the alternative presented by David Bradford's case for a personal consumption tax, which does not discuss the appropriateness of a levy on accumulation during the lifetime of the accumulator. Among prominent consumption tax advocates, only the Meade committee seems both to have coupled its recommendation for a consumption tax with specific recommendations for wealth and transfer taxation and to have conceded that the reasons for taxing wealth are inconsistent with some of the reasons offered for not taxing income.

Goode's first argument for income taxation can, it seems to me, be more forcefully presented than in its traditional ability-to-pay terms. The income tax base is, in the aggregate, the product of the society's labor and private capital during the relevant accounting period. Levying a tax on income can thus be justified as a logical concomitant of the proposition that society in general has a claim on its annual product that is anterior to the claims of its individual citizens. A possible premise of such a conclusion is that, given the role of fortuity in income distribution and the dependence of producers on consumers to create value in our society, a producer does not have a controlling moral claim over all the product of his capital and labor.

The Equity Case for Consumption Taxation

Like many recent consumption tax advocates, Bradford argues that from a lifetime perspective the consumption tax is fairer than the income tax because it treats equally taxpayers with the same endowment (that is, the present discounted value of future income streams), however that endowment is allocated in terms of consumption over their lifetimes. Yet endowment is necessarily an ex ante concept and, as such, seems to me irrelevant in discussions of fairness, which should turn on outcomes rather than expectations. If A and B have equal endowments (say, year 1 labor income of $100), which they pool and risk on the flip of a coin, the endowment concept of equity suggests that the difference between the winner and the loser should not be taken into account. It would not be under a wage tax or the prepayment version of the consumption tax. Measurement of such differences—that is, gains and losses—is, of course, the very function of the income concept.

A graduated expenditure tax would reduce the disparity between winners and losers, but such progression would itself be inconsistent with the endowment rationale. Among equally endowed taxpayers, those who defer consumption would bear heavier taxes even with lifetime averaging; thus tax burdens would vary with consumption paths, the supposed defect of the income tax under the endowment rationale. Bradford attempts to minimize this defect by (1) permitting consumers to elect the tax prepayment option, that is, *pro tanto* to choose a graduated tax on labor income alone, which is consistent with the endowment rationale, and (2) characterizing the resulting tax as progressive ex ante with regard to consumption.

Bradford also argues for the consumption tax as a matter of fairness on the basis of the utilitarian analysis found in the optimal tax literature. Alas, I react to that literature the way an economist must react to the provisions of the Internal Revenue Code dealing with corporate reorganizations: it seems interesting—perhaps—but has no apparent connection with reality. The conclusion that no taxes other than a tax on labor earnings are necessary to distinguish among individuals in a world in which people are assumed to be identical except for their wage rates does not seem to me pregnant with meaning for the world we live in.

Tax Shelters

In the section called "Defects of the U.S. Income Tax," Bradford discusses the difficult problem of tax shelters. He gives an example of a taxpayer who, under the present income tax, can annually pocket $1.62 with no personal investment. I share what I take to be Bradford's ambiguous reaction to this type of transaction. Arguably there is nothing inappropriate about the after-tax receipt of $1.62, since that is exactly what Congress has promised a taxpayer in the 70 percent bracket who invests his own cash in the favored asset;[70] the interest deduction simply makes the tax benefit from current deductibility available to taxpayers who invest borrowed funds. On the other hand, the benefit of the 50 percent deduction should arguably be limited to those who invest their own money, in which case the interest deduction should be limited. On that view, however, there would be an even greater potential for manipulation under the consumption tax because all investment expenditures are currently deductible. A taxpayer in the 70 percent bracket who borrowed $100 on the prepayment method could invest $333 for an annual after-tax yield of $6.99, if interest payments were deductible, without using a penny of his own money—more than four times the benefit from the income tax shelter.[71] Of course, interest payments on the prepayment

70. A $100 investment (paying 10 percent) would yield $3 after taxes to a taxpayer in the 70 percent bracket. The 50 percent deduction permits an initial investment of $154 and raises the after-tax yield to $4.62 ($15.40 × [1.0 − 0.7]).

71. Annual 10 percent yield ($33.30) minus interest payment ($10.00) minus tax due ($16.31 [$23.30 × 0.7]) equals $6.99.

method should not be deductible, but neither should they be in Bradford's income tax example if that result is thought inappropriate. The point is that the potential for tax shelter manipulation is present under either tax if the base is inconsistently defined. Nor is this the only kind of tax shelter that might increase in value under the consumption tax. For example, Michael Graetz's paper shows how the classic movie purchase shelter could yield even more benefits to taxpayers under the consumption tax than under the income tax.

The Corporate Income Tax

As Bradford indicates, there is no need for a corporate income tax under the consumption tax ideal, but neither is there need for one under the accretion ideal. On the other hand, the corporate income tax does fulfill a useful role under a realization income tax, since it can be used to reach income not currently distributed to individual shareholders (although the current statute is overinclusive in that it also reaches distributed earnings). If one assumes that it is unrealistic to expect the repeal of the corporate income tax, what would be its role under a regime of personal consumption taxation? The short answer is that, if earnings are to be taken into account only when converted into personal consumption, the corporate income tax has no role whatsoever.

The Meade committee report suggests that an appropriate corporate tax under a personal expenditure tax regime would provide that contributions to corporate capital be nontaxable, corporate investments deductible, and corporate disinvestments taxable. Although that levy appears similar to a personal expenditure tax in form, it is in fact equivalent to a government matching program for corporations that raise capital from private sources.[72] Such a program is not only a long way from the current double taxation of dividends

72. A shareholder who contributes $1,000 to a corporation would permit corporate management to make a $2,000 investment at a corporate tax rate of 50 percent, which at a 10 percent rate of return would yield $2,200 to the corporation on disinvestment, $1,100 in corporate taxes and $1,100 for distribution to the shareholder. The shareholder would receive the usual consumption tax treatment ($1,000 deduction and $1,100 inclusion, or neither), so the return on the shareholder's investment would not be reduced by a corporate level tax. Corporate management is, however, in the same position it would have been in had the corporate tax been repealed and the government enacted a program matching shareholder contributions to capital, with the Treasury collecting its investment and profit at the same time private shareholders did.

but seems an odd result to justify as a natural concomitant of personal consumption taxation.

There is simply no way a true corporate tax can be integrated with a personal consumption tax. Unless it is to interfere with the deferral of taxation at the shareholder level until consumption, the corporate tax must in substance be a nullity, whatever form it is given to disguise its nonexistence. Thus Graetz in his paper is driven to suggest that the corporate tax be made purely a withholding tax with full credit given against shareholder taxes. Yet even that form would interfere with the personal consumption tax if there were a lag between corporate withholding and shareholder credit, as there would be if credits were available only on the distribution of corporate earnings. It is not surprising that no consumption tax advocate to date has successfully explained what should happen to the corporate tax under a consumption tax regime, given the realistic constraint of nonrepeal.

Human Capital

The argument that human capital is incorrectly treated under the income tax misses the point of the accumulation branch of the Haig-Simons definition, which focuses on changes in the value of marketable rights. Indeed, the inability of a person in our society to become an indentured servant or to sell himself into slavery calls into question the label "human capital" in the cases usually referred to, such as education for a profession. It is true that by discounting a stream of future earnings, its value can be "capitalized," but if there is no way in which that capitalized value can be used currently to command economic resources, why should it be counted in the "store of property rights" part of the Haig-Simons calculation? Although the human capital concept has had a pervasive effect on a great range of economic theory, it seems to me as inappropriate for analyzing fairness in taxation as the endowment concept. Both are ex ante formulations.

Moreover, it is simply not true that the income tax distinguishes between human and other capital; it is true that an entirely appropriate distinction is drawn between marketable and nonmarketable assets. To the extent that a lawyer's practice—human capital indeed—is marketable and has a value in excess of its cost, that appreciation should be included in the Haig-Simons calculation and would be reached by the current realization income tax on sale. Pension plans under which the beneficiaries or their heirs have no rights (including the right to hypothecate) before retirement are an example of financial capital with no market value, even though a present value can be calculated on the basis of actuarial assumptions. Thus, the taxation of income with respect to such pension plans is appropriately deferred under both current law and the accretion concept, since the rights involved have no present market value. (Of course, present law extends deferral beyond the category of plans appropriate for deferral under this rationale.)

Conclusions

The equity case for income taxation depends either on the acceptance of society's claim (for public goods or for redistribution) to a portion of the product of capital and labor or on the acceptance of income taxation as a means of reaching the benefits of both consumption and wealth. Essentially an ex post view, this conclusion also requires agreement that outcomes rather than expectations are what matter for equity in taxation.

Much of the case for substituting a consumption tax for the income tax depends on the opposite premise—that expectations alone are relevant. The life cycle hypothesis, the human capital construct, and the discounting of income streams to present value are generally not useful for comparing the two tax bases unless it is conceded that equity and progression are no longer to be measured ex post.

The problems of tax shelters and corporate taxation are illustrative of the general proposition that consumption taxation should not be regarded as a panacea for structural difficulties under the income tax, whatever conclusion is reached about fairness. Although it is true that some structural issues can be better resolved under the consumption tax, there are many fewer such issues than consumption tax advocates claim.

WILLIAM D. ANDREWS

A Supplemental
Personal Expenditure Tax

A PERSONAL EXPENDITURE TAX has been widely discussed as an alternative to the existing personal income tax. Adoption of such a tax as a substitute for the existing tax might well be the most practical way to eliminate substantial existing disparities in the treatment of income from different capital investments.

It is not clear, however, that completely replacing the present regime is practical. It would in any event raise serious transition problems, and it might burden us with unanticipated problems affecting what would then be our principal revenue source. There is much to be said for proceeding by small changes rather than radical substitution and for preserving what we can of the value inherent in old taxes as such.

The question arises, then, whether the idea of a personal expenditure tax can be used as a critical norm for evaluating the existing tax, identifying its chief faults, and generating corrective measures. The notion of a comprehensive income tax, or accretion ideal, has been constantly so used. Many who are not ready to accept all the ramifications of a comprehensive accretion base regularly use it as a guideline for dealing with particular problems under the existing tax.

It might be argued that the accretion ideal represents a way of perfecting the existing income tax while the expenditure tax model represents the substitution of something different. But that argument rests primarily on semantic confusion. The existing tax and the accretion ideal have both been called income taxes despite their differences. In reality, the existing tax base includes some forms of accumulation but excludes others. Omission from the base of unrealized capital appreciation, accumulation of pension reserves, and most of the buildup in life insurance reserves, together with the existing treatment of owner-occupied housing, already makes the present tax in many ways more like the expenditure than the accretion model. There is no reason, therefore, why the expenditure tax ideal might not serve just as well as the accretion ideal as a guide to incremental improvement of the existing hybrid tax.

One might begin by talking about the handling of particular items, comparing their treatment under existing law and under a personal expenditure tax. Pension funds, for example, are already dealt with essentially on an expenditure tax basis, and one might use the expenditure tax model to show that this treatment is more satisfactory than the accretion ideal alone would suggest. Or one might seek to justify the nontaxation of unrealized capital gains by reference to the expenditure tax model. Indeed, following this line, one would be tempted to construct solutions for the capital gain problem by extending opportunities for tax-free rollover. Similarly, one might argue for extension of the present pension rules by authorizing establishment of various other tax-free investment vehicles, like business stock ownership plans and tax-deductible dividend reinvestment schemes.

But whatever their merits, these schemes are all of limited potential, since they continue to treat different kinds of investments differently. Many of the virtues of a personal expenditure tax, like those of a comprehensive accretion tax, depend on its being comprehensive. Selective treatment of particular investments on a cash flow basis would generate incentives and rewards for people to invest in such items rather than others. The mere creation of additional deductible investment opportunities would cause wealthy people to make qualifying investments while living off withdrawals from other investments. Even those without existing salable assets would be induced to make deductible investments while borrowing to finance current consumption. These distortions of the personal expenditure tax ideal can be avoided only if all a taxpayer's business, investment, and borrowing transactions are taken into account on a cash flow basis.

It is possible, however, to pursue the personal expenditure tax ideal or an incremental yet comprehensive basis by adopting a supplemental personal expenditure tax. The most promising course would be to substitute a supplemental expenditure tax for the highest rates of tax under the existing individual income tax. Once installed, therefore, the scheme would contain something like our present income tax, but with top rates of around 40 percent, together with a supplemental expenditure tax for most taxpayers now facing marginal rates higher than 40 percent. This paper describes such a scheme and explores its advantages, disadvantages, and problems of implementation.

General Description of the Tax

The new tax would be a graduated personal consumption expenditure tax serving as a supplement to the existing individual income tax. It would be imposed on aggregate personal consumption expenditures, which would be determined by computing net aggregate cash flow from business and investment transactions (including employment). An exemption of about $20,000 to $25,000 would be allowed as a deduction so that the tax would be confined to high-expenditure taxpayers. Personal deductions for such items as medical expenses, charitable contributions, taxes, alimony, and dependency exemptions would all be allowed, just as they are under the existing tax.

Computation of the Tax

The supplemental personal expenditure tax would be computed on a supplemental schedule to be filed with a person's income tax return. The basic items on that schedule would be as follows:

1. *Ordinary income from salaries, wages, interest, and dividends.* Since these items are reported already on the income tax return, only the totals would need to be reproduced on the supplemental tax schedule.

2. *Excluded income items.* Various receipts like municipal bond interest and social security payments are not included in gross income under the existing tax. But these provide just as good a source of funds for consumption expenditure as taxable income receipts and therefore should be included in computing taxable expenditures. (These items are considered further below.)

3. *Net sales of investment assets.* This item would include proceeds from all sales of securities and other investment properties

minus the amount of all purchases of securities and other investment properties. If a taxpayer bought more, in dollars, than he sold, then this item would be negative—net purchases of investment assets must be subtracted from income to measure consumption expenditure.

It has sometimes been suggested that net sales be computed by starting from gain (or loss) realized and adding basis to it, since gain (or loss) is the final gross income figure on the income tax return relating to these transactions. Indeed, it is sometimes suggested to go further; that is, to start from taxable income and add back the capital gain deduction as well as the basis of assets sold.

It is simpler in almost every way, however, to start from total sales proceeds, even if sales are not a final figure on the income tax return. Adding basis to gain (or loss) usually serves only to get back to total sales proceeds, from which profit was previously computed anyway.

4. *Net business and investment borrowing.* This item is net cash flow from borrowing transactions: borrowing proceeds received minus total payments made because of borrowing (both interest and principal repayments).

Moderate, personal, noninvestment borrowing should be excluded from this schedule. If particular borrowing proceeds were excluded, then of course subsequent payments made on that particular loan would be nondeductible. This would make it possible to ignore ordinary consumer credit transactions in computing the supplemental personal expenditure tax. Any borrowing secured by business or investment assets, however, and any other personal borrowing in excess of say $10,000 should be counted as investment borrowing.

5. *Net cash flow from partnerships and proprietorships.* This item consists of the excess of all receipts and withdrawals over expenditures and contributions from or to any partnership or proprietorship or other such business or investment venture. Any borrowing taken into account in computing partnership or proprietorship cash flow in this schedule should not also be included, of course, in item 4. Similarly, any sales or purchases of investment assets included in computing cash flow in this item should not also be reported in item 2. Cash flow from corporations is not included here, since it is fully and conveniently reflected in items 1 and 3.

Again it would be theoretically possible to reach the figure for this item by starting from taxable income on the basic return and then making adjustments to get back to cash flow. These would include (a) adding back deductions like depreciation, depletion, and the capital gain deduction that do not reflect any current expenditure, (b) adding back the basis of assets sold, and (c) deducting expenditures required to be capitalized under the basic income tax. It seems incomparably simpler, and therefore sounder, to require that cash flow be directly reported as such.

6. *Personal deductions.* These should be essentially the same as under the existing tax, with the following modifications.

a. At this point no deduction should be allowed for interest, since interest expense is already reflected, to the extent it should be, in item 4 (net borrowing).

b. The deduction for taxes paid should include a deduction for the basic federal income tax. One might argue for no such deduction and for lower rates of expenditure tax, because it seems anomalous to allow a deduction for some of the very tax being computed. But part of the function of the supplemental expenditure tax is to serve as a minimum tax, imposing more tax on those who have escaped regular tax liability. That function will be enhanced by making the regular tax deductible. In any event, the deduction of the regular income tax is necessary to arrive at a figure that reflects funds actually available for consumption.

Since the purpose is to measure funds spent for consumption, the deduction should be for income taxes paid during the year, not for the liability accrued. Indeed, if a deduction were allowed for accrued but unpaid liabilities and also for investment of funds set aside to meet those liabilities, the effect would be a double deduction for the same thing. The double deduction would be rectified by the inclusion in taxable receipts of the subsequent disinvestment required to pay the tax, but the net result would be an unfortunate distortion in the timing of liability for the supplemental expenditure tax.

Strong arguments can be made for allowing expenditure tax payments themselves as a deduction. The only trouble is that if a deduction is allowed for the supplemental expenditure tax itself, nominal rates have to be set at higher figures to achieve any particular level of taxation. Indeed, a 50 percent rate without the deduction is equivalent to a 100 percent rate with, and 60 percent without equals 150 percent with. The discussion of rates in this paper assumes no deduction for the supplemental expenditure tax so as to keep the nominal rates in a familiar range. Those rates could be readily translated to accommodate a deduction for the expenditure tax.

c. No deduction should be allowed for charitable contributions of investment assets. For one thing, since the cost of investment assets will already have been deducted in computing the supplemental expenditure tax, it would be unjustified to allow a second deduction for the same expenditure. For another, the function of the deduction warrants the limitation. If an asset is sold and the proceeds donated to charity, the sale proceeds will enter into the computation of expenditures as a source of available funds; the deduction is then necessary to account for the fact that they were expended on something other than taxable consumption. There is no occasion for a deduction, however, if the contribution is financed out of an unreported source of funds.

The reasoning is precisely analogous to that underlying section 170(e)(1) of the Internal Revenue Code, which requires a reduction in the amount of any charitable contribution by the amount of ordinary income that would have been produced by a sale of the property at its fair market value. For supplemental expenditure tax purposes, in effect, any sale of investment property would yield ordinary income in an amount equal to the whole sale proceeds, thus eliminating the entire charitable contribution deduction.

7. *Exemptions.* In addition to the personal exemptions allowed under the existing tax, there should be a basic exemption of about $25,000 to make the tax apply only to high-bracket taxpayers. If one takes the rate schedule of the existing tax as a starting point and then determines to substitute an expenditure tax for all marginal rates above 40 percent, the exemption should be $27,038 for married persons filing a joint return.[1] This figure is derived from the fact that marginal rates first exceed 40 percent for a couple filing jointly when taxable income (plus the standard deduction) goes over $35,200. An exemption of $35,200 is not needed, however, since the basic income tax of $8,162 at this taxable income level would already be allowed as a deduction in computing expenditure tax liability. An exemption of $27,038, when combined with the deduction for income tax paid, would just suffice to exempt a pretax income of $35,200.

By a similar line of computation the basic exemption for an unmarried taxpayer (not a head of household) should be $28,800 minus $7,434, or $21,366.

8. *Gains on sales of consumer durables.* In general, there would

1. These figures were revised after the conference to reflect changes made by the Revenue Act of 1978.

be no deduction for purchases of housing and other consumer durables, and such assets could therefore be usually regarded as tax paid. Thus sales proceeds for such assets need not be reported as a source of funds, at least when they are not in excess of cost. A case can even be made for excluding sales proceeds in excess of cost, but such an exclusion does not seem appropriate if one wishes to have the tax reflect different levels of economic well-being, however achieved. Accordingly, such gains should be included in the supplemental personal expenditure tax base.

It might well be appropriate, however, to allow the same relief for such gains as the basic income tax does. Accordingly, it would be appropriate to defer recognition of gain on a residence when proceeds are reinvested within the terms of section 1034 of existing law, and it might be appropriate to allow whatever other forms of relief, by way of indexing or otherwise, may be provided in the computation of taxable gain from such transactions. In any case, it would be simple and convenient to take gain as reported on the basic income tax return as the amount to be subjected to expenditure tax.

9. *Cash balances.* It would be most convenient simply to ignore normal cash balances, including personal checking accounts, in the computation of the supplemental expenditure tax. In effect, funds in such accounts should ordinarily be treated as having been devoted to household use upon deposit. Some special provision for deduction of very large year-end balances would be appropriate, however, with a corresponding inclusion of such balances in funds available for consumption in the following year.

Effects on the Basic Income Tax

The fundamental relation of the supplemental expenditure tax to the basic income tax here proposed is that the former should replace all marginal rates above 40 percent under the latter. Thus, the main change proposed in the basic income tax itself is to cut off the rate schedules at a top marginal rate of 40 percent. As a result, the maximum rate of tax on personal service income under existing law would become irrelevant. Moreover, it is contemplated that the present minimum tax would be dropped, since the supplemental expenditure tax would perform many of its functions.

Other changes in the basic income tax are not advanced as part of this proposal. It has been assumed that partial exclusion of capital gains would continue, as would complete exclusion of municipal bond interest. This is not to say that those provisions ought to be continued in their present form but only that changes in them are not part of this proposal.

Rates

As a starting point, for a taxpayer who spends his whole disposable income, rates and exemptions in the supplemental expenditure tax could be designed to make up exactly the loss in revenue from cutting the top marginal rate from 70 to 40 percent. Thus the top rate of the expenditure tax should be enough to make up the difference between 40 percent and 70 percent, the new and old top rates under the basic income tax. This calls for a top nominal expenditure tax rate of 50 percent. If a top-bracket taxpayer receives an additional dollar of income, 40 cents will go in basic income tax, leaving 60 cents, of which 30 cents will go in expenditure tax, leaving 30 cents to spend.

For a taxpayer who spends more or less than his total income after taxes, of course, the expenditure tax will take more or less than his saving from reducing the top income rate. That shift in burden is precisely what is intended. It seems reasonable to assume that there would not be any serious, overall revenue loss from adopting an expenditure tax on this basis, although that point deserves further investigation. If a revenue loss did appear—because on average the people affected would spend substantially less than their taxable income minus income taxes—then some compensating increase in expenditure tax rates should be considered.

Rate brackets for the supplemental expenditure tax could be initially constructed in the same way as described above for the basic exemption, by reference to taxable income minus income tax payable at various levels in the existing income tax. Thus, for example, under existing law the 70 percent marginal rate is reached on a joint return at $215,400. The income tax on that amount would be $80,242 if marginal rates were not allowed to exceed 40 percent. (Notice how near this comes to an average rate of 40 percent! For well-to-do taxpayers the basic income tax would become nearly proportional, with relief worth a total of $5,918 in the bottom brackets.) The level of expenditure at which the expenditure tax should reach 50 percent, therefore, is $135,158 (taxable income of $215,400 minus tax of $80,242). If the rate schedule were expressed in terms of taxable

Table 1. Supplemental Personal Expenditure Tax Schedule for Married Couples Filing Joint Returns

Dollars

Taxable expenditure[a]	Tax
Not over 6,360	5% of expenditure
Over 6,360 but not over 14,880	318 plus 15% of the excess over 6,360
Over 14,880 but not over 30,240	1,596 plus 23.3% of the excess over 14,880
Over 30,240 but not over 44,520	5,180 plus 31.7% of the excess over 30,240
Over 44,520 but not over 76,320	9,702 plus 40% of the excess over 44,520
Over 76,320 but not over 108,120	22,422 plus 46.7% of the excess over 76,320
Over 108,120	37,262 plus 50% of the excess over 108,120

a. Taxable expenditures are defined as expenditures net of a basic exemption of $27,038.

Table 2. Supplemental Personal Expenditure Tax Schedule for Unmarried Persons

Dollars

Taxable expenditure[a]	Tax
Not over 3,180	6.7% of expenditure
Over 3,180 but not over 7,620	212 plus 15% of the excess over 3,180
Over 7,620 but not over 15,900	878 plus 25% of the excess over 7,620
Over 15,900 but not over 31,800	2,948 plus 38.3% of the excess over 15,900
Over 31,800 but not over 47,700	9,043 plus 46.7% of the excess over 31,800
Over 47,700	16,463 plus 50% of the excess over 47,700

a. Taxable expenditures are defined as expenditures net of a basic exemption of $21,366.

expenditures after deducting the basic exemption, the 50 percent rate would be reached at $108,120 ($135,158 minus $27,038).

Tables 1 and 2 contain illustrative rate schedules for a supplemental personal expenditure tax constructed on this basis.

Variations are possible, of course, in the way this tax could be fitted to the basic income tax. In particular, it would be possible to taper off the income tax more gradually and introduce the expenditure tax before the top rate of income tax is reached. This would provide a range within which both the supplemental expenditure tax and the basic income tax are graduated, instead of having graduation shift entirely from one to the other at a certain income level.

It would also be possible, of course, to set top rates differently: one might have a top income rate of 50 percent and a top expenditure rate of 40 percent, or any of a number of other possible combinations. Indeed it would probably be a good idea to introduce the expenditure tax at relatively low rates in any event, and then extend it in small steps to take over more of the burden; experience would then help to determine an appropriate final level.

Whatever the best ultimate combination, however, the rates set forth above for a supplemental expenditure tax, together with a simple 40 percent maximum under the basic income tax, seem useful for exploring the implications of this form of tax.

Transition Provisions

The best transitional scheme would be to introduce the supplemental personal expenditure tax at very low rates and then phase it in slowly by small increases in rates. Top income tax rates would be phased out on a corresponding schedule, so that revenue and progression would be held constant. The phase-in should be gradual enough to make it unprofitable for people to try to hold large cash balances, instead of investing, when the supplemental tax is introduced or increased.

If the phase-in were gradual enough, then no other special transition provisions would seem necessary. The introduction of the supplemental tax would not have any drastic effect on property values. Moreover, it would not impose the special hardship on retirees that the wholesale substitution of an expenditure tax for the existing income tax might have.

A disadvantage of this transition scheme is that a known plan to increase rates from year to year would create some inducement to accelerate consumption expenditures. A very gradual phase-in would attenuate that inducement but also prolong it. The magnitudes of these effects need to be estimated.

General Advantages of the Tax

Adoption of a personal expenditure tax as a supplement to the basic income tax would have several distinct advantages.

Reduction of Top Marginal Rates

Speaking most generally, adoption of the tax would allow amelioration of the acute distortions caused by very high marginal rates under the existing income tax, without the sacrifice in progressivity that would result from lowering top rates without introducing a supplemental tax.

Existing law treats different forms of investment return quite differently. Some forms of return, like municipal bond interest, are exempt from tax. Others, like returns on qualified pension funds, are effectively exempted, in whole or in part, by way of deduction or postponement of recognition of gain on the amount invested. Still other forms of investment return, like capital gains, are taxed at preferential rates. Sometimes these several kinds of disparate treatment are combined.

One virtue of a complete changeover to an expenditure tax would be to eliminate or minimize these disparities in the treatment of investment returns. Adoption of a supplemental expenditure tax would not have this virtue, since existing disparities would be preserved in the basic income tax. For purists, therefore, a supplemental expenditure tax would be inadequate, except possibly as a step toward an ultimate solution. Put differently, if the case for a general expenditure tax as a substitute for the existing tax depended upon the complete elimination of disparities in the treatment of investment returns, then that case would not support the adoption of a supplemental expenditure tax, except possibly as a phase in the transition to a general expenditure tax.

But it seems clear that the worst distortions and inequities in the existing tax result from the application of very high marginal rates to a base in which there are such disparities in the treatment of investment returns. It is high-bracket taxpayers for whom capital gain rates represent the largest partial exemption from tax. It is high-bracket taxpayers who secure a benefit from the tax exemption of municipal bond interest much greater than the burden of the reduction in interest rate the market imposes on such bonds. It is only high-bracket taxpayers who can afford to invest in tax shelter schemes whose profitability depends upon their distorted tax effects. Reducing the top rate of tax applicable to investment return as such would therefore eliminate the worst effects of these disparities even if it did not eliminate the disparities themselves.

These considerations have already led others to conclude that top rates under the existing tax should be limited to, say, 50 percent, if the revenue and distributional effects of such a reduction could be made up in some satisfactory way. The most common idea about how to do this has been to increase the tax on capital gains by eliminating preferential rates and perhaps imposing constructive realization at death. But the current political climate is not hospitable to a simple increase in tax on capital gains. Perhaps a supplemental expenditure tax would be a more acceptable way of making up revenue and preserving progressivity while reducing top rates on income as such.

Consider, for example, a top-bracket taxpayer who plans to convert $100 of ordinary income into capital gain. If the possible effects under the minimum tax provisions are ignored, the conversion would reduce his tax from $70 to $28 and increase his disposable income from $30 to $72. This is a 140 percent increase in after-tax income.

Under this proposal, if a top-bracket taxpayer received all ordinary income and spent everything left after taxes on consumption, he would pay a regular income tax of $40, and a supplemental expenditure tax of $30. The total tax would thus be the same as that under present law. If he were able to convert the receipt from ordinary income to capital gain (assuming no change in the capital gain deduction), he would reduce his basic income tax from $40 to $16. But if he continued to spend whatever was left after tax, his supplemental tax would go up from $30 to $42 (half of what is left after payment of the basic income tax of $16). The total net effect would thus be to decrease taxes from $70 to $58 and to increase disposable income from $30 to $42. This represents an increase of only 40 percent instead of 140 percent.

A taxpayer might be planning to save rather than spend the income item in question. In that case the total immediate tax difference between ordinary income and capital gain treatment would be a tax of $40 instead of $16, and the income left after tax would be $60 instead of $84, again a difference of 40 percent instead of 140 percent.

Adoption of a supplemental expenditure tax would reduce disparities only in the treatment of investment items, which are excluded from the supplemental tax base in any event. It would not reduce disparities in the treatment of fringe benefits, entertainment expenses, and other consumption items, which ought to be taken into account in computing taxable expenditure as well as taxable income. Indeed, it may be argued that adoption of a supplemental expenditure tax would aggravate the distortions surrounding consumption items, especially if it were decided to increase aggregate rates to make up for revenue lost on savings. Even without higher rates, it might be argued that efforts to avoid taxes would be centered on consumption items if the chances for avoidance on investment items were reduced.

On the other hand, consumption disparities are not subject to leverage in the same way as investment disparities. That is to say, omission of a consumption item from the tax base only eliminates the tax on that item; the effective rate on the item in question only drops to zero. Taxpayers would be fully taxed on that part of their consumption that was unrelated to business activities, even if they achieved additional consumption on a tax-free, business-related basis.

By contrast, disparities in the treatment of investment items often operate to shelter income devoted to normal consumption, producing negative effective marginal rates on the return from the favored investments.

Furthermore, a supplemental expenditure tax might enable the government to focus its enforcement efforts on consumption problems. This result would stem both from the decrease in investment-item distortions and from the fact that a supplemental expenditure tax would make consumption-item issues clearer. If it were perceived that the ultimate issue is defining consumption rather than income, it might be easier to secure the adoption of a compensatory excise tax, for example, in the case of fringe benefits that cannot now be satisfactorily allocated to individual employees. (No one suggests, for instance, that the excise tax on alcoholic beverages be eliminated for liquor drunk during a business discussion.) One can, perhaps, more readily view liquor or entertainment as consumption than as income, even if consumed in a business context.

Minimum Tax Effect

Some people can almost entirely avoid income taxes while enjoying comfortable levels of income and consumption. The ways vary. Usually they involve some kind of undertaxation of investment return, often combined with deductions on a full accretion basis. For example, interest is ordinarily deductible as it accrues, even when used to finance investment whose returns enjoy substantial tax deferral or even partial exemption under the capital gain provisions. Similarly, charitable contribution deductions are allowed for the full value of appreciated capital assets, even though the appreciation is never taken into account.

One response has been to propose and impose various forms of minimum tax. As originally proposed in 1969, the minimum tax would have been a tax computed on total income at rates substantially lower than those for the regular income tax, and then, if greater, imposed instead of the regular income tax. As adopted, the minimum tax was a flat-rate tax on preference items above a certain dollar amount. There was also a deduction from the minimum tax base for regular income taxes paid, or, later, for half of regular income taxes paid.

Under the Revenue Act of 1978, the portion of capital gains deducted in computing taxable income is no longer to be treated as a taxable preference under the old add-on minimum tax. This represents a substantial dismantling of that minimum tax, since most of the revenue collected under it was attributable to capital gains. A new minimum tax has been adopted, however, which does apply to capital gains. It requires the computation of "alternative minimum taxable income," which includes capital gains in full as well as ordinary income, with an adjustment for excessive personal deductions, and the application to this base of a simple rate schedule that rises to 25 percent on income above $100,000.

One difficulty with the minimum tax approach has been that it reraises issues already disposed of one way or another under the regular income tax. If a convincing argument exists for excluding an item from gross income under the regular tax, there is nothing essentially different about the minimum tax to provide an answer to that argument. Accordingly, important exclusions from the regular income tax base, such as the imputed rental value of housing, unrealized capital gains, and municipal bond interest, have not been subject to minimum tax. The minimum tax has tended to become just another complicated way to make compromises in the treatment of debatable items.

Adoption of a supplemental expenditure tax would accomplish many of the functions of a minimum tax but without some of its defects. The great majority of people at whom the minimum tax is aimed not only have sizable real incomes but also enjoy high standards of living. A supplemental expenditure tax would impose substantial taxes on such people even if their entire income were from tax-exempt sources. It would be better than a minimum tax because it would be more comprehensive. It would reach consumption financed out of unrealized capital appreciation and would effectively impose a burden on the rental value of owner-occupied housing, things that minimum tax proposals have not even attempted to reach. Moreover, it would impose some tax on people like real estate developers who continue to pay no income tax under existing law.

A supplemental expenditure tax would be different, of course, from even an ideal minimum tax, since it would fall on consumption financed out of capital as well as out of tax-exempt income and would not reach undertaxed income items not devoted to consumption expenditure. Justification of these differences depends, of course, on a judgment that it is acceptable to put the total tax partly on a consumption rather than an accretion basis. That judgment is implicit in many provisions of existing law. A supplemental expenditure tax would result in a much more coherent implementation of that judgment.

Relief for Savers

Savings are said to be doubly taxed under an accretion-type income tax, since the tax is imposed both on the income saved and on the return from investing it. Some object to the double taxation label, but there is no real disagreement about what happens. If a taxpayer goes to work to earn money for investment to produce a particular after-tax income stream, imposition of a 50 percent accretion-type income tax would require him to earn *four* times as much as he would otherwise need, while one who earns for current consumption will merely have to double his earnings to offset the tax.

Existing law softens this effect by various provisions for deferral and exemption from tax of investment gains. Qualified pension plans permit deferral of tax on savings therein. The capital gain provisions combine substantial deferral with partial (or sometimes complete) exemption. Other provisions offer various combinations of deferral and exemption. But savings out of ordinary income continue to bear the full brunt of accretion-type taxation. As a result, at the top rates of tax, a saver's ultimate reward for his efforts is only a very small fraction of what it would be in the absence of tax.

The substitution of a supplemental expenditure tax for income tax rates over 40 percent would provide relief for savers on a much more coherent and uniform basis. Because of the structure of the change, the greatest relief would be given those whose savings are now most severely taxed.

Transitional Value

One problem in the discussion of a general expenditure tax is that we have had no direct experience with it. Neither have we had any direct experience with a true, comprehensive, accretion-type income tax. Experience with the existing hybrid tax gives some basis for inferring what a true consumption or accretion tax would be like but no direct confirmation of these inferences.

Another problem has to do with transition. However perfect once installed, an expenditure tax would raise transition problems if instituted all at once. Similarly, sudden termination of the existing tax would create difficult transition problems. These problems would occur partly because of certain characteristics of the taxes themselves. But transition problems of another kind would also arise because taxpayers and administrators would have to suddenly learn a whole new system and apply it across the board.

A supplemental expenditure tax would be a careful and conservative response to these problems. It would provide a way to generate experience and data about personal expenditure taxation without risking the whole revenue on the enterprise. If there were unforeseen difficulties and disadvantages to this form of tax, a supplemental expenditure tax would enable us to discover them. On the other hand, if experience confirmed the advantages of a general expenditure tax, a supplemental expenditure tax would represent a partial transition already effected. Finally, the experiment might suggest that continued reliance on both the basic income tax and supplemental expenditure tax would be the best course. In any event, the Treasury would have another tested device in its armory for future use if needed.

Effects on Particular Items

This section examines the impact a supplemental expenditure tax would have on selected, particular problems under the income tax.

Pension Contributions

Under existing law, contributions to qualified pension plans are not taxed to plan participants, and income from the investment of such contributions is not taxed to anyone until benefits are paid out after retirement. Formally, this is a matter of deferring tax until distribution. The effect, however, is equivalent to an exemption of investment yield from tax.

On the face of it, a supplemental expenditure tax would have no effect on the treatment of pension rights; indeed, one might say that since pension rights are treated on an expenditure basis under existing law already, adoption of a supplemental expenditure tax would make no difference.

But the treatment of pension rights under existing law creates distortions that would be mitigated by a supplemental expenditure tax. Most obviously, present law strongly favors investment through a qualified retirement plan over investment outside such a plan. A supplemental expenditure tax, by deferring part of the tax on all investments, would reduce (but not eliminate) that bias.

Moreover, present law may permit some people to defer taxes on pension contributions even though they are not net savers. This is accomplished by funneling earnings into a pension plan while financing consumption by liquidating other assets or borrowing. A supplemental expenditure tax would not be subject to deferral under these conditions, since both liquidation of other assets and borrowing would be treated as taxable sources of funds.

Municipal Bond Interest

Municipal bond interest is not taxable under the existing income tax. But that interest is just as available for consumption expenditure as any other income; therefore, it should be included as a taxable receipt under the supplemental expenditure tax. As a result, a top-bracket taxpayer who spent all his after-tax income would find his expenditures out of municipal bond interest taxable at 50 percent, while for taxpayers not subject to the supplemental expenditure tax the receipt and expenditure of such interest would continue to be tax free.

One standard criticism of the municipal bond exclusion is that it is wasteful as a subsidy: the reduction in the interest rate resulting from the exclusion is much less than the tax saving for high-bracket taxpayers. Introduction of a supplemental expenditure tax would respond nicely to that criticism, since it would make the top marginal rate of subsidy uniform for a great many municipal bond investors— at 67 percent of the nominal interest rate. With a large pool of individual investors at a marginal income tax rate of 40 percent, and with banks and casualty insurance companies at the corporate rate, perhaps the market would create an interest differential that would pass most of the benefit of tax exclusion through to the municipalities.

This does not mean, of course, that adoption of a supplemental expenditure tax would be a matter of indifference to sellers of municipal bonds. Inefficient as it is, complete exclusion from income tax at very high rates presumably makes it possible to sell more bonds to top-bracket investors than with a lower rate of subsidy. Adoption of a supplemental expenditure tax would knock out these sales, diverting investment, presumably, into something other than bonds of any kind. It is not clear how much the interest rate on municipal bonds would need to be increased to make up for these lost sales.

It would be possible, of course, to extend the exclusion of municipal bond interest to the supplemental expenditure tax to avoid opposition from those interested in the exclusion. But that would be a bad precedent. The great virtue of an expenditure tax is that it can be kept neutral with respect to taxpayer investment decisions; the exclusion of any form of investment return from accountable receipts would undermine that quality.

Essentially, it is not the supplemental expenditure tax that would hurt sellers of municipal bonds, but the reduction of the top rate of income tax. If there were to be any sort of compensation for that harm, it should take some form other than exemption from tax on expenditure of interest received.

Exclusion of Social Security Benefits

The existing law does not tax social security benefits and various other government payments for unemployment and disability. For many of the reasons applicable to municipal bond interest these receipts should also be included in the computation of expenditures subject to the supplemental tax. But the matter is perhaps less important, because such payments are not a return on any voluntary investment to which the supplemental expenditure tax is supposed to remain neutral and because such payments are not so concentrated among high-bracket taxpayers. On the other hand, inclusion of such items in the supplemental expenditure tax base would not impose the hardships on low-bracket taxpayers that income taxation might sometimes involve.

Owner-occupied Housing

Gross income does not include a homeowner's return on his investment in the form of housing services enjoyed in kind. This omission is compounded by the allowance of deductions for mortgage interest and real estate taxes. These provisions create a serious disparity between homes and other investments for high-bracket taxpayers. On the other hand, inclusion of imputed rent in the income tax base would introduce difficult questions of valuation into the determination of tax liability for a very large number of taxpayers.

One great virtue of the existing tax is that for most taxpayers, for most of the time, it depends entirely on cash transactions. As proposed, the supplemental expenditure tax would not include imputed rent as such, either, and would therefore share and extend that particular virtue.

But in the long run the value of homeowners' housing services would not be exempt from the supplemental expenditure tax, because expenditures for the purchase of housing would be taxable, nondeductible expenditures. The tax on such expenditures, under any expenditure tax, is a suitable proxy for a tax on housing services, which it is not under an income tax, since both invested funds and the return thereon are supposed to be taxed under an accretion-base tax.

Put differently, imputed rental income would not be taxed as such under the supplemental expenditure tax; in this respect housing would be better treated than investments in financial assets. But the original investment in financial assets would itself be deductible, while an investment in a house would not. This difference in the treatment of the investment itself would counterbalance the difference in the treatment of return.

The effects of transition on homeowners merit special consideration. Think of a homeowner who has paid off his mortgage; he has finished paying for the ownership of his home but continues to enjoy services therefrom. If a general expenditure tax is now introduced, he will continue to enjoy housing services without any tax either on them as such or on the earlier expenditures for the purchase of his home.

But an expenditure tax is not just being introduced into a previously taxless world; homeowners' purchases have presumably been made out of funds on which income tax was paid. The true potential inequity in moving from an income to an expenditure base affects tax-paid investment assets whose yield is taxable, especially for taxpayers planning to liquidate such assets to finance their retirement. If people near retirement are apt to be those whose homes are fully paid for, then the proposed treatment of housing will provide some relief for the very class of people otherwise likely to be adversely affected by the introduction of a supplemental expenditure tax.

Homeowners with mortgages would be directly affected by the transition to a supplemental expenditure tax, since mortgage interest would be nondeductible under it. Real estate taxes would probably be made deductible, particularly because of the effect the transition would otherwise have on elderly homeowners. A strong case can be made for extending the real estate tax deduction to renters as well as homeowners, but the argument is essentially no different than under the existing income tax.

Some real estate is used alternately for direct personal occupancy and for rental to others. If a deduction is allowed for the purchase of real estate, on the ground that it is an investment rather than a personal expenditure, then it would seem important to include subsequent personal use in the yield that is subject to tax. On the other hand, if the purchase price (including mortgage interest) is not deducted, then a case can be made for excluding moderate rental income from an expenditure base. It is not immediately obvious, however, how these considerations should be applied to preexisting investments in mixed-motive vacation housing and the like.

Employee Housing

Under certain circumstances, existing law excludes from gross income housing and meals provided in kind by a taxpayer's employer. On its face, this is a simple omission of a consumption-income item, presenting exactly the same issues under a consumption tax as under the income tax. If the inconvenience of valuing a noncash item justifies exclusion under existing law, it might similarly justify exclusion under a supplemental expenditure tax.

There is, however, an unstated justification for exclusion under existing law that evaporates under a supplemental expenditure tax. The argument is that present law largely excludes housing services enjoyed by homeowners as a return on their investment and that exclusion of employer-supplied housing is a compensating provision for taxpayers who are precluded by their conditions of employment from enjoying the tax benefits of homeownership. But under a supplemental expenditure tax, there are no special advantages to homeownership. Hence housing supplied by employers should be taken into account under a supplemental expenditure tax even if still excluded from gross income under the basic income tax. The resulting need to put a value on such housing would affect only a small minority of taxpayers.

A special argument can be made, however, for not enacting this inclusion right away. As indicated above, owner-occupied housing enjoys a transition advantage that may serve to provide some relief from the hardships of taxing people on expenditure of what they already were taxed on earning. An employer-housed taxpayer will not enjoy that particular form of transition relief. Some period of continued exemption of employer-supplied housing might tend to compensate very roughly for this transition disadvantage. But there may well be better ways.

Capital Expenditures and Tax Shelters

Capital expenditures are said to be nondeductible under existing law, but the rule is riddled with exceptions. Some of the exceptions are the product of explicit legislation; others result from early administrative rulings and interpretations. Differences in deductibility make big differences in after-tax cost and rate of return.

Even if a capital expenditure is initially nondeductible, it may often be amortized, and the rules governing rates of amortization also have unexplained disparities and incongruities.

The advantages to a taxpayer of immediate deductibility and rapid amortization can often be multiplied by leverage, since a taxpayer can deduct or amortize his gross investment without being taxed on the borrowing proceeds used to finance it. Recent legislation limits deductions for certain kinds of investments to what is at risk, but the privilege of deducting the expenditure of a lender's funds continues for real estate investments and for borrowing on personal credit.

Tax shelters are normally a matter of exploiting the forgoing rules one way or another. The net effect is frequently to make a purse out of a sow's ear by creating a negative effective rate of income tax, even after the rules for eventually recapturing tax benefits are taken into account.

The supplemental expenditure tax itself would deal with these problems in the simplest way by putting taxation on a simple cash flow basis. Capital expenditures for business or investment property would be immediately deductible in every case. But debt-financed investments would not be deductible at all until the debt was paid.

There would be no need or occasion for distinguishing between recourse and nonrecourse indebtedness, as both would serve equally to offset deductible expenditures.

Adoption of a supplemental expenditure tax would not eliminate disparities in the treatment of capital expenditures, of course, since they would persist under the basic income tax. But their impact would be greatly ameliorated by reduction of the top marginal rate to 40 percent. Tax shelters today are commonly described as unsuitable investments unless an investor is in at least a 50 percent income tax bracket. Adoption of a supplemental expenditure tax would therefore represent a simple, comprehensive, and practical way of curbing an otherwise quite intractable set of abuses.

Capital Gains

Perhaps the most intractable problem under the existing income tax has been how to treat capital gains. Under existing law, unrealized appreciation goes untaxed. This is primarily a matter of deferral, because appreciation remains potentially taxable upon realization. But even when realized, capital gains are generally taxed at bargain rates. Moreover, until recently the law permitted complete escape of unrealized gains at the death of an owner, by giving his successors a basis equal to the fair market value at the date of his death.

From one standpoint, these provisions have seemed to represent the single largest gap in the coverage of the individual income tax. Realized capital gains are just as ready a source of consumption or accumulation as any other gains or income. Even unrealized gains represent accumulation to the holder, no less valuable than accumulations out of ordinary income. The distinction between ordinary income and capital gains has proved difficult to define. Moreover, the favored tax treatment of capital gains has created a pointless inducement to try to cast income in that form. The advantages of capital gain treatment can often be magnified by taking ordinary deductions for correlative costs. Finally, since capital gains are quite concentrated among high-bracket taxpayers, their special treatment undermines the progressivity of the tax.

In response to these considerations, reformers have advocated and Congress has enacted a number of restrictive changes in recent years. Recapture provisions curb the conversion of ordinary income into capital gain. The alternative ceiling rate on capital gains has been removed. The maximum and minimum tax provisions enacted in 1969 further increased the top rate on capital gains in some cases. In 1976 a provision for carry-over basis at death was enacted. In 1978, however, the capital gain rules were revised to bring the top rate back down to 28 percent, and the effective date of the carry-over basis provision was postponed.

Underlying these continual legislative revisions are some real problems with respect to capital gains. Current taxation of unrealized appreciation would raise severe valuation and liquidity problems. But taxing realized gains fully without taxing unrealized appreciation creates excessive disparities between those who realize their gains and those who do not.

Moreover, capital gains in an inflationary period are often unreal. Though interest income may be equally illusory, the point is less clearly perceived; consequently, awareness of inflation has mainly affected attitudes toward capital gains. Even apart from inflation, many capital gains represent mere changes in the rate at which future income is discounted, not changes in the amount of income expected. Because such gains do not represent any increase in the level of consumption (or tax payments) a taxpayer can maintain, the case for taxing them exactly like ordinary spendable income is not very convincing. The restoration of the capital gain differential in 1978 seems to have been to some extent a response to inflation.

How would the introduction of the supplemental expenditure tax, as here proposed, affect the capital gain problem? The answer to this question, like the capital gain problem itself, has several facets.

So far as unrealized gains are concerned, the supplemental expenditure tax would have no direct effect, because unrealized gains would not be taken into account. But in at least two ways the supplemental expenditure tax would reduce distortions resulting from the nontaxation of unrealized gains under existing law. First, reduction in the top rate of the basic income tax would lessen the disparity between treatment of unrealized gains and treatment of accumulation out of ordinary income. Second, the supplemental expenditure tax itself would impose a tax to the extent that a person used unrealized appreciation to finance consumption either by borrowing or by selling other assets.

So far as realized gains are concerned, the supplemental expenditure tax itself would draw no distinction between sales of capital assets and other sources of funds. The distinction between ordinary income and capital gain might be preserved under the basic income tax, but the reduction of top rates under that tax would diminish the effect of the distinction. (This effect is illustrated by the example on page 138.)

In the long run the supplemental expenditure tax would decrease the taxation of inflation gains. A general expenditure tax does not involve any tax on inflation gains, since it does not involve subtracting preinflation costs from inflated revenues. All items of revenue and cost are included or deducted currently, in the period in which paid. Over time the supplemental expenditure tax would move partially toward this state of affairs, since capital costs would be currently deductible. Inflation would continue to be a problem under the basic income tax, but less of one, as the top rates would be lower.

Adoption of a supplemental expenditure tax would not relieve the inflation problem for people who are net dissavers after its adoption, because for them there would be no net deduction for investment. But even for such people, the supplemental expenditure tax itself is neutral with respect to inflation, as it simply taxes what is spent for consumption, when it is spent, at whatever price levels then prevail.

Adoption of a supplemental expenditure tax would diminish taxpayers' profits derived from converting ordinary income into capital gain by taking ordinary deductions, since the tax itself would have only a single rate schedule at which inclusions and deductions could take effect.

In sum, the effect of adopting a supplemental expenditure tax would be similar to that of putting the taxation of capital gains partly on a rollover basis: the tax would be delayed until liquidation without reinvestment. But there would not be the discrimination and distortion that would result from allowing that treatment for capital gains while denying it for accumulation financed out of other kinds of income.

Conclusion

A personal expenditure tax is free from the disparities in treatment of investment returns that have produced many of the worst problems under the existing individual income tax. The introduction of a supplemental personal expenditure tax for high-bracket taxpayers, with an offsetting reduction of the highest rates under the existing tax, would be a conservative, practical step toward ameliorating most of those problems.

Comments by Nicholas Kaldor

The issue of income tax versus expenditure tax can be discussed at various levels.

The fundamental question, which Andrews does not discuss, is whether in principle income or consumption affords the superior base for an ideal tax system. Several writers on the subject, among them Irving Fisher, have thought that the only true notion of income is consumption, and that every other definition is defective (because it involves double counting). For most economists, however, consumption and income mean something different, and as a measure of taxable capacity, income is superior because it relates to a person's spending power, or ability to spend, independently of how much of that power he actually exercises.

I do not agree, therefore, with the implication of Andrews's introductory remarks, in which he states that the changeover from an income tax system to an expenditure tax system does not mean "the substitution of something different," because the existing tax can be regarded as an approximation to an ideal expenditure tax just as much as to an ideal income tax, and hence the expenditure tax model could "serve just as well as the accretion ideal as a guide to incremental improvement of the existing hybrid tax."

I would not agree that the existing tax is a hybrid kind of an expenditure tax for the simple reason that, while there are many particular forms of savings that are exempt from tax (or taxed at preferential rates), there are no corresponding provisions to bring dissaving into charge. It is the charge on dissaving, much more than the exemption of savings, that distinguishes an expenditure tax from an income tax. The numerous special provisions that make the existing income tax different from a true income tax cannot therefore be justified by reference to the expenditure tax principle. But even if Andrews were right in suggesting that the existing tax system is a kind of halfway house between an income tax and an expenditure tax system, it would still be necessary to decide whether the direction of "incremental improvement" should be toward a proper income tax or toward an expenditure tax. In other words, it does not absolve economists of the need to discuss the fundamental issues—in the first instance in abstraction from all practical (that is, political or administrative) considerations.

This is what I attempted to do in my book on *An Expenditure Tax* written nearly a quarter of a century ago.[2] In that book I did not really dispute the dominant view of Robert Haig or Henry Simons that a comprehensive notion of income looked at as "the net accretion of economic power between two points of time" is the ideal measure for apportioning the burden of taxation between different members of the community and that the "net accretion of economic power between two points of time" is identical with the sum of consumption and net saving.

The difficulties that I found were in the definition of income insofar as it relates to net saving. As Simons rightly argued, capital appreciation is an accretion of purchasing power and therefore no different from an increase in the value of assets that results from additions to the stock of rights, such as the purchase of bonds or shares out of current income. Indeed, an appreciation in the value of ordinary shares may be no more than the equivalent of the savings made by companies on behalf of their shareholders. But the basic difficulty with the notion of net saving lies not in whether it takes the form of an appreciation in the value of assets (as distinct from an addition to the stock of assets) but in whether the increment in the value of assets is in the nature of an *accrual* (which is always a *process* in time) or a revaluation (that which occurs at a *point* of time); and, if the latter, whether (and how far) it is a *real* increase as distinct from a purely nominal one. In assessing the relative spending power of individuals, one cannot say that income consists of accruals only, to the *exclusion* of revaluations—no more than one can say that a business firm earns a true increase in profit only from selling more shoes, not from selling better shoes. A revaluation that reflects the prospects of improved earnings raises a person's spending power every bit as much as an increase in income due to the declaration of a larger dividend payment.

However, this is not true of all revaluations, and it is not possible (in theory, let alone in practice) to isolate the one kind from the

2. *An Expenditure Tax* (London: Allen and Unwin, 1955; Westport, Conn.: Greenwood Press, 1977).

other. If two taxpayers spend equal amounts over the same period, they can be presumed to have had the same real consumption— though in times of inflation this statement may only be approximately true, since one person's expenditure basket may have shown a larger rise in prices (between two points of time) than another person's. Nevertheless, the extent of arbitrariness thereby introduced is limited and can safely be disregarded for practical purposes. But when it comes to net saving, two persons who show the same net amount of saving, in terms of money—whether it is in the form of a transfer of funds from an income account into a capital account (that is, the purchase of additional shares and of income) or of appreciation in the value of shares already held—will not normally have gained equally in terms of "increment in economic power." In times of inflation one has to make some allowance for the reduced purchasing power of money, but the proper allowance depends not only on the rise in prices in a given period but also on the relationship of the current accrual of wealth to the value of a person's possessions at the beginning. Thus, suppose inflation is 10 percent a year and two men have each made a net money saving of $100; the net accretion of economic power is negative for the one who started with $2,000 but positive for the one who had less than $1,000.

As I have shown in my book, the same kind of problem may also arise when different securities increase in value because of a change in the rates of interest at which earnings are discounted; this in turn is causally indistinguishable from the revaluation due to a change in subjective uncertainty surrounding the expectation of future earnings that are discounted.

I therefore came down in favor of an expenditure tax principle not because the existing system of income taxation is defective but because the basic limitations of the income concept make it impossible to implement the Haig-Simons formulation, *no matter how the tax laws are framed.* In that sense, my advocacy of an expenditure tax was that of a second best. If spending power is measured by actual spending, there is an injustice in the allocation of the tax burden as between misers and spendthrifts. But if it is assumed that different people's propensity to spend does not vary much because of differences in "tastes and temperaments" (as Pigou called it) but only because of objective considerations that a tax system can make allowance for (for example, the number of dependents), a tax based on spending may give a better approximation of true spending power than a comprehensive tax on income, however comprehensively income is defined for tax purposes.

There is no need, however, to opt for one to the exclusion of another; and, as I argued in a later publication,[3] in a society composed of individuals who draw benefits in many forms from widely different sources, a system of personal direct taxation based on a number of criteria (such as income, expenditure, capital gains, net wealth, the receipts of gifts or inheritances) may give a more reasonable (or more reliable) allocation of taxation in accordance with taxable capacity than a system based on a single criterion.

In that respect, I am fully in agreement with Andrews that, for theoretical as well as practical reasons, it is better to use an expenditure tax as a supplement to an income tax than as a replacement. But in that case the introduction of an expenditure tax does not remove the need for dealing with the present anomalies and distortions in the income tax system—though one might argue that these anomalies would become less important if the introduction of an expenditure tax alongside the income tax made it possible to reduce substantially the present income tax rates. Indeed, my own recommendations (and the more recent recommendation of the Meade committee) are both similar to the supplemental expenditure tax advocated by Mr. Andrews.

I have little to criticize in Andrews's detailed suggestions, which are like those that I advocate in *An Expenditure Tax*. Andrews and I both agree that it is possible to administer such a tax on a cash flow basis—by measuring expenditure as the difference between all cash receipts and nontaxable outgoes. We agree on the method by which this cash flow should be computed, and we also agree that the introduction of the new tax, if combined with a reduction in the income tax, might give rise to difficult transitional problems—but these are inherent in almost any *large* change in the tax system. On a few points of minor importance I would take a different view from the author. For example, I would prefer to treat house purchase like an investment but introduce imputed rent as an addition to expenditure (though in that case mortgage repayments should not be included in taxable expenditure).

3. *Indian Tax Reform: Report of a Survey* (New Delhi: Ministry of Finance, Government of India, 1956).

We also appear to differ on another point. Andrews defines the expenditure tax on a *gross* basis, in the same way as an income tax (that is, the tax is levied on total spending, including the tax on spending as part of expenditure), whereas I think it is more logical, and more in accordance with the spirit of an expenditure tax, to define it on a *net* basis—which means treating all payments of direct taxes (that is, the expenditure tax liability as well as income tax payments) as a deduction from chargeable expenditure. The difficulty with the gross basis is that the expenditure tax must always be levied ex post—on the basis of what was received and spent in the previous year—so that last year's expenditure tax payments would enter into this year's expenditure tax liability (unless the payments were deducted when calculating the current liability and a notional charge added, which would make the calculations rather cumbersome). I think it is also important that the taxpayer have clearly in mind what his marginal expenditure tax rate is when deciding on any optional item of expenditure —for example, whether to order a second glass of whiskey in a bar, which he may do if his marginal tax rate is only 100 percent, but not if it is 300 percent. So long as an expenditure tax is levied on a gross basis, it is difficult to regard it as something other than a branch of the income tax, with a different set of exemptions. It would therefore be subject to much the same pressure as the income tax.

Indeed, the lack of awareness of the political and sociological problems involved in closing tax loopholes seems to be the more serious shortcoming of the paper. Andrews identifies numerous distortions in the present U.S. tax system (which appear to be surprisingly similar to the exemptions and loopholes in the British system) and then goes on to show that these could be eliminated if either a personal expenditure tax or a supplemental personal expenditure tax were adopted. He thus gives the impression that most, if not all, of these distortions arise from the choice of income as the tax base, not from the political process by which tax laws are framed. Everyone knows the many ways in which powerful pressure groups, using specious arguments, manage to avoid their proper share of the burden of income tax. There is no reason to suppose that these same pressure groups would take an expenditure tax "lying down" and permit the new tax to get onto the statute book in a pristine form. Indeed, they did not in 1957, when the Expenditure Tax Bill was passed by the Indian parliament. The loopholes that the Lok Sabha (the Indian House of Representatives) succeeded in putting into the bill ensured from the start that the tax could be fully evaded in practice. This was done by the simple device of defining the lower exemption limit not in terms of actual expenditure but in terms of income subject to tax; therefore, all a taxpayer had to do to avoid liability to the expenditure tax was to make sure that his taxable income was below the critical limit. In addition, numerous kinds of expenditure were exempted from this tax that were not exemptions from income tax (contributions to political parties, election expenses, the purchase of cottage industry products, expenses on the occasion of a marriage, and so forth). It was pretty clear that if the tax had not been withdrawn fairly soon after its introduction, these loopholes would have become progressively wider.

If, as Andrews argues, "the current political climate is not hospitable to a simple increase in a tax on capital gains," why does he suppose that it will be hospitable to the introduction of a progressive expenditure tax? The very idea of such a tax was unanimously rejected by the Senate Committee on Finance the only time it was introduced to Congress by a U.S. administration—and this was during a particularly critical phase of World War II (in September 1942), with the tax intended for the duration of the war only.

There are, as is well known, many millionaires in the United States, in England, and in other countries who manage to avoid paying income tax—because they can avoid having a net taxable income—and yet live in great luxury while steadily growing richer. It is easy to conceive of changes in the tax laws that would make these people just as liable to taxation as the ordinary man in the street. Since this is not done, there must be political reasons for it; and these reasons would be equally powerful whether the attempt to create a genuine system of progressive taxation were made through a supplemental expenditure tax or through reform of the income tax.

The strongest political argument in favor of a supplemental expenditure tax is that it removes (or at least greatly weakens) the case that is so frequently made against progressive taxation, namely, that it reduces the funds available for saving of those taxpayers who, on account of their high incomes, are alone in a position to save a substantial part of their incomes. If net savings are exempt from taxation (or taxed only at a low rate), it cannot be said that the well-to-do are deprived through taxation of the *means* to save.

However, this argument is not as strong as it appears—not if one believes (as I do) that the market mechanism always generates sufficient profits to finance the investment that entrepreneurs decide to undertake. An expenditure tax, by encouraging saving and discouraging spending by the well-to-do, will not cause more investment to be undertaken unless there are other incentives (of a monetary or fiscal kind) to ensure that investment increases pari passu with the reduced spending of the well-to-do. But assuming that such instruments are available, and appropriate policies of economic management are followed by the government, much the same distribution of resources between investment and luxury consumption can be secured (in principle) under either system.

Comments by William A. Klein

Upon reading William Andrews's paper I experienced considerable empathy for Egyptian and Israeli hardliners witnessing President Sadat and Prime Minister Begin in public embrace. In important parts of this paper, a seemingly schizophrenic Andrews abandons his earlier efforts to defend the proposition that expenditure is the appropriate base for personal taxation. Instead, he seems to accept the idea that income is the appropriate base and suggests that the expenditure tax structure can be used as a means for improving the present system. Having thus taken the role of a believer in the income tax, elsewhere in his argument he displays his other belief by defending his proposal as a way station to a full-fledged expenditure tax and as a half-a-loaf concession to savers.

In my view, the question that ought to be discussed is whether Andrews's supplemental personal expenditure tax proposal is the preferred incremental device for ultimately achieving a full-scale expenditure tax. But first it is necessary to dispose of the notion that the supplemental expenditure tax is a device for making the present hybrid system more consistent with income tax goals.

There can be no quarrel with the fact that, if Andrews's supplemental expenditure tax proposal were adopted, it would produce some changes that would be consistent with the goals of income tax supporters. At the same time, however, it would produce other changes that can only be defended by reference to the goals of expenditure tax advocates. It seems to me that he cannot have it both ways. True, the United States now has a hybrid system. But all proposals must be tested against a consistent set of principles. It may be difficult to choose between income and expenditure; each is supported by appealing principles. But since the principles are competing, a choice must be made before the analysis can proceed. One cannot attempt to apply simultaneously two competing philosophies of taxation. Stanley Surrey made this point quite aptly:

Each tax has its own appropriate structure and each has its advantages and disadvantages. But the scope of each such tax in actual application must be tested by *its* concepts, which concepts led to its choice in the first instance. The structure of a normative income tax is not to be tested by the values or concepts used by those who prefer that a consumption tax be chosen instead, and vice versa.[4]

Although this statement was made in the context of the comprehensive tax base debate, I think it is equally correct in the present context. It is true, as Andrews says, that an expenditure tax model can "serve just as well as the accretion ideal as a guide to incremental improvement of the existing hybrid tax." But it can do so only, I suggest, if one's tax philosophy pulls one in the direction of an expenditure tax; it cannot serve as a guide to an improved tax.

The relevance of these general comments becomes clear if one examines the supplemental expenditure tax as a device for improving the present system by eliminating those features that most seriously offend principles of *income* taxation. In this process one need not get involved in still another round of the comprehensive tax base debate. Despite the disagreements on the comprehensive tax base, there is certainly a core of agreement on the directions that income tax reform should take. It is quite clear to me, for example, that if the supplemental expenditure tax can be used to reduce the tax advantages of state and local bonds, it is to that extent a good idea. If it can be used to keep people from financing consumption by borrowing against unrealized appreciation, that is just fine. I would question the political judgment that one can sneak such reforms past the defenders of the current privileges, but that is an issue on which I choose to remain silent.

So far, so good. But now consider some of the other, seemingly

4. Stanley S. Surrey, *Pathways to Tax Reform* (Harvard University Press, 1973), p. 21.

more fundamental, claims made by Andrews for the supplemental personal expenditure tax. One of those claims is that the marginal rates of basic income tax can be reduced without sacrificing progressivity. For a person whose income is devoted entirely to consumption, there will, in effect, be no sacrifice of progressivity, though I question whether such a person will feel that there has been a reduction in the marginal rate of taxation after he or she takes into account both the basic income tax and the supplemental expenditure tax. For the saver, however, while there is no reduction in progressivity as measured against the expenditure base, there certainly is such a reduction as measured against an income base.

Another claim, that the adoption of the supplemental expenditure tax proposal will reduce "disparities in the treatment of investment returns," is justified. But it will do so only to the extent that it abandons the goals of an income tax. It is perfectly clear that, by adopting the supplemental expenditure tax proposal, we can, for example, eliminate the present disparities arising from provisions allowing accelerated depreciation. But this can be accomplished only by allowing a current deduction for all capital expenditures—which, tested against income tax goals, is scarcely an improvement. It is true that to the extent that the disparity between realized and unrealized gains is eliminated, the most convincing argument for the favorable treatment of capital gains is undercut. But the price is certainly very high —again, as tested against income tax principles.

In contrast, the arguments that the supplemental expenditure tax will help savers and facilitate a greater reliance on a general expenditure tax seem to show Andrews in pursuit of unalloyed expenditure tax goals. Here the problem of consistency with underlying principles does not exist. Expenditure tax proponents should find these arguments appealing.

Given the hybrid nature of the present system, I suggest that there is little, if any, basis for objection to the incremental approach. Assuming, however, that we should strive through incremental moves toward an expenditure tax goal, the question that seems to me worth exploring is the advantage of the supplemental expenditure tax over a variety of these options, such as expanded opportunities for saving for retirement, new opportunities for tax-deferred saving for such purposes as the purchase of a personal residence, and expanded opportunities for tax-free rollovers—combined with the taxation of borrowing against unrealized appreciation. The supplemental expenditure tax has the apparent advantage of neutrality among saving-investment choices; as Andrews puts it, the supplemental personal expenditure tax is "incremental yet comprehensive." One can, however, question what weight should be given to this feature, just as some have questioned the value of the comprehensive tax base model. Moreover, the supplemental expenditure tax is something new; it would take getting used to. Tax-deferred savings and tax-free rollovers are more familiar concepts—for better or worse. It may be that a general roll-over provision would be politically unacceptable. But if that is so, then the supplemental expenditure tax would be equally vulnerable politically—provided that tax experts and economists fulfill their responsibility and try to make sure that the tax is fully understood by the public.

Andrews's paper performs the very useful function of presenting an incremental device that deserves the attention of expenditure tax proponents. I regret that he has not devoted more attention to the advantage of this incremental strategy over others that he has previously examined.

MICHAEL J. GRAETZ

Expenditure Tax Design

ALTHOUGH the idea of a progressive tax on consumption (an "expenditure tax") is not new, it has received no serious political attention in the United States since 1942, when a "spendings tax" was proposed by the Treasury Department to help finance wartime expenditures.[1] Since then the common view has been that implementation difficulties render such a tax impractical. But in recent years several detailed discussions of expenditure taxation have tended to dispel that view.[2]

These various studies indicate that a theoretically correct expenditure tax would be easier to implement than a theoretically correct income tax. The failures of expenditure taxation in India and Sri Lanka—the only two countries to have adopted such a tax—are considered irrelevant to the United States, where a sophisticated

1. *Annual Report of the Secretary of the Treasury on the State of the Finances, for the Fiscal Year Ended June 30, 1943* (GPO, 1944), pp. 93–94, 411–13, 415.

2. See, in particular, William D. Andrews, "A Consumption-Type or Cash Flow Personal Income Tax," *Harvard Law Review,* vol. 87 (April 1974), pp. 1113–88, and William D. Andrews, "Fairness and the Personal Income Tax; A Reply to Professor Warren," *Harvard Law Review,* vol. 88 (March 1975), pp. 947–58; Advisory Commission on Intergovernmental Relations, *The Expenditure Tax* (Information Report M-84 (March 1974); U.S. Department of the Treasury, *Blueprints for Basic Tax Reform* (Government Printing Office, 1977), pp. 21–52, 113–43 (hereafter *Blueprints*); Institute for Fiscal Studies, *The Structure and Reform of Direct Taxation,* Report of a Committee chaired by Professor J. E. Meade (London: Allen and Unwin, 1978) (hereafter Meade committee report); Peter Mieszkowski, "The Cash Flow Version of an Expenditure Tax," OTA Paper 26 (U.S. Department of the Treasury, Office of Tax Analysis, 1977); Sven-Olof Lodin, *Progressive Expenditure Tax—an Alternative?* A Report of the 1972 Government Commission on Taxation (Stockholm: LiberFörlag, 1978).

progressive income tax based upon self-assessment already exists. Nevertheless, practical problems abound, and a pessimistic attitude persists.

This paper takes up the principal issues involved in implementing an expenditure tax. The first section briefly describes how an expenditure tax would operate and explores the type of rate schedule that would be necessary. The next three sections consider timing issues and the treatment of investment assets, consumer durables and housing, and gifts and bequests, followed by two sections that discuss what items would be included in receipts and allowed as deductions. The taxation of business income, international issues, and administrative problems are then considered in turn. In the last major section, transitional problems likely to arise in shifting to an expenditure tax are analyzed.

Background

Consumption taxes in the United States and other industrialized countries tend to take the form not of expenditure taxes but of flat-rate or multiple-rate retail sales taxes, turnover taxes, or value-added taxes. Like the expenditure tax, these taxes are imposed upon a base composed of expenditures on consumption items. The principal difficulties with the value-added tax and the sales tax are precisely those that a well-designed expenditure tax should avoid. First, value-added and retail sales taxes are invariably imposed on less than a full consumption base. Services are typically excluded from the tax base; for example, medical and hospital care services provided by state and local governments, public transportation, financial services provided by banks and savings institutions, foreign travel, and in some cases rental payments, including those for housing. Second, value-added or retail sales taxes are not related to a person's total amount of consumption. An expenditure tax should avoid the narrowing of the tax base that inevitably seems to accompany value-added or sales taxes and would achieve individualization of the tax burden by imposing a tax on a consumption base at progressive rates directly related to a person's overall level of consumption.

If progressivity of the tax were not desired, relatively simple mechanisms exist to ensure that a value-added tax or retail sales tax would be roughly proportional to a person's consumption; and if only a proportional tax on consumption were desired, surely a value-added tax or retail sales tax would be the preferred mechanism (if for no reason other than their widespread use in the states and in other industrialized countries). Therefore, the decision to adopt a progressive rate structure is the principal basis for choosing an expenditure tax over other taxes levied on a consumption base. The fact that the decision to impose an expenditure tax is, in the first instance, dictated by a desire for progressivity needs to be emphasized because much of the expenditure tax literature analyzes flat-rate taxes. Difficulties with such analysis will become apparent in subsequent sections of this paper.

An expenditure tax at progressive rates is also closely related to a progressive income tax, as the Haig-Simons definition of income as consumption plus accretions to wealth suggests.[3] A significant portion of the income tax base is composed of consumption expenditures, and many of the problems of implementing a consumption tax are quite similar, or even identical, to those encountered under an income tax. The sixty years of experience with and analysis of income tax issues must necessarily serve as background to any discussion of implementation issues under an expenditure tax. This paper concentrates principally on issues peculiar to an expenditure tax, with only abbreviated discussion of issues that have been examined in depth in the income tax context.

Finally, Professor Alvin Warren has suggested that a consumption tax is necessarily equivalent to a wage tax.[4] This argument requires one to ask whether a graduated payroll tax, perhaps with a base similar to that of the social security tax, would be an appropriate mechanism for the implementation of an expenditure tax. This alternative will be explored in the next section, where I discuss the two principal forms of consumption tax implementation.

General Description of an Expenditure Tax

No one suggests direct accounting for consumption expenditures of individuals as a practical approach to a progressive tax on consumption. Record-keeping in connection with numerous consumption purchases would simply be too onerous; the reliance of the Internal

3. Henry C. Simons, *Personal Income Taxation: The Definition of Income as a Problem of Fiscal Policy* (University of Chicago Press, 1938), p. 50.
4. Alvin C. Warren, Jr., "Fairness and a Consumption-Type or Cash Flow Personal Income Tax," *Harvard Law Review,* vol. 88 (March 1975), pp. 931–58.

Revenue Service on sales tax tables under the current income tax confirms this rather obvious point. Consumption expenditures would necessarily be approximated indirectly by reference to amounts available for consumption (principally income) and amounts saved.

Early discussions of expenditure tax implementation tended to regard full reporting of a person's bank balances, other accounts, and assets and liabilities at the beginning and end of each year as essential to the consumption tax computation, but subsequent commentators regard balance sheet reporting as unnecessarily complicating. Instead, consumption expenditures would be computed indirectly by calculating each year's transactions that produce funds available for consumption or savings and eliminating savings from the tax base. Later sections of this paper will fill in the details, but the general form would be as follows: amounts received minus amounts saved equals consumption.

The Expenditure Tax Rate Schedule

Though the development of a specific expenditure tax rate schedule is beyond the scope of this paper, the details of the rate schedule have important implications for issues of expenditure tax design. Enactment of an expenditure tax could serve various purposes. It might replace one or more current federal sources of revenue; for example, the individual income tax (or both the individual and corporate income taxes), payroll taxes, or estate and gift taxes (if gifts and bequests are treated as consumption). Alternatively, an expenditure tax could supplement current tax sources, perhaps limited in application to high-income taxpayers. The recent report of the Meade committee considered a two-tier expenditure tax with a proportional value-added tax applicable to the broad class of taxpayers and a progressive expenditure tax applicable only at the higher brackets.

From time to time taxes on a consumption base have been suggested to finance specific federal programs. For example, Congressman Al Ullman, chairman of the House Ways and Means Committee, has recently suggested that a national health insurance program might be financed by a value-added tax, and Senator Russell Long, chairman of the Senate Finance Committee, has proposed a value-added tax to replace social security taxes and to reduce income taxes. An expenditure tax might well merit consideration in such contexts.

Throughout this paper, in analyzing problems of implementing a progressive tax on consumption, I assume that such a tax is intended to produce revenues roughly equivalent to current federal income tax receipts. I also assume that the burden of such a tax would be distributed in a manner roughly similar to the current income tax. The Treasury Department in *Blueprints* estimated that a rather comprehensive consumption tax base would be 23 percent greater than the present taxable income base and 7 percent less than a comprehensive income tax base. The Treasury proposed expenditure tax rate schedules that it contended would roughly approximate the progressivity of present law.[5] For joint returns of married couples, the rate structure would be as follows:

Before-tax consumption bracket (dollars)	*Marginal tax rate (percent)*
0– 5,200	10
5,200–30,000	28
Over 30,000	40

For returns of single persons, the rate structure would be as follows:

Before-tax consumption bracket (dollars)	*Marginal tax rate (percent)*
0– 3,200	10
3,200–30,000	26
Over 30,000	40

The tax base might be greater under a consumption tax than under the present income tax because the addition to the tax base of many items not now included as income might outweigh the reduction of the base through the exclusion of amounts saved. Capital gains, for instance, would be included in full, and the Treasury would not allow deductions for charitable contributions or state sales or property taxes under its proposed consumption tax.

The Treasury's calculations notwithstanding, it is of course quite possible that the expenditure tax emerging from the political process might not significantly expand the present taxable income base, so that the major modification of the present tax base would be the exclusion of savings. If this were the case, and a distribution of the tax roughly equivalent to that of the present income tax were desired, a much more sharply progressive rate schedule than that proposed in *Blueprints* might be required. The current income tax rate schedule for married couples ranges from 14 percent at taxable incomes

5. *Blueprints,* p. 169.

of $3,400–$5,500 to 70 percent at taxable incomes in excess of $215,400. If, as is widely believed, people in lower income brackets annually consume more than their income, and the proportion of income allocated to savings increases with income, comparable rate schedules applied to a consumption tax base would tend to start lower than those of the current income tax and rise more gradually until about the $30,000 taxable income class. Above that amount, rates would tend to rise steeply and be higher than current marginal income tax rates.

Regardless of the base selected, it seems unrealistic to expect rate brackets as broad as the Treasury suggests. For example, the Treasury suggests one marginal rate for married couples with consumption between $5,200 and $30,000 and one marginal rate for consumption in excess of $30,000. Present law contains seven different marginal tax rates for taxable income classes between $5,200 and $30,000 and eight different marginal rates for taxable incomes in excess of $30,000. It therefore seems more reasonable to assume that, whatever the consumption tax base, a progressive rate schedule would include considerably more gradations than the three suggested in *Blueprints*. This aspect of a proposal would have significance for implementation decisions. Under the *Blueprints* schedule, the few gradations may make the allocation of consumption to a particular taxable period extremely important for persons with consumption near the amounts where the brackets shift. On the other hand, numerous marginal tax brackets make it less reasonable to assume that an individual taxpayer will be taxed at the same effective rate over a period of many years and therefore usually render the allocation of consumption to specific taxable periods more important.

I assume throughout this paper that the rate schedule for an expenditure tax would have numerous gradations, as does the present income tax, and would be set at a level to raise revenue approximately equal to that of the present income tax.

Timing Issues: The Treatment of Financial Assets and Loans

Issues of timing in income taxation—in particular, questions of when deductions are permitted or amounts included in income— have received detailed consideration by tax analysts. Economists over the years have been instrumental in developing and refining techniques designed to facilitate evaluation or comparison of events occurring at different times. Lawyers and accountants have long been concerned with allocating their clients' income and deductions to particular taxable years to minimize tax liabilities, and recently academic lawyers and others interested in revised income tax policies have carefully analyzed issues of income tax timing.

In the expenditure tax context, analysis of timing issues is critical both for an understanding of how an expenditure tax differs from other taxes, particularly income or wage taxes, and for guidance in resolving implementation questions. Proponents of an expenditure tax, such as Professor Andrews and the Treasury Department in *Blueprints,* have argued that the capacity of an expenditure tax to handle timing problems equitably and without economic distortion is one of its principal advantages over an income tax.[6]

This section compares expenditure taxes and income taxes with respect to timing issues, with special emphasis on tax deferral and the treatment of investment assets and borrowing under an expenditure tax. Discussion of the expenditure tax treatment of consumer durables and housing, each of which requires the allocation of consumption or investment to particular taxable years, is dealt with in the following section. The treatment of gifts and bequests, which also raises timing problems, is taken up after that.

The Immediate Deduction–Yield Exemption Equivalence

Income tax deferral is most commonly described by reference to taxpayers who save tax initially, usually by accelerating deductions or postponing income, but in a later year (or years) incur an identical income tax liability. The effect of such tax deferral is most often demonstrated by two alleged equivalences: (1) the equivalence of tax deferral to an interest-free loan from the government to the taxpayer, and (2) the equivalence of deducting immediately an investment's cost to imposing tax initially and exempting from tax the income from the investment (the "immediate deduction–yield exemption equivalence").

Although this second equivalence has only recently appeared in

6. *Ibid.*, pp. 127–28; Andrews, "A Consumption-Type or Cash Flow Personal Income Tax," pp. 1120–28. See also William A. Klein, "Timing in Personal Taxation," *Journal of Legal Studies,* vol. 6 (June 1977), pp. 461–81.

the legal literature, it is well known in the economic literature, having originated in an article published by Professor E. Cary Brown more than thirty years ago, and appears in the standard public finance texts.[7] The equivalence is important under a consumption tax for two reasons. First, if it holds, it would be possible to create simple and flexible rules for implementing a consumption tax. The Treasury Department in *Blueprints* bases its expenditure tax treatment of investments and loans on this equivalence. Second, since a consumption tax, unlike an income tax, is not intended to be imposed on the yield from savings per se, this equivalence has informed discussions of the fundamental nature of an expenditure tax, leading Professor Warren, for example, to assert that a consumption tax is equivalent to a wage tax.[8] Moreover, it is consistent with the widely expressed notion that the difference between an income tax and an expenditure tax is solely a matter of timing. This equivalence is therefore central not only to specific implementation decisions but may also influence one's judgment about the desirability of an expenditure tax in the first instance. Thus it, and the analytical position that it implies, must be explored in some detail.

Professor Andrews's example relating to deferred compensation is a helpful introduction to the basic timing difference between income and expenditure taxes:

a 33 percent accretion-type tax . . . would take away one-third of the original dollar when earned, leaving only 67 cents to invest; and it would cut the rate of growth from 9 percent per annum to 6 percent. At 6 percent per annum for 24 years, 67 cents will produce a retirement fund of only $2.67, as compared with $8.00 in the absence of tax. On the other hand, if the tax were deferred until retirement, the taxpayer would pay only $2.67 tax out of $8.00, leaving $5.33 to spend. Deferral of the tax, without any change in rate, would double what the taxpayer has left to spend.[9]

This example shows that tax deferral, even when an identical rate tax is subsequently imposed, is clearly inconsistent with the theo-

7. E. Cary Brown, "Business-Income Taxation and Investment Incentives," in *Income, Employment and Public Policy: Essays in Honor of Alvin E. Hansen* (Norton, 1948), pp. 300–16. See also Stanley S. Surrey, *Pathways to Tax Reform* (Harvard University Press, 1973), p. 123; and Carl S. Shoup, *Public Finance* (Aldine, 1969), p. 302.

8. Warren, "Fairness and a Consumption-Type or Cash Flow Personal Income Tax," p. 931.

9. Andrews, "A Consumption-Type or Cash Flow Personal Income Tax," p. 1125.

retically correct income tax treatment, which should tax interest earnings as they occur. But such deferral is the desired expenditure tax result; taxes on earnings and from investments should be deferred until the income is used for consumption. The deferral illustrated in the example is also consistent with the economic definition of an expenditure tax offered by the Meade committee:

It is indeed the characteristic feature of an expenditure tax as contrasted with an income tax that, at any given constant rate of tax, the former will make the rate of return to the saver on his reduced consumption equal to the rate of return which can be earned on the investment which his savings finances, whereas the income tax will reduce the rate of return to the saver below the rate of return which the investment will yield.[10]

As Professor Andrews notes, the immediate deduction–yield exemption equivalence holds in his example: the same result would be reached by taxing the original $1.00 of earnings 33 cents and allowing the remaining 67 cents to grow to $5.33 without additional tax. In terms of the Meade committee's definition of an expenditure tax, the "reduced consumption" of 67 cents would have earned the full 9 percent "rate of return which can be earned on the investment which his savings finances."

As mentioned above, the Treasury Department in *Blueprints* relies on the immediate deduction–yield exemption equivalence not only to distinguish income from expenditure taxes but also to develop its specific expenditure tax rules.[11] Thus the Treasury recommends that an expenditure tax should allow taxpayers to elect either (1) immediate deduction (cash flow) treatment, under which purchases of financial assets would be deducted and subsequent withdrawals of principal and earnings taxed, or (2) yield exemption treatment, under which no deduction would be allowed for purchases of financial assets but earnings and withdrawals of principal would be exempt from tax. Similar flexibility would be granted for loans. The Treasury defends unfettered taxpayer discretion on the ground that "the consequences . . . of the two ways of taxing the purchase of assets would . . . be the same *in present value terms*."[12] Before turning to an examination of the circumstances under which the immediate deduction–yield exemption equivalence will hold, I comment briefly on the im-

10. Meade committee report, p. 37.
11. *Blueprints,* pp. 119–27.
12. Ibid, p. 123.

portant theoretical question raised by the Treasury's analysis: is equal *present value* an acceptable basis for assessing tax?

Ex Ante versus Ex Post Approach

The Treasury proposal would, in effect, treat persons as if they were in similar circumstances whenever their tax base (consumption in this case) is the same in present value terms. Thus tax parity among persons would be approached ex ante. The Treasury recognizes that under this system, "lucky investors might become very rich and owe no additional [expenditure] tax liability on future consumption of their wealth. . . . Conversely, unlucky investors will have prepaid a tax on expected returns and will then obtain no deduction for the losses they incur." But this does not cause the Treasury to reject options or question the underlying analysis.[13] In other words, whenever people were in equivalent circumstances ex ante, the Treasury would ignore ex post differences in circumstances.

The basic argument for the Treasury's point of view is contained in the Meade committee report, which advances two competing definitions of income.[14] The first is equivalent to the Haig-Simons definition, in which income is taken as the amount of consumption during the year plus net accretions to wealth. The alternative definition regards income "as the amount which [a person] could consume in any one year and yet be left with the resources and expectations at the end of the year which would enable him to maintain that same level of consumption indefinitely in the future." By this definition people would be treated as being in similar or different circumstances according to their expectations. The definition is rejected by the Meade committee as "quite impracticable," essentially because "it is not easy to envisage the tax inspector agreeing with each taxpayer upon what may reasonably be expected." The Meade committee suggests that whether comprehensive income or consumption is used as a tax base, each should be measured with reference to historic fact rather than to subjective views about the future. This attitude is reflected in its proposals for implementing an expenditure tax, which endorse analytically the taxpayer options for the treatment of financial assets provided under *Blueprints,* but reject this method when assets on which "substantial capital gains might be made" are involved. Under

13. Ibid, p. 129.
14. Meade committee report, pp. 31–32.

the Meade committee approach, purchase of investment assets would ordinarily be deducted from the tax base and sales and income would be included in the tax base. The committee seems to reject an ex ante approach to tax implementation for reasons of practicality but accepts it as a basis for assessing various taxing schemes.

But an ex ante approach to the evaluation of taxes requires a major restructuring of the classic conceptions of tax equity. Horizontal equity, the most widely accepted notion of fairness in taxation, requires that persons in similar circumstances pay similar amounts of tax. Although the tax literature is replete with disputes over whether "similar" or "different" circumstances are being compared, the notion that similar circumstances should be evaluated ex ante in present value terms seems quite a radical departure. The better view of horizontal equity usually depends on the Haig-Simons definition of income or on similar ones, which are necessarily ex post concepts. Regardless of the precise form of the definition of income or consumption, horizontal equity must be an ex post concept. Circumstances should be considered as similar only after results are known: lucky gamblers are not the same as unlucky gamblers.[15]

An ex ante approach to vertical equity is even more troubling. Vertical equity is said to require different taxation of persons in different circumstances and is principally used to gauge the fairness of the distribution of the tax burden among persons with different amounts of income, consumption, or wealth. Certainly, if one accepts a vertical equity criterion that relates the distribution of the tax burden to "ability to pay," ex post rather than ex ante circumstances are relevant. If progressive taxation is to be justified, even in part, as a device for the redistribution of income, consumption, or wealth, the tax base must distinguish those who are lucky from those who are unlucky, even though their expectations might have been the same before the gamble. The notion of vertical tax equity is not limited to income taxation but should apply with equal force to a progressive tax on consumption designed to vary the tax burden according to the standard of living attained.

Choosing an expenditure tax necessarily implies progressivity; otherwise a sales or value-added tax would be adopted. Thus, although people may well differ on the appropriate time period for

15. See Nicholas Kaldor, *An Expenditure Tax* (London: Allen and Unwin, 1955; Westport, Conn.: Greenwood Press, 1977), pp. 60–64.

applying a progressive rate structure, or even on whether consumption is a proper base for progressive taxation, once an expenditure tax with progressive rates is chosen, the tax must be imposed with regard to ex post circumstances. People should be taxed on their actual, not their expected consumption.

Ex Post Relation of Immediate Deduction and Yield Exemption

Whether the Treasury intended to advance the radical restructuring of the traditional concepts of tax equity implied by its ex ante approach is necessarily a matter of conjecture, given its endorsement of progressive taxation and its reliance on the Haig-Simons definition of income elsewhere in *Blueprints*. The Treasury's intent is made more difficult to assess because its recommendations are based upon the immediate deduction–yield exemption equivalence, which would occur ex post as well as ex ante under a restrictive set of conditions that is present in all the Treasury's examples and that is usually assumed (although often not explicitly) in the relevant economic and legal literature.[16] The Treasury might simply have based its recommendations on an equivalence that would occur ex post as well as ex ante under the common assumptions.

Accepting an ex post perspective for implementing an expenditure tax, however, requires that the practicality of the immediate deduction–yield exemption equivalence be determined. In its most general form, the equivalence may be tested by describing the conditions under which an expenditure tax would be equivalent to a wage tax. If the equivalence between immediate deduction and exemption of yield holds, an expenditure tax should be equivalent to a tax on wages under which all income from savings is excluded from the base. It would then be a matter of indifference whether the base for an expenditure tax is computed by deducting amounts saved or by exempting investment sales and yield.

A consumption tax will indeed be equivalent to a wage tax under the following set of unrealistic conditions:

1. There is no initial period wealth.

2. The system is closed: the taxpayer exhausts his wealth by death, or the system classifies all remaining capital balances (all bequests) as consumption in the taxpayer's final tax return, or an identical tax is subsequently imposed on bequests in some other way.

16. See *Blueprints*, pp. 127–28; Andrews, "A Consumption-Type or Cash Flow Personal Income Tax," pp. 1124–25.

3. Tax rates are not progressive; moreover, they do not change over time.

4. There exists a perfect capital market with no uncertainty: all taxpayers can borrow and lend unlimited amounts at a risk-free interest rate.

5. All income can be classified as one of two types: wage income or income to capital accumulated during and after the initial period.

Under these conditions a wage tax and a consumption tax are equivalent: the discounted present value of a wage base equals the discounted present value of a consumption base when viewed from the perspective of the opening or closing period. When the conditions are relaxed, however, the equivalence disappears.

The set of conditions required for this equivalence simply will not exist when an expenditure tax is actually implemented. Under the consumption tax set forth in *Blueprints,* for example, rates are progressive and likely to vary over time, capital markets are imperfect and the future uncertain, and the system is open at the beginning. Progressivity alone, which is central to the decision to impose an expenditure tax, defeats the equivalence. The immediate deduction–yield exemption equivalence therefore will not hold ex post in practice and should not serve as the basic guide to implementation decisions.

Perhaps most important, with uncertainty and progressive rates the distributional consequences of the two methods would be different. With a progressive rate structure, the cash flow version of the tax would narrow the after-tax differences between the lucky and unlucky investor in ways that the omission alternative would not.

Under the cash flow method, the government can be regarded as automatically becoming a joint venturer in taxpayers' investments. In effect, it invests a percentage equal to the taxpayer's marginal tax rate in each venture—for example, with a 60 percent marginal rate, the taxpayer's initial tax savings is 60 percent of the cash investment and the government receives 60 percent of the gain or contributes 60 percent of the loss. An expenditure tax under either the immediate deduction or yield exemption option, then, would not reduce the before-tax rate of return on investment capital (or in the Meade committee's terms, on "reduced consumption"). But this fact does not make the options equivalent. Under the cash flow method, the government would share in any gains or losses on investments or borrowing; under the yield exemption option, it would not.

This difference may be illustrated by assuming that a taxpayer has

$800,000 cash to invest in a $2,000,000 investment asset (since the immediate deduction under the cash flow method of $2,000,000 would save a 60 percent taxpayer $1,200,000). Under the immediate deduction method, the taxpayer would in effect receive a non-interest-bearing contribution from the government, but the government would participate in any return (at the time when the proceeds are ultimately devoted to consumption). Under the yield exemption alternative, the taxpayer would have to borrow the additional $1,200,000 at the market rate of interest but would keep any excess of the proceeds from the investment over the interest payment. Thus, in cases in which the rate of return exceeds the market rate of interest, such taxpayers would be better off under the yield exemption option. Likewise, if aggregate gains exceeded aggregate losses (or if losses were not eligible for immediate refunds), government revenues would be greater under the cash flow method, even with a constant flat-rate tax.

Results equivalent to those under the cash flow option would occur, however, if only $800,000 were invested under the yield exemption option, the returns were identical with that of a $2,000,000 asset, and taxes were imposed at identical rates. Likewise, to obtain equivalent results in situations with identical tax rates and identical returns on borrowing, it would be necessary for the ratio of borrowing to after-tax investment to be the same under the two alternative tax regimes. To the extent that speculative investment opportunities (or borrowing opportunities) were limited, differences among winning and losing taxpayers would be lessened under the cash flow method.

In one sense, borrowing is simply the reverse side of the problem of asset taxation. As a theoretical matter ex ante, it should make no difference in present value terms whether borrowing would be accounted for on a cash flow basis—with loans included in receipts and deductions allowed for interest and repayments of principal— or on a yield exemption basis, with loans not included in receipts and no deductions allowed for interest or repayments of principal. This can readily be illustrated by a simple example.

Assume that in year 1 the taxpayer borrows $100 at 10 percent interest; in year 2 the loan plus interest—$110—is repaid. In general, taxpayers and the government should be indifferent to whether the $100 loan is included in receipts in year 1 and $110 is deducted in year 2 or whether the entire transaction is omitted from expenditure tax accounts. As the Meade committee indicates, the interest deduction forgone under the omission alternative would result in an increase in the individual's tax liability by an amount that would correspond to interest on the amount of tax deferred by not including the loan in receipts in year 1. Given the virtually unlimited allowance of interest deductions under the income tax, it is worth emphasizing that denying the interest deduction is critical to this result.

The equivalence would, of course, not exist ex post if the taxpayer were to fail to pay interest or repay the loan proceeds. If such a transaction were omitted from expenditure tax accounts, taxpayers could enjoy additional consumption free of tax. Thus (although such a rule is not provided by the Treasury in *Blueprints*) if loans were not initially included in receipts, forgiveness of indebtedness or default on principal or interest should result in an expenditure tax receipt for the amount of accrued interest and principal that were not paid. This treatment would be somewhat similar to the current income tax treatment of borrowing, which excludes loans from income and includes discharges of indebtedness in income.

Tax Manipulation

Opportunities for manipulations to save tax would be available whenever tax accounting rules permit distortions of the assumptions underlying the immediate deduction–yield exemption equivalence. The ability to shift assets within a single accounting period illustrates the general problem. Assume that on January 1 a taxpayer receives $1,000 of salary, which he invests in an asset under the yield exemption alternative. If the asset is worth $1,100 on December 31, the taxpayer may sell the asset and reinvest the proceeds under the immediate deduction alternative, thereby obtaining a net deduction of $100 (the $1,000 of receipts less the $1,100 investment) under circumstances in which wealth has increased by $100.

By selling the asset on January 1 of the next year and reinvesting the proceeds until December 31 in a yield exemption asset, the process could be repeated. Thus, over time, the problem would appear to be one of year-end deferral, similar in effect to techniques familiar under the income tax for accelerating deductions and postponing income. Likewise, similar results could be achieved by January borrowing on a cash flow basis and investing the proceeds in a yield exemption asset until December 31, when the loan would be repaid. Assuming 10 percent interest on the loan and a 10 percent investment return, the taxpayer could obtain a net deduction of the interest payment in a transaction that produced no change in net wealth. The January 1 loan receipt of $1,000 would be included in receipts and the December 31 $1,100 repayment deducted, with the $100 earnings excluded by a yield exemption election.

As these examples illustrate, systematic biases in favor of tax deferral would occur under an expenditure tax whenever the amount deferred plus an appropriate amount of interest would not subsequently appear in the tax base.

Additional problems occur when the Treasury's assumption that there is no basis ex ante for a taxpayer to prefer one of the two options is erroneous in fact. To the extent that tax rates are progressive or expected to vary over time, taxpayers' ex ante calculations may be affected. For example, the omission alternative would be selected whenever the immediate deduction forgone would be expected to reduce tax at a lower rate than would apply to a subsequent speculative gain. Likewise, under an elective system taxpayers could be expected to seek information about results before making an irrevocable election. Under the Treasury's proposal to elect on tax returns, information about investment results that would affect taxpayers' choices might well be available for assets purchased early in the taxable year. Delays in making elections would be likely to be sought until results became known to the taxpayers. Efforts to revoke disadvantageous elections should also be expected. Administration of the tax laws and tax planning would be simplified under a mandatory rather than elective system.

Moreover, even strict rules about the timing and irrevocability of elections would not preclude taxpayers from structuring transactions to maximize advantages from the optional forms of treatment. Common estate planning techniques would have immediate application in an expenditure tax context. In estate planning, the goal is to "freeze the size of a client's estate at its current level and direct future growth to the natural objects of the client's bounty."[17] In expenditure tax planning, the goal would be to obtain deductions for investment on an immediate deduction basis and direct future appreciation to taxpayers subject to yield exemption treatment.

One common estate planning technique is to design a corporation's capital structure by using bonds or preferred stock to freeze value in

17. George Cooper, *A Voluntary Tax? New Perspectives on Sophisticated Estate Tax Avoidance* (Brookings Institution, 1978), p. 12.

closely held corporations with substantial appreciation potential.[18] Under an expenditure tax, a parent might transfer $2,000,000 to a corporation and elect cash flow treatment, thereby obtaining an immediate deduction for the amount transferred. In return, the parent would receive preferred stock paying cumulative dividends of 10 percent. His adult child transfers $200,000 to the corporation for all the common stock and elects yield exemption treatment. If the value of the corporation appreciates, say by $2,000,000, in the next two years, the parent would receive a total of $400,000 ($200,000 each year), which would be includable in his expenditure tax receipts (and taxed, if consumed); the child could sell his stock and realize $1,600,000 free of expenditure tax. Prohibiting such transactions would require extensive and well-designed rules, and given the lack of estate tax success at inhibiting such transactions, optimism hardly seems warranted.

By the same token, expenditure tax planning techniques can be expected to shift risks of loss to taxpayers who elect cash flow treatment, while providing appreciation for taxpayers who elect yield exemption treatment. For example, a parent and his child invest $200,000 each in an oil field, arranging their ownership like squares on a checkerboard, with the parent taking the black squares, the child the red. The parent elects immediate deduction treatment and the child takes the yield exemption option. The parent spends $1,500,000 on drilling to locate the oil within the field, deducts this amount, and discovers oil worth a total of $3,000,000 now that the location of the oil is known. The parent and child then sell their interests for $3,000,000, $1,500,000 each. The parent would be required to include his proceeds in receipts but would have obtained a net expenditure tax deduction of $200,000. The child would have obtained $1,300,000 free of expenditure tax.

The Treasury proposal permits even more obvious tax avoidance possibilities by allowing inconsistent treatment of loans and assets. By electing yield exemption treatment for loans and immediate deduction treatment for assets, taxpayers would find even better opportunities for shelters under the expenditure tax than under the in-

18. Ibid., pp. 13–20. For other estate planning techniques with potential expenditure tax application, see Ralph G. Miller, Jr., "Certain Aspects of Estate Planning for the Business Owner," presented at the 33d Annual Institute on Federal Taxation (New York University, November 1975), pp. 81, 98–99.

come tax. This may be illustrated by investigating the expenditure tax consequences of a typical motion picture tax shelter. (The following example was used by the staff of the Joint Committee on Taxation in its 1974 presentation to the House Ways and Means Committee.)

Assume that a taxpayer purchases the U.S. rights to a foreign movie for $2,000,000. The taxpayer's cash investment is $200,000 and the remaining $1,800,000 is borrowed from the foreign producer. The loan is payable first out of the proceeds of the film, with the balance, if any, due and payable in twenty years. The film is unsuccessful and realizes only $1,500,000 of income, $1,200,000 in the first year and $300,000 in the second year. In year 20, the taxpayer defaults on the remaining indebtedness of $300,000.

Under the income tax, results would depend on allowable depreciation. Assuming an estimate of $1,500,000 of total income was made in the first few weeks following release, under the income forecast method the taxpayer would be allowed depreciation deductions of $1,600,000 the first year (80 percent of $2,000,000, since the first year's income is 80 percent of forecast income) and $400,000 in the second year. The tax loss for year 1 is $400,000 ($1,200,000 of income and $1,600,000 of depreciation deductions) and the tax loss in the second year is $100,000 ($300,000 of income and $400,000 of depreciation deductions). In year 20, $300,000 of income results from the default on indebtedness.

Under a cash flow expenditure tax, the $2,000,000 purchase of the film and the income ($1,200,000 in year 1 and $300,000 in year 2) would be taken into account on a cash flow basis, with the $1,800,000 borrowing and the $1,200,000 repayment counted in year 1 and the $300,000 repayment counted in year 2. No cash transaction occurs in year 20, so nothing would be reported. Under an election to treat the asset on an immediate deduction basis but to omit borrowing, the loan transaction would not enter into the expenditure tax computation until year 20, when the default on indebtedness should produce a $300,000 receipt. The results would be as follows (in thousands of dollars):

Year 1	Cash flow expenditure tax	Borrowing-omitted expenditure tax
Receipts		
Income from film	1,200	1,200
Loan	1,800	0
Total	3,000	1,200

	Cash flow expenditure tax	Borrowing-omitted expenditure tax
Deductions		
Purchase of film	2,000	2,000
Repayment of loan	1,200	0
Total	3,200	2,000
Taxable expenditure (or loss)	(200)	(800)
Year 2		
Receipts: income from film	300	300
Deductions: repayment of loan	300	0
Taxable expenditure	0	300
Year 20		
Receipts: default on loan	0	300
Taxable expenditure	0	300

Since no amount is repaid in year 20 because of the taxpayer's default on the indebtedness, that year's transaction is not included in the expenditure tax base under the cash flow computation; under the borrowing-omitted alternative, however, a receipt of $300,000 should be required. If the loan were in fact repaid, a loss of $300,000 would occur in year 20 under the cash flow method, and no amount would enter the borrowing-omitted computation. In either case, the losses under both alternatives would be the same: $200,000, if the loan were not repaid, and $500,000, if it were, although their timing, and therefore their present values, would be quite different.

Assuming 60 percent tax rates in each of the relevant years and refund of tax on losses, the tax liabilities are as follows (in thousands of dollars):

Income tax	Cash flow expenditure tax	Borrowing-omitted expenditure tax
Year 1		
Refund of 240	Refund of 120	Refund of 480
Year 2		
Refund of 60	0	Tax of 180
Year 20		
Tax of 180	0	Tax of 180

In this case the taxpayer has, in effect, shifted $300,000 of the loss to the foreign producer by the borrowing and subsequent default, thereby losing only $200,000. Both the income tax and the expenditure tax result in a total tax loss equal to the $200,000 economic loss, and at a 60 percent tax rate produce a total tax savings of $120,000. The timing of the tax savings varies dramatically, however, as would the present value effect. Under the cash flow expenditure tax, the entire $120,000 tax savings occurs in year 1, and by applying a 6 percent discount rate, the present value of this savings as of the beginning of that year equals $113,160, or 60 percent of $188,600 (the present value of the $200,000 loss discounted from the end of the year to the beginning of the year). Any distortion is due simply to the administrative convenience of accounting for taxes on an annual basis, which necessarily means that gains and losses are not taken into account at the instant they occur.

The present value of the tax savings under the income tax as of the beginning of year 1 equals $223,740, or $35,140 more than the total economic loss of $188,600 present value at that time. One might have expected a 60 percent income tax to reduce the before-tax loss by only 60 percent, but instead, by borrowing and deferring default, the taxpayer has turned a before-tax loss into an after-tax gain. (Since interest is deductible under the income tax, the omission of interest payments from the example makes no difference to this conclusion.) That such income tax results occur is well known to high-bracket taxpayers and their advisers. The Tax Reform Acts of 1969 and 1976 and the Revenue Act of 1978 have restricted many tax shelter techniques, but certain opportunities remain. Results may diverge even further from the norm if the taxpayer's income tax bracket changes over time or if the ultimate income on default or "phantom gain" is taxed at capital gains rates. Moreover, in many cases, the phantom gain is never reported by taxpayers nor discovered on audit.

The borrowing-omitted expenditure tax alternative provides an after-tax return even greater in present value than that available under the income tax before the recent reforms. Moreover, if the default were not required to be reported as a receipt in year 20, as seems possible under *Blueprints,* losses would total $500,000, even though the taxpayer was only out of pocket $200,000.

The disallowance of interest deductions under the borrowing-omitted alternative, however, would tend to compensate for the deferral that would be possible under such a scheme, and the example may overstate the problem because no stated interest is paid. If an appropriate interest rate were charged, no deductions were allowed for interest, and any interest or principal forgiven or defaulted were required to be included in receipts, the tax shelter possibilities under the borrowing-omitted alternative would generally be substantially less than under the present income tax. However, the ability to deduct immediately the full purchase price of an asset, including borrowed amounts, would create additional difficulties under a progressive rate schedule.

Implementing a cash flow approach to borrowing might encounter taxpayer resistance because people have become accustomed under the income tax to excluding borrowed amounts from receipts. As the forgoing example illustrates, however, major difficulties with the omission alternative would occur when the loan proceeds or interest were not repaid, either because the loan was from a related person and forgiven, or because the taxpayer defaulted. In either event, collection of tax when indebtedness was discharged would be difficult. For example, lawyers counseling clients regarding leveraged tax shelter investments under the income tax are frequently careful to point out that immediate deductions may produce phantom gains in a later year, that is, the taxpayer may be required to report gain and pay taxes in a year in which no cash income exists, which might be the year the investment is abandoned. But the amount of such phantom gain not reported to the Internal Revenue Service is no doubt significant, and underreporting is quite difficult to detect.

In addition, even if the gain is reported or detected on audit, the Internal Revenue Service will in many instances have great difficulty in collecting the tax. And there is no assurance that methods of avoiding ultimate inclusion of the phantom gain in the tax base that have occurred under the income tax, such as through death or charitable giving, would not exist under an expenditure tax. An omission alternative would therefore increase the problems of enforcement and collection of tax.

Moreover, as the forgoing example demonstrates, the expenditure tax treatment of borrowing must be coordinated with the treatment of related assets. Under an expenditure tax, treating loans on a cash flow basis would, regardless of how assets were treated, eliminate the potential for deferral. Likewise, if assets were treated under the yield exemption alternative, omitting related borrowing from expenditure tax accounts would not add any new problems; however, the ability to leverage investments on a yield exemption basis might with progressive rates increase the ex post advantages to lucky winners and the disadvantages to unlucky losers. But if assets could be treated on a cash flow basis and loans were permitted to be omitted from expenditure tax accounting, tax shelter opportunities would occur under an expenditure tax as they have under the current income tax.

If cash flow reporting of assets and loans were impossible for political reasons, the best alternative would be to limit expenditure tax deductions for investments, including asset purchases, to the taxpayer's equity in the investment, but such an approach would be fraught with difficulties. It would, for example, be necessary to accompany such a rule with a provision that would "recapture" deductions whenever assets were refinanced. Likewise, difficulties would occur from the need to amortize loans in order to allow deductions whenever additional principal amounts were contributed. But if interest deductions were allowed on such loans—as they should be if deductions for assets purchases were limited to equity (allowing only a deduction for equity would be equivalent to including borrowed amounts in receipts and allowing a deduction for the full cost of assets)—it would not be necessary to distinguish payments of interest and principal. It might, however, be necessary to trace indebtedness to various assets, since in other instances interest deductions might be disallowed. On balance, it seems important that expenditure tax be computed by treating assets and loans on a cash flow basis, except when a different treatment is necessary because of administrative considerations.

Summary and Recommendations

In a world of uncertainty and imperfect capital markets, a progressive expenditure tax that provided an optional treatment to exclude investments and loans from expenditure tax accounts, such as *Blueprints* proposes, would simply not be the same as a tax regime that permitted investments to be deducted and imposed tax on the yield and sale proceeds of assets whenever such amounts were devoted to consumption. The yield exemption option would be confusing to taxpayers, would increase tax manipulation opportunities, and would tend to undermine a progressive marginal rate structure designed to distinguish among taxpayers according to their actual consumption. A cash flow approach should also tend to produce less variance among ultimate winners and losers than exemption of yield. Likewise, if people systematically underestimated probabilities of success (perhaps because they were risk-averse), an immediate deduction would be more stimulative in inducing investments than an exemption of yield. Thus cash flow treatment of investment assets and loans would tend to be more equitable and more efficient than exemption of yield and should be adopted as the general rule.

Including loans in receipts would be a significant departure from the current income tax treatment and would undoubtedly require considerable taxpayer education before adoption, but the offsetting deduction for investments purchased with loan proceeds should ease a transition. Cash flow reporting of loans does not seem likely to cause new administrative problems, although the potential underreporting of loans must be considered.

Cash flow treatment of investment assets and loans would eliminate certain income tax complexities, principally those designed to mitigate the income tax distinction between realized (and therefore taxable) gains and losses and unrealized (and therefore nontaxable) gains and losses. These would include the capital gains–ordinary income distinction, the nonrecognition provisions, and installment sale provisions. Likewise, full cash flow reporting would eliminate the need for depreciation and recapture provisions, since all purchases of investment assets would be immediately deducted and all sales proceeds included in full in receipts. Finally, any need for inflation adjustments, as have been suggested for capital gains and depreciation under the income tax, would be unnecessary under an expenditure tax.

If tax-planning opportunities were not widely available, however, the yield exemption alternative might in some instances substantially simplify tax administration. In these cases, the systematic bias in favor of deferring payment of income taxes would not occur to the same extent with expenditure taxes. Under an income tax, people usually assume that deferring tax will be advantageous to them; under an expenditure tax, people may be indifferent to tax postponement, and sometimes, because of the progressive rate structure, may actually prefer to prepay expenditure taxes as an averaging technique. Thus the techniques of tax deferral familiar under an income tax would not tend to cause similar systematic distortions under an expenditure tax. Obtaining a deduction in an earlier year would be of no value to taxpayers under a constant rate expenditure tax in which an annual return equivalent to the discount rate plus the amount of the original deduction would be included in the tax base in a later year.

In cases in which progressivity and changing rates are not likely to be systematically distorting factors, in which returns are generally predictable and imperfections in the capital markets may be reasonably ignored, and in which administrative considerations argue for the yield exclusion alternative, this method of accounting for asset purchases might be used instead of cash flow accounting. Such treatment is, for example, recommended for consumer durables.

Consumer Durables and Housing

The expenditure tax treatment of consumer durables and housing requires practical resolution of two related issues, the more important of which is the timing issue discussed in the preceding section. The purchase of any consumer good that provides benefits beyond the taxable year of purchase necessarily involves an element of "savings" in the form of consumption deferred to a later taxable period. Common examples of such purchases are household furniture and appliances, certain types of clothing, automobiles, and yachts. In some instances, items not usually thought of as durables—season tickets to the theater or opera, for example—may involve purchase in one taxable year with use extending into subsequent taxable years.

In addition, certain goods, such as jewelry and works of art, have investment as well as consumption aspects. Housing is typically the most expensive and most enduring of consumer durables and, in a time of rising housing prices, often turns out to be a family's most important investment. It is therefore necessary to determine the appropriate expenditure tax treatment of gains and losses upon disposition. The basic problems are complicated somewhat because purchases of consumer durables and housing quite often involve borrowing, with larger loans usually secured by the asset purchased.

Ordinary Consumer Durables

Although the literature is somewhat confused, analysts generally agree about the theoretically appropriate treatment of consumer durables. It is, nevertheless, important to repeat the analysis so that the practical rules offered here may be measured against the theoretical norm. Only then may they be properly evaluated as concessions to the exigencies of administrative convenience or taxpayer understanding.

Initially, I assume that the goods in question will provide benefits beyond the year of purchase and will be used by the consumer as long as they endure. This second assumption permits focusing on the case in which the purchaser will enjoy all the benefits of the durable in question, thereby putting aside for the moment cases in which the good has an investment component.

Theoretically, an expenditure tax should tax consumption as it occurs and exempt amounts put aside for future consumption. Such an approach would, in effect, treat the purchaser of a consumer durable as if he had rented the good for the year in question. This could be accomplished by treating durables like financial assets; an immediate deduction would be allowed for the cost of the durable and its yield (an imputed rent) and sale price, if any, would be taken into receipts. This would have the virtue of treating purchasers and renters of consumer goods equally, since the latter would be taxed annually on nondeductible rental payments.

It would, however, be difficult to measure precisely the annual rental value to be imputed to consumer durables. For many durables, rental markets do not exist; for many others, rental prices vary depending upon terms, warranties, and other conditions. The amount to be imputed as rent could be determined by selecting an arbitrary yield on the cost of durables, say 10 percent a year, but any rules that allowed an immediate deduction for the purchase of the good and imputed annual rent as income until such time as the good is disposed of would be very difficult for the average taxpayer to understand. Allowing an immediate deduction for the cost of a durable and including only the subsequent sale price (if any) in income would permit tax-free consumption to the extent of forgone interest on the initial purchase price and depreciation of the good.

As the discussion of timing issues above suggests, if the purchase price of a consumer durable approximated the present value of the stream of imputed rents, denying an immediate deduction and ignoring income from the asset would be equivalent under an expenditure tax, given certain assumptions, to allowing a deduction and including the income and sale price of the asset in receipts. In the discussion of financial assets, the alternative of imposing tax initially, with income and sales omitted from expenditure tax accounting, was rejected principally because uncertainties about subsequent yield coupled with progressive tax rates rendered inappropriate the ex ante evaluation implicit in such a prepayment option.

In the context of consumer durables, at least two major distinctions argue in favor of the prepayment approach. First, though speculative gains and losses on consumer durables are not unknown, they are far less common than on investment assets and can be taken into account in a limited way without undermining the basic integrity of an expenditure tax. Second, the nature of the income from durables —imputed rent—renders incomprehensible to the average taxpayer the recommended alternative for financial assets (which would require imputed income to be included in receipts). Administrative considerations also argue for omitting this form of noncash income from tax accounting.

Furthermore, the real world absence of the conditions sufficient for the equivalence between immediate imposition of tax and subsequent taxation of yield and sale price is not as troublesome in the case of consumer durables as with financial assets generally. Differences among individuals that occur in returns from the use of most consumer durables are frequently attributable to consumer surplus— the fact that the individual would have paid more than the market price for the good—at the time of the purchase, rather than to subsequent events that, in effect, change the yield of the assets. Whether consumer surplus exists at the time of purchase is known only to the purchaser and simply cannot be taken into account for tax purposes. Expectations at the time of purchase must necessarily be measured by reference to market prices.

If market prices are accepted as the touchstone, returns from typical consumer durables (such as automobiles) may be regarded as more predictable than returns from financial assets (such as a motion picture or real estate investment or the purchase of common stock). Gains on consumer durables are infrequent, and losses on consumer durables will tend to occur either because the consumer was mistaken at the time of purchase about the satisfactions that the good would yield or because the product was defective. Taking the former losses into account would require exploration into consumers' minds and would be unacceptable for tax purposes. Losses from product defects are reflected to some degree in the prices of durables, which vary, for example, with the availability of warranties. If extraordinary misfortunes, such as sudden casualty losses, occurred, losses in excess of a certain amount might be deductible, as are casualty losses under the present income tax.

On balance, cash purchases of ordinary consumer durables should not be deductible, the asset's yield (imputed rental value) should be ignored, and subsequent sale price usually should be excluded from receipts. (This yield exemption treatment of consumer durables should be mandatory and not optional, to avoid problems of taxpayer manipulation.) Such rules are generally consistent with the present income tax treatment of purchases of consumer durables (I omit for the moment the deduction of interest on borrowing for consumer purchases, to be discussed later) and are similar to those recommended by others who have considered this issue.[19] Professor Andrews and the Meade committee, however, would limit the amount excluded on sale of the asset to the amount originally included in the tax base as consumption, usually the purchase price of the asset.

The discussion of consumer durables has thus far proceeded on the assumption that the original purchaser holds the consumer durable throughout its useful life. When durables are transferred to another, however, it becomes important to assure that an appropriate amount of total tax is paid and properly allocated among the owners. If the basic approach outlined above were followed, the purchase of either new or used durables would be an occasion for the imposition of expenditure tax liability. If one pays tax on the entire purchase price in the year of acquisition, sale proceeds generally should not be included in the tax base (for reasons set forth in detail in the previous section). The value of typical consumer durables, such as automobiles, furniture, and appliances, will depreciate over time and the sale price will be less than the purchase price. Though the actual sale price may reflect not only the decline in value resulting from actual use of the asset over time but also changes in market conditions that have occurred since the purchase of the asset, it seems appropriate to disregard the effect of such changes. Having imposed tax initially, it is theoretically inconsistent to impose a tax on sale; further-

19. See *Blueprints,* pp. 121–22; Meade committee report, p. 180; Lodin, *Progressive Expenditure Tax,* pp. 76–82; Advisory Commission on Intergovernmental Relations, *Expenditure Tax,* pp. 21–26; Mieszkowski, "Cash Flow Version of an Expenditure Tax"; and Andrews, "A Consumption-Type or Cash Flow Personal Income Tax," pp. 1155–57.

more, it would be administratively impossible to separate losses due to depreciation from offsetting gains (or additional losses) due to changes in market conditions.

This second difficulty seems compelling if the sale price is less than the purchase price, except when a sudden and unexpected casualty or theft cuts short actual use. Deductions for such loss could be allowed, limited to original cost (or value, if less) as under current law, and perhaps with more stringent dollar limitations. Allowing deductions for such losses only when the casualty occurred relatively early in the expected useful life of the asset might also be appropriate. Alternatively, if the cost of insuring durables was assumed to be a general cost of use, no deductions for casualty losses might be permitted. In any event, it is usually reasonable to assume that at least some portion of the decline in value of consumer durables, which have *not* suffered any casualty, is due to consumption use during the period the asset was held. As a practical matter, separating that amount from any change in price resulting from market forces would be impossible. Moreover, as the following example illustrates, such a rule would necessarily distinguish trade-ins from other forms of sales and purchases.

Assume each of two taxpayers A and B purchases an automobile for $5,000 in year 1 and that the car is worth $2,000 in year 3. Taxpayer A sells his car for $2,000 and purchases a new one. Taxpayer B trades in his car on an identical new one. First, it is virtually impossible to know what portion of the $3,000 decline in value of the old car is attributable to use and what portion is attributable to changes in market conditions having nothing to do with use. Second, in each case, the taxpayer has in effect sold an old car and purchased a new one. If no deduction is allowed for purchases of consumer durables, the original $5,000 purchase price will be taken into consumption in year 1 and, in the case of taxpayer B, the price of the new car (less the trade-in) will be accounted for in year 3. If the sale price of the old car is not included in income in year 3, taxpayer A will enjoy similar treatment. Taking the $2,000 into taxpayer A's income will, however, overstate his consumption relative to that of taxpayer B unless a deduction for an amount equal to the sale price is allowed when the new automobile is purchased. Such a rule would require limited deductions for purchases of consumer durables and would be difficult to administer; tracing the proceeds of sales of used durables or an aggregate limitation on the deduction based upon sales of used durables and purchases of other durables would be necessary.

If the sale price exceeds the original purchase price, however, different considerations obtain. In general, it seems reasonable to assume that when used goods sell for more than their original cost, market forces other than ordinary interest and depreciation have affected the price. Viewed ex post, if the expenditure tax were to impose tax initially on the purchase of a consumer durable but exempt from tax the durable's yield and sale price, and if sales were not taken into account when the sale price exceeds the purchase price, either an amount of consumption or speculative gains on durables would be excluded from the base. Although sale price will exceed purchase price only rarely in the case of typical consumer durables (for instance, when an automobile becomes a "classic car"), this state of affairs may occur frequently for certain types of durables, such as jewelry and works of art, that typically do not depreciate.

For example, assume that a person buys an oriental rug at the beginning of year 1 for $1,000 and sells it at the beginning of year 3 for $3,000. The theoretical analysis suggests that the person has enjoyed some consumption in the form of imputed rent while owning the rug. If the asset were sold for an amount equal to its purchase price plus an interest return ($1,210 in the example, assuming a 10 percent rate of interest) and the proceeds of sale were not included in receipts, this consumption would escape tax completely. If the asset were sold for an amount greater than its purchase price plus interest ($3,000 in the example) and the excess over the purchase price plus interest (the speculative gain) were not taken into account for tax purposes, an additional amount of future consumption ($3,000 minus $1,210 in the example) could be enjoyed free of expenditure tax.

Requiring any excess of sale price over purchase price to be included in the expenditure tax base would eliminate such possibilities of additional tax-free consumption. Taxpayers would not be able to purchase nondepreciating durables as a means of enjoying tax-free consumption due to speculative gains—an alternative that, if made widely available, would undermine the efforts to design rules for financial assets to assure that consumption financed out of speculative gains would be included in the tax base. To the extent, however, that a portion of the excess of sale price over purchase price represents a normal interest return, taxing such amounts at the time of sale would result in overtaxation, since by initially imposing tax on the durable's purchase price, expenditure tax would have been prepaid on normal interest returns. Nevertheless, this may usually be ignored, because for typical durables interest return is forgone in exchange for the use of the asset. In the case of nondepreciating durables, such as art or jewelry, that are enjoyed by the purchaser, an interest return has also often been forgone for using the asset, and the entire excess of the sale price over purchase price may reasonably be regarded as the result of market forces and thus an appropriate subject of tax. Theoretical purity would require distinguishing these cases in an effort to determine the portion of the sale price attributable to a normal interest return (for example, taxpayers who actually use jewelry might be treated differently from those who merely store it), but practical considerations argue against such an approach. For most durables, sale price will be less than purchase price and the issue will not arise. For durables the sale price of which is greater than historical cost, it does not seem unreasonable simply to include the excess in receipts.

Consumer Credit

Borrowing to finance consumption, particularly the purchase of consumer durables, is so common in our society that the treatment of consumer borrowing under an expenditure tax merits discrete attention. In some cases such credit is secured by a specific consumer durable—for example, an automobile or an appliance—and in others it is unsecured, as with the use of bank or gasoline credit cards or department store charge accounts. Both cases are considered here.

I suggested earlier in the paper that borrowing for investment in financial assets be treated on a cash flow basis, with loan proceeds included as receipts and repayments of principal and interest deducted. Such treatment, however, seems impractical for much consumer borrowing. With charge account purchases, for example, monthly variations are quite normal, and repayments occur throughout the taxable year. Merely to determine the total amount of annual borrowing or repayments would require onerous record-keeping and computational burdens for the average taxpayer. Comprehensive reporting of consumer borrowing might require different computations from persons who borrow in one month and repay in another than from persons who make all their purchases with cash. Matters would not be greatly simplified by requiring each taxpayer to report only annual fluctuations in consumer borrowing. Many taxpayers would find it quite difficult to determine exactly what their consumer debt totaled on December 31 of each year, and new information reporting requirements, which would be burdensome to lenders, would probably be necessary under an expenditure tax system that required unsecured consumer borrowing to be taken into account. It therefore seems necessary, as a practical matter, to omit typical unsecured consumer borrowing from receipts. This leaves two questions. (1) What is the appropriate scope of the omission of consumer borrowing from expenditure tax calculations? (2) What rules will apply when borrowing is omitted?

The guidelines for the second question have been presented above. In general, omitting consumer borrowing from expenditure tax calculations would entail excluding loans from the tax base and disallowing deduction of principal or interest repayments. If interest deductions were allowed when loan proceeds were included in receipts, parity would require that no deduction for interest be allowed when loan proceeds were omitted from receipts. The denial of deduction for interest under such circumstances may be viewed as increasing a person's tax liability by an amount that corresponds to the interest on the tax deferred by omitting loan proceeds from receipts.

When consumer durables are purchased with borrowed funds that are omitted from receipts, denying a deduction for the original purchase has an effect comparable to including in annual receipts a rental value attributable only to the taxpayer's equity in the durable, even though the taxpayer is enjoying the use of the entire durable without regard to how it was financed. Disallowing an interest deduction on funds borrowed to finance consumer durables would approximate the addition to receipts necessary to reflect the consumption value of the durable that would be taxed if its entire rental value were imputed annually. Other commentators have argued for denying an interest deduction on loans used to finance consumption purchases on the ground that such interest represents additional consumption expenditure.

Excluding consumer loans from receipts and allowing no interest deduction on such loans would ordinarily result in similar treatment of taxpayers whether or not they borrow to finance consumption purchases and would, in many common circumstances, approximate theoretically appropriate results. Including cash purchases of consumer durables in the expenditure tax base in the year of purchase and, in effect, including corresponding purchases with borrowed funds in the tax base as principal and interest on the loan were paid (since no deductions were permitted at that time), would, however, enable taxpayers to spread the taxation of consumption over a number of taxable years. When durables were financed with borrowed funds, taxation would follow the schedule for loan repayments and would therefore permit self-help averaging in some cases. Finally, the simplification advantages of this approach are substantial.

Limitations on the ability to exclude borrowing from expenditure tax receipts merits attention. If it is intended that a progressive expenditure tax be applied to a base that annually reflects as accurately as possible taxpayers' consumption, cash flow treatment of borrowing should be the general rule. Consumer loans would be permitted an alternative treatment of exclusion from receipts principally for reasons of administrative ease and taxpayer convenience and understanding. Denying deductions for interest on excluded loans would, however, significantly reduce any advantage that might occur because of the initial exclusion of the loan proceeds, and limitations on this exclusion alternative may be quite generous so long as interest deductions are denied.

There are basically two alternative methods for limiting the scope of the exclusion of borrowing from receipts in the case of consumer credit. One method, suggested by both the Meade committee's and Professor Lodin's reports, would be to allow borrowing to be omitted up to a specified amount, say $5,000 to $10,000, and require all borrowing in excess of that amount to be included in receipts and treated under the standard method. If the ceiling were sufficiently high, this alternative would exempt many low- and moderate-income families from the reporting burdens discussed above. For the family with two heavily mortgaged cars and numerous credit card and charge account purchases, however, a higher ceiling would seem necessary to eliminate record-keeping problems. But a ceiling set as high as $25,000 would permit borrowing to purchase financial assets and would tend either to greatly complicate the rules for deduction of purchases of financial assets or to permit unwarranted results like those described earlier. The Meade committee and Professor Lodin suggest limitations in the range of $2,500 to $7,500.[20]

As an alternative to a specified dollar limit, borrowing could be tax exempt and interest deductions denied only when indebtedness was incurred or continued to purchase or carry items for personal consumption. Such a rule would require tracing borrowing to its uses, but this is now required to some extent under section 163(d) of the Internal Revenue Code. Methods used under that provision for distinguishing borrowing for investment purposes from borrowing for personal purposes could be applied under an expenditure tax. These rules are not completely satisfactory, however, and are of limited application under current law because dollar limitations restrict their applicability to a relatively small number of taxpayers. On balance, a dollar limitation, say of up to $15,000, which does not require tracing loan proceeds to their use, seems preferable.

Housing

Housing may be regarded simply as a very expensive and long-lasting consumer durable. From this perspective, the theoretically appropriate treatment of housing under an expenditure tax is similar to that of other consumer durables: persons who rent housing should not be allowed any deduction for rent (which would be taxed as consumption), and an imputed rental value should be taxed to owner-occupiers. If rental value were imputed to owner-occupiers, it would be appropriate to treat the purchase and sale of housing in the same manner as financial assets generally; the cost of a home and any repairs, maintenance, or improvements would be deducted and the sale price would be included in full as a receipt at the time of sale. Likewise, home mortgage indebtedness would be treated on a cash flow basis.

As with consumer durables, however, the requirements for imputing rents to owner-occupiers would create severe problems of administration and taxpayer understanding. If such imputation were to be done precisely, it would be necessary to appraise rents annually for every owner-occupied home and take into account capital improvements made during the period of ownership. Because the duration of housing increases the likelihood that tax rate changes or unforeseen market changes will occur while it is owned, imputation of

20. Meade committee report, p. 179; Lodin, *Progressive Expenditure Tax,* p. 78.

rents is regarded by most commentators as more critical for housing than for other consumer durables.

Richard Slitor, for example, would allow a deduction for the purchase price of owner-occupied homes and include in consumption each year a ratable portion of the purchase price based upon an assumed useful life. Professor Andrews suggests allowing an owner-occupier to deduct the original purchase price (or the down payment) of his home, with income imputed to him at a specified interest rate on the amount deducted. Both the Meade committee's and Professor Lodin's reports would require a fixed annual imputation based upon a rate of return on the annual value of property; in Britain, 3 percent of the value, in Sweden, 5 percent.[21]

The principal advantage of these proposals would be to include an amount in the expenditure tax base intended to approximate the annual value of the taxpayer's consumption of housing services. Proponents argue that such an approach would achieve greater neutrality among taxpayers, whenever tax rates changed or persons moved into different tax brackets, than the prepayment method recommended here for other consumer durables and would lessen somewhat distortions in the consumption tax base caused by housing market changes unforeseen at the time of purchase.

But imputing rents to owner-occupiers would also be the appropriate theoretical treatment under the income tax, and notwithstanding the theorists' admonitions, imputation of rents has never achieved much favor with Congress for political reasons as well as reasons of administration and taxpayer comprehension. One cannot expect rent imputation to be politically easier under a consumption tax than under an income tax; therefore, as a practical matter, it seems essential to explore other alternatives.

Perhaps the best solution for expenditure taxation of housing would be to follow the treatment recommended for ordinary consumer durables. Under such a system, cash purchases of housing would be subjected to initial tax (that is, not deductible), yield (imputed rental value) would be ignored, and any excess of subsequent sale price over original cost would be included in receipts. Under such rules a pro-

21. Richard E. Slitor, "Administrative Aspects of Expenditures Taxation," in Richard A. Musgrave, ed., *Broad-Based Taxes: New Options and Sources* (Johns Hopkins University Press, 1973), pp. 227, 239–40; Andrews, "A Consumption-Type or Cash Flow Personal Income Tax," p. 1158; Meade committee report, pp. 221–22; Lodin, *Progressive Expenditure Tax,* pp. 83–89.

vision comparable to section 1034 of the Internal Revenue Code (which excludes gain on the sale of a personal residence if the proceeds are reinvested in a home) would seem desirable. An exclusion of a dollar amount of gain (such as a one-time $100,000 exclusion recently enacted by Congress) would not be necessary, however, because the general expenditure tax rules would allow offsetting deductions for the cost of investment assets purchased with the proceeds of sale. No adjustment would usually be required when houses were sold at a loss, but, as with consumer durables, a limited deduction for casualty losses seems appropriate.

Home mortgages could be treated like other consumer credit. Amounts borrowed would not be included in receipts and no deduction would be allowed for repayments of principal or interest. To better equate renters and homeowners, it would also be appropriate to deny any deduction for property taxes.

As a result, the consumption tax base would include (1) the original cash down payment on the purchase of housing, (2) mortgage payments of principal and interest, (3) property taxes, and (4) costs of repairs, maintenance, and improvements. To the extent that the return from housing approximates a typical rate of return on the owner's equity, including these costs in the consumer's tax base should put owner-occupiers on a tax basis approximately equal to that of renters. In the long run, rental payments can be expected to cover the owner's interest expenses, property taxes, repair and maintenance costs, and a rate of return on invested capital. Remaining disparities between homeowners and renters would be due principally to the difference between requiring homeowners to prepay expenditure tax on their cash investment (by including cash down payments in consumption) and requiring investors to treat rental housing on a cash flow basis as with other investments. Taxing the excess of the sale price over cost under this prepayment method would tend to eliminate any advantage that might otherwise accrue to homeowners if housing proved to be as good a speculative investment as it has been in the recent past.

As with consumer durables, this treatment implicitly assumes that when housing declines in value, the bulk of the decline is attributable to use and should be taxed. Thus when houses were sold for an amount equal to or less than their original purchase price, no amount would be entered into consumption tax receipts.

This system of taxation would avoid problems of taxing persons with limited cash incomes on an imputed rental value that might be excessive relative to their cash income. The principal theoretical objection to the recommended approach is that it would not take into account changes in a person's tax rate or value of housing that might occur during the time the house was owned. Such changes in tax rates seem likely to arise either because of changes in the statutory rate structure or because of fluctuations in a person's income under a progressive rate schedule.

Moreover, the rules that have been recommended would require the inclusion of the entire cash outlay for housing and other major durables in expenditures for the taxable year of purchase and would tend to overstate the amount of consumption for that year. Spreading of the tax burden over a period of years would then be necessary because failure to permit some form of averaging in a progressive tax system would result in the application of higher marginal tax rates to consumption. Since general self-help averaging by taxpayer election has been rejected for consumer durables and financial assets and loans, a general averaging provision would be necessary under an expenditure tax.

Notwithstanding the basic validity of the recommended approach, there are certain political obstacles. For example, including mortgage interest and property taxes in the tax base can be expected to encounter serious political resistance in Congress. Notwithstanding their theoretical inappropriateness under an expenditure tax, other benefits for owner-occupiers might also be enacted. If a significant portion of housing consumption by owner-occupiers were excluded from the tax base by special provisions, allowing a deduction for rent might then become appropriate to ensure equal treatment. The outcome might well be to exclude from the expenditure tax base most taxpayers' housing costs. Such a scheme would tend to misallocate resources by encouraging taxpayers to overconsume housing relative to other taxable forms of consumption and would tend to create inequities, since the deductions and exclusions that would probably be enacted would tend to be of greater value for people in higher tax brackets. Similar inefficiencies and inequities currently exist under the income tax, however, and do not seem to engender much congressional concern. In any event, under an expenditure tax, no distortions would be created by the failure to include unrealized housing appreciation in income, since appreciation would not usually be included in receipts until devoted to consumption. On balance, it seems likely that even if housing were completely excluded from the expenditure tax base, distortion would be less than under the current income tax.

Recommendations

I recommend an identical approach for the taxation of consumer durables and the taxation of housing.

—No deductions should be permitted for the purchase of consumer durables and housing; yield in the form of imputed rents should be ignored; and when the sale price does not exceed the original cost, no amount need be included in the expenditure tax base upon sale. When the sale price of a house or consumer durable exceeds original cost, such excess should be added to expenditure tax receipts, when received.

—Loans for the purchase of consumption goods or housing should ordinarily not be included in expenditure tax receipts, and no deduction should be allowed for interest or principal payments. A dollar limitation might be used in implementing this rule.

—No deductions should be allowed for property taxes on consumer durables or owner-occupied homes.

—A limited deduction for sudden and unexpected uninsured losses due to theft or casualties involving consumer durables or housing might be allowed. This deduction should be limited to cases occurring early in the expected useful life of the asset or to a dollar amount equal to the original purchase price (which was included in the expenditure tax base) reduced to reflect actual use, or value, if less. No deduction should be allowed in excess of the amount originally included in the expenditure tax base. Limitations could be adopted so that this deduction would be allowed only for extraordinary losses, and they could be set high enough to encourage most people to insure against such losses.

Gifts and Bequests and the Taxation of the Family

In designing any personal tax system, an important issue is whether the filing unit is to be the individual or a group, such as husband and wife or the entire family, including minor children. In general, the arguments relating to the choice of the filing unit under the income tax apply with similar force in an expenditure tax context, although it does seem more reasonable to regard the family as the appropriate unit for measuring consumption than for measuring the accumulation of income or wealth. But the principal advantage of a family filing unit under an expenditure tax would be its effect on the taxation of gifts and bequests.

Individual versus Family Filing

Under the present income tax law, the income of husbands and wives may be aggregated and joint returns may be filed; taxation is then based on a rate schedule in which brackets are twice as wide as those for married persons who file separate returns. The income of children or other dependent family members is not aggregated with that of parents but is taxed separately under a rate schedule that is applicable to single persons generally. Until 1969 single persons were usually subject to the same rate schedule as married persons filing separately, but since 1969 they have been eligible for a separate rate schedule. Since 1951 a still different rate schedule has been applicable to so-called heads of households—unmarried persons with dependents in the household—with rates about midway between those applicable to married couples filing jointly and single persons.

Under this system, when a person marries someone with little or no income, his taxes are reduced, because he becomes eligible for filing a joint return. On the other hand, when a husband and wife earn relatively equal incomes, they would reduce tax by divorcing, because they obtain little benefit from the income-splitting privilege accorded joint returns and would pay less tax if they filed as single persons. The nonneutralities produced by the current system have prompted detailed analyses by lawyers and economists that have greatly increased our understanding of the issues at stake.[22] Unfortunately, however, recent discussions about whether the individual or the family is the more appropriate unit for the assessment of income

22. See Boris I. Bittker, "Federal Income Taxation and the Family," *Stanford Law Review*, vol. 27 (July 1975), pp. 1389–1463; Harvey S. Rosen, "Applications of Optimal Tax Theory to Problems in Taxing Families and Individuals," in *Compilation of OTA Papers*, vol. 1 (GPO, 1978); Michael J. McIntyre and Oliver Oldman, "Treatment of the Family," in Joseph A. Pechman, ed., *Comprehensive Income Taxation* (Brookings Institution, 1977), pp. 205–34.

tax have largely served to confirm that neither choice is free of difficulties.

Whichever choice is taken, conflict between fundamental principles, each of which is independently embodied in current law, is inevitable. No progressive tax schedule can satisfy both the following criteria: (1) the tax on a family should depend on its total income regardless of how each family member contributes to that income; and (2) the total tax liability of two persons who marry should be the same as the total tax they paid before marriage. It is simply impossible to have a progressive rate schedule, a marriage-neutral tax system, *and* equal taxes on families of equal size with equal incomes. One must choose which of these principles should be paramount.

A tax system based on individual filing has the advantages of being easy to define and familiar, since it approximates the system under the present income tax. On the other hand, a family filing unit treats the family as the main economic unit for assessing tax and bases taxation on consolidated income or consumption without regard to legal ownership of receipts and property within the family. The fact that a family filing unit ignores individual property rights within the family has both advantages and disadvantages. It would permit simplification of the taxation of gifts and bequests and would eliminate most tax-planning problems relating to intrafamily transfers of property. On the other hand, whenever individual family members behave as autonomous persons in exercising their legal property rights, taxing the family as a unit would produce inevitable conflicts. To the extent that family practices regarding property rights and consumption decisions vary, any definition of the family for aggregation of the tax base would produce some arbitrary results.

Further study is necessary to know what rules would be required for taxation of family units.[23] For example, when adolescent children are involved, it would probably become necessary to enact an "innocent parent or child" rule analogous to the innocent spouse rules under the current income tax. Likewise, defining the family unit would create difficulties when parents are separated or divorced and children share their time with the two parents. The application of a progressive rate schedule to family units would have the effect of tax-

23. See "Evaluation of the Proposed Model Comprehensive Income Tax, Special Committee on Simplification, Section of Taxation, American Bar Association," *The Tax Lawyer,* vol. 32 (Spring 1979).

ing the children's income or consumption at their parents' highest marginal rates and seems likely to result in certain inequities.

Taxation of family units might include a special deduction for two-earner families, and differences in family size might be taken into account either through personal exemptions or tax credits. An exemption seems the more appropriate mechanism for adjusting the tax base to reflect the changes in the standard of living that occur because of the addition of new family members. Tax rates can be adjusted to achieve the desired level of progressivity, while taking into account any credits or exemptions used to differentiate among families of different sizes.

Gifts and Bequests

In my analysis of the treatment of gifts and bequests, I assume that filing status under an expenditure tax will be equivalent to that under the current income tax, with separate rate schedules for married couples filing jointly, married couples filing separately, unmarried individuals, and heads of households.

Taxation of donor or donee. Some income tax commentators, such as Henry Simons and the Carter Commission in Canada,[24] have argued that gifts and bequests should be included in the incomes of both the recipient and the donor. But the better view is that income tax should be imposed only once on gifts within a family—whether on the donor or on the donee—since there is only one source of earnings and one case of spending.

Under current law, gifts and bequests are excluded from the gross income of the donee or heir. If a person earns income and donates some portion to another, the income is taxed to the donor but not to the donee. Whether the current income tax rules are theoretically appropriate is debatable. Because the selection of an income tax implies some reliance on sources rather than uses of funds, present income tax rules are defensible; the choice of the donor as the appropriate taxpayer may be justified, since he is the income earner in the first instance and has exercised control over his receipts. Besides, since donors tend to be subject to higher marginal income tax rates than donees, present law inhibits somewhat the shifting of income

24. See Simons, *Personal Income Taxation,* chap. 6; and *Report of the Royal Commission on Taxation,* vol. 3 (Ottawa: Queen's Printer, 1966), chap. 17.

among family members to take advantage of lower marginal tax rates, which usually apply to children.

Under an expenditure tax, the structural issue is basically the same —whether gifts should be taxed to the donor or donee—but the theoretical result seems somewhat more obvious. An expenditure tax is intended to impose a progressive levy on consumption, and the donee, not the donor, will spend the amount of the gift or bequest. The commentators tend to agree, therefore, that an expenditure tax should exclude gifts and bequests from the donor's tax base and include such amounts in the donee's receipts.

On the other hand, if the family is considered the basic economic unit for consumption, taxation should be imposed at the marginal rates resulting from the aggregation of total family consumption. Such a result seems more nearly approximated under a system that treats gifts as consumption of the donor. Failure to tax gifts to the donor would enable families to shift tax to the family member subject to the lowest marginal rates. For example, under a system taxing gifts to donees, if consumption by parents were subjected to a 60 percent marginal rate of tax and a 20 percent rate applied to their children's consumption, a cash gift of $1,000 would result in a deduction to the parents worth $600 in tax savings and a receipt that, if consumed, would produce only $200 of tax liability to the children.

Even commentators who consider taxing gifts to donees theoretically appropriate under an expenditure tax have voiced concern about such results. Two responses to this problem are common: it is considered necessary either to treat the family as the appropriate taxable unit under an expenditure tax, or to impose a separate tax on donative transfers, similar to the unified transfer tax on gifts and estates of current law, to inhibit expenditure tax avoidance through gifts and bequests. Taxing gifts to donors is generally not recommended; given cash flow treatment of investment assets, developing rules that would tax gifts at the marginal expenditure tax rates of the donee is reasonably straightforward, but taxing gifts as if they were consumption of the donor is somewhat more difficult.

Adopting expenditure tax rules that follow the basic income tax treatment of gifts—which allows no deduction to donors and requires no inclusion in receipts by donees—would be ineffective in prohibiting shifting of expenditure tax to lower marginal rates. By purchasing a $1,000 investment asset the parents in the above example would obtain an immediate deduction worth $600. If the asset were transferred to their children, only $200 of tax would be due if the asset were sold for $1,000 and its proceeds consumed. To impose expenditure tax at the donor's marginal rate, it would be necessary to treat gifts and bequests of assets as if they were sales by the transferor, thereby including in the donor's receipts the fair market value of the asset at the time of the gift and permitting no offsetting deduction for making the gift.

Such a rule would most likely be rejected for two reasons. First, under an expenditure tax, such a provision would make gifts disadvantageous relative to both retention of assets and actual sales. If an asset were retained by the donor, no tax would be due; and if the asset were sold, no tax would be due if the proceeds were reinvested. Second, from time to time during the past fifteen years, income tax proposals have been advanced to treat gifts and bequests of appreciated property as if the transferred asset had been sold by the donor. Such proposals have consistently been rejected by Congress. In fact, until recently it has been possible to completely avoid income tax by holding appreciated assets until death, and the limited carry-over basis provision enacted in 1976 to deal with this problem was postponed by legislation in 1978 and may well be repealed.

Under the income tax, therefore, in the case of lifetime gifts of appreciated property, taxation of gain is deferred until the asset is sold by the donee; it is then subjected to tax at the donee's rates. This rule enables taxpayers with appreciated assets to shift taxation of gain to family members with lower rates, notwithstanding the general rule that taxes donors on amounts transferred. Similar results can be achieved through bequests, and for most taxpayers income tax on bequests can be avoided altogether. It seems quite unlikely that Congress would respond more favorably to a proposal to tax gifts or bequests as sales under an expenditure tax, even though the tax avoidance possibilities would be greater, since the cost of assets would be deductible at the time of purchase. Results comparable to those under current law would occur only if amounts previously deducted were "recaptured" and included in the donor's tax base at the time of the gift.

If gifts were taxed to donees, however, the treatment of investment assets would be substantially simpler. Usually when assets are transferred, the donor will have deducted the original purchase of the asset as savings, and no additional deduction should be allowed at the time of the gift. By the same token, including the current value of investment assets in the donee's receipts would usually serve no purpose, since an offsetting deduction should be allowed. If the donee were to sell the donated asset and reinvest its proceeds in another investment asset, proceeds would be included in receipts and a deduction would be allowed for the reinvestment. The taxation of gifts of investment assets would, in effect, be deferred until the asset were sold and its proceeds used by the donee for consumption. Thus when investment assets are transferred, no deduction would be allowed the donor and no amount would have to be included in the donee's receipts until the asset was sold.

This treatment should apply whether assets have appreciated or depreciated in value while held by the donor. If consumption were to be allocated to the donee, treating a gift as if it were a sale by the donor would be unnecessary. (With such a rule, the donor would merely include the sale price in receipts and receive an offsetting deduction for the value of the gift.) Likewise, the donee would include the gift in receipts and receive a deduction. No tax would be due until the donee sold the assets and used its proceeds for consumption.

Since the donor would be allowed an immediate deduction for the purchase of investment assets, the problems of basis of gifts under the income tax would ordinarily disappear under an expenditure tax. The donee's basis in the asset would in effect be zero; all sale proceeds would be included in receipts. Thus an expenditure tax avoids many of the complexities and record-keeping difficulties that occur under the income tax in connection with determining basis of donated or bequeathed property.[25]

Under a regime that taxes gifts to donees, transfers of cash should be deductible by the donor and includable in receipts of the donee. This rule would merely eliminate any need for donors to purchase investment assets to achieve similar results. As with other cash re-

---

25. Expenditure tax rules comparable to the current income tax rule of code section 267, which disallows forever any loss deduction in the case of gifts, would be inappropriate and unwieldy. Since the donor would have deducted the original purchase price of the asset, such a rule would probably have to take the form of a "recapture" provision that would reinstate into the receipts of either the donor or the donee a portion of the previously allowed deduction equivalent to the amount of the loss on the asset. There is no reason for such a rule.

ceipts, the donee should be allowed a deduction if the money is invested but not if the amount transferred is consumed. *A de minimis* provision should be adopted so that small gifts among family members need not be taken into account for tax purposes. Furthermore, donative intent by the transferor should not be required; transfers to provide consumption by the donee should, for example, be covered under these rules even if providing such consumption is a legal obligation of the donor.

Transfers of consumer durables. Professor Andrews has suggested special rules for gifts of assets (like works of art or valuable jewelry) that are relatively long-lived consumption goods not likely to depreciate and that would be subjected to a modified yield exemption treatment, with no deduction allowable at the time of purchase.[26] He argues that the recipient should be treated as if he received cash and purchased the durable in question, because the inclusion of the consumption value of such a durable in the tax base of the donor at an earlier time might not accurately reflect the good's consumption value at the time of the gift. Unanticipated events subsequent to the time of purchase might have increased or decreased its value, and tax rates might have changed. In the absence of Professor Andrews's proposed rule, donees would enjoy greater consumption than they would under the theoretically correct treatment of consumer durables, which would include an imputed annual rental value in the receipts of the person who holds the durable.

The basic problem arises, however, because of the treatment of consumer durables recommended above, but if that treatment were generally acceptable, no additional tax should be imposed at the time of a gift or bequest. The donor could hold and enjoy the asset in question without paying additional expenditure tax. Allowing the shifting of such enjoyment within the family might permit such enjoyment over several generations (estate and gift tax considerations aside), but, under the rules described above, whenever the asset is sold, the entire amount of gain, if any, would be included in the seller's taxable receipts. Imposing tax on a donee who receives a work of art that has appreciated since purchase by the donor, for example, would require the donee to pay tax to retain the asset within the family, whereas no tax would be due if the work of art were held

26. Andrews, "A Consumption-Type or Cash Flow Personal Income Tax," pp. 1159–60.

by the donor or sold and investment assets purchased. Expenditure tax rules that would encourage a Rockefeller to sell art to buy securities at least once each generation do not seem wise. Moreover, delaying taxation until assets are sold would avoid difficulties when donees are given assets, such as grandmother's grand piano, that they do not really want, but that, for family reasons, they cannot sell. On balance, assuming a regime that taxes gifts to donees, I recommend that the treatment of gifts and bequests of consumer durables be consistent with that of other assets: no deduction should be allowed the donor and no amount should be includable in the donee's receipts until he sells the asset. Because the donor was taxed on the purchase of the asset (since no deduction was allowed), the donee should, in effect, receive a basis in the property equal to the purchase price to the donor; in other words, the donee should receive a carry-over basis similar to that under current law.

If the Andrews rule were preferred, however, donees would be taxed on the value of assets received and no offsetting deduction would be allowed. Given the congressional proclivity for enacting exceptions to estate and gift tax rules for gifts of certain types of assets or to certain recipients, such a rule would most likely be burdened with exceptions. It is easy to imagine, for example, forgiveness of tax on donations of a residence or even of a work of art to a spouse or orphan. If numerous exceptions were required for political reasons, special rules for gifts of consumer durables should be rejected on the ground of complexity alone.

Gifts in trust. As with outright gifts, taxing gifts or bequests in trust to donors rather than donees would introduce complexities under an expenditure tax. If donees and heirs were taxed, gifts of investment assets or cash in trust would pose no special problems, and the taxation of trusts, which is very complex under the income tax, would be quite simple. Since trusts do not engage in consumption, there would usually be no expenditure tax at the trust level, whether income or assets were accumulated or distributed. A gift from a donor to a trust would be treated by the donor like any other gift. The trust would not be taxable on receipt of cash or assets, but its beneficiaries would include in receipts any distributions made from a trust, whether out of income or corpus. If amounts distributed by the trust were reinvested by the beneficiary, a deduction would be allowed; if the trust proceeds were consumed, the beneficiary would be taxed.

The deferral of tax that would occur as a result of investments and accumulations of income at the trust level would provide no particular expenditure tax advantage, since similar deferral could be obtained through investments at the individual level. It would therefore not be necessary to adopt rules similar to those under the income tax that distinguish simple trusts (which distribute all their income) from complex trusts (which accumulate income). Likewise, the income tax throwback rules would not be necessary under an expenditure tax. Regardless of the terms of the trust, trust income and corpus would be taxed only when distributed to and consumed by the trust beneficiaries. It would, however, be necessary to adopt rules to ensure that tax avoidance is not possible through the purchase or receipt of consumer durables, including works of art and jewelry, by trusts.

Rules that distinguish grantor trusts from other trusts under the income tax could also be eliminated if the basic scheme of taxing donees on gifts were adopted. If, under the terms of the trust, property actually reverted to the grantor, for example, through the exercise of a power of revocation, distributions from the trust would be included in the grantor's receipts in the year of revocation.

On the other hand, if it were desired to tax the donor on amounts transferred by gift or bequest, the taxation of transfers to trusts would be more difficult. As with outright gifts, it would seem necessary to treat gifts of assets in trust as if the donor had sold the asset at the time of the transfer (or, at a minimum, to "recapture" amounts previously deducted with respect to the asset). In addition, if taxing gifts and bequests to donors were intended to ensure tax on appreciation at least once a generation, rules taxing generation-skipping trusts would become necessary.

Commercial gifts. Taxing gifts and bequests to donees would have the advantage of simplifying the taxation of donative transfers to persons outside the family. Under the income tax, there have been considerable difficulties in determining how to treat transfers that occur in the context of a commercial relationship. Payments to widows of deceased employees have proved especially troublesome. If a transfer is characterized as a gift, it is excludable from the recipient's income and, if over $25, not deductible by the payor. On the other hand, if the transfer is compensation for services, it is includable in the recipient's income and often deductible by the payor. Under the income tax, the resolution of this issue depends upon the intent of the payor; the Supreme Court has ruled that whenever the issue is litigated, the trial court should determine the payor's intent by applying its "experience with the mainsprings of human conduct."[27] Taxing gifts to donees would tend to eliminate these problems; transfers of cash, for example, would be deductible by the payor and includable in the recipient's receipts regardless of the motives of the parties. Some problems, however, would remain for gifts by private persons in a nonbusiness context. While such amounts would be taxed to the donee in any case, they should not be deductible if they are in fact payment for consumption services.

Summary and Recommendations

Taxing gifts to donees rather than donors has two advantages under an expenditure tax. First, it seems theoretically consistent with the selection of a consumption base for taxation; the donee, not the donor, will spend the amount of the gift or bequest. Second, assuming that (in accordance with my recommendations above) financial assets are taxed on a cash flow basis, such rules would be much more simple than taxing gifts and bequests to donors in cases of outright transfers of property, transfers in trust, and commercial gifts. If taxation to donees were desired, it should be implemented by allowing donors to deduct gifts of cash (in excess of *de minimis* amounts) and requiring donees to include such amounts in receipts. No deductions should be allowed for gifts of property, and donees should include in receipts only proceeds from sales of donated property.

The major disadvantage of taxing gifts to donees is that it would permit families to use gifts to determine who shall be subject to tax. Under a progressive rate schedule, transfers from parents to children would be used to shift tax to lower brackets; opportunities for such tax shifting would be much greater under an expenditure tax than under the current income tax, where such opportunities are ordinarily limited to transfers of appreciated property. Taxing gifts to donors would solve this problem but would require treating gifts of investment assets as sales of such assets with no deduction allowed for gifts. Alternatively, results no worse than those that occur under the current income tax (which allows transfers of appreciated property to

27. *Commissioner* v. *Duberstein,* 363 U.S. 278 (1960); compare *Estate of Sydney J. Carter* v. *Commissioner,* 453 F.2d 61 (1971).

persons in lower brackets) could be achieved by recapturing amounts previously deducted as a receipt of the donor.

If direct taxation of gifts to donors were regarded as unduly complex or politically impractical, taxing shared family consumption at appropriate marginal rates would probably require treating the family as the taxable unit. If a family unit, which would include husband and wife and any minor (or perhaps full-time student) children, were selected as the unit for expenditure taxation, the most troublesome opportunities for shifting taxation to lower marginal rates would disappear. Gifts would not vary tax consequences until amounts were transferred out of the family unit, and when such transfers were made, imposing expenditure taxes at donees' marginal rates would usually seem appropriate.

Even with filing based upon a family rather than an individual unit, however, it does not seem likely that the expenditure tax will significantly limit the amount of wealth that can be accumulated and transferred within a family. Consequently, some observers argue that donors should always be taxed on gifts and bequests, even if that requires complex rules, such as taxing unrealized gains at death, grantor trust rules, and expenditure tax rules similar to the generation-skipping trust rules of current law. To the extent that the problem is regarded as one of undue accumulation of wealth, however, it would be better addressed by employing an effective and comprehensive wealth tax (perhaps in the form of an estate and gift or accessions tax and perhaps coupled with a periodic tax on trust assets) than by taxing gifts and bequests under an expenditure tax, which presumably would be enacted with a progressive rate schedule designed to tax periodic consumption.

Amounts Available for Consumption: Receipts

Computation of the expenditure tax base requires deduction of amounts saved or invested from amounts available for consumption, with the balance treated as consumption expenditures. If this is to be an accurate measure, amounts available for consumption should, to the extent practical, include all categories of receipts. Failure to include in receipts amounts available for consumption would translate directly into an understatement of consumption; taxpayers would be able to deduct amounts saved from a limited number of receipts and enjoy consumption tax free.

In fact, a comprehensive definition of consumption may be more critical to an expenditure tax than to an income tax. Under an income tax, if a taxpayer's consumption is omitted from the tax base, some of his savings may nevertheless be subjected to tax. Under an expenditure tax, there would simply be no tax base if consumption escaped taxation. Moreover, the comprehensiveness of the tax base would have an important effect on the expenditure tax rate structure. If the base were significantly less than the current income tax base, the rate structure would have to be higher and more steeply progressive than current income tax rates for similar revenue and distribution of tax burden to obtain. Omission of substantial amounts of consumption from the tax base because of their form would offend the concepts of horizontal and vertical equity and induce allocative inefficiencies.

Notwithstanding the differences in expenditure tax receipts and income, the concepts are more similar than different. All items of income includable under the income tax would constitute receipts available for consumption under an expenditure tax. For many taxpayers, expenditure tax receipts and income would be identical in most years; this would, for example, be true for taxpayers who received only wages and interest or dividends.

Some of the differences between income and expenditure tax receipts have been described above; others are taken up in this section. The issues considered here have been thoroughly discussed in the income tax context, particularly in connection with debates over "comprehensive income taxation," and it is neither possible nor desirable to review in detail such well-traveled ground.[28] In some instances, however, differences between income and expenditure taxation produce important variances in the analysis. In a few other instances, the issues seem important enough to warrant a brief discussion. I consider in turn the taxation of fringe benefits; the taxation of imputed income and consumption; the exclusion from receipts for interest on state and local bonds; the taxation of life insurance investments and proceeds and annuities; payments from the government, including social security benefits; distributions from charities; and, finally, other statutory exclusions under the income tax.

It has recently become apparent that Congress has little desire to

28. See Boris I. Bittker and others, *A Comprehensive Income Tax Base? A Debate* (Branford, Conn.: Federal Tax Press, 1968); Joseph A. Pechman, ed., *Comprehensive Income Taxation* (Brookings Institution, 1977).

tax the above items undcr present law, but in general I assume here
that this political attitude would not exist under an expenditure tax.
My inquiry will suggest practical solutions from a perspective that
recognizes that it would be better expenditure tax policy to include
all items in the tax base that can reasonably be viewed as serving to
satisfy personal needs and desires.

Nonstatutory Fringe Benefits

The Internal Revenue Code provides little guidance for assuring
the taxation of consumption obtained in a business context. Important exclusions have occurred, particularly through the provision of
nontaxable fringe benefits by employers and through the deduction
of business expenses, such as entertainment and travel, that have a
substantial consumption component (business deductions are considered later).

Section 61 of the Internal Revenue Code defines income as including compensation for services whether in cash or in kind, but statutory
exceptions to that rule operate to exclude certain fringe benefits from
income. Examples are employer contributions to certain group legal
services plans and meals and lodging under certain circumstances.
Moreover, a wide variety of employee benefits usually referred to as
"nonstatutory fringe benefits" has been excluded from income by
Internal Revenue Service regulations, rulings, or administrative practice. Examples are employees' discounts, airline and railroad passes,
physical examinations, and meals in free or subsidized company
cafeterias. The ability of certain taxpayers to obtain tax-free fringe
benefits violates standards of tax equity and produces allocative inefficiencies.

The horizontal equity standard will be violated whenever the availability of tax-free compensation varies significantly among jobs; for
example, as between union and nonunion workers. Likewise, to the
extent that the taxation of an item depends upon whether it is furnished by employers, whether employers reimburse employees' expenses in obtaining the item, or whether employees bear the costs of
the item directly, horizontal equity will tend to be violated. Close
coordination is therefore required between rules that include employee benefits in the tax base and those that allow employees or
self-employed persons to deduct items of consumption as business expenses. Particular care would have to be exercised under an expendi-

ture tax to prevent highly compensated persons from structuring their remuneration so as to receive a maximum amount of compensation in the form of fringe benefits. Otherwise, the same classes of persons principally able to reduce taxes by deductions for savings would also obtain a disproportionate exemption of consumption, and the prospect of genuine progressivity would be undermined.

Moreover, if significant amounts of compensation were excluded from the tax base, employers would be given an incentive to provide such compensation. For example, if employees were, on average, subjected to a 25 percent marginal expenditure tax rate, they would prefer $76 of tax-free compensation in kind to $100 of taxable wages. Employers would likewise prefer paying $76 to paying $100, since there would be no difference in treatment at the employer level. Such lower relative cost of in-kind benefits would produce economic nonneutralities, and a significant proportion of employees' compensation would probably take the form of excluded benefits. By the same token, such exclusions would tend to induce labor to shift to situations amenable to the provision of excluded compensation.

Given the variety of fringe benefits, developing practical rules that include most of such benefits in the expenditure tax base will be extremely difficult. Under the existing income tax, the Internal Revenue Code and current regulations are general and largely uninformative. Little published guidance is available to taxpayers or revenue agents. A discussion draft of proposed regulations relating to fringe benefits was published in 1975 by the Treasury but was subsequently withdrawn, and the Internal Revenue Service has recently been precluded by Congress from publishing either a comprehensive set of regulations or a complete set of examples through issuance of revenue rulings.

Under an expenditure tax, a comprehensive set of principles of fringe benefit taxation must be adopted either by legislation or regulation. The basic rules must distinguish working conditions from in-kind compensation. The former would be regarded as primarily for the benefit of the employer and therefore not includable as receipts to the employee. An important noncompensatory business purpose for providing to an employee the good or service in question should be prerequisite for exclusion. In other words, benefits would not be excluded unless the good or service were related to the nature of the employee's work and were something ordinarily useful to someone in the employee's position. A benefit provided at the employer's place of business should be more likely to be characterized as a working condition, but this should not be determinative.

Other relevant factors, but none of which alone should be determinative, would include the following. (1) Did the employee have an option to accept or reject the good or service? If so, this would argue for inclusion. (2) Was the good or service something that the employee would normally pay for out of after-tax dollars? If so, this would argue for including an amount as consumption. (3) Was the good or service provided to the employee's family? If so, it would most likely be regarded as compensation. (4) Was the good or service provided routinely or only sporadically? If the former, inquiries should be made to determine whether it was part of the negotiated wage structure and therefore something the employee expected as compensation.

When the compensation or consumption element of a good or service provided to employees by employers is readily identifiable and a reasonable allocation is possible, allocation should be the general rule. This occurs under the current income tax, for example, when employer-provided automobiles are available for the personal use of employees; amounts are included in income based upon an allocation of mileage between business and personal use.

To convert a set of general principles like these into a workable system, Congress or the Treasury must provide a reasonably comprehensive set of examples indicating whether particular goods or services are includable in an employer's receipts and, if so, at what value. *De minimis* rules and reasonable rules for the valuation of fringe benefits are essential to fringe benefit taxation.

For any fringe benefits taxation system to work, employers should withhold tax on amounts that will be included in employees' receipts. The Supreme Court's recent income tax opinion in *Central Illinois Public Service Commission* v. *United States*, 98 S.Ct. 917 (1978), suggests that a greater degree of certainty is required for withholding than for including amounts in income. Under the rules suggested above, record-keeping burdens and the requirements of allocating compensation to particular employees would often be onerous to employers. It would be virtually impossible, for example, to allocate the benefit of a company-owned swimming pool to employees according to their use. Under the income tax, rules could be enacted to disallow deductions to employers when allocating fringe benefits to specific persons was difficult or impossible. Such an alternative would not, however, be available under an expenditure tax, since a decision to tax consumption implies the elimination of business income taxes on production.

If the principles described above were adopted, items such as supper money, employee discounts, free admission to athletic or entertainment events, employees' use of vacation facilities and country club memberships, meals and lodging provided to employees, and interest-free loans provided to employees would be includable in expenditure tax receipts, and withholding would be required. Although the alternative of disallowing business deductions would not be available, it might be possible to impose a special excise tax on fringe benefits that were difficult to allocate to individual employees.

Taxation of such items would not be easy under an expenditure tax, either politically or administratively. The only practical alternative, however, seems to be the exclusion of such items from the tax base, which seems even less acceptable than under an income tax.

Imputed Income or Consumption

Imputed income or consumption normally takes the form of benefits from labor on one's own behalf or benefits from the ownership of property. Such benefits are usually regarded by economists as income that should be taxed under an income tax and that should be included in receipts under an expenditure tax. Imputed income from the ownership of property—from housing and consumer durables—has been discussed above and rejected in favor of other methods.

Although, in general, imputed income from labor on one's own behalf has been excluded under the income tax, the case law is somewhat inconsistent. For example, cases decided the same year held that the value of farm products consumed by the owner of a farm is not income, but that the owner of a grocery store must include in income groceries used for home consumption.[29]

The largest amount of imputed income from services in the United

29. Compare *Morris* v. *Commissioner,* 9 B.T.A. 1273 (1928) with *Dicenso* v. *Commissioner,* 11 B.T.A. 620 (1928). See also *Commissioner* v. *Minzer,* 279 F.2d 338 (2d Cir. 1960) (insurance agent's commissions on policies on his own life includable in income); *Commissioner* v. *Daehler,* 281 F.2d 823 (5th Cir. 1960) (real estate broker's commissions on his own purchases taxable).

States comes from services rendered by homemakers to their families. Recent estimates have suggested that income taxation of imputed income from domestic services of homemakers might increase the income tax base by as much as $200 billion. Nevertheless, it is inconceivable that imputed income from housework, from farming, or from other forms of personal services would as a rule be included in receipts under an expenditure tax. The exclusion of imputed income of homemakers is, however, related to other aspects of the tax law—for example, deductions for child-care expenses. A special deduction or exclusion for two-earner families seems appropriate as a means of somewhat reducing the relative tax advantage of spouses who perform domestic services.[30] Nevertheless, nonneutralities resulting from the failure to include imputed income and consumption in the expenditure tax base are likely to occur as they have under the income tax.

Interest on State and Local Bonds

Notwithstanding periodic attacks from tax reformers, the exclusion from income of interest on state and local bonds is among the most enduring features of the income tax, having been in the law since its adoption in 1913. Though the exclusion was originally justified on the ground that income taxation of state and local obligations would be unconstitutional, the basic justification for its continuation is that an interest exclusion reduces the costs to state and local governments of capital outlays for such projects as schools and other public buildings, highways, water and sewage systems, and anti-pollution facilities.

The effect of the income tax exclusion is to allow state and local governments to borrow at interest costs lower than those incurred by private corporations on bonds of comparable risk. An ancillary effect of the exclusion is to provide windfall tax savings to individuals who would be subject to federal income tax rates higher than the rate of marginal purchasers. Historically, the ratio of yield on tax-exempt bonds to that of taxable bonds has been as low as 60 percent but in recent years has hovered around 75 percent. The higher the ratio of yields on tax-exempt to taxable bonds, the greater the windfall to

30. See *Blueprints,* p. 25, which recommends that only 75 percent of the wage income of secondary earners be included in income under a "comprehensive income tax."

individuals and institutions otherwise subject to high marginal rates of tax, and the greater the total revenue cost to the federal government relative to state and local government savings in interest charges.

In recent years various proposals have been advanced to tax state and local bond interest while maintaining reduced interest costs for state and local governments through a direct federal subsidy. In general, however, even partial replacement of the tax benefit with a direct subsidy has been unattractive to state and local governments and has failed to muster a majority in Congress. In light of this attitude, it may be useful to inquire about the expenditure tax effect of an exclusion from receipts of interest on state and local obligations.

As outlined earlier, investment assets would usually be taxed on a cash flow basis, with purchases of assets deducted when made and yield and sales price of assets includable when received. The effect of these rules would be to permit an after-tax rate of return on investments equal to the before-tax rate of return on the amount of consumption forgone by making the investment. But if the tax system is to provide a lower interest cost for state and local debt than for corporate bonds generally, some additional benefit would be necessary.

If the yield and sales price of state and local bonds were excluded from receipts and no deduction were allowed for the purchase of such bonds, there would be no reason to expect that the interest on state and local bonds would be lower than that on ordinary corporate bonds. Thus, to maintain an advantage for borrowing by state and local governments, both a deduction and an exclusion of yield would have to be provided, or some other benefit besides the generally available deduction—perhaps some sort of tax credit—would have to be enacted. Permitting both a deduction and an exclusion for state and local bonds would create a *negative* tax rate on income from that source (or expenditures financed from that source) that would vary directly with purchasers' marginal rates of tax. A tax credit would also produce a negative tax rate but would be somewhat more neutral with regard to marginal tax rates.

Proponents of an expenditure tax may take solace from the fact that it is more difficult to provide relative advantages for particular kinds of investment under an expenditure tax than under an income tax. On the other hand, observers of congressional behavior may suffer apoplexy thinking about the distortions and inequities that would probably occur if Congress were to persist in its income tax policy of offering relative expenditure tax advantages to investments in particular sectors of the economy.

Life Insurance

Life insurance is normally of two types: "term insurance" and "permanent insurance." Term insurance represents a payment designed to protect a person's family against economic loss due to premature death. In effect, term insurance is a gamble that the person will not outlive the period predicted by mortality tables. Permanent insurance provides a combination of term insurance and a significant element of savings in the form of reserves accumulated out of premium payments that earn interest for the insured's benefit. The precise combination of savings and pure insurance varies from policy to policy.

Under the income tax, life insurance premiums are not deductible and amounts that are paid "by reason of the death of the insured" are not subject to income tax—regardless of the amount of mortality gain or loss or return of interest earnings that may be involved. These rules result in preferential income tax treatment of interest earned on savings in the form of cash value life insurance.

The appropriate treatment of term insurance under an expenditure tax may be controversial, since life insurance is the only widely available method by which individuals may protect their families against the economic consequences of premature death. Most commentators have recommended that term insurance be treated similarly to purchases and receipts of investment assets generally; premiums paid for life insurance would be deductible by the payor and proceeds would be taxed to beneficiaries. The Treasury Department in *Blueprints* justifies this treatment on the grounds that purchasing an insurance policy "lowers the lifetime consumption of the policyholder and raises the expected lifetime consumption of the beneficiary," and Professor Andrews argues that allowing a deduction for premiums would enable individuals to purchase greater amounts of insurance and would therefore offset any hardships resulting from taxation of mortality gains.[31] Moreover, simplification considerations argue for

31. Ibid., p. 132; Andrews, "A Consumption-Type or Cash Flow Personal Income Tax," p. 1164.

rules that treat life insurance in the same way as other investment assets. If such rules prove acceptable to Congress, they should be adopted.

On the other hand, allowing life insurance to be treated under the yield exemption option would avoid imposing tax upon the death of the insured, when the family may well suffer a net economic loss even if it receives insurance proceeds. In fact, it is entirely possible that the actual economic loss to the family will be greater as mortality gains increase. If insurance proceeds are used to enable the insured's dependents to maintain their standard of living during the period shortly following his death, assessing expenditure tax at the time of death may be burdensome to the family. But any hardship from taxing proceeds under an expenditure tax would be offset somewhat because investments made with such proceeds would be immediately deductible. Thus applying graduated rates to the payment of life insurance proceeds would create fewer difficulties for the deceased's family under an expenditure tax than under an income tax.

By contrast, the arguments against taxing mortality gains from term insurance do not apply to life insurance proceeds attributable to the buildup of life insurance reserves. Expenditure tax should be applied to the savings. With yield exemption treatment limited to mortality gains, however, such an approach would allow deductions for premiums in excess of term insurance premiums, and the portion of proceeds that represented interest income and return of savings would be included in the beneficiary's receipts. Allocating taxable amounts to individual beneficiaries would create difficult information and policing problems, and if tax were not withheld by life insurance companies, collection might prove difficult. At a minimum, beneficiaries would have to be provided information by life insurance companies that indicated the portion of proceeds to be included in receipts. Taxpayers would find this system difficult to understand.

These problems argue for a relatively simple solution to the entire life insurance problem—either cash flow treatment, as with other investment assets, or a yield exemption alternative, under which no deduction would be allowed for life insurance premiums, whether for term or for permanent insurance, and life insurance proceeds realized at the time of death would be excluded from beneficiaries' receipts. The political pressure for exempting life insurance proceeds from receipts will very likely be great, so that instead of the normal cash flow treatment, the result may well be both an immediate deduction for premiums and an exemption for proceeds. Thus yield exemption treatment—denying deductions for term life insurance premiums and excluding such proceeds from receipts—should be an acceptable alternative, assuming that the coordination of such a rule with the cash flow treatment of annuities were feasible.

If a yield exemption treatment of life insurance were adopted, proceeds received upon surrender of cash value life insurance policies during the lifetime of the insured should also be excluded from tax receipts. Rules would have to be developed, however, to ensure that application of the yield exemption option to life insurance would not become a general opportunity to obtain exclusion of speculative gains—for example, through "variable life insurance" policies, in which premiums are invested in the stock market by the life insurance company and proceeds depend upon how well the investments perform.

Annuities

The treatment of annuities under an expenditure tax would be much simpler than under an income tax. Under the latter, a portion of each annuity payment is taxable and a portion is excludable as a recovery of capital. In the case of life annuities, the taxable amount is determined by the life expectancy of the person or persons whose lives measure the period of the annuity. The annuitant's income tax may be excessive if he dies prematurely and capital is not returned free of tax, but annuitants may also receive tax free more than the amount that was paid for the annuity. Although considerations like those advanced above regarding the expenditure taxation of life insurance might seem to argue for the yield exemption treatment of annuities, annuity returns represent mortality gains only if the taxpayer outlives the prediction of the issuer, and similar hardships do not seem likely to occur. An annuity should be treated under an expenditure tax like any other investment; a deduction would be allowed for purchases of annuities, and annuity proceeds would be included in receipts as they were paid.

The policing of private annuities however, might prove quite important under an expenditure tax. The extent of the difficulties resulting from such transactions would depend in part upon the rules for the taxation of gifts. If cash gifts were deductible by the donor and includable in the donee's receipts, private annuities for cash would cause no additional problems. But if gifts were taxed to donors, it would be necessary to determine whether private annuities were partly gifts.

Commercial and private annuities purchased in exchange for property (for example, when a father transfers property to a son and the son agrees to pay the father a monthly sum as long as the father lives) are somewhat more troublesome. It is important that the annuitant not be allowed a double deduction from the transaction. Thus any deduction allowed for the purchase of an annuity should be reduced by amounts previously deducted on the property transferred, usually its cost. In general, no deduction should be allowed on transfers of property for annuities unless the fair market value of the property is included in receipts as if the property were sold and the proceeds then applied to purchase the annuity.

Transfers from the Government and Charities

Payments from the government, such as social security benefits, railroad retirement benefits, and veterans' pensions, may be used to finance consumption in the same manner as wages and therefore should be included in receipts. If such items were not included in receipts, the advantages gained by recipients would depend upon their marginal tax brackets, with higher bracket taxpayers obtaining a relatively greater advantage from the exclusion. (Deductions should be allowed for individuals' contributions to such plans.)

When payments from the government are based on a test of need, the question is more difficult. If cash transfers were included in receipts, similar results should obtain for in-kind transfers like food stamps and subsidized rental housing, but valuation problems would probably result in administrative costs in excess of the revenue from taxing such amounts. Payments based upon means tests are presumably determined on the assumption that they are tax free; taxation would tend to produce a subsequent increase in the level of such payments. On balance, such payments should probably be excluded from an expenditure tax base. Likewise, transfers from charities should be excluded from receipts. If for no other reason, the administrative burden of taxing those who receive food from the Salvation Army or health care from the Red Cross compels exclusion.

In addition, benefits that individuals receive from general government services would necessarily be excluded from the expenditure tax base. To the extent that individuals can persuade governments to provide consumption benefits, such as recreational facilities, that are not completely financed through user charges, consumption will escape taxation.

As a practical matter, expenditure tax receipts would most likely include only cash transfers and easily valued in-kind transfers not based on need.

Other Statutory Exclusions from Gross Income

The Internal Revenue Code specifically excludes certain items from gross income. The exclusion under section 119 of the code for meals and lodging provided to employees by employers under certain conditions was discussed in connection with fringe benefits. Other than deferred compensation (discussed earlier), the principal statutory exclusions from gross income under the current income tax are as follows.

1. *Life insurance.* An employer's payments of premiums for up to $50,000 of group term life insurance are excludable from an employee's income.

2. *Employer-provided health insurance.* In certain cases employees may exclude amounts provided by employers in the form of health insurance premiums and reimbursements of an employee's uninsured medical expenses.

3. *Sick pay.* Subject to dollar limitations and other stringent requirements, disability payments under an employer-financed accident or health plan may be excluded from an employee's income.

4. *Qualified group legal service plans.* Amounts contributed by an employer to a prepaid legal services plan for employees and the value of legal services received under such a plan are excluded from employee's income under certain conditions.

5. *Scholarships and fellowships and prizes and awards.* Scholarships and fellowships are generally excluded from gross income, and prizes and awards are excluded in certain limited circumstances.

The Internal Revenue Code provides other, somewhat less important, exclusions from income for: (1) combat pay, mustering-out pay, and certain retirement pay of members of the armed services;

(2) veterans' disability, survivor, and pension benefits; and (3) the rental value of parsonages and rental allowances paid to ministers.

Various arguments have been advanced for repealing each of these statutory exclusions from income, and, with the possible exception of exclusions relating to health benefits, none would be excluded from a "comprehensive" income tax base. Most of these provisions, however, reflect congressional decisions to favor income or consumption of a particular kind. The recently enacted exclusions for group legal services plans, for example, create a tax preference for the consumption of legal services relative to other forms of consumption. An equitable and efficient expenditure tax system would generally provide no special advantages for such items. But whether these exclusions or others would be adopted if an expenditure tax replaced the income tax would ultimately depend upon congressional decisions. Even though such exclusions would be difficult to justify theoretically, there is no reason to imagine that their proponents (for example, labor unions) would be less effective in persuading Congress to enact such provisions under an expenditure tax.

Summary and Recommendations

In this section I have described how some of the more important categories of receipts would be treated under an expenditure tax, on the assumption that, to be effective, the indirect expenditure tax computation of consumption would require a broad definition of receipts. Specifically, I recommended:

—that rules be promulgated (either through legislation or administratively) that would have the effect of including most fringe benefits in receipts;

—that imputed income from services generally be ignored for expenditure tax purposes, but that a special deduction or exclusion be allowed to families in which both spouses have significant earned income;

—that life insurance be treated on a cash flow basis in the same way as other investment assets, but if this proves politically unacceptable, that no deduction be allowed for premiums on life insurance and that proceeds from life insurance policies be usually excluded from receipts;

—that annuities be treated on a cash flow basis in the same way as other investment assets: a deduction would be allowed for the purchase of an annuity and amounts received would be included in receipts (special rules would apply to exchanges of property for an annuity);

—that government transfers of cash and easily valued in-kind transfers not based on need be included in receipts; and

—that the statutory exclusions from gross income of the current income tax not be duplicated under an expenditure tax.

But, as I have suggested throughout, two major difficulties will occur in any effort to enact as comprehensive a definition of receipts as proposed here. First, problems of administration and taxpayer understanding will require that certain kinds of receipts be excluded from the expenditure tax computation. Second, political considerations will very likely bring about certain exclusions even when neither taxpayer understanding nor administrative convenience is a problem.

Deductions

To distribute the tax burden in a manner that varies directly with consumption, an expenditure tax must distinguish as precisely as possible between nondeductible consumption expenditures and deductible expenditures for savings or investment. In some instances this task is relatively straightforward. For example, when someone spends money on goods or services for the sole purpose of personal pleasure, such expenditures are clearly consumption. By the same token, if someone deposits $100 in a savings account with a financial institution, the deposit plainly constitutes savings. Likewise, purchasing stock of an unrelated company in the hopes of obtaining a return offers a clear case of investment, as does lending money to unrelated parties for an expected interest return. Many individual expenditures, however, are made with mixed motives. Money is often spent not only to provide personal satisfaction but to make more money.

The practical problems of distinguishing between personal expenses and expenses made for business or investment purposes are familiar under the income tax. Professor Chirelstein accurately assesses the magnitude of the tax collector's task when he observes that "the notion of a sharp division between pleasure-seeking and profit-seeking is alien to human psychology and essentially unrealistic."[32]

32. Marvin A. Chirelstein, *Federal Income Taxation: A Law Student's Guide to the Leading Cases and Concepts* (Mineola, N.Y.: Foundation Press, 1977), p. 87.

Professor Bittker has remarked on the essential dilemma in greater detail:

There is, unfortunately, no theoretically satisfactory boundary between business expenses that provide incidental personal benefits and personal expenditures that incidentally serve business purposes. No matter how generously the Code defines business expenses in an effort to insure that all business-related expenses can be deducted, there will always be some non-deductible items beyond the line that contribute in some way to the production of income, whether it is the basic cost of living—one cannot work, after all, unless one is fed and housed—or the cost of luxuries that contribute to the taxpayer's willingness to work and to his initiative and reliability while on the job. On the other hand, no matter how severely the term "business expense" is defined, many items will continue to qualify for deduction although they confer "personal" benefits on the taxpayer. Taxpayers may be forbidden to deduct entertainment expenses because they are suspected of enjoying dinners and theater parties with their business customers, for example, but even the most puritanical definition of business expense is not likely to prevent self-employed taxpayers from deducting the cost of air conditioning their offices, upholstering their swivel chairs, or adding gadgets to their telephones, even if they derive personal pleasure from these amenities.[33]

In some instances the Internal Revenue Code permits deductions for expenses without requiring the taxpayer to show any profit-seeking motive. These include the so-called itemized deductions for charitable contributions, medical expenses, interest, and state and local taxes. In other cases the taxpayer must demonstrate a business or profit-seeking motive to obtain a deduction. In this section I consider both these categories of expenses under an expenditure tax. First I take up expenses that require a profit-seeking motive for deduction under the income tax, then I discuss the principal itemized deductions. Finally, I consider the need for a deduction for expenditure taxes—the question of a tax-exclusive base.

The Distinction between Business and Personal Expenses

Under the income tax, the struggle to distinguish deductible business or investment expenses from nondeductible personal, family, or living expenses has been largely left to the Internal Revenue Service and the courts. The statutory standards are quite general. Sections

33. Boris I. Bittker, "Income Tax Deductions, Credits and Subsidies for Personal Expenditures," *Journal of Law and Economics,* vol. 16 (October 1973), pp. 203–04.

162 and 212 of the Internal Revenue Code provide for the deduction of "all the ordinary and necessary expenses" incurred in carrying on any trade or business or other income-producing activities, while section 262 states that "no deduction shall be allowed for personal living or family expenses." Beyond these general principles, Congress has provided the Internal Revenue Service and the courts little help in distinguishing business and investment expenses from consumption expenditures.

A variety of standards has developed, depending upon the particular type of expense involved. For some kinds of expenses, the courts ask only whether the expense is appropriate and helpful to the taxpayer's business, and if so, allow a deduction. For other expenses, courts attempt to discern the objective motive of the taxpayer and disallow a deduction unless the expense would not have been made "but for" the existence of the business or investment motive. The courts occasionally will require that a taxpayer's profit-seeking activities be "reasonable" and will review the business or investment judgments of taxpayers even if it is established that the decision to spend money was profit-oriented rather than personal. Some types of expenses are regarded by courts as "inherently personal," and nondeductible even if shown to enhance profit-making activity. It is difficult to know—other than by looking at the precedents—when the courts will apply this test; the cost of haircuts, for example, satisfies the inherently personal test, but the cost of meals does not.

It is not possible in this paper to review each of the types of expenses that have been allowed or disallowed deduction under the income tax, but a review of the current treatment of legal expenses may help to illustrate how an expenditure tax might modify the courts' income tax approach.[34]

The basic income tax rule is set forth in *United States* v. *Gilmore,* 372 U.S. 39 (1963), where a taxpayer attempted to deduct legal expenses incurred in defending a divorce action that involved a contested property settlement. The taxpayer argued that such expenses were deductible because they were incurred for the conservation of income-producing property. The Supreme Court concluded that de-

34. The analysis in the text of the appropriate expenditure tax treatment of legal expenses is generally consistent with income tax arguments advanced in Richard A. Epstein, "The Consumption and Loss of Personal Property under the Internal Revenue Code," *Stanford Law Review,* vol. 23 (February 1971), pp. 454–72.

ductibility turned not on the potential consequences of the divorce action on the defendant's property but on "the origin and character of the claim with respect to which an expense was incurred." The Court held that the wife's claim stemmed from the marital relationship and that the taxpayer's expenses incurred in defending the claim were therefore personal and not deductible.

In a subsequent proceeding involving the same taxpayer, however, a district court held that the attorneys' fees incurred in defending the divorce action were costs of defending title to the taxpayer's property and, even though not deductible, could be added to the property's basis. Moreover, divorced spouses are usually allowed to deduct legal expenses incurred for the collection of alimony, even though these expenses originate in a personal context. On the other hand, application of the "origin of the claim" test of *Gilmore* has led courts to conclude that legal fees incurred in preparing a will are nondeductible personal expenses, as are a legatee's expenses in contesting a will.

Besides the basic distinction between personal and business investment expenses, there is a significant income tax timing issue involved when expenditures are made in connection with property. For example, capitalization rather than deduction should be required of expenses incurred to defend title to property, because the benefits of successful litigation will obtain throughout the period of ownership. In some instances courts have denied income tax deductions under the business/personal rubric for expenditures that should be capitalized.

Under an expenditure tax, the timing issue disappears, and expenses should be deductible unless the payments can be fairly treated as consumption. If in *Gilmore* the question were rephrased to ask whether the legal expenses constituted consumption, a different answer might be forthcoming. If the expenses were costs of rearranging ownership of property within a family group, this would seem to be not consumption but a prelude to consumption. Rather than proceeds from the assets being consumed, ownership is being rearranged so that consumption will be facilitated when the consumer—the new owner—sells the property. The cost incurred is not a cost of consumption, but a cost of deferring consumption, and deferred consumption is usually treated as savings under an expenditure tax. Expenditure tax deductions might therefore be allowed for any expenses incurred in rearranging the ownership of property, including those for the preparation or contest of wills and those related to divorce settlements.

By the same token, expenses incurred in defending lawsuits might normally be deductible under an expenditure tax without asking (as is now done under the income tax) whether, for example, the expenses were incurred to protect the taxpayer's reputation, whether they were incurred in criminal rather than civil proceedings, or whether they were incurred to acquire or protect title to business or personal property. In no case would such legal expenses be properly viewed as consumption.

This brief discussion of legal expenses is chiefly intended to show that income tax precedents that distinguish personal from business or investment expenses might be reexamined under an expenditure tax. Courts faced with expenditure tax issues would probably tend to resolve them by inquiring whether a particular expenditure could be fairly characterized as an expense of immediate consumption rather than of deferred consumption (or a loss). If this approach were adopted, many expenditures made in connection with property ownership that are not deductible now would be deductible under an expenditure tax.

Professor Daniel Halperin has advanced a general approach to business deductions for personal expenses under the income tax.[35] This approach emphasizes consumption aspects of such expenses rather than taxpayers' motivation or potential business or investment benefits and seems consistent with the goals of an expenditure tax. Professor Halperin argues that deductions should be disallowed whenever personal satisfaction is obtained from an expenditure. If personal satisfaction is equal to cost, no deduction should be allowed; in other cases a deduction should be permitted only to the extent that cost exceeds the personal benefits from the expense. Professor Halperin recognizes the practical difficulties of measuring consumption when the possibility of profit also contributes to a person's decision to incur an expense, and he suggests that practical rules be developed that approximate as closely as possible the theoretical test offered. Professor Halperin's recommendations for particular expenses can

35. Daniel I. Halperin, "Business Deductions for Personal Living Expenses: A Uniform Approach to an Unsolved Problem," *University of Pennsylvania Law Review,* vol. 122 (April 1974), pp. 859–933.

serve as a guide to implementation decisions under an expenditure tax.

(1) *Education:* Allow amortization of the cost of professional and certain other postgraduate education and vocational training after high school.

(2) *Job seeking:* Allow a deduction for, or amortization of, job-seeking costs not involving travel or education.

(3) *Clothing:* No change in present law. [Deductible only if required as a condition of employment and not adaptable to ordinary wear.]

(4) *Office in the home:* Deny a deduction unless the principal purpose of acquiring the space is business. . . .

(5) *Travel:* Deductions permitted for travel would be in the ratio of time spent on business to total time on the trip. Attention should be devoted to an effort to limit the portion of the trip allocated to business to the actual time so spent. Consideration should be given to whether a deduction can be fully denied for certain trips, e.g., conventions at vacation spots, which appear to result in personal satisfaction equal to cost. If so, meals and lodging on such occasions also should not be deductible.

(6) *Food:* Deny all deductions for the cost of food. If this is not acceptable, do not allow a deduction for food consumed at home or for lunches wherever they take place. Place a low dollar limit on deductions for breakfast and dinner. The exclusion for meals provided for the convenience of the employer should be consistent with the dollar limit.

(7) *Lodging:* Deny a deduction unless lodging duplicates housing otherwise available and in all cases for days not spent on business. A dollar limit should apply.

(8) *Entertainment:* Deny any deduction.

In addition to the issues mentioned above, expenditure tax rules would be needed to deal with so-called hobby loss investments, in which individuals seek to obtain personal satisfaction in the guise of profit-seeking activities. In general, the income tax rules for such activities have been quite unsuccessful and seem inadequate to ensure that a proper amount of consumption would be included in the expenditure tax base.

Itemized Deductions

The Internal Revenue Code, without requiring any show of profit-seeking motive, currently allows deductions for some expenses that are personal in nature. The most important of these are for charitable contributions, interest on personal indebtedness, medical expenses

and casualty losses, and state and local taxes. The income tax literature is replete with disputes over the propriety of these various personal deductions, and those arguments are not repeated here. But
certain issues that relate to these deductions under an expenditure tax
are considered.

   Charitable contributions. Deductions are allowed under the income tax for contributions to charitable organizations, including
educational, religious, and scientific organizations. The charitable
deduction is subject to numerous limitations, which depend upon the
donor's income, the kind of property donated, the recipient's status,
and the use by the recipient. The tax treatment of a gift of appreciated
property, for example, depends on whether the recipient is a private
foundation or a public charity, whether the appreciation would be
taxed as capital gain or ordinary income, and whether the gift is
personal property, real property, or securities.

   Income tax deductions are also allowed for gifts to charity when
property is split between charitable and noncharitable beneficiaries.
This most frequently occurs when property is transferred to a trust
under provisions requiring income from the property to be paid to
noncharitable beneficiaries (usually the donor's spouse or children)
for a period of time after which the remainder of the trust will be
transferred to charity. The income tax deduction allowed is intended
to approximate the present value of the charitable remainder interest.

   Various proposals for revising the income tax charitable contribution deduction have been advanced in recent years. Those who view
it as basically inconsistent with a comprehensive definition of income
or who otherwise regard it as inequitable (since it is worth relatively
more to high-income taxpayers and nothing to persons who take the
standard deduction or who are not taxable) have argued for replacing
the deduction with direct government assistance (or with tax credits)
providing identical benefits per dollar of charitable giving.[36] On the
other hand, those who regard the charitable deduction of current
law as an insufficient incentive to charitable giving have proposed
that charitable deductions be allowed in addition to the standard
deduction or that deductions in excess of the amount contributed
be allowed. The Filer Commission in 1975, for example, recom-

   36. See Paul R. McDaniel, "Federal Matching Grants for Charitable Contributions: A Substitute for the Income Tax Deduction," *Tax Law Review,* vol. 27 (Spring
1972), pp. 377–413.

mended that a double deduction be provided for charitable gifts of families with annual incomes of less than $15,000, and a 150 percent deduction for gifts of those with incomes between $15,000 and $30,000 a year.[37]

The Treasury Department in *Blueprints* argues that charitable contributions are consumption of the donor and that no deduction should be allowed for charitable giving under either a comprehensive income tax or an expenditure tax. The Treasury, however, acknowledges that basic policy issues are at stake, notes that "the question of how to treat charitable contributions extends beyond issues of income measurement," and concludes that "the decision whether or not to allow the deduction of charitable contributions is not essential to the basic integrity of the overall proposal."[38] Professors Andrews and Bittker have argued that the charitable contribution deduction is proper because it is inappropriate to regard amounts given to charity as consumption by the donor.[39]

Without addressing the merits of the debate, I simply assume that under an expenditure tax a deduction would be allowed for gifts of cash to charities on the ground either that an incentive for charitable giving is necessary for policy reasons or that it would be theoretically inappropriate to treat charitable gifts as consumption of the donor. Discussion here will be limited to two issues: the treatment of gifts of property and the treatment of charitable gifts in which the donor receives value in return for the contribution.

A brief description of the income tax rules for charitable gifts of property is essential before considering the appropriate expenditure tax rules. When a sale of property (for example, inventory) would produce ordinary income (or short-term capital gain), the donor's income tax deduction is limited to the cost of the asset. Deductions for gifts of appreciated property to private foundations and gifts of appreciated personal property not to be used by the charity in a manner relating to its exempt purpose or function are limited to cost

37. *Giving in America: Toward a Stronger Voluntary Sector,* Report of the Commission on Private Philanthropy and Public Needs (Commission on Private Philanthropy and Public Needs, 1975), p. 135.

38. *Blueprints,* pp. 95–97, 116–17.

39. William D. Andrews, "Personal Deductions in an Ideal Income Tax," *Harvard Law Review,* vol. 86 (December 1972), pp. 309–85; Boris I. Bittker, "Charitable Contributions: Tax Deductions or Matching Grants?" *Tax Law Review,* vol. 28 (Fall 1972), pp. 37–63.

plus one-half of any accrued gain, but gifts to public charities of appreciated securities or real property are allowed a full fair market
value deduction.[40] In 1969 Congress rejected proposals for limiting
deductions for gifts of appreciated property to public charities, even
though the unrealized appreciation of donated property escapes income taxation. Congress was apparently convinced that the continuation of a full fair market value deduction was essential to the continued well-being of charities, particularly colleges and universities.
Gifts of appreciated property are most common for persons in upper
income tax brackets and are an important source of private voluntary support for colleges, universities, museums, and hospitals.

Under an expenditure tax, a deduction would be allowed upon
purchase of investment property, including securities or real estate.
If an additional deduction were allowed for the fair market value of
property given to charity, its cost would be deducted twice, once
when purchased and again when donated. If marginal expenditure
tax rates exceed 50 percent, the tax savings from such a double
deduction would exceed the cost of the asset, thus providing high-
bracket taxpayers with a simple way of making money. To maintain
the integrity of the tax, it is essential that one deduction at most be
allowed and that no charitable contribution deduction be allowed for
amounts that have previously been deducted. Thus, at a minimum,
the deduction for charitable contributions of property must be reduced by amounts previously deducted, usually the cost of the asset.
If the excess of fair market value over cost were allowed as a deduction when property was contributed to charity, the income tax advantage for giving property to charity over selling property and donating
the proceeds would be retained under an expenditure tax. Such a
rule would therefore maintain the current tax preference for gifts of
appreciated property over cash.

There is, however, no theoretical justification for this kind of
preference under an expenditure tax, and such a rule would introduce considerable complexity into the tax system. Taxpayers would

---

40. The rule stated in the text was changed by the Revenue Act of 1978, so that
gifts of appreciated property to private foundations and gifts of appreciated personal
property not to be used by the charity in a manner relating to its exempt purposes or
function are limited to cost plus 60 percent of any accrued gain. The rule was
changed to conform with a general increase to 60 percent in the exclusion from
income for long-term capital gains. Gifts to public charities of appreciated securities
or real property continue to be allowed a deduction for full fair market value.

be required to know the basis of assets donated to charity and to retain records and make computations that would not otherwise be required. A simpler and more theoretically appropriate rule would be to limit expenditure tax deductions of charitable contributions to gifts of cash. But this rule might seriously reduce donations to institutions of higher education, since gifts of appreciated property would be denied tax advantages currently available. Likewise, split-interest gifts of property in trust, which also are important to colleges and universities, would no longer be eligible for deduction.

A deduction only for cash gifts to charities also would produce lesser advantages to donors than the current income tax deduction. Allowing an expenditure tax deduction for cash gifts to charity merely equates such gifts with purchases of investment assets that are also deductible. Under the income tax, a donor faced with the choice of giving to charity or saving for his own or his family's subsequent consumption can obtain only a before-tax rate of return on savings that is a function of his tax rate times the before-tax rate of return. Thus, for example, a taxpayer subject to a 60 percent marginal tax rate will obtain only 4 percent after tax of a 10 percent before-tax return. Under an expenditure tax, however, his after-tax return on his reduced consumption would equal the 10 percent before-tax return, and the relative cost of instead donating the cash to charity would be greater than under the income tax. If recent empirical studies showing a high price elasticity of charitable giving are correct, high-income persons would probably reduce their charitable contribution substantially as giving became more costly. It is therefore quite possible that an expenditure tax would either have to permit charitable deductions for more than 100 percent of cash gifts or be accompanied by additional tax incentives or direct subsidies for charities. Given their popularity in Congress, tax credits for college tuition would seem to be a likely candidate for addition to the law.

The income tax law denies charitable contribution deductions when taxpayers receive consumption value in return for the charitable contribution. Although the Internal Revenue Service has been able to disallow deductions in certain "abuse" cases, it has been ineffective in dealing with this problem generally. Deductions have been disallowed, for instance, for large contributions to churches where weddings of the donor's family members have been performed and for gifts to schools where the donor's children are to be educated.

On the other hand, gifts have been allowed to be deducted when substantial benefits are received by the donor. One taxpayer, for example, was permitted to deduct amounts given to a nursing home, even though she subsequently moved to the nursing home and paid a reduced rental charge because she was a donor.[41] The Internal Revenue Service has issued a ruling that requires deductions to be reduced by the value of theater tickets or dinners that the donor receives in return for contributions, but enforcement is spotty at best. The service has been unsuccessful in disallowing deductions for gifts to colleges and universities when choice football or basketball seats are provided to those who contribute a specified amount.

Failure to disallow charitable contribution deductions when the recipient receives a consumption benefit would permit such consumption to escape the expenditure tax base. While no change in the income tax rules would be necessary, more effective enforcement seems warranted. But since such enforcement appears unlikely, the use of this technique for excluding consumption from the tax base would probably continue or even increase under an expenditure tax.

Interest. The appropriate treatment of interest payments under an expenditure tax has been considered in some detail in previous sections. It was argued that loans other than consumer credit should be accounted for on a cash flow basis and that an expenditure tax deduction would be proper for interest on indebtedness that was included in expenditure tax receipts. (Alternatively, if loans for investment were excluded from receipts and deductions limited to equity investments, interest on such loans should be deductible.) No deductions should otherwise be allowed for interest on indebtedness incurred or continued to finance consumption, whether consumption is to occur in the current year or over a period of years. Though it might appear that such rules would require distinctions not now necessary under the income tax (because interest is now generally deductible for most taxpayers regardless of its purpose), this would not be the case. Deductibility of interest would turn only on whether indebtedness was included in receipts when the loan was obtained. If the loan proceeds were included in receipts, interest on the loan would be deductible; if the loan proceeds were excluded, no interest deduction should be allowed.

Given the income tax treatment of interest expenses, it might be a

41. *Estate of Wardell* v. *United States,* 301 F.2d 632 (8th Cir. 1962).

difficult political matter to enact rules that disallow deductions for interest on indebtedness to finance consumption in all cases in which loan proceeds were excluded from expenditure tax receipts. If so, interest on a certain amount of indebtedness might be allowed by Congress to be deducted without regard to its purpose. Such a rule would, however, undercut the theoretically correct result, and, to the extent interest on borrowings to finance consumption is allowed to be deducted, would favor present consumption over future consumption.

State and local taxes. The Internal Revenue Code currently allows a deduction for state and local income taxes, property taxes, general sales taxes, and certain miscellaneous taxes (not covered here). All state and local taxes incurred in connection with a business or investment are deductible. The arguments for allowing federal income tax deductions for state and local taxes are basically that (1) deductions are necessary to aid in fiscal coordination in a federal system, and (2) payment of such taxes is compelled and therefore should not be regarded as consumption.

If federal income tax deductions for state and local taxes are justified in order to coordinate federal taxation with that of state and local governments, similar arguments should result in such deductions under an expenditure tax. If this is not the case, however, certain modifications seem desirable; for instance, as was argued above, no deduction should be allowed for property taxes on a personal residence.

Whether or not deductions should be allowed for state and local income and sales taxes is debatable. For example, Professor Bittker contends that, because state and local tax payments are compelled rather than voluntary, "it strains reality to count state and local taxes as consumption expenditures."[42] On the other hand, the Treasury Department in *Blueprints* argues that under either a comprehensive income tax or an expenditure tax, no deduction should be allowed for state and local sales taxes, but that state income taxes should be deductible. The rationale for this distinction is somewhat difficult to follow. The Treasury apparently believes that income taxes "reduce the resources available to the payor for consumption or accumulation," but that general sales taxes do not reduce income reported by households and individuals, and asserts that the sales tax "has al-

42. Bittker, "Income Tax Deductions," p. 201.

ready been deducted from income sources" except to the extent that
sales tax rates vary among states and localities. The Treasury's analysis seems to assume that sales taxes have no important income effect
and that they do not influence work-leisure choices.[43] But if people
work additional hours to earn enough income to pay sales taxes on
goods they wish to consume, that argument would not seem to apply.

In any event, individual taxpayers are likely to regard both state
income and sales taxes as reducing the resources available for private
consumption. Perhaps state sales taxes should be denied deduction
on the ground that they are merely a cost of consumption, but if so,
a portion of state income taxes should be denied deduction for a
similar reason. The Treasury's argument that "income taxes would
be fully deductible because they are not regarded as part of consumption" is not persuasive.[44] As the Haig-Simons definition teaches,
taxes on income are in large part taxes on consumption. Allowing a
federal deduction for state income taxes but not for sales taxes would
tend to induce states to rely more heavily on deductible income taxes.
It is difficult to know why a federal government shifting from income
taxes to a consumption tax should at the same time revise its policies
so as to encourage state and local governments to shift from taxes
on consumption to income taxes. It seems quite likely that deductions
for state and local income taxes and sales taxes would be retained
under an expenditure tax. There have been few problems in administering such deductions under the income tax, and no additional
problems should arise under an expenditure tax.

Medical expenses. The deductibility of medical expenses is based
principally on the argument that such expenses are not voluntary
consumption. Under the income tax, medical expenses are allowed to
be deducted to the extent that they exceed 3 percent of the taxpayer's
adjusted gross income. The floor of the medical expense deduction is
intended to treat normal medical expenses as other consumption but
to allow deduction of extraordinary medical expenses. Many would
agree that the current floor is too low for this purpose and should be
raised.

Those who would repeal the medical deduction altogether con-
tend that consumers exercise a high degree of choice about most
medical expenses and that extraordinary medical expenses should

43. *Blueprints,* pp. 92–94; quoted material from p. 93.
44. Ibid., p. 117.

be insured against, with such insurance regarded as any other normal consumption expenditure. Professor Andrews has argued that extraordinary medical expenses are not voluntary consumption and that an income tax deduction is necessary to properly reflect differences in individuals' abilities to pay tax.[45] This argument has great force in the context of an expenditure tax. A person who is hospitalized for a long time is simply not enjoying consumption in a manner equivalent to that of a healthy person who spends the same amount of money on personal satisfaction; an expenditure tax base should reflect such differences.

The most persuasive argument for denying deductions for medical expenses is that people should be encouraged to insure against medical catastrophes and that allowing a deduction tends to discourage the purchase of such insurance. If medical expense deductions are to be denied, however, it seems essential that the government take steps to make certain that adequate insurance against medical catastrophes is available for everyone. Until such insurance exists, continuation of a medical expense deduction under an expenditure tax seems desirable, although substantially increasing the floor would very likely improve tax equity and simplify tax administration.

A variety of arguments have been advanced in income tax cases in which taxpayers have attempted to obtain deductions for consumption expenditures by characterizing them as medical expenses. Effective enforcement seems to depend on whether the person's total medical expenses are high enough to produce a careful audit of medical deductions. The case law, however, has tended to be reasonably sensible in distinguishing personal consumption from genuine medical expenses. Nevertheless, consideration should be given to additional precautions to preclude taxpayers from claiming normal consumption expenditures as deductible medical expenses. One approach would be to deny any deductions for payments that mirrored normal consumption expenditures, for example, for meals and clothing.

Standard Deduction

The income tax contains a provision, known generally as the standard deduction (now called the zero bracket amount), which is allowed to taxpayers in place of itemized deductions. The amount of

45. Andrews, "Personal Deductions in an Ideal Income Tax," pp. 337–41.

the standard deduction has been adjusted from time to time to ensure its use by a substantial majority of taxpayers and therefore to eliminate many taxpayers' need to keep records of expenses that qualify for itemized deductions. If itemized deductions were allowable under an expenditure tax, as seems likely, a similar desire to avoid record-keeping and audit argues for a comparable expenditure tax standard deduction. Such a deduction should be set at a level that would allow the majority of taxpayers to use it.

Under the income tax, however, increases in the standard deduction over time have created pressure on Congress to enact tax credits instead of itemized deductions and to consider allowing other deductions (for example, the charitable deduction) along with the standard deduction. This trend has caused at least one commentator to argue that a "standard tax credit" is needed as an alternative to the specific credits allowable under the income tax. This tendency toward complexity under the income tax should be avoided under an expenditure tax.

Deduction of Federal Expenditure Taxes

Under the income tax, tax is imposed on a "tax-inclusive" basis; in other words, no deduction is allowed for the income tax itself. Most commentators agree that an expenditure tax should be imposed on a "tax-exclusive" basis, with the expenditure tax itself excluded from the tax base.[46] But much higher rates are required to produce equivalent revenues on a tax-exclusive base, as the following table illustrates.[47]

Tax-inclusive rates (percent)	Equivalent tax-exclusive rates (percent)
35	54
40	66⅔
50	100
75	300
83	488
98	4,900

46. Kaldor, *An Expenditure Tax,* p. 237; Lodin, *Progressive Expenditure Tax,* pp. 63–65; Meade committee report, p. 167. For an opposing view, see Andrews, "A Consumption-Type or Cash Flow Personal Income Tax," pp. 1119n, 1151n.
47. The table is taken from the Meade committee report, p. 28, which also provides a general formula for converting tax-exclusive into tax-inclusive rates and vice versa.

Obviously, the psychological and political consequences of the choice between a tax-inclusive base and a tax-exclusive one may be quite significant; taxpayers and legislators may feel quite differently about a tax of 75 percent on a base that includes the tax and a tax of 300 percent on the same base with the tax removed. Nevertheless, it seems important that an expenditure tax be calculated on a tax-exclusive base so that the withdrawal of funds from savings to pay taxes would not affect the actual amount of taxes due. A tax-exclusive base would be implemented by allowing a deduction for expenditure taxes actually paid during the year. Expenditure taxes would, in effect, be treated on a cash flow basis in a manner similar to savings.

Failure to treat payments of expenditure tax as deductible would create oscillations in the amount of tax due, depending on the timing of tax payments as compared with amounts saved. To the extent that taxpayers adjust their savings to meet tax liabilities, a tax-exclusive expenditure tax base will tend to produce more stable results.[48] Though the problem is not limited to divergences between amounts withheld and final tax liability, a simple example of underwithholding will illustrate the advantage to taxpayers under a tax-inclusive computation of delaying payment of expenditure taxes and temporarily increasing savings.[49]

Assume that a taxpayer had a salary of $100 and after-tax consumption of $50, with expenditure tax of 50 percent on a tax-inclusive base or 100 percent on a tax-exclusive base. If no amount of tax were withheld, but the taxpayer put $50 in a savings account, a tax-inclusive computation would produce an expenditure tax liability of $25 for that year (since the tax base would be $100 receipts minus $50 savings). This tax liability presumably would be paid by withdrawing the $25 from savings in the following year. Since no deduction for expenditure tax would be allowed in a tax-inclusive system, the taxpayer's tax liability would increase in future years: by $12.50 in year 2 (50 percent of the $25 additional receipts withdrawn from savings to pay taxes); $6.25 in year 3 (50 percent of the $12.50 additional receipts withdrawn from savings in year 3 to pay expenditure tax), and so on. In contrast, a taxpayer subject to accurate withholding of $50 in year 1 would owe tax of $50 for that year ($100

48. Meade committee report, p. 167.
49. More detailed examples may be found in Meade committee report, pp. 162–67.

of receipts and no deduction for savings). A tax-exclusive computation, on the other hand, would allow deduction for expenditure tax payments and, with a rate of 100 percent, produce an identical tax of $50 in year 1 whether taxes were withheld or saved.

Under the income tax, tax payments are treated like amounts saved: no deduction is allowed, and taxes are computed on a tax-inclusive basis. Under an expenditure tax, treating tax payments like amounts saved requires deduction for tax payments on a cash flow basis, that is, a tax-exclusive base.

Most expenditure tax proponents tend to regard a tax-exclusive base as an advantage because it leads to better taxpayer understanding of the tax consequences at stake, especially as between spending and saving. But the political and psychological implications of tax-exclusive rates, including rates in excess of 100 percent, may prove quite disadvantageous to the adoption of an expenditure tax. If so, it might be possible through mathematical maneuvering to express tax rates in tax-inclusive language. In other words, tax liability might be described in terms of a tax-inclusive rate schedule, with actual computations of the base on a tax-exclusive basis.

Summary and Recommendations

The practical problems that would arise under an expenditure tax in distinguishing spendings to earn income from those intended to satisfy personal needs and desires are quite similar to those familar under an income tax. Given the difficulties under the income tax of resolving these issues, there is no reason to expect that expenditure tax rules will be more satisfactory. I have tried to suggest some practical solutions and have argued for limiting deductions when expenses are induced by mixed personal and business or investment motives. Deductions for travel, meals, lodging, and entertainment should, for example, be more limited than under the current income tax. On the other hand, items like legal expenses, which do not tend to provide consumption benefits, should probably be more generally deductible than under the income tax.

Itemized deductions would most likely be allowed under an expenditure tax for state and local sales and income taxes, for charitable contributions, and extraordinary medical expenses, but the precise rules governing these deductions would be somewhat different from those under the income tax. Interest should be deductible on indebtedness that is includable in expenditure tax receipts and should not be deductible when loan proceeds have been excluded from receipts. The arguments for a standard deduction under an expenditure tax are similar to those under an income tax and seem likely to prove compelling.

Finally, it seems necessary that an expenditure tax be applied to a tax-exclusive base rather than to a tax-inclusive one. This would probably require expenditure tax rates in excess of 100 percent and might require that tax liability be described in terms of a tax-inclusive rate schedule but with actual computations made on a tax-exclusive basis.

Taxation of Business Income

Before considering the impact on corporate taxation of a shift from an income tax to an expenditure tax, it is essential to explore briefly the role of the corporate income tax in the current system. The dominant analytical position justifies a progressive individual income tax (and likewise a progressive personal expenditure tax) by reference to individuals' "ability to pay," and based on this criterion argues that all income should be taxed equally regardless of its source. Under this view, taxation of income at the corporate level is merely a mechanism necessary to ensure that undistributed corporate income does not escape taxation. This theoretical position suggests a criticism of the current corporate income tax. Corporate earnings distributed to shareholders are taxed more heavily than other kinds of individual income, since they are subject to the corporate income tax and taxed at shareholders' marginal rates. Undistributed corporate earnings are, by the same token, undertaxed if the corporate tax rate is less than the shareholder's marginal rate and if the shareholder's tax can be deferred for a long period of time and/or taxed at favorable capital gains rates. Thus present law creates an incentive for retention rather than distribution of corporate profits and for distribution of corporate income as deductible interest to bondholders rather than as dividends to shareholders. The theoretically correct reform of the current corporate income tax thus becomes evident. The separate corporate income tax should be repealed and undistributed corporate income should be directly attributed to shareholders and taxed at their marginal rates. If any tax were continued at the corporate level, it would be only a withholding tax that would be credited to shareholders as corporate income is distributed or attributed to them. Corporations would be treated merely as conduits for tax purposes and be taxed similarly to partnerships and subchapter S corporations.

From this analytical position, the fate of a corporate income tax under an individual expenditure tax also becomes clear. Substitution of an expenditure tax for an income tax would eliminate the need to allocate undistributed corporate income to shareholders because an expenditure tax would not in any case apply until funds were devoted to consumption. To the extent that taxation of business is regarded as complementary to the taxation of individuals, a decision to move to a tax on consumption at the individual level therefore implies elimination of taxes on business income; businesses are engaged in production, not consumption. Amounts earned by businesses and retained for additional investment would be exempt from tax just like amounts invested and saved by individuals. Amounts distributed from businesses to their owners would be included in the owners' receipts and taxed unless invested or saved, but no additional tax would be imposed on the business itself. Individuals would generally be allowed deductions for purchases of corporate stock, and cash receipts relating to stock ownership would be includable for expenditure tax purposes whether in the form of dividends, return of capital, or proceeds from the sale of stock.

The Treasury's *Blueprints,* consequently, calls for a repeal of the corporate income tax.[50] Most proponents of expenditure taxation, however, disagree; they would like to retain a separate corporate tax in some form or other.

Forms of Corporate Taxation

The Meade committee report advances three reasons for the continuation of a separate corporate tax under an expenditure tax regime:

1. Incorporation confers special privileges, in particular the benefits of limited liability.

2. A corporate tax may be a convenient source of significant revenues.

3. The existence of a corporate tax argues for its continuation—otherwise shareholders would enjoy "unexpected windfall gains."[51]

50. *Blueprints,* p. 133.
51. Meade committee report, pp. 227–58.

In attempting to devise a corporate tax that would be appropriate under an expenditure tax regime, the Meade committee does not completely divorce corporate taxation from individual taxation, but endeavors to describe the form of corporation tax that would best "harmonise business taxation" with an expenditure tax at the individual level. The guiding principle is that any corporate tax should preserve the "distinguishing feature" of an expenditure tax: that the taxpayer receive a rate of return on savings equal to the before-tax yield on investments. A tax on corporate profits would necessarily violate this principle, and therefore the Meade committee recommends a flow-of-funds corporate tax base—essentially the excess of total receipts from the sale of goods and services over total expenditures on the purchase of such goods and services, including purchases of capital assets. In effect, the tax would be levied on the "net amount of funds that were taken by shareholders out of the corporate sector of the economy,"[52] usually the excess of dividends over new equity investments. Rather than repeat the Meade committee's analysis here, I shall illustrate a flow-of-funds form of corporate tax by a simple example, which should make clear the relation of such a corporate tax to the expenditure tax treatment of investments at the individual level.

Assume a person has a salary of $400 and wishes to consume $150 after tax. Assume further that an expenditure tax with a uniform rate of 50 percent applies to individuals and that investments will yield a before-tax return of 15 percent. Investments will be made in period 1, and the investment and its return will be consumed in period 2. If in period 1 the taxpayer invests $100, he will be entitled to deduct that amount and will pay a tax of $150 on the remaining $300 tax base, leaving $150 for consumption after tax. In period 2 the $115, representing the return of his investment and its yield, will be included in the tax base, leaving $57.50 for after-tax consumption. The person's reduced consumption in period 1 was $50 and his $7.50 after-tax return is a 15 percent return on reduced consumption.

The basic question is how to structure a corporate tax to produce similar results if the $100 investment were in the form of a contribution of capital to a corporation. If the $100 capital contribution were treated as a receipt at the corporate level, and the $100 corporate investment, say in capital goods, were treated as an offsetting

52. Ibid., p. 257.

deduction, any tax at the corporate level imposed in addition to the tax at the individual level would reduce the amount of after-tax consumption available to the taxpayer below $57.50. The only mechanism for maintaining the same after-tax rate of return to the individual when the contributions of capital were treated as receipts to the corporation would be a corporate tax that would in effect be only a withholding tax on amounts distributed to shareholders. Under a withholding tax, any corporate tax would be refunded (probably through tax credits) when amounts were distributed to shareholders and included in their receipts.

On the other hand, if, as under the Meade committee's proposal, the $100 of contributed capital were not treated as a corporate receipt, the corporation would be able to purchase a capital asset costing $200 (assuming that the corporation could immediately deduct the cost of capital assets, that the corporate tax rate was 50 percent, and that an immediate refund was available on losses or that the corporation had other income against which it might offset the $200 deduction). Under such circumstances, the corporation would be investing $100 and the government contributing an additional $100 in the form of reduced tax or tax refund. If the asset produced a 15 percent yield, it would return $230, which, when subjected to a 50 percent corporate tax, would still leave $115 to be distributed to the shareholder. This $115 distribution would enable the shareholder to consume $57.50, assuming again a 50 percent expenditure tax on individuals.

The flow-of-funds tax recommended by the Meade committee would operate in this way, with imposition of corporate tax deferred until funds were distributed to shareholders. Thus if the funds were reinvested, no corporate tax would be imposed, but the government would continue to share in future yields and would collect tax whenever funds were taken out of the corporate sector by shareholders. If, for example, the corporation in the above example were to reinvest the $30 yield from its $200 asset, a $30 deduction would be allowed at the corporate level and no tax would be collected. The government would, of course, be entitled to its 50 percent share of corporate profits whenever funds were distributed to shareholders, and at the latest when the corporation terminated its existence (for example, through a liquidation). Collection would, of course, be possible in the case of a liquidation only if termination occurred when the company still controlled the assets and accumulated yield. In effect, the government would have a share in the company's assets that would be realized upon distributions to shareholders, and, in general, the government would be indifferent about the timing of such distributions.

Under such a system, it would be important to ensure that shareholders could not obtain corporate earnings without imposition of the corporate tax. If, in the above example, a shareholder/employee (or lessor) were able to obtain the entire $30 return in the form of deductible salary (or rent), greater individual consumption would be possible as a result of corporate investments. Furthermore, if such a tax system were adopted at the corporate level, it would be inappropriate to allow any tax credits or other relief on amounts distributed to shareholders as dividends; allowing such relief would reduce the tax on corporate investments below that applicable to other investments.

The appropriate treatment of debt and interest payments under a flow-of-funds type of corporate tax is not free of doubt. Some analysts recommend that payments to suppliers of finance—whether in the form of dividends or interest—should be taxed and therefore that no interest deduction should be allowed.[53] The Meade committee, on the other hand, under its version of the flow-of-funds tax, would permit deductions for interest and in general would treat corporate debt on the same cash flow basis as individual debt under the general expenditure tax rules. The Meade committee determined that this would require rules distinguishing debt from equity (as are necessary under the current U.S. and British corporate income taxes), noting that "it would be necessary to prevent companies from issuing debt to their shareholders at abnormally high interest rates, so that the return on capital which had in fact been financed by share issues . . . would be paid out as [deductible] interest on debt."[54] In this connection, the Meade committee regards it as necessary to treat interest in excess of a specified rate as a dividend distribution. Since postenactment loans would be includable in receipts, however, while equity contributions would not, it would seem possible simply to correlate the imposition of tax on distributions to suppliers of capital

53. See J. A. Kay and M. A. King, *The British Tax System* (Oxford University Press, 1978), p. 200.
54. Meade committee report, p. 241.

with the treatment of that capital when initially supplied. If no inclusion in receipts were required when capital was received by the corporation, the government would have a contingent tax claim when returns on such capital were distributed; if capital were originally included in receipts, returns would be regarded as deductible interest.

The Meade committee argues that imposing a corporate tax in this way would produce revenue, even though it would not reduce the rate of return on corporate investment. As to future transactions, this revenue allegedly would be produced because "the government would receive a tax revenue from any profits made by companies on their real transactions in excess of the rate of interest on government debt."[55] This would occur because the government becomes, in effect, a joint venturer with the corporation, contributing one-half of the original cost of the asset ($100 in the above example) and receiving one-half of any returns distributed to shareholders. Revenue would also be derived from gain relating to corporate assets on hand at the inception of the tax. Distributed income from such assets and proceeds from their sale would be fully taxed, even though the full cost of the asset might not have been deducted in prior years.

Putting aside for the moment the question of "windfall gains" for existing shareholders who presumably invested with the expectation of a continuing tax on corporate income, unless the Meade committee's argument depends upon expected increases in the aggregate level of investment, it is difficult to understand why its proposed corporate tax would be preferable to elimination of any separate corporate tax (or conversion of the corporate tax to a withholding tax). The government would, in effect, be participating as a joint venturer in investments made by corporations in a manner different from investments made directly by individuals. Returning to the earlier example, if the individual had invested in an unincorporated business, only $100 of assets could be purchased, whereas under the Meade committee's corporate tax system, if he invested in a corporation, he could obtain an additional deduction at the corporate level and thereby purchase $200 of assets. To reach equivalent results at the individual level, a deduction would have to be allowed for an amount double the amount of the investment. It is difficult to understand why $50 of forgone consumption at the individual level should produce $200 for investment if contributed as capital to a corporation, but only $100

55. Ibid., p. 232.

if otherwise saved or invested. Elimination of the corporate tax would seem a better alternative.

If only a cosmetic corporate tax were desired (presumably for political reasons), a corporate tax could be designed that would include contributions of capital in corporate receipts but would be offset by a system of imputation and tax credits at the shareholder level. Such a corporate tax would serve simply as a withholding tax to be refunded to shareholders whenever amounts were distributed and included in the shareholder's receipts. Distortion would result, however, from lags between collection of the tax at the corporate level and refund at the shareholder level. Moreover, an entire corporate tax system might be necessary, even though no additional revenue were intended to be collected from corporations. Conversion of all or a portion of the corporate income tax to a withholding tax on dividends might involve difficult practical problems (which have been adequately discussed in connection with recent proposals to integrate the individual and corporate income taxes through a system of imputation and tax credits).[56]

Alternatively, a straightforward withholding tax on distributions by corporations to shareholders could be enacted to apply at a flat rate, without any calculation of corporate income or profits. Such a tax would be available as a credit against shareholders' expenditure tax liability.

The distinguishing feature of the Meade committee's proposed flow-of-funds tax is that it provides a mechanism for collecting some corporate taxes on existing investments made under an income tax regime without distorting new corporate investment decisions made in the environment of an individual expenditure tax. In so doing, it would eliminate any need to distinguish dividends from returns of capital, to determine a taxpayer's basis in corporate stock, to distinguish capital purchases and improvements from deductible expenses, or to adjust corporate taxes for inflation. For these reasons, such a tax merits consideration. If phasing out the corporate income tax over a long period of time proves to be the only practical alternative, the Meade committee approach may be preferable, but such a

56. See Charles E. McLure, Jr., *Must Corporate Income Be Taxed Twice?* (Brookings Institution, 1979); John S. Nolan, "Integration of Corporate and Individual Income Taxes," in *Proceedings of the University of Southern California Tax Institute, 1978* (USC, 1978), pp. 899–929.

tax would probably produce substantially less corporate tax revenue than is generated under current law.

The Meade committee estimates that the revenue yield from a flow-of-funds corporate tax would be greater than that now produced from income taxes on the corporate sector.[57] Certain differences between the U.S. and British tax systems are noteworthy, however. First, many British companies currently pay little or no corporate income tax because of a system of "stock relief," enacted in 1974, that has had the effect of eliminating the corporate tax liability of British manufacturing companies.[58] Second, since 1973 British corporate tax is imputed to shareholders and credited against shareholders' individual income tax liability on dividends. This means that a large amount of total British corporate tax revenues are really withholding taxes. Finally, the Meade committee bases its revenue estimates on the obviously unrealistic assumption that the behavior of corporations would remain the same under the new tax system. Though a similar effort to estimate the effects on revenue of a change to a flow-of-funds corporate tax in the United States is beyond the scope of this paper, it seems quite likely that the revenue consequences would be substantial. A reduction in corporate tax receipts on the order of 50 percent or more would not be surprising.

Methods of Accounting

The commentators seem to agree that only the cash method of accounting for receipts and expenditures would be appropriate under an expenditure tax.[59] In the case of a proprietorship, any excess of net receipts over business expenditures would be added to the owner's receipts, and the owner would be allowed a deduction if expenditures exceeded receipts. Likewise, cash distributions from partnerships would be included in partners' receipts, and contributions to a partnership or amounts paid to purchase partnership interests would be deductible by the individual partner.

The cash method of accounting is considered appropriate because an accrual accounting system would often tax individuals on amounts not currently available for consumption and would allow deductions for amounts not yet paid and therefore currently available for con-

57. Meade committee report, p. 245; see also ibid., pp. 61–65.
58. Kay and King, *British Tax System*, p. 176.
59. *Blueprints*, p. 135.

sumption. Certain cash method accounting problems that have occurred under the income tax would continue under an expenditure
tax; the constructive receipt doctrine, for example, would still be
applied. On the other hand, the cash equivalency doctrine that has
produced considerable litigation under the income tax would probably not produce significant expenditure tax problems, since such
issues tend to arise most frequently with regard to notes or other investment assets for which offsetting deductions would be available
under an expenditure tax. By the same token, prepayments of expenses other than year-end prepayments would not cause as many
problems under an expenditure tax as under an income tax. Requiring businesses to keep books and records on a cash basis might produce some additional costs for companies that now maintain their
books on the accrual method, but it is difficult to know if these costs
would be large.

It is interesting to observe that in methods of accounting the expenditure tax differs significantly not only from income taxes but
also from value-added taxes, under which accrual accounting is the
preferred method for businesses. In Europe, for example, the value-
added tax usually attaches at the time products are delivered or services rendered and when the recipient becomes obligated to pay,
whether or not a cash payment is actually made. Similar results occur under manufacturers' excise taxes in the United States.

If a separate corporate tax were continued in an expenditure tax
regime, there would be no compelling reason to base such a tax on
the cash method of accounting. Accrual accounting should probably
be allowed for purposes of the corporate tax, but this should be regarded as a concession to taxpayer convenience rather than a result
required by theoretical considerations.

Summary and Recommendations

If an expenditure tax were enacted to replace the income tax on
individuals, a separate corporate income tax would become inappropriate. If some corporate tax were to be maintained, it should basically serve as a withholding tax on corporate distributions to shareholders.

Repealing the corporate tax or converting it to a withholding tax,
however, has serious implications that have not been explored here.
Elimination of the corporate tax might, for example, require enact-

ment of direct subsidies to induce corporate investments that now receive tax-preferred treatment or regulations or excise taxes to discourage corporate expenses, such as those for grass roots lobbying, that are now disallowed under the income tax.

Moreover, concern with "windfall gains" from repealing the corporate income tax might produce long-delayed effective dates or a phaseout so gradual as to interfere with the fundamental economic justifications for converting to an expenditure tax. If this seems likely, the Meade committee's proposal for a flow-of-funds corporate tax merits serious consideration. (Other possibilities, such as a lump-sum tax on assets payable over a number of years or a "windfall profits" tax, should also be analyzed.) If, on the other hand, retention of a separate corporate tax is predicated on considerations of revenue alone or of corporate privileges (like political power or limited liability), various possibilities for corporate excise taxes (on total assets or gross sales, for example), which have not been discussed here, should be given attention.

An expenditure tax implies that business accounting should be based on the cash method, but if a general corporate level tax were retained, accrual accounting by corporations might be permitted.

International Issues

A shift by the United States from income to expenditure taxation would have major implications for international transactions. In recent years hotly contested political battles have been waged over income tax provisions affecting international flows of capital and labor, and the opposing sides in the debates have relied on conflicting principles of international taxation.

The industrialized countries have tended to assert rights to tax residents and citizens on all income, regardless of where earned, and to tax all income earned in their jurisdiction, regardless of the residence of the person who earns it. The United States taxes its citizens, resident aliens, and domestic corporations on their worldwide income. Nonresident alien individuals and foreign corporations are taxed on income "effectively connected with" the conduct of a U.S. trade or business and on other items of U.S. source income through withholding taxes. U.S. citizens and residents are allowed tax credits for foreign income taxes on foreign source income, subject to rules limiting such credits to an amount no greater than that determined by applying U.S. income tax rates to foreign source net income. U.S. shareholders of foreign corporations are normally not taxed on foreign corporate earnings until such earnings are distributed to them. The United States also provides income tax relief to its citizens residing abroad, in the form of an exclusion from income of a specified amount of earnings. Preferential income tax treatment is granted to domestic corporations on income derived from the active conduct of business in a U.S. possession and to "domestic international sales corporations" engaged in the export of goods manufactured in the United States. Precise relations among the income tax rules of the various industrialized countries are usually governed by treaties.

It should be clear from this brief summary of U.S. income taxation of international transactions that no single principle has governed congressional policy. Although current policy tends to favor establishing neutrality among the industrialized countries for the taxation of income, there are important divergences from this principle.

Only the Meade committee and Professors Lodin and Mieszkowski have discussed the international aspects of a shift from income to expenditure taxation.[60] The Treasury Department in *Blueprints* does not discuss international issues arising under an expenditure tax but does argue (in connection with its discussion of a comprehensive income tax) for adoption of the principle of residence, under which countries would tax the worldwide incomes of their residents.[61] Although the definition of residence is difficult, the residence principle, if accepted internationally, would also seem an appropriate basis for assessing a progressive consumption tax. Receipts would be includable regardless of source; investments or savings, whether in the United States or abroad, would be deductible; and consumption would be taxed without regard to where it occurs. The need for foreign tax credits would be eliminated, and the progressive rate structure would be applied only once to all consumption. A graduated expenditure tax imposed on the basis of residence would differ from other taxes on consumption, such as the value-added tax, which are

60. Meade committee report, pp. 411–30, 433–42; Lodin, *Progressive Expenditure Tax,* pp. 108–14; Mieszkowski, "Cash Flow Version of an Expenditure Tax."
61. *Blueprints,* pp. 98–101.

generally applied only to consumption within the boundaries of the taxing jurisdiction.

The practical barrier to an expenditure tax system based upon the residence principle is that international harmonization would come slowly, if at all. Some industrialized countries would probably retain income taxes, and taxing income based upon its source (rather than its owner's residence) would remain attractive to countries that are net importers of capital. Rather than yield to the temptation to assume that with patience international harmonization would occur and expenditure taxation on the residence principle would be adopted throughout the industrialized world, I briefly explore the problems that would arise if the United States were to shift to expenditure taxation while taxation in the rest of the world remained unchanged.

Consumption Abroad

The decision to individualize the tax on consumption through a progressive rate structure clearly implies that U.S. residents (and perhaps nonresident citizens) should be taxed on their consumption whether the consumption takes place here or abroad.

Nonresident Aliens

Notwithstanding a general shift from income to expenditure taxation of U.S. citizens and residents, it does not seem appropriate for the United States to eliminate its income taxes on nonresident aliens or foreign corporations or its withholding taxes on U.S. source income earned by foreign residents until it obtains concessions from other countries on foreign source income earned by U.S. residents. Thus for quite some time—at least until treaties could be renegotiated —the basic income tax provisions applicable to foreign residents would have to be retained. Even though this state of affairs would produce complexity and run counter to U.S. tax treaty undertakings to handle foreign investors from treaty countries and domestic investors in the same way, limiting U.S. taxation of nonresidents to their expenditures on consumption in the United States does not seem immediately feasible or desirable.

Foreign Investments

The treatment of earned income under a progressive expenditure tax would not be very different from that under an income tax. Thus the arguments advanced whether foreign-earned income should be excluded from tax or whether foreign tax credits should be allowed under an expenditure tax for foreign-earned income of U.S. residents are basically the same as those advanced under the income tax. Since Congress has continued exclusions for foreign-earned income and has resisted income tax proposals to convert the foreign tax credit into a deduction for foreign taxes, it seems likely that an expenditure tax would continue such provisions for foreign-earned income.

The appropriate treatment of foreign source investment income of U.S. citizens and residents is more difficult to discern. If adopting an expenditure tax at the individual level were accompanied by repeal of the corporate income tax, the most important question would be whether foreign tax credits relating to income of foreign subsidiaries of U.S. corporations should be allowed as credits to U.S. shareholders. Allowing such credits could become quite complex; it would be particularly difficult to determine the applicable individual tax rate to serve as a limitation on allowable credits. Since income that was reinvested would be subject to a zero rate of tax, no credits should be allowed for undistributed income. Since income earned domestically would be taxed on a cash flow basis, similar treatment should apply to income earned abroad. Corporate income distributed to individual shareholders would first be reduced by any income taxes paid. If, in addition, tax credits were allowed for foreign taxes on income earned abroad, foreign investments would be favored over domestic ones.

If individuals were allowed both an immediate deduction for the purchase of investment or business assets and foreign tax credits for such investments, the after-tax rate of return on reduced consumption would *exceed* the before-tax rate of return on foreign investments, while the after-tax rate of return would equal the before-tax rate of return on domestic investments. Assume, for example, that a person subject to a 50 percent expenditure tax rate wishes to reduce his consumption by $500 and invest $1,000. He is considering choosing between two investments in similar companies. Company A will earn $100 domestically, which will be distributed as dividends. Company B will earn $100 through foreign subsidiaries abroad, will pay foreign income taxes of $20, and will distribute the remaining $80 as dividends. If the taxpayer invests in company A, he will receive $100, which will be included in his receipts and subjected to a 50 percent tax unless saved or reinvested. The $50 after-tax return on the $500 of reduced consumption will equal the before-tax return of 10 percent. If he invests in company B, he will receive an $80 dividend, which, if a $20 foreign tax credit is allowed, will produce a $60 after-tax return—or a return of 12 percent on reduced consumption if the company earns 10 percent before tax. In fact, the higher the foreign tax rate, the higher the after-tax rate of return.

To achieve neutrality for the two investments, it would be necessary to impute creditable foreign taxes as receipts to the shareholder. Then $100 from company B would be included in the shareholder's receipts and $20 would be allowed as a tax credit, which would produce an after-tax return to the shareholder of $50, as would the investment in company A. Including foreign taxes in income and crediting such taxes should achieve neutrality between domestic and foreign investments regardless of the tax rate of the foreign country or of the individual investor, assuming that the returns on investment in the two countries are identical except for the reduction for income taxes in the foreign country. If the foreign tax were a tax on consumption, there would be no need for a tax credit or imputation to preserve neutrality between foreign and domestic investments.

On the other hand, it might be argued that allowing imputation and credit would, in effect, treat foreign income taxes on the corporation as if they were withheld expenditure taxes of the individual, and that foreign taxes should not be imputed and credited with respect to the foreign investment, because any lesser return from the investment abroad would be due to the foreign country's decision to impose an income tax rather than an expenditure tax. This argument suggests denying foreign income tax credits altogether.

Limiting either imputation and crediting of foreign taxes or denial of foreign tax credits to instances in which investments have been subject to U.S. expenditure tax treatment would require distinguishing preenactment from postenactment investments, an extremely difficult rule to administer. It would be simpler to continue to allow the foreign tax credit for all foreign source income, but to deny immediate deduction for investments abroad. Though such a distinction might create controversy under the General Agreement on Tariffs and Trade, there are precedents; the investment credit, for example, does not apply to foreign investments by U.S. corporations or individuals. Such a rule, however, would require retention of income tax treatment for foreign source income. It would then be necessary, for example, to distinguish depreciable from nondepreciable assets and to provide depreciation allowances for the former as under the current income tax. The prospect of an expenditure tax system for domestic investments coupled with an income tax system for foreign investments is not appealing.

A far simpler solution would be to treat all foreign source investment and income on a cash flow basis, and either impute and credit foreign income taxes to shareholders or disallow foreign tax credits altogether. The impact of such rules on the international flows of capital and labor merits further study.

The issue of deferral of taxation of income earned abroad, which has engendered great controversy under the income tax, should disappear under an expenditure tax. Foreign source receipts, like receipts from other investments, would be includable in expenditure tax accounts on a cash flow basis.

Emigration

The Meade committee and Professor Lodin argue that there will be a substantial incentive for people to leave an expenditure tax country when they intend to dissave by living on previously accumulated capital. To deal with this problem the Meade committee proposes a special tax on emigrants that is intended to recapture relief initially granted when taxpayers were allowed deductions for savings.[62] The committee would require taxpayers to know the total value on the date of emigration of all assets previously deducted in calculating expenditure taxes; the value, adjusted for inflation, of assets as of the date the expenditure tax was introduced; and the value, adjusted for inflation, of gifts and bequests subjected to transfer tax. Additional adjustments would be required if the taxpayer were previously an immigrant. As an alternative, the Meade committee suggests a special tax on the entire value of an emigrant's assets. Professor Lodin's proposals are similar, although easier to adopt in Sweden, where a net wealth tax is currently in place.[63]

Lengthy discussion of these proposals does not seem necessary;

62. Meade committee report, pp. 438–42.
63. Lodin, *Progressive Expenditure Tax*, pp. 108–10.

they are unworkable and probably impossible to enforce in the United States—certainly impossible without controls on the movement of capital to foreign countries. Although the predictions by the Meade committee and Professor Lodin of widespread avoidance of British and Swedish expenditure taxes through emigration are troubling, the problem may be more significant for European countries than for the United States. It is simply impossible to know in advance whether the shift from an income tax to an expenditure tax will induce U.S. citizens to emigrate in any great number. In one sense at least, the tax avoidance problem seems likely to be less important under an expenditure tax than under an income tax. Under an income tax, a person need only move capital to a tax-haven country to avoid tax; under an expenditure tax he himself would have to move. And if nonresident U.S. citizens were subject to expenditure tax on worldwide consumption, they could avoid tax only by abandoning citizenship. However, any such tendency of U.S. citizens and residents to emigrate should be offset by the countervailing tendency of people to immigrate to the United States to avoid income taxes abroad. Elaborate mechanisms to deal with emigrants, such as the proposals by the Meade committee, should be avoided unless expenditure tax experience demonstrates that they are essential.

New problems of enforcement and collection, however, do seem likely to arise under an expenditure tax when individuals obtain deduction upon purchase of an asset and attempt to exclude the sale price of the asset from receipts, perhaps by selling it abroad. Under an income tax, all that is at stake when assets are sold is the tax on the gain from the asset; under an expenditure tax, the entire sale price of the asset would normally be included in the base, and, if excluded, tax-free consumption in an amount equal to the sale price could be achieved. It is difficult to know how these problems will arise in practice, but greater policing of foreign sales, including those of foreign trusts, may prove necessary.

Immigration

Because expenditure tax deductions would be allowed for the purchase of investment assets, it would seem necessary to include in receipts for the year of immigration the amount of cash (or consumption goods) imported by an immigrant or otherwise to limit the amount he can deduct against subsequent receipts. If such rules were not adopted, immigrants would consume imported cash free of expenditure tax. The treatment of cash imported by immigrants is related to the general treatment of cash balances upon enactment of an expenditure tax, a problem that is discussed below.

Summary and Recommendations

The impact on international arrangements and transactions of a shift from income to expenditure taxation needs considerable attention before enactment of an expenditure tax in the United States. In this section I have mentioned some of the problems and have tentatively advanced several recommendations.

—Pending treaty renegotiations, the United States should continue income taxes on nonresident aliens and foreign corporations and withholding taxes on U.S. source income earned by foreign residents. In addition, the United States should not allow any expenditure tax credits for foreign income taxes on investment or business income earned abroad or, alternatively, if credits were allowed, should impute to receipts any creditable amounts. The arguments for revising the rules for taxation of foreign-earned income are similar to those under the income tax.

—Foreign consumption expenditures by U.S. citizens and residents should be treated like domestic consumption expenditures.

—No special expenditure tax rules should initially be enacted to deter emigration, but special rules would be necessary with respect to cash brought to the United States by immigrants.

In addition, the various rules suggested in this section must be subjected to further scrutiny, to determine their probable impact on the U.S. economy. The practical consequences of the various mechanisms for dealing with international transactions will undoubtedly overwhelm the application of tax logic.

Administrative Considerations

In this section I consider some administrative problems likely to arise under an expenditure tax, assuming that an expenditure tax would be administered in approximately the same way as the income tax.[64] The first formal determination of a person's expenditure tax liability would occur when the taxpayer filed his expenditure tax return, and an expenditure tax system, like the current income tax system, would depend significantly upon self-assessment and voluntary compliance. Collection procedures, procedures for the resolution of disputes, and sanctions under an expenditure tax would be similar to those under the current income tax. Three issues of tax administration are taken up here: withholding, information reporting, and audit problems. I assume that the audit capability of the Internal Revenue Service would not be expanded under an expenditure tax, and therefore that, as with the current income tax, only a small percentage of total expenditure tax returns would be audited, with audit selection usually based upon statistical sampling techniques.

Withholding

Since more than 75 percent of total individual income tax liability is collected through withholding, the need for current tax payment through a withholding system should be apparent. Collection of the bulk of taxes at the source through withholding would be essential to an expenditure tax. But withholding would very likely present certain difficulties not present under the current income tax.

The withholding provisions of the current income tax provide a variety of methods intended to take into account fluctuations in taxpayers' wages during the year and to permit reduced withholding when taxpayers expect greater than average deductions. Withholding exemptions are provided for taxpayers who are likely to be nontaxable when their final income tax returns are filed. Notwithstanding efforts to devise income tax withholding rules that approximate final income tax liability, a substantial amount of overwithholding occurs; in fiscal year 1977 more than $35 billion (including overpayments of estimated taxes) was refunded to taxpayers. The Treasury estimates that the bulk of income tax overwithholding is voluntary.

64. See Meade committee report, pp. 478–86; Lodin, *Progressive Expenditure Tax,* pp. 115–23. The British and Swedish reports are not as useful in connection with expenditure tax issues as elsewhere because of differences in the administration of the tax system in those countries and in the United States. For example, the Meade committee report discusses at some length the difficulties in adopting a self-assessment system in the United Kingdom, and Professor Lodin relies heavily on the existence in Sweden of a tax on wealth to facilitate the administration of an expenditure tax.

Producing accurate withholding under an expenditure tax should prove more difficult than under an income tax. Under an income tax, wage withholding depends only on the amount of the taxpayer's wages and estimated credits and deductions based upon these wages. Under an expenditure tax, the amount of final tax liability would also depend on the taxpayer's annual savings or investment. The best withholding approximation would estimate consumption relative to wages based upon typical patterns of consumption and saving. There would probably be a tendency to err on the side of overwithholding to assure collection of the tax. An expenditure tax seems likely to produce greater variations in tax liability than the income tax, both among taxpayers with similar amounts of gross income and for the same taxpayer from year to year. The greatest variations would tend to be concentrated in the middle and upper brackets.

Withholding on expenditure tax receipts other than wages does not seem practical. Under the income tax, the Internal Revenue Service has recently urged dividend and interest withholding on the ground that the current information reporting system, under which payors notify recipients of the amount of interest or dividends paid during the year, is inadequate to assure income tax collection. Recent estimates of annual underreporting of income taxes on interest and dividends have ranged as high as $1.5 billion. Income tax withholding for interest and dividends has been rejected largely because it would have to be based upon a fixed rate of tax, and fixed percentage withholding would tend to overwithhold for low-income taxpayers and underwithhold for high-income taxpayers. Applying graduated withholding rates to interest and dividends has been considered impractical, as payors would have to know the marginal income tax bracket of their creditors and shareholders. Reasonably accurate withholding on interest and dividends would be even more difficult under an expenditure tax than under the income tax, because no expenditure tax would be due whenever dividends and interest were reinvested. On the other hand, the problem of expenditure tax understatement might be less significant, since payment of investment returns would produce tax less frequently.

As indicated in the previous section, conversion of the corporate tax to a withholding tax on dividends through a system of imputation and credits merits attention. Because the expenditure tax concept of receipts would be somewhat broader than the current definition of income, withholding on other categories of receipts should also be considered. Such withholding, however, would tend to suffer the same difficulties as withholding on dividends and interest and also does not seem practical. Withholding would very likely not be possible on gifts or sales of assets, and withholding on loans seems neither practical nor necessary. (If loans for investment purposes were included in receipts, an offsetting deduction would eliminate tax.) Reliance on increased information reporting and requirements for current payments of estimated tax, with additional enforcement for amounts not now included in gross income but included in expenditure tax receipts seems necessary.

As indicated in the section on deductions, divergence between current payments of tax (through withholding or estimated tax payments) and final tax liability would, however, create special problems under an expenditure tax imposed on a tax-inclusive base. If, for example, underwithholding were to occur, amounts could be saved that would otherwise be taxable, and expenditure tax liability would be reduced. Overwithholding, on the other hand, would eliminate the possibility of saving withheld amounts and thus obtaining expenditure tax deductions. Imposing expenditure tax on a tax-exclusive base, that is, allowing deductions for current payments of expenditure tax, would, however, eliminate such problems. In any event, interest should probably be paid to taxpayers on amounts overwithheld.

Information Reporting

Increased information reporting might be necessary under an expenditure tax. If loans had to be reported on a cash flow basis, lenders should be required to provide annual information statements to taxpayers informing them of both amounts borrowed and repaid. If gifts and bequests were includable in receipts of donees, information reporting should probably be required for gifts and bequests. If individuals had to report receipts from businesses on a cash flow basis, information reporting of such payments should be required.

Likewise, expenditure tax information reporting might be required for purchases and sales of investment assets and for net annual additions or reductions in savings account balances with financial institutions. For the typical stock market transaction, however, it would be difficult to require sellers to report social security numbers of purchasers, but some aid to enforcement would seem essential. Without an enforcement mechanism, deductions for purchases of investment assets might be overstated and sales of such assets understated. Since the entire sales price of investment assets would be includable in expenditure tax receipts, incentives for underreporting sales would be greater than under the income tax, where only gain is includable in the tax base. Kaldor and Slitor, for example, urge the use of an expenditure tax voucher system, under which purchasers would be required to furnish vouchers to sellers, which presumably would be forwarded to the Internal Revenue Service to confirm transactions.[65]

Excessive reliance on information reporting as an enforcement device should be avoided, however. The Internal Revenue Service's ability to cross-check information reports under the present income tax system is quite inadequate. In 1975, for example, the Service collected about 435,000,000 interest and dividend information returns, but less than half were processed for possible computer matching. When information returns are submitted on individual papers, the process of transferring such information onto magnetic tape is alone a sufficient burden to preclude cross-checking. If the number of information returns were to increase greatly because of the expansion of the category of receipts under an expenditure tax, information might have to be submitted in a way readily usable by the Internal Revenue Service. For example, general information reporting might be required to be on magnetic tape. But such a requirement would be burdensome to certain taxpayers. In any event, greater cross-checking of information returns would be desirable, and sufficient funding would be necessary for the Internal Revenue Service to handle the additional workload.

Audit

Expenditure tax audit selection would tend to mirror the current income tax process. A mathematical technique would probably be used similar to the so-called discriminant index function that now identifies returns with a high potential for significant understatement of income tax. Assuming that the cash flow method of reporting investment assets were adopted, the construction of a similar expenditure tax formula would be facilitated if taxpayers were required to report beginning and ending cash balances. Otherwise, variations among taxpayers in the amount of cash on hand might produce

65. Kaldor, *An Expenditure Tax*, p. 217; Slitor, "Administrative Aspects of Expenditures Taxation," pp. 254–55.

consumption variances that would not be explained by information contained in the return. If the yield exemption option for reporting financial transactions were made widely available, identification of returns for audit from information appearing on the return would be extremely difficult.

If businesses were required to shift to a cash method of accounting for the expenditure tax while continuing to use an accrual method of accounting for financial reporting, revenue agents' ability to use business books and records in auditing tax returns would very likely be lessened and audits rendered more difficult. In business audits, revenue agents currently make great use, for example, of the form 1120, schedule M, reconciliation of book accounting and tax accounting. Greater divergences between book and tax accounting would tend to increase enforcement costs and might require additional training of revenue agents. If an expenditure tax were adopted as a supplement to the income tax, expenditure tax accounting and income tax accounting should be closely coordinated.

As under the current income tax, expenditure tax enforcement would be largely dependent upon taxpayers' reliability in complying with stated requirements. If the "tax lottery" were played aggressively, with tax returns serving chiefly as opening bids, serious enforcement problems would occur. Such expenditure tax problems, however, do not seem likely to differ from those under the current income tax. The expenditure tax avoidance game, however, would emphasize efforts to exclude consumption from the tax base, as contrasted with tax avoidance efforts under the income tax, which are often concentrated on excluding investment income from tax or deferring tax on such income.

Where significant underreporting is suspected, excessive conspicuous consumption relative to the reported tax base may prove a more reliable measure of expenditure tax understatement than income tax understatement. Looking at taxpayers' consumption in an effort to reconstruct income has occurred most frequently when the Internal Revenue Service has tried to collect income taxes on illegally obtained income. Results have been mixed.

Summary and Recommendations

An expenditure tax does not seem likely to produce administrative problems significantly greater than or different from those familiar under an income tax. Withholding would probably have to be limited to wages, and the variations between amounts withheld and a person's final tax liability would probably be greater than under the income tax. Interest should therefore be paid on amounts overwithheld. Information reporting should be extended to such items as gifts and bequests not now reportable under the income tax, and the ability of the Internal Revenue Service to cross-check such data should be increased. Audits of individual returns would most likely be similar to those under the income tax.

Transitional Problems

The change from income to expenditure taxation would constitute a major revision of the tax system requiring careful consideration of transitional problems. But the transition would affect various categories of taxpayers differently. The expenditure tax base of low-income taxpayers who spend more than their income would be greater than an income base, but rates and exemptions could be adjusted to eliminate any increase in tax. For many low- and moderate-income taxpayers whose income and consumption expenditures are approximately equal, the change from income to expenditure taxation would not significantly affect tax liability and should cause no special problems. Special transitional rules should not be needed for those two categories of taxpayers.

The situation of other taxpayers, however, who have accumulated wealth under an income tax system that would be spent under an expenditure tax, has brought forth special transitional proposals from the Treasury Department, the Meade committee, and Professor Lodin, the three commentators who have considered transitional problems.[66] Although the details of their recommendations vary, the underlying analysis seems quite similar.

The commentators have usually focused on persons who have accumulated wealth out of income that has been taxed and who would spend such wealth after enactment of the expenditure tax. Problems, however, would also arise when persons have made investments that are granted preferential treatment under an income tax

66. *Blueprints*, pp. 181–215; Meade committee report, pp. 187–92, 198–200; Lodin, *Progressive Expenditure Tax*, pp. 123–27.

and that would not receive preferential expenditure tax treatment. Here the alleged inequity would be due not to prior income tax burdens on the individual, but rather to the frustration of expectations that the investments would continue to receive tax-favored treatment.

The Two Basic Approaches to the Problem of Transition

In general, there are two basic attitudes that might inform recommendations for transition. First, the politically dominant view argues that significant changes in the tax laws should be adopted in a way to minimize losses to persons who have planned their affairs on the expectation that current tax laws will remain unchanged. This attitude is reflected in recent tax legislation that has tended to protect taxpayers' expectations through the enactment of grandfather rules, which exempt from the change in the law transactions entered into before the date of change. Proponents of grandfathering usually argue that such rules would minimize adverse wealth effects that would otherwise result from changes in the tax law. The Treasury, for example, identifies two problems "requiring special transitional rules": (1) carry-over problems and (2) price changes. These problems are described as follows:

Carryover problems would occur to the extent that changes in the tax code affect the taxation of income earned in the past but not yet subject to the tax or, conversely, income taxed in the past that may be subject to a second tax. Price changes would occur in those instances where changes in the tax code altered the expected flow of after-tax income from existing investments *in the future.*[67]

The basic problem, however, in both cases is that relative wealth would be changed because of a tax law revision. The Treasury illustrates the carry-over problem by reference to a retiree who has accumulated wealth that he expects to consume during his retirement. If an expenditure tax were introduced, his wealth would purchase less consumption than if the tax were not introduced. His wealth would, in effect, be reduced and his expectations frustrated.

"Price changes" would occur whenever a change in the tax law altered the relative taxation of future earnings from an asset. Changes

67. *Blueprints,* p. 181.

in relative rates of income taxation would produce changes in asset values, as would a shift to expenditure taxation. If the relative rate of taxation on future income were increased, the value of the asset would fall; if the relative tax were decreased, the asset would become more valuable. By the same token, if the relative rate of taxation on income from the other kinds of assets were decreased, the relative value of the asset would be lessened.

In general, *Blueprints* adopts a policy that would favor grandfathered effective dates to protect taxpayers who have "relied" on existing law, whether price changes or carry-over problems were involved. This analysis therefore argues for protecting not only retirees but also persons who enjoy tax-preferred income from investments that would be treated like other investments under an expenditure tax. The issue in the second case is similar to that which would arise if a tax advantage were repealed under the income tax or if the income tax itself were repealed.

The second basic attitude toward tax law transitions, which I have advanced in greater detail elsewhere, is that neither fairness nor efficiency demand grandfathered effective dates, and that when the magnitude of change is large, the impact should be reduced through delayed or phased-in effective dates rather than grandfathering.[68]

Though it may be possible to distinguish some so-called carryover problems from price changes (because the wealth effects of the former will not necessarily be reflected in the market price of individual assets), the two kinds of problems are usually similar in their effect on individuals. For the retiree, consumption would necessarily be less than was anticipated because of a change in the tax law. Likewise, when an asset declines in value because of a tax change, the owner's ability to consume is also decreased. Assuming the decrease in consumption in each case were similar in magnitude, I would treat the problems analytically as one—as a wealth reduction caused by a change in law.

The principal argument advanced by the proponents of "prospectivity" in tax law changes is that considerations of fairness and efficiency require the protection of those who probably altered their behavior on the expectation that a tax rule would remain unchanged.

68. Michael J. Graetz, "Legal Transitions: The Case of Retroactivity in Income Tax Revision," *University of Pennsylvania Law Review,* vol. 47 (November 1977), pp. 47–87.

The argument, in effect, would treat the recipient of a tax benefit as
if he had entered into a contract with the government and would preclude the government from disadvantaging such a person by changing the law. An evaluation of this argument requires a determination
of what kinds of expectations are to be generally eligible for protection.

Economists, for example, would usually not describe a competitive
market as unfair or inefficient, although it is certainly not unchang-
ing or even predictable. Persons make long-term capital investments
under conditions that produce in them "expectations" that these investments will be profitable. But tastes and societal conditions
change; technological advances, for example, may render production
methods obsolete, and changes of this sort may be of such magnitude
that investors will suffer sizable losses. It is, however, the ability of
the market to adjust output to reflect changes in tastes and technology
that is often described as its greatest achievement. Protection by law
of those who invest in a product or process that is subsequently dis-
dained in the marketplace is not demanded, nor even suggested, by
efficiency or fairness criteria. Why should efficiency or fairness require a different result when losses occur because a change in tastes
or societal conditions is reflected through the political process rather
than through the market? Would not those who fervently argue for
compensation (or other protection, perhaps through a grandfathered
effective date) for losses suffered because of a change in law be ap-
palled if similar protection were proposed for those who invested in
Edsel or hula hoop production? But what is the difference between
market and political processes that justifies such protection against
political change? Such a justification becomes particularly difficult
in a mixed economy, where the market is so often affected by political
decisions.

Fairness and efficiency do not require individuals to assess a zero
probability of change in law before they respond to a legal rule.
Political output should be expected to change. The risks of a change
in law do not seem necessarily different in kind or magnitude from
the risks of a change in market demand or technology. A priori, it
cannot be said that the latter are less random, or more predictable.
Since there are no convincing empirical data showing that the losses
from political change are disproportionately distributed or more
burdensome on productive output than market-reflected changes,

efficiency and fairness criteria seem to make no demands for grand-fathered effective dates. In fact, efficiency may demand that people expect changes in law. In the market context, only behavior that takes into account probabilities of change is treated as reasonable. Reasonable expectations in the political context may also include only those that assess some subjective probability of change in law.

Fairness arguments grounded upon individuals' reliance have tended to concentrate on protecting those who are nominally affected by a change in the law. For example, in the case of an exemption for state and local bond interest, advocates of compensation to losers would compensate only the holders of tax-exempt bonds. A grand-fathered effective date rule would similarly tend to protect those who hold tax-exempt bonds. Thus, though some argue that people who purchase tax-exempt bonds should be entitled to tax-free interest for the life of the bond, it has not been suggested that issuers of tax-exempt bonds, who may well have structured their financing plans on the expectation that exempt status would continue into the future (or, perhaps more appropriately, with a high subjective probability that the exemption would remain unchanged), are entitled to continuation of the tax exemption because of their "reliance" interest. Nor has it been argued that those who demanded or supplied substitutes, on the assumption that the exemption would continue, should also be protected. If the fairness of change depends upon individual reliance, this fairness concept should demand the protection of everyone who might have altered behavior because of a specific tax rule.

If fairness demands protection of everyone whose expectations are upset by a change in law, grandfathered effective date rules will usually be inadequate. Nothing short of the perfect stability of legal rules seems likely to suffice. Uncertainty will necessarily produce winners and losers. But a requirement that once a law is enacted it must remain unchanged raises fairness problems itself, particularly in the context of law produced by representative democratic political institutions subject to periodic changes in representation and political leadership.

The Problem of Income Tax—Favored Investments

Most of the literature concerned with transitional problems in taxation considers the repeal of the tax-favored treatment for particular investments, such as would occur in a move to a comprehensive income tax rather than to an expenditure tax.[69] The following statement captures the dominant sentiment:

In general, the repeal of code provisions that provide an incentive for certain business-related expenditures or investments in specific assets should be developed to minimize the losses to persons who made such expenditures or investments prior to the effective date of the new law. The principal technique to effectuate this policy would be to grandfather actions taken under current law.[70]

Similar considerations argue for protection from change through special transitional rules if the income tax on competitive investments is significantly reduced or eliminated. For example, Frederic Hickman, former assistant secretary of the treasury for tax policy, has argued that special rules are necessary to ensure that persons who now receive tax-favored treatment would be protected if proposals to reduce the corporate income tax on dividends were enacted:

Once [so-called tax-preference items] are in place, the market adjusts to them, or, in the words of the economists, they are "capitalized." . . . If the subsidies are taken away, [persons] will make an abnormally low return and suffer a loss in . . . value.[71]

If the income tax were replaced by an expenditure tax, similar problems would arise. This can be illustrated with reference to state and local bonds, on the assumption that interest on such bonds would be included in receipts under an expenditure tax and therefore treated like other investment assets.

If owners of state and local bonds were not protected through a grandfathered effective date rule, the value of their bonds would decline relative to other investment assets, and there would be no difference in the value of state and local bonds and, for example, corporate bonds of similar risk. Protecting holders of tax-favored assets, however, might result in an increase in the value of the tax-favored asset. For example, under the income tax, if exclusion of interest on municipal bonds were repealed only for bonds issued after

69. See ibid.; *Blueprints*, pp. 181–215; Committee on Tax Policy, New York State Bar Association, "Retroactivity of Tax Legislation," *Tax Lawyer*, vol. 29 (Fall 1975), pp. 21–30; "Setting Effective Dates for Tax Legislation: A Rule of Prospectivity," *Harvard Law Review*, vol. 84 (December 1970), pp. 436–55.

70. *Blueprints*, p. 200.

71. *The President's 1978 Tax Reduction and Reform Proposals*, Hearings before the House Committee on Ways and Means, 95 Cong. 2 sess. (GPO, 1978), pt. 9, p. 6120.

the date of enactment, interest on previously issued bonds would remain exempt from tax. Since the bonds are not perpetuity obligations, once all the bonds outstanding as of the enactment date reached maturity, all interest would be subject to tax. The maximum supply of tax-exempt bonds would be fixed as of the date of enactment; with varying maturity dates for the bonds outstanding as of the date of enactment, the supply of tax-exempt bonds would subsequently shrink until all the bonds had matured. With a grandfathered effective date, the value of existing municipal bonds would rise as higher-bracket taxpayers purchased these bonds from lower-bracket taxpayers.

Whenever a subsidy is provided to producers of specified goods, through favored tax treatment or otherwise, the introduction of the subsidy will usually result in a decrease in the price of the subsidized good and an increase in the output of the good. The precise effects of the subsidy on price and quantity would depend upon the elasticities of the supply of and the demand for the good. If the subsidy were repealed, other things being equal, the output and price would be expected to return to the equilibrium in effect before the subsidy was introduced. But if the product of certain firms were grandfathered so that the subsidy was continued for those firms, the grandfathered firm would enjoy economic rents (in this case, increased relative value).

For example, if a subsidy were provided (either directly or through the tax system) to suppliers of housing, the output of housing would increase and rental prices would fall. If the subsidy were subsequently removed, rental prices and output would tend to return to the original equilibrium. But an owner of a grandfathered apartment building would enjoy increasing rental prices as he would then be competing with owners who were not subsidized. The grandfathered apartment building would increase in value relative to nonsubsidized housing.

The repeal of tax-favored treatment without grandfathering would result in a decline in wealth of people who held the tax-favored investments before the repeal. With a change from income to expenditure taxation, if, as the Treasury recommends, all assets were treated as though expenditure tax were prepaid and yield and sales prices were exempted from receipts, the value of state and local bonds would tend to decline to a value that would render their yield equal to that of corporate bonds with similar risk. The number of such valuation effects is difficult to estimate, since it would vary according to the kinds of assets that would be affected by the change in law. If, for instance, a fixed-obligation tax-exempt bond were at issue, one might ignore the possibility of shifting the burden of the repeal of the tax exemption to the supplier of the bond. On the other hand, if the tax-favored asset were rental property, before the repeal landlords and tenants might share the benefits of the tax reduction, and both groups might be affected by the repeal of the tax exemption. Moreover, elimination of such a tax exemption would affect the supply of housing. Even in the case of the fixed-obligation bond, the expectations of suppliers would most likely be affected by the change in law. Issuers of tax-exempt bonds might have developed their long-range financing plans expecting continuation of the relative advantage resulting from the tax exemption.

The repeal of tax-favored treatment without grandfathering or neutralization of a tax advantage through the elimination of the income tax on other investments would result in a decline in the wealth of those who held tax-favored investments before the change. To protect the position of those who enjoy favored treatment under the income tax, special rules would be needed to distinguish the expenditure tax treatment of such assets from that of other assets. If most other preenactment assets were included in initial expenditure tax receipts, the exemption of yield or the deduction for basis (or value) of income tax–favored assets would protect the owners of such assets. If, on the other hand, most preenactment assets were given a special transitional expenditure tax deduction or exclusion, as recommended by Professor Lodin, the Treasury, and the Meade committee, an additional benefit would have to be provided to maintain the relative advantage of the tax-favored investment. For example, if preenactment corporate bonds were treated as expenditure tax prepaid (either through the yield exclusion option, which would exclude the interest and sales price of such bonds from expenditure tax receipts, or through an immediate deduction for the basis or value of the assets), it would be necessary to provide *both* an expenditure tax exclusion and a deduction for state and local bonds issued before the date of enactment.

The problem of the special transitional treatment of assets favored under the income tax is further complicated by arguments that certain assets that have received preferential treatment should be treated *less* favorably in a transition from income to expenditure taxation. The Meade committee, for instance, argues that pension benefits that have received expenditure tax treatment under the income tax should not be eligible for the transitional exclusion treatment proposed for assets that have previously been accumulated out of after-tax income. In fact, the Meade committee would reduce the amount of assets otherwise eligible for transitional relief by the amount of accumulated pension benefits.[72] State and local bonds might also be characterized as having approximately received expenditure tax treatment under the income tax (although they are advantaged through yield exemption rather than immediate deduction). This fact, however, would be of little comfort to persons concerned about the adverse wealth effects (due to the decline in value of such bonds) that would occur if no special treatment were provided.

In general, special rules should not be enacted to grandfather assets that have received favored treatment under the income tax. I have argued elsewhere, in the context of income tax repeal of tax-favored treatment, that grandfather rules should usually be rejected in favor of delayed or phased-in effective dates. In transition to an expenditure tax, the owners of such assets would suffer a decrease in wealth that would, in effect, be attributable to the termination of the income tax on *other* investments. Under these circumstances, the arguments for protecting those who hold tax-favored investments seem even less compelling, even though their disappointment (and the decline in the value of their assets) would be identical.

The Problem of Wealth Accumulated after Payment of Income Taxes

The expenditure tax commentators have been principally concerned with people who have accumulated wealth out of taxed income that would be spent after enactment of an expenditure tax. The taxation of such expenditures is considered inequitable when a person in those circumstances is compared with one whose income, savings, and consumption all occur after or before enactment of an expenditure tax. The combined income and expenditure taxes on a person caught in the transition might be greater than the total taxes

72. Meade committee report, p. 190.

that would have been imposed if he had always lived under either an income tax or an expenditure tax.

To protect such people, *Blueprints* and Professor Lodin recommend that, at the inception of an expenditure tax, all existing assets be treated as tax prepaid; in other words, preenactment assets would not be taxed on a cash flow basis but instead would be excluded from expenditure tax computations. To minimize the "inequitable distribution effects" of such treatment, the Treasury recommends that for a ten-year period taxpayers be required to compute both income and expenditure tax liability and pay the greater amount. It also suggests that this requirement might be limited to those with adjused gross incomes above a certain level; for example, $20,000 or more.[73] All unrealized capital gains would be subjected to income taxation at the end of the ten-year transition period.

The Meade committee also recommends a ten-year phase-in of the expenditure tax, which would be accomplished by adding one-tenth of the expenditure tax adjustment to the income tax in the first year, two-tenths in the second year, and so on. The "expenditure tax adjustment" is described as involving "adding purchases and deducting sales" [*sic*] of financial assets from the income tax base.[74]

As an alternative transitional measure, the Meade committee would provide tax relief for people who held assets on the date of enactment. Such relief would be limited by an unspecified lump sum that would vary directly with the taxpayer's age. The lump-sum limitation is presumably intended to ensure that wealthy people would not avoid indefinitely all payment of expenditure taxes simply because they had paid income taxes in the past. If, for example, such relief were not subject to dollar limitation, a person with $1,000,000 of assets treated as expenditure tax prepaid on the date of enactment could consume $100,000 a year tax free for ten years even if he earned no additional income. If additional income were earned and saved, the imposition of expenditure tax might be delayed indefinitely.

Assuming that the alleged inequity due to a shift from income to expenditure taxation for persons with preenactment wealth should be addressed, the principal objection to the Treasury and Meade committee recommendations is that they are unduly complex. Each involves a ten-year phase-in during which taxpayers are required either

73. *Blueprints*, pp. 209–11, 215n.
74. Meade committee report, p. 188.

to compute both income and expenditure taxes or to make fractional expenditure tax adjustments to income tax calculations. The Meade committee requires full valuation of assets at the date of enactment, and both the committee and the Treasury require realization of all unrealized gains before the expenditure tax is made fully effective. Furthermore, the Treasury's transitional proposals are complicated by the decision to permit the expenditure tax yield exemption option for financial assets.

If relief is to be granted for preenactment assets, it should take the form of an immediate deduction of the basis of assets held on the date of enactment (perhaps limited to a maximum dollar amount, with a carry-over or required spread over a period of years). This would eliminate the need for a realization date for unrealized capital gains and would also eliminate any need for taxpayers to sell pre-enactment assets to obtain expenditure tax deductions. Moreover, it would avoid any subsequent increase in tax-free consumption due to postenactment speculative gains, such as might occur under the Treasury's proposal to exempt preenactment assets from expenditure tax computations.

Because of the variety of fully and partly exempt sources of income under current law, limiting relief to assets that have been purchased with taxed income would add complexity to the transition. For example, pension benefits have not been taxed, and realized capital gains have been only partly taxed. Inherited wealth has been taxed only to the extent that unrealized gains have not escaped income taxation through stepped-up basis provisions. Investments in state and local bonds, real estate, oil and gas, motion pictures, farming, and so forth might have been untaxed, partly taxed, or subsidized. Although one might argue for special rules either to deny transitional relief or to preserve tax-favored treatment in such cases, complexity would necessarily result from either choice.

On balance, I would deny special transitional relief to all assets without attempting to determine whether they were accumulated from taxed or untaxed income. Providing transitional relief limited to cases in which income was previously taxed (since the equity case seems somewhat stronger) would necessarily require higher tax rates on consumption (and therefore a greater tax burden on wages) and would cause undue complexity in compliance and administration.

In the short run, at least, the change from an income tax to an expenditure tax should increase the after-tax return from savings and investments and would thus benefit those who are able to save, whether from wages or accumulated wealth. The principal difficulties of transition would fall on people who consume a large portion of their wealth in the early years following enactment and would thus be unable to enjoy the increased after-tax returns from savings that would most likely accrue in the short run under an expenditure tax. (The question whether any increase in after-tax return would occur in the longer run or whether increases in the supply of capital would result in a reduction of before-tax and therefore of after-tax returns is beyond the scope of this paper.) This situation is likely to occur most frequently for retired elderly taxpayers (and occasionally in other special circumstances, such as when a handicapped person is dis-saving).

The income tax contains three principal benefits available to tax-payers aged sixty-five or over. The first of these benefits is the ex-clusion from income of social security benefits (which have been recommended for taxation under an expenditure tax). The second is an extra personal exemption (of $1,000) available to every person aged sixty-five or over. The third is the retirement income credit, which is designed to reduce the tax on elderly people's income (in-cluding a certain amount of earnings) so long as total income is limited. Because of the limitations, the retirement income credit chiefly benefits low- and moderate-income taxpayers.

These income tax provisions have been adopted over the past forty years without any comprehensive rationale, but some form of re-duced income taxation for the elderly can be supported on the ground that the income tax penalizes deferred consumption relative to pres-ent consumption. Although the precise benefits of current law are quite difficult to justify theoretically, it might be argued that some offsetting income tax benefit should be provided when consumption has been deferred until retirement. Under an expenditure tax, future consumption would not be penalized more than present consump-tion, and, therefore, taxpayers who defer consumption until retire-ment would not face any relative expenditure tax disadvantage. Thus the argument for special benefits for the elderly largely disappears under an expenditure tax.

The current generation of elderly people, however, has been sub-ject to income tax during their working years and would be subject to expenditure tax after retirement without the offsetting benefit of being able to save for a substantial period of time under advantageous expenditure tax conditions. It would therefore seem appropriate to continue some special benefit for the elderly during the early years of expenditure taxation. This could take the form of a special dollar exclusion available to people aged sixty-five or older (and perhaps to disabled people with moderate wealth or income), which could be a large amount when the tax was first introduced and be gradually phased down. (To avoid an abrupt difference in tax burdens because of age at enactment, the special benefit would also probably have to be phased in for taxpayers between ages sixty and sixty-five.) It should be recognized, however, that there will be tremendous political pressure to maintain a special benefit for the elderly at a high level. Thus, though such a special exclusion is considerably simpler (and in my view preferable on other grounds) than other forms of transitional relief, its attendant political risks are serious.

For taxpayers other than the elderly, a delayed effective date would provide an opportunity to make adjustments to the new regime and would reduce the impact of the change. A phase-in of the expenditure tax seems less feasible than a delayed effective date, because it would be necessary to retain all or part of the income tax during the phase-in period to maintain aggregate revenues. A phase-in would therefore require computations of both income and expenditure tax liabilities during the transition.

A delayed effective date would enable those who could receive more favorable treatment under an income tax to realize gains or losses before the effective date of an expenditure tax. Transactions subsequent to the effective date would result in expenditure taxation if proceeds were consumed, and if proceeds were reinvested, no expenditure tax would be due. It would seem appropriate, however, to provide greater ability during the transition period than under current law to obtain income tax deductions for capital losses. If further relief were considered essential, a deduction for a limited amount of basis of preenactment assets could be provided, but no such rule is recommended.

The Problem of Initial Cash Hoarding

Because financial assets would be taxed on a cash flow basis and gain on consumer durables would be included in receipts (as recommended earlier in this paper), the widespread preenactment shifting to "tax-prepaid" assets, which was feared by the Meade committee and the Treasury, would have to take the form of preenactment hoarding of cash or preenactment purchases of consumption for post-enactment use. If, for example, taxpayers were to stuff their mattresses with currency before the tax was implemented, these amounts could then be consumed without being taken into receipts and therefore without incurring any expenditure tax liability. Cash hoarding would be a problem only before the enactment of the expenditure tax. Subsequent to enactment, it would be to taxpayers' advantage to put cash into savings or investments, which would produce an immediate deduction. If, as has been recommended in this section, no transitional relief were provided for assets generally, initial cash balances should be included in receipts. To detect such cash, it would probably be necessary, as a practical matter, to rely on information reports of large withdrawals from savings accounts and of substantial sales of investment assets. Such detection would nevertheless be quite difficult.

As an aid to enforcement, it would probably be desirable to require taxpayers to file an initial report listing all assets on hand at the inception of the expenditure tax. If willful misstatements were subject to fraud penalties, truthful information would very likely be forthcoming. Furthermore, if an expenditure tax were implemented with a delayed effective date, requiring a statement of assets immediately following enactment would result in a loss of earnings on assets converted to cash before enactment. This would probably have some further impact on deterring cash hoarding.

A report of initial wealth could also be required if, as a transitional matter, tax-free expenditures out of savings accumulated before enactment of the expenditure tax were permitted. Conversion of assets to cash would not be a problem under such transitional rules, but any requirement for an initial wealth statement would burden both the Internal Revenue Service and taxpayers and should be avoided unless potential cash hoarding was expected to be substantial.

Summary and Recommendations

The transitional proposals of the Meade committee and the Treasury Department reflect excessive concern about prohibiting gains and losses from the changeover to an expenditure tax. Their elaborate transitional proposals are unnecessarily complex and should be rejected. Instead, the impact of the change should be reduced by a delayed effective date that would give taxpayers opportunity to take advantage of beneficial income tax provisions. A delay of about five years would seem appropriate.

In addition, a special exemption should be provided to elderly (and perhaps handicapped) people who have paid income tax and who would be burdened rather than benefited by a shift from income to expenditure taxation. This special exemption should be phased out over time. If further general relief were considered necessary, a fixed dollar deduction limited to a person's aggregate basis in assets should be provided. Sales of preenactment assets would be treated on a cash flow basis in the same way as was outlined above for assets in general. Other expenditure tax rules, such as those relating to gifts and other receipts and deductions, should be made effective immediately following the general delay. Special grandfather rules should be avoided.

This approach to the transition would enable an expenditure tax to be enacted with a significantly lower rate schedule than under the proposals of the Treasury and the Meade committee. The immediate narrowing of the tax base that would result from their elaborate and extensive grandfather rules would necessarily require higher rates to make up the revenue cost of transitional exemptions.

If the amount of cash hoarding before the enactment of an expenditure tax were considered likely to be significant, an initial report of assets and liabilities would facilitate enforcement, but would impose substantial administrative burdens on the Internal Revenue Service and taxpayers alike.

Conclusion

The forgoing analysis suggests that the obstacles to implementing a progressive personal tax on consumption would be substantial, but not absolutely prohibitive. An administratively feasible expenditure tax is possible in the United States today, but it is impossible to know whether a consumption tax that would emerge from the political process would in fact achieve the efficiency and fairness advantages that its proponents claim are theoretically possible. Moreover, the problems of implementation that have been identified in this paper suggest the need for great caution in going forward with expenditure tax proposals.

Given the practical difficulties, proponents of an expenditure tax should be required to demonstrate that its claimed advantages in terms of equity and economic efficiency are real and cannot be achieved in a simpler fashion—either through changes in the income tax, such as new deductions for some amount of individual savings and increased opportunities to rollover and defer taxation of investment gains, or, more dramatically, through a value-added or national sales tax for most taxpayers and an income tax for people with high incomes. Unless and until this burden is met, replacing the income tax with a progressive personal tax on consumption should remain low on the list of political priorities, and the principal utility of expenditure tax analysis should continue to lie in illuminating issues of income taxation and increasing our understanding of tax policy.

Comments by Sven-Olof Lodin

In evaluating the expenditure tax as an alternative to the income tax, it is important to consider not only today's tax problems but also those that will arise in the future. In spite of recent developments in the United States, I believe that in the longer run higher taxation and steeper progression are to be expected. Thus the analysis should be carried out against the background of the problems of the high-tax society, though not necessarily one with as high tax rates as now exist in Sweden. As long as tax rates are kept to a moderate level, the income tax seems to function fairly well. However, for technical and political reasons, rising taxation and increased emphasis on redistribution require a more sophisticated and consistent tax technique than can be achieved under an income tax regime. The Swedish experience demonstrates clearly that the distorting effects of the income tax are unacceptable at high tax rates.[75]

The general feeling in Sweden is that the income tax has been pushed too far (see table 1) and therefore we must choose between two alternatives. The first is to keep the income tax, but at much lower and less progressive rates, and to raise the value-added tax

75. For more detailed discussion of the questions raised in these comments, see my Swedish report: *Progressive Expenditure Tax—an Alternative?*

Table 1. Average and Marginal Rates of Income Tax of a Married Person in Sweden, 1977[a]

Income in U.S. dollars; tax rates in percent

Income before tax	Average tax rate	Income after tax	Marginal tax rate	Percent increase in post-tax income resulting from a 10 percent increase in pretax income
3,400	7	3,180	29	7.6
5,700	16	4,790	33	8.0
8,000	21	6,320	49	6.5
11,500[b]	30	8,050	62	5.4
17,000	42	9,860	75	4.3
23,000	50	11,500	78	4.4
35,000	60	14,000	85	4.2

a. Includes the local income tax of 26.63 percent.
b. Average salary of industrial worker.

rates to recover the revenue loss. This would mean a much less ambitious use of the tax system for redistributional purposes than the present use. The second alternative is to switch to a graduated expenditure tax; such a move would enable us to keep our present redistributional objectives. There is now a very lively public debate in Sweden on the merits of these two alternatives.

Starting with high taxes is a new point of departure for most participants in this conference. But I believe it is fruitful to discuss the issues from this vantage point. The demand for consistent technical solutions and great precision are thereby much stronger, and the weaknesses of a new tax are likely to show up.

I agree with the proponents of the expenditure tax that a theoretically correct expenditure tax would be easier to implement than a theoretically correct income tax. Because of technical and political problems, however, the plans discussed in the United States have not always applied a consistent tax technique. This inconsistency is justified on the ground that the distortions will be of very minor importance. Although that may be true now, it is far from certain that it will be equally true in the longer run.

In comparing the income and expenditures taxes, it is important to distinguish among the conceptual, technical, and political issues. Especially in the United States, many of the problems seem to be primarily of a political nature. Political considerations are, of course, very important, but I think they should be left out of the discussion until the conceptual and technical problems have been resolved.

I have just two points to make about the political issues. First, the shortcomings of income taxation are in some ways a result of politically motivated actions. It is unrealistic to assume that this problem can be avoided just by changing to a new tax system. Instead, the United States must count on as much political interference with an expenditure tax as there has been with the income tax. It may be, however, that the simplicity of the basic concept of the expenditure tax will make it a little easier to prevent the excessive erosion of the tax base. Second, if the expenditure tax is regarded as a tax on consumption, the specter of regressivity, and issues such as whether medical and educational expenses should be taxed, will be central to the debate, thus creating the usual emotional problems. If, instead, the expenditure tax is regarded—as Fisher did—as a tax on income differing conceptually from the traditional income tax only in the timing of tax payments, the approach to the technical issues will be different and politically less risky.

In the beginning of his paper, Michael Graetz argues convincingly that in general the cash flow method should be adopted for the expenditure tax. All purchases and sales of assets and changes in saving and borrowing must be taken into account. Otherwise, he points out, there will be numerous tax avoidance opportunities. I fully agree with this position. But the paper later deviates from this principle in several ways; in my view, these deviations are technically unnecessary and will create serious distortions.

For instance, given the precedent of the U.S. income tax, Graetz rejects an imputation system for housing. Yet the proper treatment of housing is much more important under the expenditure tax than under the income tax. If imputation is rejected, the entire housing sector must be kept outside the expenditure tax system—no deductions would be allowed for housing investments, home mortgages would not be taxed, and deductions would not be allowed for mortgage interest. These deviations would probably create more administrative problems than the imputation system itself would.

The purchase of a home is a typical example of a mixed investment that can for that reason be treated as either saving or consumption. Graetz has chosen the consumption approach. But as soon as progressive tax rates are introduced, it becomes urgent for practical reasons to treat the purchase of a home as a deductible investment. Otherwise, for example, it will be almost impossible for a taxpayer to use deductible savings to cover the down payment. And it will also introduce all the distortions now created by inflation under the income tax, which the expenditure tax otherwise would avoid.

Imputation may not be as difficult as Graetz describes it. The imputation systems proposed in the Meade committee report and in my Swedish report do not require the calculation of an imputed rental value. Instead, an imputation is made only for the return on the gross investment; then a deduction is allowed for interest paid. The difference represents the net return on the capital that the owner has put into the house. Of course, some difficulties arise with regard to assessing the value of the home, but for the rest the technique is simple. Sweden has had an imputation system since 1955, and it is working smoothly at the technical level. However, the politicians have not had the courage to keep the imputed income in line with rising house values and interest rates—except in the case of the more expensive homes—and this has caused serious inequities. Technically, there is no reason to hesitate to use imputations for housing. Then housing investments, loans, and interest paid could be treated fully in accordance with the principles of the expenditure tax. (I refrain from discussing the political implications of introducing such a system.)

Differences in approach toward the expenditure tax will also lead to different decisions on how gifts should be treated. If the tax is regarded as a tax on income net of savings, it becomes quite natural to tax the donor on his gifts because he is not saving any longer. If the tax is regarded as a tax on consumption, it is doubtful that gifts should be taxed. Graetz prefers not to tax gifts to the donor. For reasons of principle and administration, I believe the donor should be taxed. With rising marginal tax rates, exempting the donor will provide unacceptable tax avoidance opportunities for wealthy people with children. The donee should also be taxed, but only when he or she consumes the gift. This "double taxation" is consistent with the underlying principles of the expenditure tax and cannot be considered harassment. In fact, the same kind of double taxation is to be found in the income tax with regard to earnings from personal services.

The treatment of international flows is one of the most troublesome features of an expenditure tax. As Graetz points out, the residence principle seems to be the appropriate base for an expenditure tax, and residents should be taxed on a worldwide basis. International transactions do not cause any special problems; they can be solved by using existing techniques for avoiding international double taxation under the income tax. The real problems are immigration and emigration. Graetz states that some kind of adjustment will be necessary whenever income taxes have been paid by immigrants on accumulated assets in the country of origin. But he rejects any kind of taxation on emigration as unworkable and probably impossible to enforce. Some tax on emigration, however, is conceptually correct if the expenditure tax is regarded as a cash flow income tax (with deferral of tax on savings). And also for reasons of equity, I believe it is essential to tax the accumulated assets of emigrants under an expenditure tax. Failure to do so would be a decisive argument against it.

To calculate tax due from emigrants, it is necessary to require taxpayers to provide with their annual tax returns listings of all their registered assets and debts. (Such simple balance sheets are now required for a net wealth tax.) The availability of year-end balance sheets would provide a good check on purchases and sales of registered assets. It would also automatically provide the basis for calculating the tax due at the time of emigration.

It is not necessary, however, that tax be paid immediately upon emigration. Deferral of the tax payment is possible in several ways. One possibility is to require the emigrant to submit a bank guarantee covering the amount of tax due. This would be especially necessary in the case of temporary emigration. Of course, there is a risk that taxpayers will try to emigrate without paying the tax. In Europe this risk will eventually be reduced because of special tax treaties providing for cooperation in tax enforcement.

The increasing movement of capital across borders is a complicating factor. The Meade committee report contains a somewhat drastic, but effective, solution that would also somewhat improve the equity of the expenditure tax. The suggestion is that every resident possessing net registered assets exceeding a certain amount should submit to the tax authorities a bank guarantee of an amount approximately corresponding to the deferred tax on the net value of the assets. The bank guarantee would be drawn down if anyone emigrated without paying the tax. Aside from preventing tax evasion by emigrants, this solution will have an important side effect. Since the bank guarantee reduces the usability of registered assets as collateral for loans, taxpayers who defer tax by saving will increase their opportunity to borrow only by the amount of savings net of prospective expenditure tax; in this respect they will be in a no better position than under an income tax regime.

Another troublesome problem is the transition. I will not go into the economic effects of a transition from the income tax to an expenditure tax. But it is obvious that the removal of the distortions of the present system would produce a dramatic realignment of asset values. Indeed, the impact of the present system on values may be so significant as to make a change to another system virtually impossible without causing chaos on the markets. The greater the distortions of the income tax system, the harder it will be to abolish it. As for the technical transition problems, Graetz rejects the introduction of elaborate rules. I think, however, he underestimates the problem of double taxation of net savings from the preexpenditure tax period and the reciprocal problem with regard to borrowing.

The transition rules can be designed in a number of different ways. I believe that a tax credit model—one of three different solutions discussed in my Swedish study—would have great advantages. If the taxpayer had assets on the date of enactment of the expenditure tax, he would be given a tax credit calculated on the basis of an average expected tax rate. The tax credit could then be used to offset the expenditure tax incurred later when he dissaved. Conversely, if the taxpayer was, on balance, in debt on the date of enactment, he would have a tax debit that would be offset against future saving (including the repayment of the original debt). This method would permit the introduction of an expenditure tax that would take preexisting assets and debts into account. It would also protect the progressivity of the tax when the assets were used later for consumption purposes.

Graetz argues that it would be too burdensome for the taxpayer to prepare yearly balance sheets. But on the basis of the Swedish experience with yearly balance sheets for net wealth tax purposes, I believe that Graetz overestimates the problems. The use of balance sheets would solve many of the problems that Graetz is forced to leave unsolved. Furthermore, I believe that the use of balance sheets will be unavoidable. For redistributive reasons the expenditure tax should be supplemented with a net wealth tax, which by its very nature would require that balance sheets be filed. A general net wealth tax that applied even to people with modest amounts of wealth would help to regulate the net-of-tax return on saving in all wealth classes. It is also possible to conceive of the net wealth tax as an interest charge payable by the saver for the deferral of the tax on his saved income.

I do not believe that there are any serious technical problems in deciding whether to retain a corporate tax in an expenditure tax system. It is basically a matter of choosing among several possible techniques, and the choice will depend primarily on political considerations.

A more technical question is whether the expenditure tax should be calculated on a tax-inclusive or a tax-exclusive basis. At first glance, a tax-inclusive basis may seem simpler to apply. But in spite of the problems involved, the tax-exclusive basis is probably the more realistic alternative. This is especially true if the expenditure tax is combined with other taxes, such as a net wealth tax, a proportional income tax, or an inheritance or estate tax.

In summary, Graetz has produced a valuable paper, but I feel that he should have more closely observed the distinction between the political issues and the purely technical ones. His analysis of how an expenditure tax system could be implemented suffers from self-imposed inhibitions that reflect political taboos.

Comments by Paul R. McDaniel

Michael Graetz's paper is a significant contribution to the growing literature on the expenditure tax. It gives a more complete picture than has heretofore been available of what an expenditure tax might actually look like in the United States. My comments further explore some matters that were raised in his paper either explicitly or implicitly.

The Basic Implementation Questions

In designing any kind of tax, the draftsman must be given the answers to six fundamental questions.
1. What is the tax base that the tax statute is to embody?
2. What rates of tax are to be applied to that base?
3. How often is the tax to be imposed?

4. What is to be the taxable unit?

5. How are such juridical entities as corporations, mutual associations, and trusts to be treated?

6. How is the tax to be applied to taxpayers who engage in activities across national borders?

There is little or nothing in tax law theory as such—nor, I should add, in tax economics or accounting—that provides the correct answers to these questions. They must be answered by political leaders drawing upon the broad social, philosophical, economic, jurisprudential, and historical perspectives of the society. What the tax expert can do is supply the policymaker with a variety of possible solutions to each problem and an analysis of the equity, economic, and administrative implications of each solution. Although it is sometimes implied to the contrary, the selection of a particular tax base (question 1) does not dictate the answers to the remaining questions; in fact, that selection may make it more difficult to solve some of them.

Graetz clarifies several important points about the expenditure tax proposals that have been advanced to date (notably the Treasury's *Blueprints for Basic Tax Reform*) in the U.S. context.

First, an expenditure tax will be no more immune to the introduction of tax preferences than the income tax, although there may be some restructuring of the form of the preferences.

Second, even in seeking an ideal expenditure tax, most expenditure tax proposals deviate from the norm and settle for second-best solutions. In the real world such deviations may be manipulated to secure a relative tax advantage for some, or they may produce a relative tax disadvantage for others (see, for example, Graetz's discussion of the tax prepayment proposal made in *Blueprints*).

Third, many of the intractable definitional problems in an income tax are encountered in an expenditure tax. The adoption of an expenditure tax provides no better answers to the borderline issues, and in some instances the matters are more difficult to resolve.

Fourth, the answers provided by expenditure tax proponents to the fundamental questions listed above have been different in some respects from those the United States has adopted under its income tax, but little or no justification has been given for those answers.

I should like to elaborate on these points in my comments.

Deviations from the Ideal Expenditure Tax Base

One of the fallacies frequently encountered in expenditure tax discussions is the comparison of the pure expenditure tax with the present preference-riddled income tax. This is not a helpful comparison and provides no basis for concluding that the United States should convert to an expenditure tax. *Blueprints* avoids this particular problem by comparing a (near) ideal expenditure tax to a (near) ideal income tax. Graetz's paper drives us to an examination of the more fruitful issue: which of the tax preferences now contained in the income tax would be retained in an expenditure tax and in what ways would an impure expenditure tax be superior to the present impure income tax?

Tax preferences have been introduced in the income tax in various forms (special exemptions, credits, deductions, deferral of tax, and reduced rate of tax) and for various purposes (to provide relief from hardship and to encourage specific types of economic or social actions). These tax preferences are identified and quantified as tax expenditures.

Table 2 lists the various categories of tax expenditures for individuals under the present income tax. Is it likely that identical or restructured tax expenditures for the same purposes would be found in an expenditure tax?[76]

Tax expenditures that could be carried over to an expenditure tax. The tax expenditures in this group are serious omissions from the income tax base. But simply shifting to an expenditure tax will not reduce the pressure from powerful special interest groups to keep those tax preferences. The crucial question is whether such an expenditure tax loaded with similar preferences is superior in efficiency and equity to the existing income tax. To date, expenditure tax advocates have not addressed this issue.

Items 1–23 and 29–31 represent funds available to a taxpayer for general consumption or deductions and credits for specific consumption purposes. They would clearly constitute tax preferences if carried over into an expenditure tax.

---

76. Tax expenditures that benefit only corporations are not discussed. It is assumed that some form of corporate income tax would be employed after adoption of an expenditure tax and that corporate tax expenditures as such would be unaffected by the decision to adopt an expenditure tax.

Expenditure tax discussions to date have sometimes asserted that items 24–28 (and perhaps 32) do not represent consumption expenditures and hence should not be taxable under an expenditure tax. So far the analyses of this issue have not been convincing, but the following observations are relevant.

First, if such items as charitable contributions, medical expenses, and political contributions are regarded as personal consumption expenditures, the continuation of the present deductions (or credits) will constitute tax preferences in an expenditure tax.

Second, even if such items are not regarded as consumption expenditures, Congress may wish to continue present tax differentials to encourage or support such expenditures. But a mere deduction for charitable contributions will not prove attractive to charitable organizations under an expenditure tax. With such a deduction, there would be no difference between the tax consequences of buying a share of stock and giving the same stock to charity. Recent studies for the Commission on Private Philanthropy and Public Needs (the Filer Commission) indicate that, in the absence of an incentive, high-income taxpayers would tend to reduce charitable giving relatively more than lower-income taxpayers.[77] Accordingly, to maintain an incentive for charitable giving under an expenditure tax, a deduction in excess of 100 percent of the gift must be allowed. Thus, for example, the deduction might be 200 percent for cash contributions to public charities, a 160 percent deduction for contributions of assets (with no taxation of fair market value in excess of cost), and 140 percent for gifts to private foundations. Similar techniques would be required for other incentive-type individual tax preferences, such as that for political contributions.

Nor is there any reason why adoption of an expenditure tax would dissipate enthusiasm for the investment tax credit (item 33) or a jobs tax credit (item 34). The fact that business costs are immediately deductible does not mean that some subsidy in place of the credit would not be added under an expenditure tax. Similarly, tax credits to subsidize or encourage the installation of energy saving equipment in personal residences can be expected to be carried over. After all, these tax credits have just been introduced into a world in which in-

77. *Research Papers Sponsored by the Commission on Private Philanthropy and Public Needs*, vol. 3: *Special Behavioral Studies, Foundations and Corporations* (Department of the Treasury, 1977).

**Table 2. Selected Tax Expenditures under the U.S. Individual Income Tax,
Fiscal Year 1979**[a]

Millions of dollars

Tax expenditure	Estimated amount
Tax expenditures that could be carried over to an expenditure tax	
1. Exclusion of benefits for armed forces personnel	1,370
2. Exclusion of military disability pensions	120
3. Exclusion of income earned abroad by U.S. citizens	385
4. Exclusion of excess of percentage over cost depletion	370
5. Exclusion for ($100 or $200) of corporate dividends	505
6. Exclusion of scholarships and fellowships	330
7. Extra personal exemption for students	790
8. Exclusion of certain employer-provided meals and lodging	325
9. Exclusion of employer contributions to prepaid legal services plans	15
10. Exclusion of employer contributions for medical care	7,225
11. Exclusion of social security benefits	6,345
12. Exclusion of railroad retirement benefits	280
13. Exclusion of workers' compensation benefits	970
14. Exclusion of benefits for disabled coal miners	50
15. Exclusion of unemployment insurance benefits	1,135
16. Exclusion of public assistance benefits	360
17. Exclusion of sick pay	60
18. Exclusion of premiums on employer-provided group term life insurance	955
19. Exclusion of premiums on employee accidental death plans	80
20. Exclusions for veterans' benefits	1,040
21. Additional exemption for elderly	1,215
22. Additional exemption for blind	20
23. Deduction of state gasoline taxes	840
24. Deduction of property taxes on homes	5,180
25. Deduction for charitable contributions	6,470
26. Deduction for medical expenses	2,655
27. Deduction of casualty losses	395
28. Deduction of nonbusiness state and local taxes	9,440
29. Tax credit for elderly	255
30. Earned income credit	1,165
31. Credit for child and dependent care costs	575
32. Deduction and credit for political contributions	75
33. Investment tax credit	2,725
34. New jobs tax credit	860
35. Maximum tax on earned income	800
Tax expenditures that could be carried over in modified form to an expenditure tax	
36. Exclusion of interest on pollution control bonds	130
37. Exclusion of interest on other exempt industrial development bonds	135
38. Exclusion of benefits under qualified pension plans	13,255
39. Exclusion of benefits under supplementary unemployment benefit plans	10

Table 2 (continued)

Tax expenditure	Estimated amount
40. Exclusion of interest on life insurance savings	2,225
41. Exclusion of interest on state and local bonds	2,150
42. Deferral of interest on U.S. savings bonds	670
43. Deduction of home mortgage interest	2,350
44. Deduction of consumer credit interest	2,585
Timing of deductions for capital investment	
45. Expensing of research and development costs	30
46. Expensing of intangible drilling, exploration, and development costs	300
47. Five-year amortization for costs of rehabilitating certain historic structures	5
48. Expensing of certain agricultural costs	460
49. Expensing of construction period interest and taxes	90
50. Excess first-year depreciation	155
51. Accelerated depreciation on buildings	405
52. Asset depreciation range (ADR) system	135
53. Five-year amortization for rehabilitating low-income housing	5
Gains on disposition of assets	
54. Capital gain treatment for sales of long-term capital assets	7,990
55. Capital gain treatment of coal and iron ore royalties	70
56. Capital gain treatment for timber income	65
57. Capital gain treatment for certain assets used in agriculture	365
58. Deferral of gains on sales of homes	980
59. Exclusion of gains on home sales by elderly	70
60. Exclusion and deferral of gains on property transferred at death and by gift	8,975

Source: *Tax Expenditures: Relationships to Spending Programs and Background Material on Individual Provisions*, prepared for the Senate Committee on the Budget, 95 Cong. 2 sess. (GPO, 1978), pp. 9–189.
a. The table does not reflect tax expenditure changes effected by the Revenue Act of 1978 or subsequent tax legislation.

come attributable to residences is untaxed, and there is no reason to suppose that the same advantage will not be regarded as necessary under an expenditure tax.

Tax expenditures that could be carried over in modified form to an expenditure tax. Expenditure tax advocates seem to be much too optimistic in believing that a zero rate of tax on all forms of saving will eliminate pressures for preferential treatment of particular forms of saving. The function performed by items 36–44 in an income tax is to create a *differential* in favor of the particular form of saving over other forms. Neutrality of treatment among all types of saving is pre-

cisely what beneficiaries of these tax preferences do not want. Therefore, under an expenditure tax one should expect pressure to provide
not only an immediate deduction for the particular types of investment in items 36–42 but also an exclusion from receipts for the interest earned.

The treatment of items 43 and 44 in an expenditure tax depends
on the treatment of consumer durables and housing. It would not be
surprising to find a deduction for investment in housing, the exemption of imputed net rental income, deductions for mortgage interest
and property taxes, and exclusions for the gain on sale. Similarly, the
present preference for consumer durables purchased on credit would
probably be continued, perhaps by excluding purchases from the tax
base and allowing a deduction for interest payments (with no taxation of imputed income).

Timing of deductions for capital investment. One of the virtues asserted for an expenditure tax is that it eliminates timing differences
attributable to capital investments. This is true if the expenditure tax
merely provides an immediate deduction for all capital investments.
But timing differences could be introduced into an expenditure tax.
The income tax preferences in items 45–53 reflect priorities that
Congress and various administrations have accorded to certain kinds
of investments. The purpose of these preferences is to distort investment decisions in favor of the indicated activities. What reason is
there to believe that the adoption of an expenditure tax would eliminate the congressional desire to make tax distinctions (that is, eliminate subsidies) for different kinds of activities? Realistically, it
should perhaps be assumed that an expenditure tax would, for example, provide a 200 percent deduction for equity invested in low-
income housing, a 150 percent deduction for the equity investment in
nonresidential buildings, and a 125 percent deduction for the equity
investment in used residential buildings with a useful life of twenty
years or more.

The capital expenditure issue is closely related to the tax shelter
transactions that bedevil the income tax. As Graetz points out, an
expenditure tax could be structured to provide even greater tax shelter benefits than are now available under the income tax. But it must
also be kept in mind that a properly designed expenditure tax (which
produces only a zero rate of tax on investment income) would increase the relative tax burdens of those who now invest in tax shelters;

these taxpayers are now enjoying a negative tax rate on their investment income from oil and gas, real estate, and other tax-preferred activities. Thus the advantage of an expenditure tax that is so frequently emphasized—a reduction in the tax on investment income—is a disadvantage to investors in tax shelters. The pressure from such investors as well as the lobbies for "good causes" like low-income housing and pollution control can be expected to produce tax preferences for certain capital investments in an expenditure tax just as they have under the income tax.

Income tax shelters have also been built on the cash method of accounting in situations in which accrual accounting is necessary to reflect income properly. Under a cash flow expenditure tax, there would be pressure to allow special accrual treatment to permit deductions in advance of payment.

Gains on disposition of assets. Items 54–59 provide preferential rates of tax on certain kinds of income and investments. Such preferences could easily be transferred to an expenditure tax. A special calculation similar to the present maximum tax calculation on earned income might be provided for income from timber. Alternatively, a deduction of, say, 60 percent of such income could be granted, even if that income was used for consumption.

As to item 60, expenditure tax proponents have yet to agree whether gifts and bequests constitute consumption expenditures. If they were not taxed (as proposed in *Blueprints*), the present income tax preference would actually be magnified, since the gain as well as the original cost of the transferred asset would be excluded from the transferor's expenditure tax base.

Finally, consideration needs to be given to the question whether the introduction of an expenditure tax might create a demand for new tax preferences. For example, as taxpayers focused on the fact that an expenditure tax imposed a tax on purchases of food and clothing, pressure for preferential treatment of expenditures for necessities would be generated. The European experience with the value-added tax and the U.S. experience with state sales taxes give grounds for such concern.

Other tax base problems. Many of the difficult definitional issues in an income tax would not be resolved merely because an expenditure tax was adopted. It would still be necessary to distinguish between (1) taxable fringe benefits and nontaxable outlays to improve

working conditions, (2) deductible business expenses and nondeductible consumption expenditures (work clothes, travel, entertainment, and so on), and (3) capital costs and personal consumption
outlays (education expenses).

Indeed, the definitional issues may be more difficult under an expenditure tax. Consumption must be defined under an expenditure
tax; under an income tax the question is whether an outlay is a cost
of producing taxable income. The analysis may be the same in some
cases, but as a practical matter it is often easier to determine whether
a given cost is associated with taxable income in an accounting sense
than whether it constitutes consumption.

The Accounting Period

Blueprints asserts, without much analysis, that the proper time
horizon for taxation is the individual's lifetime. Why this is so is not
clear. Individual taxpayers are at different points in their respective
life cycles. It is not apparent why it is equitable to levy the same tax
on a twenty-two-year-old person who consumes all his income (and
perhaps borrows) and on a forty-five-year-old person who consumes
the same amount and saves an additional 25 percent. The assurance
that both will ultimately pay the same tax if they live out their life
expectancies *and* they have the same lifetime consumption *and* tax
rates remain unchanged is unlikely to appeal to those who believe in
equal tax treatment of equals. Moreover, as Graetz points out, even
the hoped-for lifetime equality will never be realized if the expenditure tax rates are progressive.

The Taxable Unit

Graetz links the issue of the taxable unit with the treatment of gifts
and bequests. This linking obscures some problems and creates others
that might be resolved if the two issues were separated.

The proper treatment of gifts and bequests is best resolved as a tax
base matter. The fundamental determination must be whether gifts
and bequests constitute consumption expenditures by the transferor.
Advocates of the expenditure tax disagree on this issue. My own view
is that, to prevent unacceptably large accumulations of family wealth,
gifts and bequests out of the taxable unit must be taxed to the transferor. In light of recent U.S. legislative experience, it seems unlikely
that stiffer estate and gift taxes will be enacted.

The problem of defining the taxable unit needs more extended analysis than is contained in the Graetz paper. Several points require further study.

First, how should the taxable unit be defined? Many troublesome problems might be resolved if, for instance, the taxable unit were to include spouses and children up to age twenty-five. In that case, no gift would be involved until there was a transfer out of the taxable unit. Thus, for example, an interspousal transfer at death would not be a taxable event. All receipts and consumption of the unit would, of course, be aggregated.

Second, how should assets be treated for expenditure tax purposes when there is a transfer into a new taxable unit (marriage) or out of it (divorce)? If the taxable unit includes spouses, the treatment of marriage in view of death and of transfers to divorced spouses will create difficult problems.

Third, if qualified and nonqualified accounts are employed (as in *Blueprints*), how are the accounts of two single persons to be treated when they marry and when they divorce?

Fourth, what adjustments, if any, are required for two spouses who produce cash income?

The Treatment of Juridical Entities

The tax treatment of such juridical entities as corporations and trusts would be an important consideration if an expenditure tax were to be adopted. *Blueprints* assumes that since corporations and trusts do not consume, such entities would not be taxable. Beneficiaries or shareholders would be taxed, but only when they consumed the income distributed by these entities.

The adoption of an expenditure tax for individuals, however, does not necessarily mean that the tax on corporations and trusts should be eliminated. If the separateness of these entities from their shareholders or beneficiaries were accepted (as the law now does for many purposes), a separate tax could be justified. Indeed, the case for the taxation of trusts as separate entities would be strong under an expenditure tax that allowed deductible transfers to be made to accumulation trusts, since the property and income could be held untaxed for as long as 100 to 150 years. For corporations, an excise tax on the privilege of operating in corporate form, measured by net income, could still be employed in conjunction with an expenditure tax. Of course, many of the claimed advantages of an expenditure tax would disappear, because the important simplification advantages from the standpoint of tax accounting—depreciation, inventories, and so forth —involve the corporate income tax far more than the individual income tax.

This is not to suggest that trusts or corporations should be taxed separately if an expenditure tax were enacted. It is intended to clarify a point frequently assumed in the expenditure tax literature: the adoption of an expenditure tax does not necessarily imply that separate taxation of juridical entities will disappear. The treatment of such entities will be based on many other factors besides tax logic (which does not really point in either direction); it involves broad issues of jurisprudence and social and political philosophy that go well beyond the issues posed by an expenditure tax (or any other tax on individuals).

International Issues

Graetz rightly calls attention to the need for further analysis of the application of an expenditure tax in the international context. Several issues warrant closer study.

The jurisdictional base. Under an expenditure tax at least three bases for the assertion of U.S. international tax jurisdiction appear possible: (1) U.S. citizenship, (2) U.S. residency, or (3) U.S. consumption.

If the citizenship basis were used, U.S. citizens would be taxed on their worldwide consumption; this corresponds to the present income tax jurisdictional basis. *Blueprints* recommends the residency principle. By and large, other consumption taxes—that is, U.S. sales taxes and European value-added taxes—apply the third (geographical) jurisdictional principle.

It is sometimes assumed that an expenditure tax necessarily implies the adoption of the residence principle, but this is not the case. The jurisdictional basis is quite distinct from the tax base adopted and must be determined by reference to both tax and nontax factors. A priori, it is not at all clear why, if the United States has chosen the citizenship principle under its income tax—contrary to the rest of the world—the concept would be dropped if an expenditure tax were adopted.

The adoption of the citizenship principle would solve the emigration questions that plagued the studies by the Meade committee and Professor Lodin. U.S. citizens would be taxed wherever and whenever their consumption occurred. If citizenship were abandoned by a taxpayer, it might be appropriate to tax or recapture at the time of emigration previous deductions for savings; as a less drastic measure, a tax might be applied to the emigrant's U.S. consumption for the following ten years.

Proponents of the residency-based expenditure tax who favor deductions for gifts must give serious attention to gifts by resident U.S. parents or grandparents. Otherwise there would be significant opportunities for tax avoidance.

Double taxation. Regardless of the jurisdictional base adopted, the potential for the taxation of the same income or consumption by two different countries would still exist. The income tax techniques to mitigate double taxation appear to apply equally to an expenditure tax; that is, a tax credit could be given by the United States for taxes imposed by foreign countries, or the United States could exempt foreign consumption that was taxed by the other country.

If the credit technique is adopted (and, again, it is not clear why the United States should change over to the exemption method just because it replaced its income tax by an expenditure tax), the question becomes what foreign taxes are creditable. Under the present income tax, foreign consumption taxes, such as value-added taxes, are not creditable against the U.S. income tax; only foreign income taxes may be credited. Traditionally, it has not been thought necessary to allow credits against the income tax for other types of foreign taxes that are imposed on U.S. citizens. Moreover, a foreign tax—even though denominated an "income tax"—is actually creditable only if it is an income tax according to the U.S. meaning of that term.

If these traditional principles were applied by the United States under an expenditure tax, the following questions would require answers.

1. Which foreign taxes are creditable against the expenditure tax —foreign income taxes or foreign consumption taxes, such as the value-added tax? (It is presumably not necessary to credit both.) In answering this question, principles would have to be developed to identify the elements in a foreign tax that would qualify it for a credit

under an expenditure tax. It is possible, for example, to reverse the
present rules: value-added taxes would be creditable taxes and income taxes would be deductible only if incurred in a trade or business.

2. How are creditable taxes, if any, paid by a foreign corporation
in which a U.S. citizen has invested to be treated?[78]

3. What limitations on tax credits are appropriate to protect U.S.
revenues?

4. What rules are required to allocate consumption expenditures
between countries to prevent manipulation between high- and low-tax
countries?

Treatment of nonresident aliens. At present, nonresident aliens
are subject to tax only on certain U.S. source income.

One approach under an expenditure tax would be to tax only the
U.S. consumption of nonresident aliens out of income from U.S.
sources; any excess of income over consumption would not be subject
to U.S. tax on the assumption that the country of residence would tax
consumption out of that income. But here the question must be asked
whether the United States would tolerate an exemption of purchases
in the United States by a nonresident alien out of foreign-source income when tax was imposed on the identical items purchased by a
U.S. citizen. As in the case of the present income tax, detailed allocation rules for receipts and expenditures would be required to prevent
tax avoidance.

It is also possible, as Graetz recommends, to continue present income taxation of nonresident aliens. Before adopting this approach,
it would be necessary to determine whether it violated the nondis-
crimination clauses of U.S. tax treaties.

Conclusion

Proponents of the expenditure tax cannot assume that they can
persuade Congress to adopt an ideal expenditure tax base. Realism
suggests that they should examine the list of income tax expenditures
to see whether the same preferences, or variants of them, would creep
into the expenditure tax. Moreover, many of the same issues that
plague the income tax (such as the accounting period, the treatment

78. The treatment of U.S. corporations is not considered here, as that depends
on the answer to the U.S. domestic treatment of the corporation under an expenditure tax.

of trusts and corporations, and taxation of international flows) will be difficult to resolve equitably under an expenditure tax. The relative merits of an expenditure tax and an income tax can be evaluated only after those issues have been resolved. I believe that the superiority claimed for the expenditure tax will disappear when an imperfect expenditure tax is compared with the present imperfect income tax.

JOSEPH J. MINARIK

Conference Discussion

THE PRECEDING PAPERS provided the background for a conference of economists and tax lawyers held at the Brookings Institution
on October 19 and 20, 1978. The discussion was spirited, with advocates and opponents of the expenditure tax relying on theory, applied
economics, political judgments, and international perspectives to
bolster their positions, while the undecided participants questioned
the contentions of both sides. Many issues were clarified, but differences of opinion persisted.

Four broad issues were discussed at the conference. (1) Would
the substitution of an expenditure tax for the income tax increase
saving and capital formation? (2) Would an expenditure tax be more
equitable than an income tax? (3) Would an expenditure tax be
easier to administer than an income tax? (4) What are the problems
of transition to an expenditure tax? The opinions of the conference
participants on each topic will be summarized in turn.

The Expenditure Tax and Saving

Many of those who advocate an expenditure tax as a complete or
partial replacement for the individual income tax[1] believe that the
rate of national saving is too low and that saving would increase if it
were not subject to tax. For each additional dollar saved, potential
future consumption would be larger under an expenditure tax than
under an income tax, and households would presumably save more

1. The treatment of the corporate income tax under an expenditure tax regime
is also an issue (see the discussion below).

to take advantage of the opportunity to consume more in the future. A contrary theoretical argument can be made, however: some taxpayers might choose to save less under the expenditure tax, because less personal savings would be required to attain a planned level of consumption. Thus each household would be faced with two offsetting influences under the expenditure tax: the opportunity to consume more later for each dollar of forgone consumption (that is, saving) today, and the need to save less to achieve any given level of consumption later. Theory cannot predict which force would be stronger and hence whether personal saving would go up or down.[2] That question must be answered by empirical measurement—the aim of the paper by E. Philip Howrey and Saul H. Hymans.

Howrey and Hymans wrote against a backdrop that included a recent paper by Michael J. Boskin.[3] In sharp contrast to most earlier research, Boskin found a relatively large and significant elasticity of saving with respect to the real after-tax rate of return. This would indicate that a higher rate of return to saving, such as would be produced by a change from the income tax to an expenditure tax, would significantly increase saving. Boskin's analysis was an attempt to explain consumption in the years 1929 to 1969 on the basis of a number of variables, including the unemployment rate, household wealth, the inflation rate, and disposable personal income, as well as the long run expected real after-tax rate of return on saving. Howrey and Hymans performed a similar time series analysis and found no significant evidence of a positive effect on saving. Much of the discussion of the response of saving to the rate of return dealt with the technical merits of the two studies.

2. Total national saving will increase, however, if the change from an income tax to an expenditure tax shifts some of the government's tax receipts from the taxpayers' later years to their earlier ones. The government must then increase public saving in the early years if the time pattern of government purchases of goods and services is to remain unchanged. Thus, even though private saving decreases, total national saving will necessarily increase. The crucial point is that the government increases its surplus to maintain the original time pattern of public spending during the transition from income to expenditure taxation. Martin Feldstein, "The Rate of Return, Taxation and Personal Savings," *Economic Journal,* vol. 88 (September 1978), pp. 482–87.

3. Michael J. Boskin, "Taxation, Saving, and the Rate of Interest," *Journal of Political Economy,* vol. 86 (April 1978), pt. 2, pp. S3–S27. For an earlier estimate of the response of saving to a change in the rate of return, see Colin Wright, "Saving and the Rate of Interest," in Arnold C. Harberger and Martin J. Bailey, eds., *The Taxation of Income from Capital* (Brookings Institution, 1969), pp. 275–300.

One of the difficult problems about this type of analysis is the choice of the precise variable to be explained. Given Boskin's definition of consumption, his implicit concept of saving was close to that used in the flow-of-funds accounts, which includes consumer spending on housing and other durables. Howrey and Hymans were critical of Boskin's use of this concept on the ground that expenditures on consumer durables are not available for business capital formation. They used as the basis for their analysis a new concept called *personal cash saving*. This concept excludes from saving durable goods expenditures (which are included in the flow-of-funds definition of saving) and the changes in reserves of private pension and insurance plans (which are included in the national income accounts definition of saving).

The views of the conference participants regarding the proper definition of saving were mixed. Some argued that pension and insurance reserves could be loaned to businesses for productive investment, so that those items should be included in saving. Others pointed out that consumer investment in durables (such as housing) is as productive as business investment for ultimate consumer use (such as rental housing); they felt that durables should be included in the saving variable. Some agreed that personal cash saving is the appropriate variable but were concerned that its small size—an average of only about 0.2 percent of disposable personal income in 1951–74—makes it an unpromising goal for policy. Howrey and Hymans countered that the year-to-year variance of the personal cash saving rate is almost as large as that of flow-of-funds saving, and therefore any new policy that influences the variation of personal cash saving can have a substantial effect on capital formation. Furthermore, they found that saving is not responsive to the rate of return even when a flow-of-funds or national accounts concept is used.

A second concern was the rate-of-return concept. All the conferees agreed that the real after-tax rate of return is the appropriate variable but that measurement of this concept is difficult. Boskin's rate-of-return variable was estimated "from an adaptive expectations model of price expectations, truncated after 8 years, with varying speeds of adjustment,"[4] but the precise method of calculating this variable was not explained before or during the conference. Howrey and Hymans found no rate-of-return variable other than the particular formula-

4. Michael J. Boskin, "Taxation, Saving and the Rate of Interest," pp. S5–S11.

tion used by Boskin to show a positive and significant interest effect on saving in his model. This led the discussion to focus on the interest rate.

Though data limitations forced both Boskin and Howrey-Hymans to restrict themselves to one explanatory rate-of-return variable, many of the participants felt that an array of potential interest rates is needed to capture all the opportunities available to the saver—including the passbook saving rate plus an appropriate liquidity premium, and the interest rate at which households borrow. Given the data limitations, therefore, the choice of the interest variable was critical. Howrey and Hymans tested a number of interest rates as the basis for their regression and found that the Baa corporate rate had the greatest effect on saving. They adjusted for expected inflation by subtracting from the interest rate the mean expected inflation rate as measured by consumer surveys conducted by the Survey Research Center of the University of Michigan.[5] To allow for changes in taxation, the average marginal personal income tax rate on dividend and interest income was used.

One conferee argued that both Boskin and Howrey-Hymans, in computing their after-tax rate of return on saving, did not adequately reflect the complexities of the tax laws—in particular the exemption of many forms of saving (especially pensions and insurance) from current taxation. Others criticized Howrey and Hymans for using a one-year measure of inflationary expectations rather than an average for a longer period.

The participants also stressed the weakness of the basic data used in both papers. The small number of observations (resulting from the use of annual data) limited the number of explanatory variables that could be employed and the degrees of freedom that remained, clouding all the results. Boskin's data period was longer than that of Howrey and Hymans, but even so, some conferees felt that the Howrey and Hymans sensitivity tests of the Boskin results suffered from a shortage of degrees of freedom. Several conferees stated that any clear improvement over the results presented at the conference would have to come from panel data that traced how households changed

5. Howrey and Hymans obtained similar results using inflation rates measured by the consumer price index and by the national income accounts consumption deflator.

their consumption and saving behavior as economic conditions changed. Such data are not now available, nor are they expected to become available in the foreseeable future, and research using such data would be quite complex.

Technical questions aside, the conferees had much to say about the implications of the interest elasticity of saving—whatever it might be—for tax policy in general and the expenditure tax in particular. Most felt that the United States would be better off with more business capital formation, although they disagreed on how much more was needed. Less widely accepted was the notion that an increase in personal saving would result in an increase in capital formation. As already noted, Boskin's saving concept includes investment in several forms of consumer durables that do not add to industrial capacity; increased saving in this form would not add to productivity in the business sector. Furthermore, personal saving in the form of cash or other liquid assets might be lent to borrowers from abroad; this would not increase capital formation at home.

Several conferees expressed a preference for less radical changes in the tax system than an expenditure tax—for example, larger investment credits, faster depreciation, or more exemptions for selected forms of saving. Such policies, it was claimed, would increase rates of return and thereby increase saving and capital formation to the extent that saving is elastic with respect to the rate of return. It was also noted that, without changing the tax system, saving and finance for investment could be directly increased by reducing the federal government's budget deficit.

Several conferees argued that even if the elasticity of personal saving with respect to the rate of return were zero, the substitution of an expenditure tax for an income tax would increase welfare through a more efficient allocation of consumption over a lifetime. They pointed out that the appropriate measure of the welfare effect of a tax exemption for saving is not the elasticity of saving (which is an expenditure elasticity) but rather the elasticity of future consumption (which is a quantity elasticity). The same rate of saving would yield greater future consumption because of the higher after-tax rate of return; the additional after-tax consumption in later years is a measure of the welfare gain. Thus a change to an expenditure tax would encourage individuals to reallocate consumption and saving over their life cycles (that is, save more early in life to pay for greater consumption later) and thereby would improve welfare even if personal saving did not increase.

It was agreed that this argument was correct at the theoretical level. But some conferees pointed out that, as compared with an income tax, the expenditure tax would increase taxes on the young and the old (because needs generally are higher relative to income at those stages of life and saving most difficult) while reducing taxes on people of middle age (when income generally reaches its highest level and personal needs are not affected by family formation or retirement).[6] It is not obvious that this shift in relative tax burdens is equitable, and proponents of the income tax claimed it would be politically unacceptable.

Both the capital formation and welfare effects of expenditure taxation would depend in part on the tax rates that were ultimately adopted. Since an expenditure tax is theoretically an income tax with a deduction for saving, the revenues under a comprehensive expenditure tax would be lower than the revenues under a comprehensive income tax with the same tax rate. No one can guess how far from the theoretically correct base an actual expenditure tax might turn out to be, but several participants argued that the deviations would be at least as large as those experienced under the income tax. If government revenues were to be held constant, other taxes would have to be increased or the expenditure tax rates would have to exceed the income tax rates. One conferee pointed out that the additional taxes or higher tax rates could reduce capital formation; another noted that a higher tax rate on labor income coupled with the recent payroll tax increases would reduce work incentives. Thus until the expenditure tax rates were known, the net welfare effect would be unpredictable.

The Expenditure Tax and Equity

The advocates of the expenditure tax stressed its efficiency advantages, while the opponents put more emphasis on equity. The discussion of equity dealt with six topics: the choice of the appropriate tax base, the time perspective of the tax system, the relative treatment of

6. This is mainly a timing question: a proportional expenditure tax would tax equally in present-value terms consumption streams of equal present value regardless of the timing of income and consumption flows.

different types of income, the progressivity of the system, implications for the distribution of wealth, and the tax treatment of gifts and bequests.

The Choice of an Appropriate Tax Base

The traditional equity arguments for expenditure taxation are based on a notion of the relative social value of income and consumption. Income, this view holds, represents a contribution to society's output, whereas consumption is a withdrawal or use of that output. On this basis, income is to be favored and encouraged, while consumption should be penalized and discouraged. This view is now considered fairly old-fashioned and even puritanical, but a more subtle version has survived: some conferees support consumption as the appropriate tax base because it is the best measure of the taxpayer's enjoyment or satisfaction.

Income tax advocates generally respond that saving out of income yields its own satisfaction, particularly because it accumulates as a store of wealth and economic power. Richard Goode argued in his paper that savings increase a person's power to consume marketable output and therefore do not lessen his capacity to pay taxes. According to this view, ability to pay tax is no different whether a taxpayer chooses to save or consume his income.

Other aspects of the choice rest on empirical grounds. Nicholas Kaldor, who revived academic interest with his book *An Expenditure Tax,* published in 1955, argued that many taxpayers, while maintaining comfortable living standards, can reduce their *taxable* income to trivial levels through tax preferences or dissaving from accumulated wealth. For this reason he and others supported William D. Andrews's proposal to use the expenditure tax as a supplement to the income tax, not as a replacement. Other participants argued that expenditure is in fact the best measure of a taxpayer's permanent or lifetime income. They claimed that income may fluctuate from year to year, but households tend to consume according to the income they expect to receive over the long run.

One participant argued that people with equal options (that is, equal potential consumption) should pay equal tax. Under this view, with a truncated year-by-year approach, accretion is the correct tax base. But the consumption base is preferable if a lifetime approach is used, because individuals with equal potential consumption would be subject to the same present-value tax. If gifts and bequests are considered, this participant contended, the consumption base is no longer correct unless it is broadened to include such transfers.

The Time Perspective of the Tax System

The time perspective of the income tax is explicitly annual. While short-term income averaging is available to reduce the tax penalty of progressive rates on fluctuating income, the aggregation of income over somewhat longer periods is still not necessarily a good measure of long-term well-being. Although consumption is a purely current concept, it is much more stable than income, and expenditure tax advocates believe that it is a better measure of long-term well-being. In a world of certainty, if all income is consumed over a lifetime and there is no tax on saving and no gifts or bequests, the present value of the lifetime consumption expenditures of two persons with the same lifetime income (also discounted to the present) is the same regardless of when they consume their incomes. Thus the expenditure tax has a lifetime perspective.

At the conference, supporters of the expenditure tax claimed that the lifetime perspective is a major advantage of that tax. Opponents of the expenditure tax argued that the lifetime perspective is a dubious advantage in a world of extreme political and economic uncertainty. In their view, a person's income history taken much beyond a modest averaging period has very little effect on current economic behavior. Though one year might be too short a horizon for tax purposes, they contended that a lifetime is too long.

Treatment of Various Types of Income

Expenditure tax advocates claim that income from different sources would be treated more uniformly under an expenditure tax than under the income tax because the consumption base does not depend on the source of income. Most of the conference participants agreed that a theoretically correct expenditure tax (or a theoretically correct income tax) would in fact be more neutral among income types than the present imperfect income tax. However, a number of participants insisted that preferences could easily be carried over into an expenditure tax for the same reasons that they were inserted into the income tax and that other preferences for particular items of consumption would creep in.

Progressivity

In theory, it should be possible to design a rate schedule for an expenditure tax that achieves the same degree of progressivity as the present income tax. But there are no reliable data on savings rates by income class.[7] Even if such data could be obtained, there would be considerable uncertainty as to how the savings rates would be altered by the substitution of an expenditure tax for an income tax. Further, tax preferences and loopholes might turn out to be larger or smaller at any given income class under the expenditure tax. Thus there is little basis for choosing a rate schedule for an expenditure tax that would achieve the desired degree of progressivity. One conferee pointed out that the efficiency gains from an expenditure tax are quite sensitive to the tax rates chosen, so that the flexibility for choosing a rate schedule to achieve distributional goals is limited.

Another consideration is that, to achieve the same yield, expenditure tax rates will at least appear higher than those under the income tax. Assuming no savings, a 50 percent income tax rate is equivalent to an expenditure tax rate of 100 percent; on the same assumption, the current top bracket income tax rate of 70 percent would be equivalent to a 233 percent tax rate in consumption. Some conferees considered it unlikely that the public would understand or tolerate marginal tax rates over 100 percent. On the other hand, proponents of the expenditure tax argued that the tax rates could be expressed on a gross basis (that is, as a percentage of consumption plus the amount of the tax), even though this would understate the true tax rates on consumption. If the stated top bracket tax rate on consumption had to be held below 100 percent on a net basis, the loss in revenue and progressivity would make the tax unattractive to many analysts.

Implications for the Distribution of Wealth

By the very nature of the consumption tax, taxpayers who save large fractions of their income will, over time, be able to accumulate wealth. Several conferees raised the possibility that the tax would increase the concentration of wealth.

A basic question is whether the shift to an expenditure tax would

7. The lack of data is the result of the inevitable failure of sample surveys to successfully account for the upper tail of the income distribution and of the absence of savings information from existing tax returns.

significantly increase the tax-saving opportunities of high-income people. Some argued that the present income tax preferences for saving, such as the provisions for private pensions, individual retirement accounts (IRAs), and Keogh plans, are used mainly by people at the top of the income distribution. Reinforcing this view, the best available data indicate that most of the population saves very little and has very small or negative net worth. The expenditure tax, however, would allow taxpayers to defer tax on any type of saving, thereby broadening the opportunity for saving. Taxpayers with small amounts of wealth might have particularly strong incentives to save more. The result might be to increase wealth holdings among households of comparatively modest means.

Opponents of the expenditure tax argued that it would have just the opposite effect. They contended that savings are small in the lower part of the income distribution because needs are large relative to income, not because the rate of return is too low. The shift to an expenditure tax would not increase after-tax rates of return for low-income taxpayers very much (because they are already subject to low tax rates), so that the effect on their saving would probably be minimal. If saving should increase among upper-income taxpayers, before-tax rates of return would be bid down, thus reducing the savings incentives for those with modest incomes. Some expenditure tax advocates agreed with this proposition.

Thus the benefits of a switch to an expenditure tax could accrue largely to high-income taxpayers with above average savings, who might accumulate even more wealth than under the present system. Some conferees were therefore concerned about the distribution of wealth if an expenditure tax were enacted, but there was little agreement on what should be done about it.

A final wealth consideration concerned the transition to an expenditure tax. Wealth held at the time of enactment of an expenditure tax would be accumulated from taxed income. Full taxation of such wealth when consumed plus the prior income tax would be a greater burden than the taxes that would be paid on the consumption of wealth accumulated after the expenditure tax was enacted. At the same time, the full exemption of prior wealth accumulations would validate the past use of tax loopholes to achieve tax-free consumption, which many expenditure tax advocates decry. Further, the exemption of accumulated capital at current market prices would forgive the tax liability on any appreciation that had not been realized when the income tax was in effect. This issue was regarded by the participants as a major roadblock to the adoption of an expenditure tax, but there was no agreement on how to solve the problem.

Tax Treatment of Gifts and Bequests

The treatment of gifts and bequests under an expenditure tax was one of the most controversial topics discussed at the conference. As was noted earlier, the identity of the present value of lifetime aggregates of consumption of persons with equal discounted incomes holds only if there are no gifts and bequests. Accordingly, several conferees recommended that under an expenditure tax gifts and bequests be regarded as consumption of the donor. Such treatment is also justified on the ground that, since the donor has the option of making the gift or bequest, doing so must give him satisfaction or he would choose to consume more himself. Other conferees pointed out that this technique would in fact amount to double taxation—the gift would be counted as consumption of the donor and taxed to him; then it would be counted as a receipt of the donee and taxed again when it was consumed. They felt that this would inordinately encourage consumption at the expense of saving for the purpose of making gifts and bequests. Some of this group preferred that the gift or bequest not be considered consumption of the donor, but be taxed only to the donee when it was consumed.

A lively debate ensued over the equity implications of taxing a gift in that way. Some of the conference participants felt that it would result in wholesale tax avoidance by wealthy families through transfers from members in higher tax rate brackets to those paying at lower rates, but one participant argued that taxpayers would try to minimize the total tax by dispersing their gifts among many low-rate taxpayers, thus tending to equalize wealth. Other conferees argued that the tax on both donor and donee was not offensive because both could derive utility from the same gift—one by giving it and the other by consuming it—and that the donee would not be taxed so long as he did not consume the gift. One lawyer lamented that taxation of the donor would continue many of the problems in the present estate and gift tax laws, including the use of generation-skipping transfers and the need for distinguishing between gifts and support for dependents. It was pointed out that, in all these matters, the definition of the taxable unit would be crucial in determining whether a transfer was in fact a gift, a support payment, or a reward for services rendered.

A different element in the debate on taxation of the donor or donee under an expenditure tax was the role of the present estate and gift taxes. One conferee suggested that transfers need not be included in the expenditure tax base at all, because the estate and gift tax, possibly redesigned for the new tax environment, could perform the function of taxing such transfers. He contended that the expenditure tax would deal with continuous flows of expenditure but could not properly handle discrete transfers that were bunched into a single year. Others responded that transfers should be included in the bases of both taxes; they argued that the expenditure tax would tax the utility derived from giving or receiving the gift, whereas the transfer tax was a tax on the right given by society to transfer property.

A final suggestion was for an annual or periodic wealth tax as an alternative or supplement to the inclusion of transfers in the expenditure tax base. Such a tax would explicitly deal with wealth concentrations, and one conferee argued that a wealth tax would not alter incentives to consume or give. But others feared that any increase in the taxes on wealth, by the adoption of a wealth tax or by an increase in the estate and gift taxes, would greatly reduce the incentives of wealthy people to save. If such taxpayers decided that consumption would be the best use of their wealth, the outcome would be a drawing down of the nation's capital stock.

Administration and Measurement under an Expenditure Tax

Expenditure tax advocates claim that a tax based on consumption would be easier to administer than the present income tax and that the measurement of the appropriate economic flows would be easier and subject to fewer anomalous results. These claims are sometimes presented in a simplified form using the familiar Haig-Simons definition of income as consumption plus the change in net worth. The reasoning is that a measure of change in net worth is needed to determine income but not to measure consumption. In contrast, income tax advocates point out that consumption is income less saving. It follows that it is necessary to measure saving to determine consumption, so that the consumption tax has all the administrative problems of the income tax plus those that involve the measurement of saving. Some of the flavor of this controversy (greatly simplified here) carried over into the detailed discussion of the merits of the two taxes on administrative grounds.

The discussion in this section is divided into three parts. The first examines two possible simplifications of the expenditure tax that attracted considerable attention at the conference: the prepayment option for investments and the equivalence of a consumption tax and a wage tax. The second describes several features of the expenditure tax that are alleged to be inherently simpler than the corresponding features of the income tax. The third discusses the areas in which the income tax is alleged to be simpler than the expenditure tax.

Ways to Simplify the Expenditure Tax

It has long been assumed that the measurement of saving under an expenditure tax would require a considerable amount of record-keeping and would greatly complicate the tax return. First, in the year an investment was made, the amount invested would be deducted from receipts to determine taxable expenditure. In each subsequent period, the returns on the investment would be included in receipts. Later, when the investment was sold, the sales proceeds would also be included in receipts. This process, known as the cash flow approach, was taken to be relatively cumbersome because one of the operations —the reporting of the purchase of assets—is not required under the income tax.

In recent years it has been suggested that the procedure could be simplified by allowing the taxpayer to forgo deductions for purchases of assets and to ignore the sales, at his option.[8] Because the present value of an asset is the discounted value of its future receipts, the lump sum tax payment at the time the asset was purchased would presumably equal the discounted value of the future tax payments omitted, thus leaving the government indifferent to taxpayers' choices.[9] Beyond the fact that there would be no need to account for investment income, this "prepayment" option has an interesting implication: it would treat identically two taxpayers identically situated in

8. U.S. Department of the Treasury, *Blueprints for Basic Tax Reform* (Government Printing Office, 1977), pp. 113–39.

9. It is assumed the expenditure tax is a proportional tax or, if it is progressive, the taxpayer remains in the same tax rate bracket.

terms of their investment *opportunities* rather than their investment *outcomes* over a lifetime (given the tendency of consumption to reflect a lifetime or "permanent" income).

The prepayment option (or the ex ante view of taxation) was one of the most discussed topics of the conference. David F. Bradford, under whose supervision the Treasury's *Blueprints for Basic Tax Reform* was prepared, defended the prepayment option in his paper, while Michael Graetz opposed it in his.

Some advocates of the expenditure tax supported Bradford's position for two reasons. First, the prepayment option would greatly simplify tax compliance and administration. Second, they regarded the ex ante view of tax equity as more appropriate than the ex post view—that is, that income opportunities are a better basis for taxation than actual outcomes. The net effect would be a tax on endowments from a lifetime perspective, which they felt was ideal. One participant noted that the prepayment option might increase saving and capital formation if investors set aside reserves at the time investments were made in order to pay the expenditure tax on unprofitable ventures.

Many conference participants, however, agreed with Graetz. For some, this position was grounded on their perceptions of the principle of fairness in taxation. Several argued that taxation based on outcomes is widely accepted and that the public at large would not understand a tax based on opportunities. They also felt that ex ante taxation of investments with substantial variation of returns would be inequitable. Others disagreed with the lifetime perspective implicit in the ex ante view of tax equity; they believe that, even if an annual accounting period is too short, a lifetime is much too long for tax purposes.

Still others pointed out that, because the federal budget imposes a liquidity constraint year by year, the government would not be indifferent among different streams of tax revenue with the same present value. Bradford responded that prepayment would probably accelerate the receipt of revenues, thereby increasing rather than decreasing the government's options, and that in any event the government could meet its constraints by altering its borrowing behavior.

It was also pointed out that the prepayment option could have a negative rather than a zero net effect on government revenues over the long run. Although marginal investments can be expected to have a zero return, there are many inframarginal investments with positive expected returns. The election of the prepayment option for those investments would reduce government revenue relative to a mandatory cash flow treatment. Furthermore, since taxpayers would make the prepayment election with a year's worth of information when tax returns were filed, they would choose the option that would be to their advantage and thus reduce the government's revenue below the level to be expected from a random outcome. Finally, unless the prepayment option were modified, it would in effect allow short-term gains to be realized tax free.

Beyond these problems, the prepayment option could create extensive opportunities for tax avoidance and manipulation by taxpayers. One participant pointed out that two persons, for example parent and child, might organize a joint oil exploration and development enterprise. One of the participants—most likely the parent—would do the initial exploratory drilling of selected areas in the field at a low expected payoff and would use the cash flow option; the other would capture the high returns of subsequent development drilling and would use the prepayment option and pay a minimal amount of tax. Alternatively, any individual or group might set up a corporation heavily capitalized with preferred stock (taking the cash flow option) and lightly capitalized with common stock (taking the prepayment option). Another type of avoidance scheme would be for one person to use two interest-bearing accounts, one to be taxed under the prepayment method and the other under the cash flow method. Any money put into the cash flow account at the beginning of the year would generate a deduction, and if the funds were then moved to the prepaid account for the remainder of the year, the interest would not be taxable. The funds would then be transferred at the beginning of the next year to a cash flow account and the process repeated.

Bradford acknowledged that these avoidance opportunities would exist, but he argued that each arrangement has a counterpart under the present income tax and that the expenditure tax problems would be no worse. He felt that such problems could be dealt with through regulations or other procedures. For example, it should be possible to take care of the mineral exploration and preferred–common stock arrangements by regulations for financial transactions at less than arm's length, and the coordinated use of separate cash flow and prepaid accounts could be stopped by withholding on interest receipts. But other participants expressed the judgment that the regulatory and administrative complexity of these procedures would be considerable. Many thought that a cash flow approach would have to be used for most important financial transactions. Some felt that the rejection of the prepayment method weakened the case for the expenditure tax, while others felt that a cash flow tax would be readily administrable.

Another potential simplification of the expenditure tax derives from the theoretical equivalence, discussed in the tax literature, of the expenditure tax and a tax on wages and salaries. If the two were in fact equivalent, a wage tax would be an attractive substitute for an expenditure tax since it would be easier to administer. It was generally agreed, however, that the equivalence held only in the aggregate and only under specified conditions and that the divergence between consumption and earnings in individual cases was far too great to justify considering a wage tax to be a proxy for an expenditure tax.

Advantages of the Expenditure Tax

Proponents of the expenditure tax cited several ways in which it would be inherently much simpler than the income tax. The first is the elimination of differences in the tax treatment of the various forms of income from capital. Under the income tax, capital gains are treated differently from interest, dividends, or rent; corporate income is taxed differently from unincorporated business income; and income from mineral extraction, timber, farmland, and low-income housing are all given some form of preferential treatment. An alleged advantage of the expenditure tax is that, at the personal level,[10] there would be no distinctions among different forms of property income. Each dollar that entered into consumption would be taxed the same as every other, regardless of its source, because distinctions based on sources of income would be harder to justify. This was seen as providing several advantages: efficiency would be served by the removal of incentives to realize income in preferred forms; equity between those who can and cannot alter the form of their income receipts would be improved; and the tax system would be easier to administer. Further, the difficulties of measuring business income, including such perennial problems as accounting for depreciation and inventories, would be eliminated.

Critics of the expenditure tax generally acknowledged these theoretical advantages but doubted that they could be achieved in prac-

10. The incorporated vs. unincorporated business aspect is discussed below.

tice. They pointed out that the groups who obtained passage of depletion allowances for minerals and exclusions for capital gains under the income tax would attempt to obtain the same or similar advantages under an expenditure tax. Paul R. McDaniel pointed out that if charitable contributions were excluded from the expenditure tax base, a taxpayer would pay the same tax as he would if he had put the money in the bank for himself. He feared that charitable organizations would therefore use their influence to obtain an exclusion of more than 100 percent for charitable contributions in order to provide some tax incentive to the donors.[11] Similarly, the rapid amortization of low-income housing under the income tax could be replaced by a deduction of more than 100 percent of the amount of the investment under the expenditure tax. The issue boiled down, therefore, to a question of whether any expenditure tax that would be enacted would be closer to, or further from, the ideal than the present income tax is; the conferees were divided in their opinions.

Another advantage of the expenditure tax is that a consumption tax *base* is automatically adjusted for inflation. Since property income would be taxed only when it was consumed and then in full, an adjustment of the tax base for inflation would be unnecessary. In contrast, inflation adjustments are extremely complicated under the income tax because it is necessary to allow for price level changes over various periods of time in computing depreciation, inventory costs, changes in the value of outstanding debt, and other elements of taxable income. It might be desirable to index the personal exemptions, standard deductions, and tax rate boundaries for inflation, but this would be just as easy under the expenditure tax as it would be under the income tax.

A final advantage of an expenditure tax is that, in principle, there would be no need for a corporate income tax to supplement it. Corporate income would be taxed when distributed and consumed or when realized in the form of capital gains and consumed. Without a corporate tax, the complications of accrual accounting for depreciation and inventory valuation would be eliminated, and the distinction between the taxation of incorporated and unincorporated business income would be removed.

Nevertheless, even the expenditure tax supporters disagreed about

11. Of course, value judgments on this issue differ; another conferee expressed concern that the Congress might *not* provide such a subsidy for philanthropy.

the desirability of eliminating the corporate tax. Some felt that the simplicity and efficiency benefits of eliminating the tax are very large and therefore worth pursuing. A second group was concerned about the distributional consequences of eliminating the tax; they felt that repeal would provide windfall gains to shareholders and therefore favored something like the current tax, at least for foreign stock owners. A third group thought that the repeal of the corporate tax was unlikely, even though it would be appropriate; this group sought a corporate tax that would be as inoffensive as possible conceptually and operationally, but that would at least maintain a facade of corporate taxation to satisfy the political constraints. One possibility was the cash flow tax proposed by the Meade committee in the United Kingdom—a tax based on the notion of a partnership and sharing of risk between the government and the business enterprise. Another was a kind of integration of the individual and corporate income taxes, with the corporate tax considered to be withholding on behalf of the individual taxpayer.

Opponents of the expenditure tax felt that the question of the corporate tax cannot be easily resolved. It was pointed out that the elimination of the corporate tax would increase the revenue needed from the expenditure tax and thus require a much higher tax rate. The risk-sharing idea of the Meade committee was criticized because it would provide an implicit government share in corporate enterprises that was higher than in unincorporated firms. One conferee stated that if a corporate tax were required for political or other reasons, the burden should be on expenditure tax advocates to explain the type of tax that would be needed and whether it would negate the conceptual advantages claimed for the expenditure tax. Another conferee was quick to reply that the political need for a corporate tax is not a unique disadvantage of the expenditure tax—the corporate tax is an essential element of an income tax system.

Disadvantages of the Expenditure Tax

Although the expenditure tax would be simpler than the income tax in some respects, it would be more complicated in others.

Housing. Housing is perhaps the most difficult problem. The theoretically correct treatment of housing under the income tax is to include the rental value of the house, net of interest, depreciation, and maintenance expenses, in taxable income. Few countries rigorously tax the rental value of owned homes because it is extremely difficult to measure and would require payment of tax on income not received in cash.

Because the use of housing is a form of consumption, the net rental value of owner-occupied homes should be included in an expenditure tax base. An alternative solution, suggested by Michael Graetz, is to regard the purchase of a house as a taxable event and to include it in its entirety in the expenditure tax base (the prepayment option). Later, when the house was sold, only the gain on the sale would be included as a taxable receipt. The same treatment could also be applied to durable goods purchases.

Few of the conference participants believed that the legislative process would reach the correct result under either approach. Congress is no more likely to tax imputed rent under an expenditure tax than under the income tax. The entire purchase price of a house would probably not be taxable upon purchase, because taxpayers would be liable for large amounts of tax at the same time that they were committing themselves to large contractual expenditures. This bunching problem complicates the treatment of housing under the expenditure tax even more than under the income tax. In effect, housing purchases under the expenditure tax are analogous to the realizations of long-term capital gains under the income tax—the first are long-term expenditures that would be taxable in one year, while the second are long-term income that is taxed in one year. The bunching problem has led to the adoption of preferential treatment for capital gains and would be likely to lead to generous preferences or complete exemption for housing under an expenditure tax.

Defenders of the expenditure tax responded that there are workable solutions for the housing problem. Some suggested a simplified method of calculating the net rental value of an owner-occupied home on the basis of its purchase price, for example, imputing the value on the basis of an average rate of return. Some would adjust the imputed net rent for the aggregate inflation rate (rather than rely on periodic reassessments of each individual house), while others would not change the taxable rent after the time of purchase. One conferee suggested that a fraction of each mortgage payment (corresponding to the ratio of down payment to total purchase price) be added to taxable receipts each year, to avoid taxing the down payment in full in the year of purchase.

The conference participants were not satisfied with any of the suggested formulas for taxing housing and other durables. It was conceded that this was one of the most difficult problem areas in tax policy, and many of the conferees felt that the case for or against the expenditure tax should not depend on our ability to devise a workable solution. The expenditure tax advocates claimed that the difficulties of handling housing and other durables under the expenditure tax could hardly be considered a serious disadvantage in light of the widely acknowledged failures of the income tax in those areas.

Monitoring of transactions. A second inherent complexity of an expenditure tax is the need to devise methods of checking asset transactions. A traditional argument is that complete balance sheets would be necessary for this purpose. Participants argued that the incentive to conceal a transaction is much larger under an expenditure tax than under the income tax; under the income tax, only a fraction of the sale price—the gain or loss—is included in the calculation of taxable income, but the entire proceeds would be included in receipts under an expenditure tax. It was also pointed out that it would be essential to obtain individual balance sheets during the transition to an expenditure tax in order to prevent the accumulation of cash balances that could be used to pay for subsequent consumption on a tax-free basis.

Some defenders of the expenditure tax contended that records of asset holdings or full balance sheets would not be necessary. They based their arguments largely on the work of William D. Andrews, who has explained how a cash flow expenditure tax could be based entirely on current income flows and without regard to asset stocks.[12] Under the Andrews model of a cash flow tax, it would not be necessary to report receipts and payments in any more detail than under the income tax. Some conferees maintained that, to take advantage of the deduction for saving, asset purchasers would have every incentive to report their costs and that this would prevent sellers from attempting to conceal their side of the transaction. They further maintained that balance sheets are mainly useful in accounting for holdings of assets, which would not be taxable in any event, but they

12. William D. Andrews, "A Consumption-Type of Cash Flow Personal Income Tax," *Harvard Law Review,* vol. 87 (April 1974), pp. 1113–88.

would be of no use in identifying sales of assets, which would be taxable.[13]

Some conferees suggested that it might be possible to limit the record-keeping to certain specified types of assets. Such a register might be prepared as part of the transition procedures and for the administration of any wealth tax that would accompany the expenditure tax. One conferee pointed out that an initial register plus annual reporting of sales and purchases might be sufficient for enforcement purposes. Such a register could also be used for controlling the emigration of people with assets accumulated from tax-exempt funds (see below for a discussion of the problem of emigration). However, there was no real consensus on just how thorough the asset record-keeping would have to be under an expenditure tax.

International aspects. The third set of issues that would be encountered in administering an expenditure tax would be the treatment of emigration and immigration and of domestic consumption by foreigners and foreign consumption by U.S. citizens. These issues are not confined to the expenditure tax; they are inherent in any tax that might be adopted in an income tax world. Many procedures have been developed over long periods of time to enable income tax nations to handle international income flows, but it is not clear how an expenditure tax nation would fit in.

Opponents of the expenditure tax pointed out that the inclusion in the tax base of income received and taxed outside the country and not saved would be unorthodox and awkward. If Americans earned income overseas, it would theoretically not be proper to credit foreign income taxes paid against the domestic expenditure tax. One possibility would be to allow a credit only for value-added tax or other consumption taxes levied in foreign countries. When foreigners earned income here without spending, their liability would be zero under the tax as defined for Americans; some other form of tax would have to be imposed if it were felt that the taxation of such income was appropriate.

Unless some form of emigration tax were collected, it would be highly profitable for Americans to earn and save in the United States

13. David Bradford also pointed out that other enforcement devices were described in the Treasury's *Blueprints for Basic Tax Reform,* pp. 114–44 and 181–216.

under an expenditure tax and then go to an income tax country to do their spending. The opposite problem would be the taxation of spending by immigrants from income already taxed in the country of origin. It was also pointed out that an expenditure tax world would leave developing countries with far less tax revenue than they now have, because much of the income earned in such countries is transferred to the developed countries to be spent there.

Several conferees concluded that the emigration problem could best be handled by taxing all wealth taken from the United States as if it were consumed at that time, with exemption provisions for temporary emigration. One participant suggested that a list of assets be required from all taxpayers and that a portion of the total value of the specified assets be held as a bond to ensure against permanent tax avoidance through emigration. Other conferees were concerned about the international political implications of a large tax levied upon emigration, since it could be made to appear much like the fees some nations now impose to discourage emigration of political dissidents. Paul McDaniel suggested that taxation on a citizenship rather than a residence basis would minimize tax avoidance through emigration. Michael Graetz, who felt that emigration from the United States would be much less of a problem than it might be from other nations, suggested that explicit remedies might not be needed. Many conferees felt that our knowledge of these problems was far too limited and that much more research was needed to reach firm conclusions. But the expenditure tax advocates felt that satisfactory compromises could be written into the law and negotiated with other nations.

Accumulation of wealth. A final area of complexity that would be created by an expenditure tax would be the need for the revision of the taxation of wealth. Some form of taxation of exempt accumulation would be necessary to relieve the concern of many of the conferees (proponents as well as opponents of the expenditure tax) that the substitution of an expenditure tax for the income tax would increase the concentration of wealth. Such a tax could be an explicit annual or periodic net wealth tax, or the treatment of gifts and bequests as if they were items of consumption, or simply improved gift and estate taxes.

The conferees were divided on the form that such a tax should take, but they did agree that any solution would involve greater complexity than at present. Gifts and bequests could be taxed under the expenditure tax itself only if some form of averaging were provided. Averaging for bequests would be limited to carry-backs and would of course involve compliance by persons other than the donor. Explicit wealth taxation would involve its own complications of valuation and assessment (plus the possible need for a constitutional amendment). And if reliance were placed on the present estate and gift taxes, considerable improvement would be needed to meet the requirements of an expenditure tax regime.

Transition to an Expenditure Tax

It is widely recognized that transition to an expenditure tax would be troublesome; this topic was therefore given a good deal of attention at the conference. A related topic was the Kaldor-Andrews supplementary expenditure tax proposal, which can be used either as a permanent supplement to the income tax or as a transition mechanism between the income tax and an ultimate expenditure tax system.

Treatment of Accumulated Assets

As mentioned earlier, a major issue of the transition to an expenditure tax is the treatment of savings that were accumulated and taxed under the income tax. If such accumulations were taxed again when consumed, they would bear a heavier burden than would later accumulations from tax-exempt savings. The equity implications of alternative approaches have already been discussed, but there are also difficult problems of rule making, compliance, and verification.

The population group most seriously affected by the enactment of an expenditure tax would be the retired elderly, who would not benefit from the tax exemption for savings, because they would be drawing down their assets to finance current consumption. (Indeed, the elderly might even lose income before taxes if before-tax rates of return on savings declined.) But various forms of saving, such as contributions to pension, Keogh, and IRA accounts, are already exempt from the income tax. These produce tax outcomes that are not unlike those under the expenditure tax itself. Thus a blanket exemption of the accumulated assets of the elderly would give many of them a windfall. Graetz maintained that special rules for previously taxed assets might be needed only for the currently retired and those close to retirement. For younger people the extent of double taxation would be small because most saving accumulations take place at, or after, middle age.

It was generally agreed that it would be inequitable simply to exempt the value of accumulated assets at the time the expenditure tax went into effect. Many wealthy people could maintain their consumption levels out of their assets for many years without paying expenditure tax. Furthermore, there could be a double deferral for unrealized capital gains, which are not taxed under the income tax and which would not be taxed under the expenditure tax until they were consumed. Graetz's solution to that tax avoidance problem was to exempt only the cost basis of accumulated assets. He also suggested that taxpayers who wished to be taxed on their unrealized capital gains under the income tax system (to avoid higher consumption tax rates later) could be permitted constructive realization for such gains without actually selling the assets. Other participants, citing the recent deferral to 1980 of the effective date of the carryover-of-basis provision enacted in 1976, pointed out that the calculation of basis of assets during transitions is difficult for administrative and political reasons. They expected that if an expenditure tax were enacted, there would be an exemption for the total market value of assets accumulated up to the effective date, which would leave a wide loophole for people with large wealth holdings.

Tax evasion during the transition would also be possible by the manipulation of portfolios prior to the enactment of the expenditure tax. A taxpayer could liquidate assets (with or without a taxable gain) before the effective date of the expenditure tax, hide the cash, and then claim a deduction for saving by repurchasing the same or other assets after the tax went into effect. Such evasion could be prevented by requiring taxpayers to file comprehensive personal balance sheets on the effective date of the expenditure tax, including cash balances. Alternatively, the balance sheets might be required long enough in advance of the effective date to make the hoarding of cash for the entire period unattractive. Sven-Olof Lodin suggested that the latter course could be the beginning of record-keeping for any wealth tax to be imposed simultaneously with the expenditure tax. He added that workable transition procedures were critical because the announcement of the expenditure tax could have drastic effects on asset values.

A somewhat different effect of the announcement of an expenditure tax was suggested by another participant. Taxpayers would have incentives to accelerate consumption before the effective date of the expenditure tax and to postpone income receipts until later. Some procedure might be devised to account for such actions, but no one came up with any practical solution.

A Supplementary Expenditure Tax

The discussion of the supplementary expenditure tax, which was proposed by Andrews and supported by Kaldor, centered on equity as well as administrative problems.

A traditional argument for a supplementary expenditure tax is that it would tax those who avoid income tax through preferences in the current law and through dissaving. One participant argued, however, that a supplementary expenditure tax proposal might have peculiar distributional effects. An expenditure tax confined to the higher tax brackets would permit wealthy taxpayers to reduce their tax liability by saving a large fraction of their income, while less affluent taxpayers would not have the same opportunity. A second participant pointed out that the coexistence of two progressive taxes might result in excessive tax liabilities unless the combined burdens were taken into account.

With regard to administration, some conferees saw the supplementary expenditure tax as a suitable transition mechanism to a full expenditure tax. They felt that the supplementary tax would show how a full tax could be administered, what the tax rates might be, and how the tax would affect saving and the economy. But concern was expressed that the tax authorities would be hard-pressed to administer two different personal taxes simultaneously. One participant argued that the imposition of the expenditure tax problems on top of the problems of the income tax would give the administrators the worst of both worlds. Another participant tentatively suggested that an expenditure tax might coexist with the income tax as a kind of minimum tax, but it was pointed out that the minimum tax is a preference tax based on income tax principles and that an expenditure tax could not fill that role.

Summary and Conclusions

It is not surprising that the conference did not produce a consensus on the feasibility or desirability of expenditure taxation. Many of the problems have been discussed in the technical literature for many years, and most of the participants had formed their opinions before the conference. Moreover, the resolution of the major issues depends on value judgments that can hardly be changed in a two-day meeting.

Nonetheless, the conference provided a useful forum for the exchange of ideas among people who have opposing views of the expenditure tax, and it clarified their principal differences. The blending of economic and legal considerations was particularly helpful. It gave the economists an opportunity to appreciate the problems of implementing an expenditure tax, and lawyers an opportunity to understand the economic arguments for and against expenditure taxation.

An important issue for the economists is whether the substitution of an expenditure tax for the income tax could have a significant effect on personal saving. Many participants felt that the available data do not support the contention that the interest elasticity of saving is high, though they were not prepared to agree that it is zero. Proponents of the expenditure tax stressed that, even if personal saving did not increase, the reallocation of saving over the lifetime of individuals would increase economic welfare and efficiency.

The discussion of equity brought out a number of important points. The lifetime perspective of the expenditure tax was thought to be a great advantage by its proponents, whereas its opponents felt that a much shorter accounting period (though not necessarily as short as a year) was more appropriate for tax purposes. The close association between a tax on endowments and an expenditure tax was duly noted, but most of the participants were persuaded that the tax system should continue to be based on outcomes. It was agreed that the distributional effects of an expenditure tax on various income, consumption, and wealth groups cannot be predicted on the basis of currently available data. To prevent an inordinate increase in the concentration of wealth and economic power, effective estate and gift taxes or periodic wealth taxes were regarded by most of the participants as essential supplements to an expenditure tax.

There was no meeting of minds on the administrative feasibility of an expenditure tax, but a number of technical issues were clarified. It was agreed that there is no easy way to treat housing and that whatever solution emerged would probably be as unsatisfactory under the expenditure tax as it is under the income tax. The use of the prepayment option as a method of taxing housing, consumer durables, and other assets was explored; the consensus was that elaborate rules and regulations would be needed to prevent the manipulation of prepayments and postpayments. The treatment of wealth accumulated before the transition and the treatment of the untaxed wealth of emigrants from the United States were acknowledged to be extremely troublesome.

Thus any decision on whether or not to implement an expenditure tax rests both on scientific questions, which remained unresolved but are subject to further research, and on value judgments, on which there was and most likely will be no consensus.

Conference Participants

with their affiliations at the time of the conference

Henry J. Aaron *U.S. Department of Health, Education, and Welfare*
William D. Andrews *Harvard Law School*
Martin J. Bailey *University of Maryland*
Wayne G. Barnett *Stanford University Law School*
Walter J. Blum *University of Chicago Law School*
Michael J. Boskin *Stanford University*
David F. Bradford *Princeton University*
Gerard M. Brannon *Georgetown University*
Harvey E. Brazer *University of Michigan*
George F. Break *University of California (Berkeley)*
John A. Brittain *Brookings Institution*
E. Cary Brown *Massachusetts Institute of Technology*
Edwin S. Cohen *Covington and Burlington*
Bruce Davie *House Committee on Ways and Means*
Peter A. Diamond *Massachusetts Institute of Technology*
Larry L. Dildine *U.S. Treasury Department*
Martin S. Feldstein *Harvard University and National Bureau of Economic Research*
Harvey Galper *U.S. Treasury Department*
Martin D. Ginsburg *Weil, Gotshal and Manges*
Richard Goode *International Monetary Fund*
Michael J. Graetz *California Institute of Technology and the University of Southern California Law Center*

Daniel I. Halperin *U.S. Treasury Department*

Arnold C. Harberger *University of Chicago*

Frederic W. Hickman *Hopkins, Sutter, Mulroy, Davis and Cromartie*

E. Philip Howrey *University of Michigan*

Saul H. Hymans *University of Michigan*

Nicholas Kaldor *Cambridge University*

John A. Kay *Oxford University*

Mervyn A. King *University of Birmingham*

William A. Klein *University of California Law School (Los Angeles)*

Robert Z. Lawrence *Brookings Institution*

Sven-Olof Lodin *University of Stockholm*

Donald C. Lubick *U.S. Treasury Department*

Paul R. McDaniel *Boston College Law School*

Charles E. McLure, Jr. *Rice University and National Bureau of Economic Research*

Kenneth C. Messere *Organisation for Economic Co-operation and Development*

Peter Mieszkowski *Federal Reserve Bank of Boston*

Joseph J. Minarik *Brookings Institution*

Alicia H. Munnell *Federal Reserve Bank of Boston*

Richard A. Musgrave *Harvard University*

Harry A. Olsher *Fund for Public Policy Research*

Joseph A. Pechman *Brookings Institution*

Rudolph G. Penner *American Enterprise Institute*

Alan R. Prest *London School of Economics*

Carl S. Shoup *Columbia University (Emeritus)*

John B. Shoven *Yale University*

Joseph E. Stiglitz *Mathematica, Inc.*

Emil M. Sunley, Jr. *U.S. Treasury Department*

Stanley S. Surrey *Harvard Law School*

William Vickrey *Columbia University*

Alvin C. Warren, Jr. *University of Pennsylvania Law School*

James W. Wetzler *Joint Committee on Internal Revenue Taxation*

Bernard Wolfman *Harvard Law School*

Index

Aaron, Henry J., 54n, 75n, 86n

Accounting systems: audit and, 259–60; capital gains, 83; characteristics, 81; corporate tax and, 246–47; record-keeping, 70–71, 163–64, 247, 281, 316–17; time frame, 290, 310. *See also* Cash flow method; Prepayment method

Andrews, William D., 52, 70, 75n, 81n, 113, 114, 161n, 167, 168, 169, 172n, 187, 194, 204, 216, 229, 235, 236n, 303, 316

Annuities, 218–19

Asset depreciation range system, 83

Atkinson, Anthony B., 39, 40, 75n, 98n, 101, 103, 104, 105, 106, 107n

Auerbach, Alan J., 103n

Bailey, Martin J., 19n, 57n, 298n

Barro, Robert J., 9n, 17n, 19n, 26

Baumol, William J., 1, 3n

Becker, Gary S., 60n

Bergstrom, Theodore C., 1n

Bittker, Boris I., 198n, 209n, 223, 229, 233

Blinder, Alan S., 99n

Blueprints for Basic Tax Reform, 67, 80n, 83, 86, 175, 249; charitable contributions, 229; corporate tax, 84, 240, 291; expenditure tax structure, 165, 166, 167, 168–70, 172, 173, 176, 177, 290; gifts and bequests, 53; inflation problems, 64; life insurance, 216; tax payment deduction, 233–34; tax systems comparison, 75–76, 167; transition scheme, 67, 262–63, 268, 270–71, 274–75

Borrowing: consumer credit, 33, 130, 190–93; corporate tax and, 122–23, 243–44; information reporting, 258; interest deductions, 122–23, 174–75, 180–82, 190–93, 232–33, 243–44; investment, 130, 173–75, 177–83; tax shelters, 177–82; tax timing, 174–75

Boskin, Michael J., 2n, 9, 10–13, 16, 17, 20, 33, 35n, 39n, 43n, 45–47, 54n, 75n, 298–301

Bossons, John, 76n

Bradford, David F., 90n, 97n, 102n, 317n

Brannon, Gerard M., 57n

Break, George F., 76n

Brinner, Roger E., 65n

Brown, E. Cary, 59n, 168

Brudno, Walter W., 69n

Bulow, Jeremy I., 87n

Businesses: audit, 260; capital expenditures, 147–48, 288–89; expenses, 82, 222–27, 238; receipt measurement, 130–31. *See also* Corporate tax

Capital formation: saving and, 2, 4, 42, 301; tax systems and, 61, 62, 302

Capital gains: expenditure tax, 64–65, 183, 270–71, 289; income tax, 64–65, 66, 83, 91, 92, 94–95, 140, 148–49; supplementary expenditure tax, 149–50

Carter Commission, 84, 200

Cash equivalency doctrine, 247

Cash flow method: advantages, 182–83; annuities, 218, 219; audit and, 259–60; borrowing, 173, 174–75, 182–83, 232–33; foreign investments, 251–52, 253; gifts and bequests, 207; housing, 193–94, 278–79; investments, 173, 174–75,